The Blue Wave

The Blue Wave

The 2018 Midterms and What They Mean for the 2020 Elections

Larry J. Sabato and Kyle Kondik

ROWMAN & LITTLEFIELD
Lanham • Boulder • New York • London

Executive Editor: Jon Sisk
Assistant Editor: Chelsea Panin
Production Editor: Elaine McGaraugh
Cover Designer: Sally Rinehart

Published by Rowman & Littlefield
A wholly owned subsidiary of The Rowman & Littlefield Publishing Group, Inc.
4501 Forbes Boulevard, Suite 200, Lanham, Maryland 20706
www.rowman.com

Unit A, Whitacre Mews, 26–34 Stannary Street, London SE11 4AB

British Library Cataloguing in Publication Information Available

Library of Congress Cataloging-in-Publication Data

Names: Sabato, Larry, editor. | Kondik, Kyle, editor.
Title: The blue wave : the 2018 midterms and what they mean for the 2020
    elections / edited by Larry Sabato and Kyle Kondik.
Description: Lanham, Maryland : Rowman & Littlefield, [2019] | Includes
    bibliographical references and index.
Identifiers: LCCN 2019012249| ISBN 9781538125267 (cloth) | ISBN
    9781538125274 (pbk.) | ISBN 9781538125281 (electronic) Subjects:
    LCSH: United States. Congress—Elections, 2018. | United States.
    Congress—Elections, 2020. | Presidents—United States—Election—2020. |
    United States—Politics and government—2017-
Classification: LCC JK1968 2018 .B58 2019 | DDC 324.973/0933—dc23 LC record
    available at https://lccn.loc.gov/2019012249

Contents

Preface and Acknowledgments

Our subtitle for the 2016 iteration of this book (*Trumped*) argued that election "broke all the rules." In 2018, a similar subtitle might be "the election that followed all of the rules," or at least many of them.

The 2018 midterm was a normal midterm in that the president's party lost substantial ground in the U.S. House of Representatives. Throughout the cycle, Democrats said that a "blue wave" was coming, and that was apparent in the House. It's also part of the reason we picked *The Blue Wave* as the title of this book—not only does it aptly describe what happened in the House, but it also is, to us, perhaps the most memorable term used to describe the election before and after it happened.

That said, the results in other kinds of races—definitely the Senate, where Republicans actually netted a couple of seats thanks in large part to a very favorable map, and arguably in the races for state-level offices—did not necessarily suggest a Democratic advance comparable to other classic "wave" elections in American history. This book, therefore, will not just explain what happened, but also how this midterm fits in with other midterms.

One of us, Larry J. Sabato, provides a broad overview of the results in chapter 1; the other, Kyle Kondik, will specifically assess the House results in chapter 5. Additionally, we have a dozen other chapters from accomplished outside contributors who will assess the 2018 midterm from many different angles.

Alan Abramowitz (chapter 2) points out how the 2016 election results provided a rough guide for the 2018 results and how impressions of President Donald Trump played such a large role in the results. David Byler (chapter 4) also explores the continuity and change from 2016 and 2018 in a more granular fashion, showing how the results shifted in different states and regions. Rhodes Cook analyzes the primary season (chapter 3), which featured a lot of notable outcomes despite the near-perfect record for incumbents in seeking renomination.

Following Kondik's look at the House, James Hohmann (chapter 6) assesses the Senate results in detail, and Madelaine Pisani (chapter 7) does the same for the gubernatorial outcomes. Michael Toner and Karen Trainer (chapter 8) explain the role of money in the election, while Emily C. Singer (chapter 9) addresses one of the other main themes of this election: the rise of women candidates and increase in women elected to Congress. In chapters 10 and 11, Theodore Johnson and the team of Matt Barreto, Gary Segura, and Albert Morales assess the voting power of African Americans and Latinos, respectively. Diana Owen (chapter 12) explores the media's role in both covering an unusual president and a midterm election that generated more interest than most off-year contests. Josh Putnam (chapter 13) looks ahead to the upcoming Democratic presidential nomination process, and Sean Trende (chapter 14) concludes by pondering whether 2018 was a "wave" election or not, and what that means.

For the past couple of decades, our University of Virginia Center for Politics has released a review of the most recent national election every two years, and we appreciate the diligence of our contributors in helping us release this volume as quickly as possible following the election. We also want to thank the Center for Politics staff, most notably Associate Director Ken Stroupe, Chief Financial Officer Mary Daniel Brown, and Executive Assistant Tim Robinson. We also want to thank our publisher, Rowman and Littlefield, most notably Jon Sisk and Kate Powers.

Republicans ultimately were unable to avoid the electoral price a party typically pays when one of its members, in this case Donald Trump, is a largely unpopular occupant of the White House. That's where the normal rules that usually apply to midterms emerged in this instance. Yet there was a substantial enough variation in the individual results that some nuance is required to differentiate the circumstances of this election from other midterms. In *The Blue Wave*, we will try to provide that nuance as well as a detailed accounting of one of the most notable midterms in recent U.S. history.

Larry J. Sabato and Kyle Kondik
University of Virginia Center for Politics
February 2019

1

The Blue Wave

Trump at Midterm

Larry J. Sabato

The only thing Americans can agree on these days is that we have never had a president like Donald Trump. He dominates the news on a daily, sometimes hourly, basis. He yields center stage to no one at home or abroad. Agree with him or not, he has had a major impact on vital policies, from taxes to immigration to trade. He has already secured his legacy on the Supreme Court with two conservative appointees that have tipped the balance of the court from middle to right. Under Trump, broad economic indicators such as the unemployment rate and growth in the gross domestic product have generally been strong, and the president's business tax cuts and his deregulation of many industries, his supporters would argue, are a significant part of the reason for this.

And then, there's the other, much uglier side of the checklist. President Trump has uttered 6,420 falsehoods, lies, and misrepresentations since he took office, according to the count assembled right before the midterm by Glenn Kessler, Salvador Rizzo, and Meg Kelly of the *Washington Post*.[1]

Trump and his staff almost never bother to correct them, often doubling down instead whenever they are identified. The president is relentlessly petty and mean, refusing to rise above the fray, hurling insults by the dozen on Twitter and at rallies. All presidents are egotistical, but Trump can fairly be described as egomaniacal. As he often says, he knows more about almost any topic than anyone else—more about the military than the generals, and so on. All good things can be attributed to him, all bad things to others, in his view. (One example: When the stock market goes up, his brilliant policies produced the gains; when the market tumbles, he had nothing to do with it.) Trump has greatly worsened race relations, not just on account of insensitivity but by winking and nodding at the white nationalist movement that has avidly backed him. He identifies with, and encourages, authoritarian leaders abroad, and calls many U.S. journalists "the enemy of the people," a favorite term used by fascist and communist regimes for a century.

What is most interesting about the 2018 midterm is that, as a whole, voters balanced the good and bad in the Trump ledger and decided that providing a check on the president was more important than embracing the solid economy and the Trump agenda. For certain, this was a decision mainly reached by Democrats in blue Democratic states and districts, while most red Republican voters stayed loyal to their party and president. Yet there was a distinct shift to the Democrats among suburban voters, especially well-educated white women in the suburbs, that powered Democrats to victory in the U.S. House of Representatives, some Senate races, and gubernatorial contests around the nation. An extraordinarily high number of Americans, just over half the electorate, voted in these midterm elections, the highest since 1914 and a great improvement over the last midterm turnout mark of 36.7 percent in 2014.

It's certainly true that Republicans held their Senate majority and even added two seats, but that was as much a product of the heavily Republican map in the 35 Senate seats being contested. Yet the net gain of 40 seats in the House by the Democrats, giving them a majority of 235–199 for the GOP, was unmistakably a rebuke of Trump (one seat, in North Carolina, remained vacant as of this writing thanks to credible accusations of fraud that may have tilted the close race to the Republican in the disputed vote count). Moreover, this was the Democrats' biggest seat gain since the Watergate election of 1974. The party managed to win the nationwide House vote by 8.6 percentage points, a larger margin than any of the recent House-flipping midterms in 1994, 2006, and 2010. By contrast, Republicans have lost a net total of at least 47 House seats combined in the two elections where Trump has dominated (2016 and 2018). Thus, the GOP has gone from holding 247 seats in 2015 (the highest since 1929) to 199 as of this writing, the lowest level since 2009–2011, when 178 Republicans were elected to the House.

Adding seven governorships brought the Democrats up to controlling 23 of the 50 state executives. Their most significant additions came in the swing states of Michigan and Wisconsin, while Pennsylvania's Democratic governor easily won another term. These states were, of course, the three that put Donald Trump over the top in the 2016 presidential election. Nationally, Democrats gained 334 state legislative seats and seven state legislative houses. This dented but did not overcome the large Republican advantage collectively in state legislatures, where the GOP still has control of 61 of the 99 state legislative houses and fully 52 percent of the 7,383 state legislators across the country. Moreover, Florida, Ohio, Georgia, and Iowa yielded disappointing results for Democrats, as all four states' governorships remained in GOP hands despite aggressive Democratic campaigns.

Overall, there was no Democratic tsunami that swept aside many Republicans considered safe or even favorites, as happened to the Democrats in the GOP tidal waves of 1994 and 2010. Nonetheless, there was a distinct blue wave of considerable size. Given gerrymandering that favors the GOP in many of the competitive states, and the uneconomical distribution of Democratic voters who cluster, for example, in heavily minority districts, adding 40 House seats was remarkable. Once the solid state of the economy is taken into account, the Democratic triumph in the House is even more impressive. Voters ignored economic good times to send a message of deep concern to the sitting president.

There are well established principles that help us to understand the 2018 election and put it into historical context.[2] First, there is a "surge and decline" quality to American elections (and for that matter, the elections in most small "d" democratic countries) that has long been visible. Voters regularly seek to elevate one party in order to limit or replace the other.

Second, the recent U.S. pattern has emphasized the very different electorates of presidential and midterm years. The turnout of eligible adults hovered around 60 percent in 2008 and 2012 while voter participation in 2010 was 42 percent and, in 2014, just 37 percent—the lowest midterm turnout since 1942, when the United States was almost a year into World War II and experiencing severe disruption in the patterns of normal life. It matters greatly, because the presidential electorate is made up of larger numbers of Democratically inclined minority and young voters, while midterm voters usually skew more toward Republican-tilting seniors and whites. Even in 2018, as we hail much greater voter participation in a midterm election, we should stress that the turnout was still millions below the presidential level. What changed in 2018 was that Democrats and others unhappy with President Trump were more motivated to cast a ballot than is usually the case, expanding the electorate in a Democratic direction.

We must not forget the powerful effect that presidential job approval (or disapproval) has on the midterm. It is not accurate to say that a midterm election is a pure referendum on the occupant of the White House. The president's name isn't on the ballot, and too many other factors have some effect, such as candidate quality and campaign financing. Nonetheless, in competitive states and districts, presidential popularity matters. In early November

2018 President Trump's RealClearPolitics national job approval polling average was 43.4 percent (versus 53.4 percent disapproval). What was especially revealing was the intensity of views[3] that weighed against Trump: 40 percent *strongly disapproved* compared to 22 percent that *strongly approved.* There is simply no question that Trump was a heavy weight on the shoulders of Republicans who, for example, represented House districts won by Hillary Clinton and themselves in 2016. Of 25 such districts, Democrats picked up 22 House seats. Overall, House Democratic candidates won 31 districts that Trump carried in 2016, while House Republicans won a mere 3 districts carried by Clinton in 2016.

THE EFFECT OF THE MIDTERM ELECTIONS: COURSE CORRECTION

The midterm election is a remarkable phenomenon that has become a critical part of democracy's superstructure in the United States. Coming at the midpoint of each presidential term, the elections for about a third of the U.S. Senate, the entire U.S. House of Representatives, and nearly three-quarters of the state governorships give voters an opportunity to pass preliminary judgment on the person in the White House.

In the strictest sense, as noted earlier, a midterm is not a referendum on the president. But increasingly, political scientists have come to realize that campaign outcomes for Congress, governors, and even thousands of state legislative posts around the country have a strong relationship to the voters' level of approval for the White House administration.

Of course, it is not a perfect measure because, as mentioned earlier, a lower proportion of Americans turns out to vote in a midterm year than in a presidential year, and the circumstances of each election can vary depending on the overall political climate. One party's activists may be more enthused and thus turn out at a higher rate than the other party's, giving them a leg up in producing victories—as was true for Republicans in both 2010 and 2014, and for Democrats in 2018.

Another reason why a midterm is not a perfect measure of popular opinion is that some states and districts do not have competitive contests in any given year. For example, in 2018, 14 states had no election for governor, 17 lacked a Senate contest, and hundreds of the 435 U.S. House races were either unopposed by one major party or (more commonly) lightly opposed. Naturally, voter turnout was generally lower in the locales that lacked any high-profile, contested race.

Yet another basis on which to question midterm elections can be found by examining the contests individually. While the balance of the voters' identification with one major party versus the other is the overarching factor in most states and districts (plus turnout of the two party bases), the skills of the candidates, as well as the campaigns they run, influence the results. Especially in competitive places where the two parties are closely balanced, election outcomes can depend heavily on the abilities and characteristics of the people running for office—their strengths, weaknesses, financial war chests, policies, etc. Some politicians are a better fit for their states or districts than their opponents, and they may raise more money and run smarter campaigns. Also, incumbents running for reelection can skew the results because they usually have higher name recognition and better contacts with donors (though in 2018, Democrats in competitive contests proved able to outdraw their Republican opponents—incumbent or not—by a wide margin among small donors). A combination of these factors can occasionally produce victory for a candidate even though the national tide is running in the other party's direction.

Most analysts start from the national perspective because the conditions existing in the nation set the tone for virtually every campaign across the United States. From the second midterm of Franklin Roosevelt's presidency in 1938 through the first midterm of Bill Clinton's presidency in 1994, the party in charge of the White House lost House seats in the congressional elections without exception.

Political scientists have laid out logical reasons why this is the case. Some have theorized that midterms serve as electoral reflexes to counterbalance strong party showings in presidential cycles—an often irresistible "surge and decline" in the White House party's fortunes, as mentioned earlier. The notion of checks and balances is deeply rooted in our Constitution and our national psyche. Generally, we recoil from giving one political party too much power for too long. Republicans managed to win the presidency and both houses of Congress in 2016, and the two years that followed were exceptionally controversial. This is an ideal breeding ground for a change in party control of the House.

In the over 70 years since the end of World War II, Americans have switched control of the presidency from one party to another nine times, control of the Senate 10 times, and control of the House eight times. Unified party control of both the executive and legislative branches is becoming rare. More than half the time (44 of the 72 postwar years), the parties have shared power in one combination or another, and the 2018 election has guaranteed that two more years will be added to the split-control total. This is quite remarkable: Since President Richard Nixon came to power in 1969, there have been just 14 years when one party simultaneously had the White House and majorities of both houses of Congress.

This has considerable implications for governance. It is much easier for a party to enact its platform if its officials are in charge across the board. It was only because of large Democratic majorities in both houses of Congress that President Obama was able to (narrowly) secure passage of an $800 billion stimulus bill, health care reform ("Obamacare"), and financial services reform from 2009 to 2010. Similarly, President Trump needed nearly every GOP member of Congress, especially in the closely divided Senate, to get his tax cut and deregulation agenda passed. (Even then, Trump failed by one vote in the Senate to overturn Obamacare.)

Divided control usually produces gridlock, and not as much is accomplished legislatively. On the other hand, some conservatives would argue, invoking Henry David Thoreau and Thomas Jefferson, "That government is best which governs least." To those who favor smaller and less government, gridlock may be a good thing, though of late, spending and the national debt appear to grow by leaps and bounds whether there is one-party control or divided government.

Almost always, voters view the midterm as the designated time for a course correction in the White House, and they send messages by means of their ballots. Even in good times, voters are inclined to trim at least a few seats from the governing White House party, perhaps to remind those in power that the people are the boss. In rocky stretches, when the economy seems to be underperforming or a president has embraced controversial stands, Americans eagerly express their frustrations at the polls. In the last four consecutive midterms (2006, 2010, 2014, and 2018), the electorate has applied the brakes to Presidents Bush, Obama (twice), and Trump's agendas.

Usually, but not always, the president's party loses fewer seats in the first midterm than in the second, which occurs in the sixth year of a two-term presidency. There have been eight of these sixth-year elections in the post–World War II era: 1950, 1958, 1966, 1974, 1986, 1998, 2006, and 2014.[4] This tendency is called the "sixth-year itch." But history can play tricks. There are no iron laws in politics, and the two Obama midterms proved this yet again. Republicans gained 63 House seats in 2010, but only 13 in 2014—in part because the GOP already controlled the vast majority of territory friendly to Republican candidates before the 2014 voting commenced. In the Senate, the pattern was reversed. Back in 2010 the GOP gained just six seats in the Senate, but in 2014 it won nine net seats. It will be interesting to see which precedent prevails in 2022, which will be President Trump's second midterm should he be reelected in 2020.

Lately, we have had a couple of other midterm elections that didn't precisely follow the usual pattern. The durability of the sixth-year itch prior to 1998 led most analysts to speculate about how many seats President Bill Clinton's Democrats would lose, especially in the midst of an impeachment effort following Clinton's sex scandal involving a White House intern. Yet the Democrats actually gained a few House seats and held their own in the Senate, as voters appeared to resent Republican efforts to oust Clinton. The next midterm election in 2002, the first of the George W. Bush presidency, also broke the pattern. In the wake of the terrorist attacks on Sept. 11, 2001, the narrowly elected Bush soared to near-unanimous approval in the opinion polls, and a year later he retained enough of that popularity to add GOP seats in both the House and Senate. This was something that had not occurred in the first midterm election of a presidency since 1934, when Franklin Roosevelt's New Deal program to combat the Great Depression was exceptionally popular.

In truth, every midterm differs from its predecessors in one respect or another. In 2018, Democrats added an impressive number of House seats, yet lost ground in the Senate—a pattern that does not really match any other recent midterm. As an introduction to the rest of this volume, a short history lesson is in order, so that you can see for yourself the ebb and flow of public opinion in modern midterm years.

CHRONOLOGICAL COUNTDOWN TO 2018

Just for starters, let's glance at the midterm results from 1946 to 2018 (also see Tables 1.1 and 1.2, as well as Figures 1.1, 1.2, and 1.3 for reference). It is easy to analyze in retrospect, and every bit of it falls neatly into a sentence or two:

- 1946: After 14 years of solid Democratic control under Franklin D. Roosevelt (FDR) and Truman, voters wanted change. The end of World War II and postwar economic dislocation encouraged the "time for a change" theme. Truman did not seem up to the job—who would, after an icon such as Franklin Roosevelt?—and the mantra became "To err is Truman." So Republicans captured both houses of Congress, grabbing 55 House seats and 12 Senate seats, plus two more governorships (for a total of 25 out of 48).
- 1950: Truman's come-from-behind presidential victory in 1948 had restored Democratic rule by adding 75 House and nine Senate seats. But 18 straight years of Democratic presidencies and an unpopular war in

Korea took their toll again in the midterm, and Democrats gave back 29 House and five Senate seats. Democratic losses in 1950 were nearly identical to the Republican losses in 2006, when another unpopular foreign war, this time in Iraq, dealt the governing party a severe setback.

- 1954: Eisenhower's triumph two years earlier gave the GOP narrow majorities in Congress, even though his coattails were not particularly long. By the time of the midterm, a slight swing away from the Republicans cost 18 of the party's 22 newly gained House seats and two Senate seats, restoring the Democrats to the majority in both the House and the Senate.
- 1958: This is a dramatic modern example of the so-called "sixth-year itch," when voters decide to give the other party sizable congressional majorities after the first six years of a two-term presidency. While Democrats had already held control of Congress in 1956, despite Eisenhower's landslide reelection, the additional 47 House and 13 Senate berths for Democrats ensured that Ike's legislative influence would be minimal in his final two years in office.
- 1962: John F. Kennedy had almost no coattails in his 1960 presidential squeaker; Democrats actually lost 20 House seats and one Senate seat. JFK feared more losses in his 1962 midterm, but the Cuban Missile Crisis—the "Missiles of October"—boosted support for his administration just before the balloting. The result was a wash, with Democrats losing five House seats but picking up four Senate seats. "October Surprises" can affect congressional elections every bit as much as presidential contests do.
- 1966: Lyndon Johnson's historic 61 percent landslide in 1964 appeared to presage a new era of Democratic rule, as he carried in 37 House freshmen and two additional senators to an already heavily Democratic Congress. But that was before the Vietnam War began to devour LBJ. Already by 1966, voters were turning against the president's conduct of the war, and it cost the Democrats 47 House seats and three Senate seats—though not overall control of Congress.
- 1970: Richard Nixon's close 43 percent victory in 1968 did not stop him from dreaming of a "silent majority" of Republicans and conservative Southern Democrats, and he made a major effort to improve the GOP's weak position in Congress. (Nixon had added but five House members and five senators to the Republican minority in 1968.) His efforts paid off to a certain degree, as the GOP added one Senate seat in 1970, while holding House losses to a relatively small 12 seats. Democrats still ruled the Capitol Hill roost, though.

Table 1.1   Gain or Loss for the President's Party: Presidential Election Years

Year	President	House	Senate	Governor
1948	Truman (D)	+75	+9	+5
1952	Eisenhower (R)	+22	+2	+5
1956	Eisenhower (R)	−2	0	−2
1960	Kennedy (D)	−20	−1	+1
1964	Johnson (D)	+37	+2	−1
1968	Nixon (R)	+5	+5	+5
1972	Nixon (R)	+12	−2	−1
1976	Carter (D)	+1	0	+1
1980	Reagan (R)	+34	+12	+4
1984	Reagan (R)	+16	−2	+1
1988	Bush (R)	−3	−1	−1
1992	Clinton (D)	−9	0	+2
1996	Clinton (D)	+3	−2	0
2000	Bush (R)	−2	−4	−1
2004	Bush (R)	+3	+4	0
2008	Obama (D)	+23	+8	+1
2012	Obama (D)	+8	+2*	−1
2016	Trump (R)	−6	−2	+2

Notes: Because of Independents or third-party members, vacancies, and other factors, gains or losses for the president's party do not imply the exact opposite result for the other major party.
*Counts Maine Senator Angus King's victory as a party flip in favor of the Democrats. He took over for a Republican and caucused with Democrats despite being elected as an Independent.
Sources: *Crystal Ball* research, *Vital Statistics on American Politics 2011–2018*.

- 1974: Oddly, Nixon's 61 percent reelection landslide in 1972 almost precisely returned his party to its paltry 1968 levels in both chambers. The Republicans could ill afford a coattail-less election, given what was soon to happen: Nixon's resignation in disgrace, a recession, and an unelected successor GOP president (Gerald Ford) who squandered his initial popularity by pardoning Nixon—all just in time for November 1974. Democrats picked up 48 House seats and four Senate seats; Ford was left mainly with his veto power for his remaining two years in office.
- 1978: Jimmy Carter's narrow 1976 election left Congress virtually unchanged, though still heavily Democratic. And Carter's fall from grace had barely started in 1978. A quiet midterm before the storm of 1980 nonetheless subtracted 15 House and three Senate seats from the Democratic totals.
- 1982: Ronald Reagan's 10-point slaughter of Carter in 1980 was a coattail election, as the GOP also won 34 House seats and 12 Senate seats, defeating many longtime Democratic incumbents. That was enough to

Table 1.2   Gain or Loss for President's Party: Midterm Election Years

Year	President	House	Senate	Governor
1946	Truman (D)	−55	−11	−2
1950	Truman (D)	−29	−5	−6
1954	Eisenhower (R)	−18	−2	−8
1958	Eisenhower (R)	−47	−13	−5
1962	Kennedy (D)	−5	+4	0
1966	Johnson (D)	−47	−3	−8
1970	Nixon (R)	−12	+1	−11
1974	Ford (R)	−48	−4	−5
1978	Carter (D)	−15	−3	−5
1982	Reagan (R)	−26	0	−7
1986	Reagan (R)	−5	−8	+8
1990	Bush (R)	−7	−1	−1
1994	Clinton (D)	−54	−8	−10
1998	Clinton (D)	+4	0	0
2002	Bush (R)	+8	+2	−1
2006	Bush (R)	−30	−6	−6
2010	Obama (D)	−63	−6	−7*
2014	Obama (D)	−13	−9	−3
2018	Trump (R)	−40	+2	−6

Notes: Because of Independents or third-party members, vacancies, and other factors, gains or losses for the president's party do not imply the exact opposite result for the other major party.

*This total of seven includes Florida, which switched on Election Day from an Independent governor, Charlie Crist, to a Republican governor, Rick Scott. Crist was elected as a Republican in 2006 but left the party in spring 2010 to run unsuccessfully for the U.S. Senate (and later became a Democrat to run unsuccessfully for governor again in 2014). We traditionally count party switches in this fashion, though one could argue that there was no change between the elections of 2006 and 2010, and thus the national gain for the GOP in 2010 was six governorships. Take your pick.

Sources: Crystal Ball research, *Vital Statistics on American Politics 2011–2018.*

take over the Senate outright and obtain a working majority on some issues with conservative House Democrats. But this tumultuous period in American politics continued through 1982, when a serious recession deprived the GOP of 26 House seats. The Senate stayed Republican, however, with no net change.

- 1986: After yet another coattail-less reelection of a president—Reagan's massive 59 percent win in 1984—the sixth-year itch returned in 1986, at least in federal elections. Voters handed eight Senate seats to the Democrats, and thus control of that body. The GOP lost only five House seats, but the Democrats were solidly in charge of the House in any event. Remarkably, the Republicans did gain eight governorships, in part because of a large number of Democratic incumbents were either term-limited or didn't seek reelection.
- 1990: Vice President Bush had won Reagan's "third term" in 1988 with

53 percent of the popular vote, but the Republicans suffered from having no coattails again, losing three House seats and one Senate seat. With partisan politics somewhat at abeyance due to the pre-Persian Gulf War military buildup, a quiet midterm saw Republicans lose seven House seats and one Senate berth. Much like Carter in 1978, Bush did not see the gathering storm clouds due to this eerie calm.

- 1994: A recession and a disengaged administration took George H. W. Bush from the all-time height of 90 percent popularity to a humiliating 37 percent finish in the 1992 election. With Ross Perot securing 19 percent, Bill Clinton's 43 percent victory was not impressive, and Democrats lost nine House seats and stayed even in the Senate. A disastrous overreaching by new President Clinton on health care reform, gays in the military, and other issues, coupled with a slow economy, produced a sixth-year itch in the second year. In 1994 Republicans gained an eye-popping 54 House seats and eight Senate seats (nine when Democratic Alabama Senator Richard Shelby switched parties the day after the election) to win control of both houses.

- 1998: Proving that every defeat can yield the seeds of victory, Clinton let Republicans overreach just as he had in the run-up to the 1996 election. Running against both ex-Senate Majority Leader Bob Dole (the GOP nominee) and Speaker Newt Gingrich (the unpopular foil), Clinton won a 49 percent reelection. But Democrats captured only three House seats and actually lost two more Senate seats, leaving Republicans in charge of Congress. Would Clinton have another catastrophic midterm election in 1998? It certainly looked that way as the Monica Lewinsky scandal unfolded. But Republicans again overplayed their hand, beginning unpopular impeachment proceedings that yielded a Democratic gain of four House seats (with the Senate unchanged).

- 2002: "The George W. Bush Midterm," plain and simple. In an election dominated by terrorism, Iraq, and the president himself, the Republicans defied conventional wisdom by gaining seats in both houses of Congress, making Bush the first president since FDR in 1934 to net seats in both chambers in a midterm election. The Democrats were unable to link the poor economy to Bush, and the media's extensive coverage of the impending confrontation with Iraq and the Washington, D.C.-area sniper incidents overshadowed the somewhat fuzzy Democratic election agenda. In the final two weeks of the general election, key White House adviser Karl Rove sent Bush on a whirlwind campaign tour of the battleground states, which ended up reaping rich rewards for the GOP. The Republicans gained two seats in the Senate and eight House seats. The only positive note for the Democrats was a net gain of one governorship, but the GOP maintained a narrow overall statehouse majority (26 to 24).

- 2006: The unpopularity of the Iraq War, the failure of much of President Bush's second-term legislative agenda, and a series of financial and sex scandals that rocked the Republican congressional caucus combined to produce a major sixth-year itch. On Election Day, Democrats won 30 net House seats, six Senate seats, and six governorships. With the help of two Independents, Democrats took control of the Senate by a narrow 51–49 margin, while the party also won a comfortable majority of 233 in the House. The 2006 election marked the effective end of George W. Bush's domestic presidency. He was unable to influence Congress, at least until the bank and Wall Street crisis of September 2008, when both parties joined together to prevent what they feared would be a descent into another Great Depression.
- 2010: When Barack Obama won the White House, he added 23 House seats and eight Senate seats for Democrats, swelling their congressional majorities. But only two years later, the electorate applied the brakes to President Obama's agenda in dramatic fashion. After just four years of

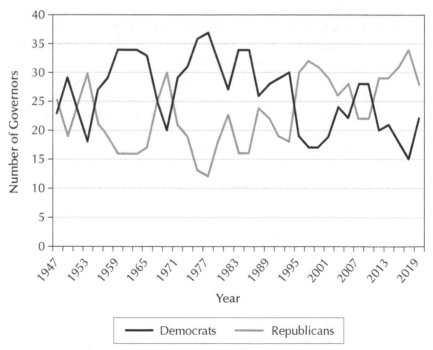

Figure 1.1   Number of Governors by Party, 1949–2019.

control in the House, Democrats gave way to Republicans as the GOP scored a massive landslide, gaining 63 seats and posting a majority of 242 seats. Democrats also lost six net seats in the Senate, but still managed to hold on to a 53-seat majority (again with the help of two Independents). In the statehouse ranks, Democrats lost a net seven governorships. The congressional results at the second year of Obama's presidency were reminiscent of 1994. Voters reacted strongly and negatively to reforms introduced by the new president. In both Clinton's and Obama's cases, health care programs and other liberal initiatives appeared to be the motivators for a large GOP base turnout. Also, for both new Democratic presidents, a balky economy that was only slowly recovering from a recession contributed significantly to low job approval and thus produced large congressional turnover. History does not repeat itself, but it does rhyme.

- 2014: The same slow economy continued right through President Obama's reelection campaign in 2012, yet Obama won by four percentage points and carried in a modest number of additional Democrats (eight in the House and two in the Senate). Following the first-term path, conditions changed rapidly. With Obama once again registering job approval in the low 40s—and much lower approval in many states with key contests—voters completed the transition of Congress from Democratic to Republican control in 2014 by giving the Senate to the GOP. On Election Day, Republicans added eight Senate seats, which was expanded to nine once the Louisiana runoff was held in early December. The new GOP Senate majority of 54 seats guaranteed trouble for President Obama's final two years in the White House. Republicans also added 13 seats to their House total, bringing their majority to 247, one seat greater than the GOP delegation at the start of 1947 and the highest number for the party since 1929. Two additional net governorships went to Republicans, leaving the GOP occupying the top executive office in 31 states.

- 2018: Pundits were far more cautious than usual in projecting Donald Trump's midterm, and with good reason. The near-unanimous prediction that Hillary Clinton would win the presidency in 2016 had proven to be dead wrong, and some battleground state polls were especially inaccurate. The Trump victory was arguably the greatest modern upset in any race for the White House; only Harry Truman's defeat of Republican Thomas E. Dewey, the heavy favorite in 1948, comes close. However, it must be noted that Trump's upset was paper-thin. A mere 77,700 votes in the states of Michigan, Pennsylvania, and Wisconsin *combined* gave Trump the 46 electoral votes that put him over the top in the Electoral College. At the same time, the president lost the popular vote by a record number. Clinton had a plurality of 2.89 million votes over Trump, with 48.0 percent of the national popular vote to Trump's 45.9 percent. This lack of a mandate never affected Trump's behavior. Trump simply dismissed the large popular-vote loss as due to "massive vote fraud," such as voting by illegal immigrants. Not a single recognized expert in the electoral field has found the slightest proof of Trump's reckless charge. President Trump's assertion has undermined confidence in America's political system, especially among millions of his followers who have been inclined to believe a bizarre variety of conspiracy theories. Instead of trying to broaden his popular support after the election, Trump played to his devoted base with consistently inflammatory language that thrilled them but alienated just about everyone else. Trump is the only president in the era of polling (which began in the 1930s) to have failed to achieve majority support for any part of his first two years in office, as measured by the polling averages. Even though Republicans maintained control of both houses of Congress in 2016, Trump's loss of the popular vote assisted Democrats in adding two Senate seats and six House seats. With low popularity, Trump helped to produce the 2018 GOP defeat in the House (-40 seats) and loss of seven state governorships, while gaining only Alaska. The Senate was the bright spot for Republicans in 2018; the GOP majority increased from 51 seats to 53 seats. Yet given the number of Democratic senators (10) up for election in states Trump had won in 2016 by margins of up to 42 percentage points, Republicans were a bit disappointed they were unable to build a larger majority.

MAKING SENSE OF THE 2018
MIDTERM ELECTIONS

Elections can be sliced and diced in numerous ways and from many perspectives in order to augment our understanding. Partisan gerrymandering of the House and self-sorting have made most congressional districts uncompetitive (except potentially in primaries), so usually, even in years when one party has a big edge, relatively few House seats register a party turnover. Yet 2018 is an exception. Mainly, the negative reaction to President Trump in suburbs across the country turned normally red districts to blue, but it is also true that Democrats were better funded than Republicans (thanks to groups like Act Blue collecting tens of millions of small contributions). Democrats also recruited an unusually able class of candidates, with women especially prominent in the top echelon.

Meanwhile, in the Senate's 35 races, a single Republican was defeated (one-term Senator Dean Heller of Nevada) and a total of four Democratic incumbents lost (Senators Joe Donnelly of Indiana, Heidi Heitkamp of North Dakota, Claire McCaskill of Missouri, and Bill Nelson of Florida, the first two being one-termers while McCaskill and Nelson were two- and three-termers, respectively). This was only the second time since 1980 that Republicans had managed to defeat more than two incumbent Democratic senators; the other election year was 2014, when five sitting Democratic senators were defeated. Of the 22 senators in the 11 Southern states, the GOP now has 19 (all but the two in Virginia, Mark Warner and Tim Kaine, and one in Alabama, Doug Jones).

In the 36 gubernatorial contests of 2018, just eight states switched parties. The GOP captured Alaska (which had been held for the last four years by an Independent), while Democrats flipped seven GOP states: Illinois, Kansas, Maine, Michigan, Nevada, New Mexico, and Wisconsin. The most valuable properties in this list are Michigan and Wisconsin, two states that helped propel Donald Trump to the presidency. Perhaps the most surprising is Kansas, a deeply red state that turned blue because Republicans narrowly nominated a candidate viewed as extreme even by many rank-and-file Republicans. However, Democrats again lost Ohio and Florida, two immensely important states where they thought they had a good chance, as well as Georgia. The latter two states had African-American Democratic nominees, and while they came close, close only counts in horseshoes. (More detailed analysis of these contests is contained in later chapters.)

Democrats finally started cutting into the massive gains Republicans had achieved during President Obama's tenure—gaining 334 seats of the nearly 7,400 seats in all 50 state legislatures. These lower-level posts fill the benches from which parties draw many of their nominees for top offices, so this will assist Democrats even though 52.2 percent of all state legislators are Republican. Democrats gained control of seven legislative chambers, though Republicans still have the lion's share of chambers: 61 out of the 98 partisan legislative houses in the 50 states. (Nebraska has a unicameral and technically nonpartisan legislature.) Amazingly, Minnesota is the only state left with Democrats and Republicans splitting control of the two legislative chambers. Every other bicameral state has one party in control of both chambers—yet another measure of the polarized nature of American politics today. Trifecta states—where one party controls the governorship and both houses—still lean to the GOP, too. 14 states have a Democratic trifecta, while 22 states have a Republican trifecta.

Table 1.3   Defeated House Incumbents, 1980–2018

Year	Primary	General
1980	6	30
1982	10	28
1984	3	15
1986	3	6
1988	1	6
1990	1	15
1992	19	24
1994	4	34
1996	2	21
1998	1	6
2000	3	6
2002	8	8
2004	2	7
2006	2	22
2008	3	19
2010	4	54
2012	13	27
2014	5	14
2016	5	8
2018	4	30

WHO TURNED OUT TO VOTE?

Every election is determined by the subsample of Americans who show up—and it differs widely from year to year. This truism is demonstrated anew in the 2018 election. As I mentioned at the outset, the turnout in 2018 of the voting eligible population (VEP; see definition in Table 1.7) was a robust 50.3 percent—the highest since 1914, the year of President Woodrow Wilson's first midterm election. This is well above the average turnout of about 40 percent in the nation's midterm elections in the previous four decades, beginning in 1974 (the first midterm that included the newly enfranchised 18–20-year-olds). The previous GOP landslide year of 2010 had produced a 41.8 percent voter participation rate.

In looking at the total votes by party (Table 1.9), remember that there are different combinations of states and districts electing the Senate, House, and governors in 2018. Yet Democratic candidates garnered a plurality of the vote in all three categories (53.4 percent for House races, 53 percent for Senate seats, and 50.4 percent for gubernatorial contests). By contrast, Republican candidates won 44.8 percent for the House, 39 percent for the Senate, and 47.3 percent for governorships.

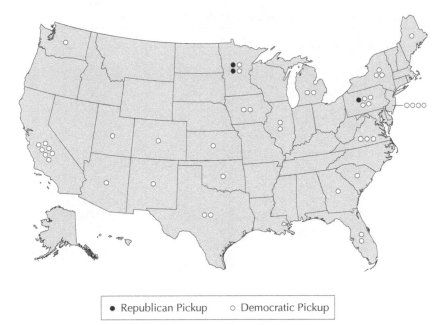

● Republican Pickup   ○ Democratic Pickup

Figure 1.2   U.S. House Seat Pickups in the 2018 Midterm Election. *Source*: Tim Robinson, University of Virginia Center for Politics.

These proportions constitute an overall Democratic victory, even though Democrats lost ground in the Senate due to the combination of states that had seats on the ballot. In the House alone—the only category where an election was held everywhere in the United States—Democrats out-polled Republicans by 8.6 percent. This percentage was greater than the 5.7 percent by which the GOP won the House in 2014 and also the 7.5 percent of 2010, which was the largest GOP advantage since the 9 percent gap that occurred in 1946.

Take a glance at Table 1.8. The 2018 electorate was tilted toward the Democrats thanks to their higher turnout: 37 percent of those voting identified themselves as Democrats, 33 percent as Republican, and 30 percent as Independents. Furthermore, as we shall see later in this chapter, the Independents who cast a ballot were much more inclined to vote Democratic.

The Democratic coloration of the 2018 voters—and the sharp distinctions with the 2016 presidential voters—can best be seen in the exit poll data. There were two exit polls in 2018 by different combinations of media organizations, but for simplicity's sake we have chosen only one for the analysis that follows. The exit poll featured here was conducted by a professional,

Table 1.4   **Defeated Senate Incumbents, 1980–2018**

Year	Primary	General
1980	4	9
1982	0	2
1984	0	3
1986	0	7
1988	0	4
1990	0	1
1992	1	4
1994	0	2
1996	1	1
1998	0	3
2000	0	6
2002	1	3
2004	0	1
2006	0*	6
2008	0	4
2010	2†	2
2012	1	1
2014	0	5
2016	0	2
2018	0	5

Notes: *In 2006, Senator Joseph Lieberman (D) of Connecticut was defeated for renomination in an August 8 primary but won the general election as a petitioning Independent, so he is not included.
†In 2010, Senator Robert Bennett (R) of Utah lost renomination at a convention and is included in the total. Also that year, Senator Lisa Murkowski (R) was defeated in the Republican primary, but won the general election as a write-in, so she is not counted in the total.

nonpartisan polling organization and financed by a consortium of news organizations. In total, 18,788 voters were interviewed by telephone or at polling places. Early and mail-in voters (especially in Colorado, Oregon, and Washington state, where most voters vote by mail, as well as California) were included in the sample by means of telephone polling.

The comparisons between 2018 and 2016 are revealing. Most, though not all, subgroups moved at least a few points in the Democratic direction compared to the presidential election that Donald Trump won. One of the most Democratic groups in the electorate, young voters aged 18–29, gave 55 percent of their votes to Democrats in 2016 but 67 percent in 2018. The other age categories also saw Democratic percentage increases, though only marginally among the oldest voters who are now the most Republican of the age cohorts. Table 1.10, which you will find at the end of this chapter, gives all the key exit poll breakdowns, including many not commented upon directly in this text. It is well worth a read.

Whites as usual voted Republican by a substantial margin (54 percent to

Table 1.5 Senate Races, 2018

State	Candidate	Percentage	Total
Arizona	Kyrsten Sinema (D)	50	1,191,100
	Martha McSally (R)	48	1,135,200
California	Dianne Feinstein (D)*	54	6,019,422
	Kevin de León (D)	46	5,093,942
Connecticut	Chris Murphy (D)*	60	825,579
	Matthew Corey (R)	39	545,717
Delaware	Tom Carper (D)*	60	217,385
	Robert Arlett (R)	38	137,127
Florida	Rick Scott (R)	50	4,099,505
	Bill Nelson (D)*	50	4,089,472
Hawaii	Mazie Hirono (D)*	71	276,316
	Ron Curtis (R)	29	112,035
Indiana	Mike Braun (R)	51	1,158,000
	Joe Donnelly (D)*	45	1,023,553
Maine	Angus King (I)*	54	344,575
	Eric Brakey (R)	35	223,502
	Zak Ringelstein (D)	10	66,268
Maryland	Ben Cardin (D)*	65	1,491,614
	Tony Campbell (R)	30	697,017
Massachusetts	Elizabeth Warren (D)*	60	1,633,371
	Geoff Diehl (R)	36	979,210
Michigan	Debbie Stabenow (D)*	52	2,214,478
	John James (R)	46	1,938,818
Minnesota	Amy Klobuchar (D)*	60	1,566,174
	Jim Newberger (R)	36	940,437
Minnesota (S)	Tina Smith (D)	53	1,370,540
	Karin Housley	42	1,095,777
Mississippi	Roger Wicker (R)*	58	547,619
	David Baria (D)	39	369,567
Mississippi (S)†	Cindy Hyde-Smith (R)*†	41	389,995
	Mike Espy (D)	41	386,742
	Chris McDaniel (R)	16	154,870
Missouri	Josh Hawley (R)	51	1,254,927
	Claire McCaskill (D)*	46	1,112,935
Montana	Jon Tester (D)*	50	253,876
	Matthew Rosendale (R)	47	235,963
Nebraska	Deb Fischer (R)*	58	403,151
	Jane Raybould (D)	39	269,917

Table 1.5 (Continued)

State	Candidate	Percentage	Total
Nevada	Jacky Rosen (D)	50	490,071
	Dean Heller (R)*	45	441,202
New Jersey	Bob Menendez (D)*	54	1,711,654
	Bob Hugin (R)	43	1,357,355
New Mexico	Martin Heinrich (D)*	54	376,998
	Mick Rich (R)	31	212,813
New York	Kirsten Gillibrand (D)*	67	4,056,931
	Chele Farley (R)	33	1,998,220
North Dakota	Kevin Cramer (R)	55	179,720
	Heidi Heitkamp (D)*	44	144,376
Ohio	Sherrod Brown (D)*	53	2,355,923
	Jim Renacci (R)	47	2,053,963
Pennsylvania	Bob Casey, Jr. (D)*	56	2,792,437
	Lou Barletta (R)	43	2,134,848
Rhode Island	Sheldon Whitehouse (D)*	61	231,477
	Robert Flanders (R)	38	144,421
Tennessee	Marsha Blackburn (R)	55	1,227,483
	Phil Bredesen (D)	44	985,450
Texas	Ted Cruz (R)*	51	4,260,553
	Beto O'Rourke (D)	48	4,045,632
Utah	Mitt Romney (R)	63	665,215
	Jenny Wilson (D)	31	328,541
Vermont	Bernie Sanders (I)*	67	183,649
	Lawrence Zupan (R)	27	74,815
Virginia	Tim Kaine (D)*	57	1,910,370
	Corey Stewart (R)	41	1,374,313
Washington	Maria Cantwell (D)*	58	1,803,364
	Susan Hutchison (R)	42	1,282,804
West Virginia	Joe Manchin (D)*	50	290,510
	Patrick Morrisey (R)	46	271,113
Wisconsin	Tammy Baldwin (D)*	55	1,472,914
	Leah Vukmir (R)	45	1,184,885
Wyoming	John Barrasso (R)*	67	136,210
	Gary Trauner (D)	30	61,227

Source: Official Sources
* Indicates incumbent.
(S) Indicates a special election.
† None of the candidates in the Mississippi special election received more than 50% of the vote, resulting in a runoff election. Hyde-Smith (R) beat Espy (D) 54% to 46%.
Note: Percentages may not total 100 because of rounding

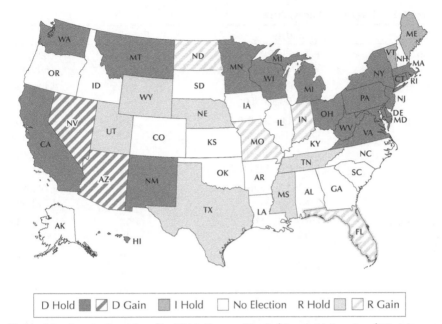

| D Hold ■ | ▨ D Gain | ■ I Hold | ▢ No Election | R Hold ▢ | ▨ R Gain |

Figure 1.3   Senate Race Results, 2018. *Source*: Tim Robinson, University of Virginia Center for Politics.

44 percent) yet all other racial classifications were heavily Democratic, as the table indicates. Also as usual, white men were very Republican, 60 percent to 39 percent. However, white women gave 49 percent to both parties, after having tilted Republican in 2016 by 10 percentage points.

Unmarried women continued their allegiance to the Democrats by a wide (two-to-one) margin; unmarried men were also Democratic by about 10 percent. Those who are married are somewhat more conservative than unmarried Americans, but in 2018 married men voted GOP by a very small margin, while married women shifted to the Democrats by 10 percentage points. About three-quarters of LGBT Americans voted Democratic, one-quarter chose Republicans—more or less the standard split in this segment of the electorate.

While Democratic voting percentages grew in most subgroups, the normal divisions of American politics were still visible, and not just among the races, genders, and age groupings. Democrats handily won voters making less than $50,000 a year, with those over $50,000 splitting their votes fairly evenly between the parties. Those who benefitted most from the Trump tax cuts (Americans with incomes over $100,000) voted Republican, but just by a few percentage points.

Table 1.6 Governors' Races, 2018

State	Candidate	Percentage	Total
Alabama	Kay Ivey (R)*	59	1,022,457
	Walt Maddox (D)	40	694,495
Alaska	Mike Dunleavy (R)	51	145,631
	Mark Begich (D)t	44	125,739
Arizona	Doug Ducey (R)*	56	1,330,863
	David Garcia (D)	42	994,341
Arkansas	Asa Hutchison (R)*	65	582,406
	Jared Henderson (D)	32	283,218
California	Gavin Newsom (D)	62	7,721,410
	John Cox (R)	38	4,742,825
Colorado	Jared Polis (D)	53	1,348,888
	Walker Stapleton (R)	43	1,080,801
Connecticut	Ned Lamont (D)	49	694,510
	Bob Stefanowski (R)	46	650,138
Florida	Ron DeSantis (R)	50	4,076,186
	Andrew Gillum (D)	49	4,043,723
Georgia	Brian Kemp (R)	50	1,978,408
	Stacey Abrams (D)	49	1,923,685
Hawaii	David Ige (D)*	63	244,934
	Andria Tupola (R)	34	131,719
Idaho	Brad Little (R)	60	361,661
	Paulette Jordan (D)	38	231,081
Illinois	J.B. Pritzker (D)	54	2,479,746
	Bruce Rauner (R)*	39	1,765,751
Iowa	Kim Reynolds (R)*	50	667,275
	Fred Hubbell (D)	48	630,986
Kansas	Laura Kelly (D)	48	506,509
	Kris Kobach (R)	43	453,030
Maine	Janet Mills (D)	51	320,962
	Shawn Moody (R)	43	272,311
Maryland	Larry Hogan (R)*	55	1,275,644
	Ben Jealous (D)	44	1,002,639
Massachusetts	Charlie Baker (R)*	67	1,781,341
	Jay Gonzalez (D)	33	885,770
Michigan	Gretchen Whitmer (D)	53	2,266,193
	Bill Schuette (R)	44	1,859,534
Minnesota	Tim Walz (D)	54	1,393,096
	Jeff Johnson (R)	42	1,097,705

Table 1.6 (Continued)

State	Candidate	Percentage	Total
Nebraska	Pete Ricketts (R)*	59	411,812
	Bob Krist (D)	41	286,169
Nevada	Steve Sisolak (D)	49	480,007
	Adam Laxalt (R)	45	440,320
New Hampshire	Chris Sununu (R)*	53	302,764
	Molly Kelly (D)	46	262,359
New Mexico	Michelle Lujan Grisham (D)	57	398,368
	Steve Pearce	43	298,091
New York	Andrew Cuomo (D)*	60	3,635,340
	Marc Molinaro (R)	36	2,207,602
Ohio	Mike DeWine (R)	50	2,231,917
	Richard Cordray (D)	47	2,067,847
Oklahoma	Kevin Stitt (R)	54	644,579
	Drew Edmondson (D)	42	500,973
Oregon	Kate Brown (D)*	50	934,498
	Knute Buehler (R)	44	814,988
Pennsylvania	Tom Wolf (D)*	58	2,895,662
	Scott Wagner (R)	41	2,039,899
Rhode Island	Gina Raimondo (D)*	53	198,122
	Allan Fung (R)	37	139,932
South Carolina	Henry McMaster (R)*	54	921,342
	James Smith (D)	46	784,182
South Dakota	Kristi Noem (R)	51	172,912
	Billie Sutton (D)	48	161,454
Tennessee	Bill Lee (R)	60	1,336,106
	Karl Dean (D)	39	864,863
Texas	Greg Abbott (R)*	56	4,656,196
	Lupe Valdez (D)	43	3,546,615
Vermont	Phil Scott (R)*	55	151,261
	Christine Hallquist (D)	40	110,335
Wisconsin	Tony Evers (D)	50	1,324,307
	Scott Walker (R)*	48	1,295,080
Wyoming	Mark Gordon (R)	67	136,412
	Mary Throne (D)	28	55,965

Source: Official Sources
* Indicates incumbent.

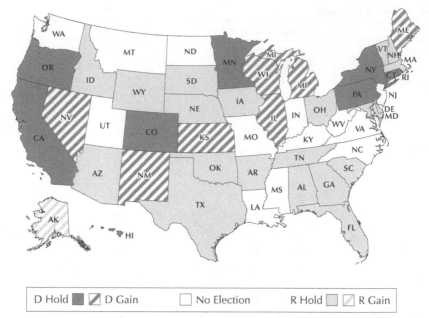

Figure 1.4 Governors' Race Results, 2018. *Source*: Tim Robinson, UVA Center for Politics, University of Virginia.

The GOP won Protestants by 14 percentage points, Catholics split about evenly, and those with other religions as well as no religion chose Democrats by very wide margins.

As would be expected in this polarized era, Democrats won almost all Democratic Party identifiers in the electorate (95 percent), and the Republicans swept the GOP voters (94 percent). It was among Independents that preferences changed from 2016 to 2018. Trump won Independents by 6 percent, but two years later Democrats won them by double that, 12 percent. Partly, of course, turnout among Democratic-leaning Independents was up in 2018. Still, we always look at the Independents as an indication of how the election will likely swing.

The Democratic-dominated identity of the 2018 electorate is also revealed in the job approval numbers for President Trump: 45 percent approved, 55 percent disapproved. Moreover, those strongly disapproving of Trump (46 percent) were much more numerous than the group of voters strongly approving of Trump (31 percent). Opinions about Trump's job performance were mainly predictive of the 2018 congressional election results state by state and district by district. It is very difficult today for candidates to separate themselves from their party label; the presidential shadow is pronounced and reduces split-ticket voting, as later chapters will suggest.

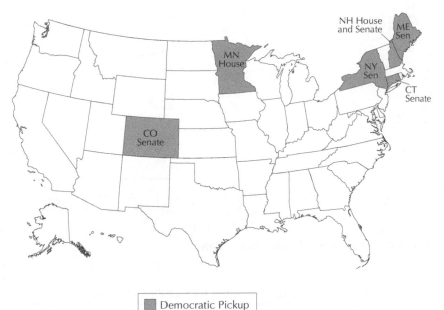

Figure 1.5 **State Legislature Changes, 2018.** *Source*: Tim Robinson, University of Virginia Center for Politics.

Table 1.7 Voter Turnout in Midterm Elections

Year	Turnout of Voting Eligible Population (VEP)
1962	47.7%
1966	48.7%
1970	47.3%
1974	39.1%
1978	39.0%
1982	42.1%
1986	38.1%
1990	38.4%
1994	41.1%
1998	38.1%
2002	40.5%
2006	41.3%
2010	41.8%
2014	36.7%
2018	50.3%

Note: Voting eligible population (VEP) means the voting age population (adults age 21 and over from 1962–1970, and age 18 and over from 1974 until present) minus those ineligible to vote, such as non-citizens, felons, and mentally incapacitated persons, but adding persons in the military or civilians living overseas who are eligible to cast ballots in U.S. elections.
Source: United States Elections Project, http://www.electproject.org/

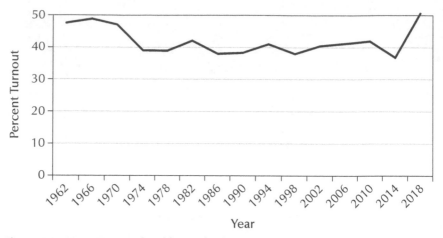

Figure 1.6   Voter Turnout in Midterm Elections.

Table 1.8   Party Identification among Voters Who Cast a Ballot, 1998–2018

	2018	2016	2014	2012	2010	2008	2006	2004	2002	2000	1998
Republican	33	33	36	32	35	32	36	38	40	32	33
Democrat	37	36	35	38	35	39	38	38	31	37	34
Independent	30	31	28	29	29	29	26	25	23	27	30

Sources: 2004, 2006, 2008, 2010, 2012, 2014, 2016, & 2018: Conducted Election Day by Edison Media Research for the Nat'l Election Pool; surveyed 19,441 voters as they left the polls or early voters who said they had already voted via phone; margin of error +/− 1%. 2002: Exit poll conducted November 6–7, 2002, and released on November 18, 2002, by Ayres McHenry and Associates (R) for the American Association of Health Plans. The company surveyed 1,000 voters and had a margin of error +/− 3 percent. This is the only exit poll available for 2002, because the Voter News Service network consortium had an organizational meltdown on Election Day and was unable to provide verifiable polling data for 2002.

CONNECTING THE DOTS

In the last dozen years, 2006 to 2018, every election but one has been a change election. After a dozen years of GOP control in the House, Democrats took over Congress in 2006. Barack Obama swept to power in 2008, ending GOP control of the White House. A backlash to Obama led to a GOP landslide for the House in 2010. Republicans completed their takeover of Congress by capturing the Senate in 2014. Two years later, Donald Trump shocked the world in a repudiation of both Obama and his chosen Democratic presidential nominee, Hillary Clinton. But two years after that, in 2018, Democrats grabbed the House back by a comfortable margin as voters punished Trump for his excesses. Only in 2012 did American voters endorse the entire status quo, reelecting Obama, a Democratic Senate, and a Republican House.

Table 1.9   Total Votes by Party, 2018

Party	Number of Votes	Percentage
Governors		
Republicans	43,452,881	47.3
Democrats	46,253,757	50.4
Independents/Others	2,132,664	2.3
Total	91,839,302	
Senate		
Republicans	34,868,108	39.0
Democrats	47,388,765	53.0
Independents/Others	7,227,961	8.1
Total	89,484,834	
House		
Republicans	50,983,895	44.8
Democrats	60,727,598	53.4
Independents/Others	1,967,161	1.7
Total	113,678,654	

Source: Calculations by author. Percentages may not total 100 percent because of rounding.

How to explain so many shifts in so few years? Usually it was presidential unpopularity caused by a corrosive war (Iraq), a bad economy, and/or scandal. Yet all indicators do not have to be pointing down for the White House to experience an electoral setback. As we discussed before, even a very good economy could not save Trump's Republicans from a House shellacking in 2018.

There was a solid midterm voter turnout in 2018, but the next election in 2020 will be decided by a considerably larger electorate than the one that showed up last November. President Trump's record and job approval rating will undoubtedly matter enormously. We address the 2020 possibilities later in this volume.

It is vital to remember that every election follows a different drumbeat, created by the special combination of issues and candidates in a particular year. None of this is especially predictable two years in advance; the next White House contest viewed solely through the lens of its previous midterm results is distorted, sometimes severely. Occasionally, though, a midterm can project the themes that will dominate the next contest for the presidency.

Be careful about connecting the dots too quickly. The Democratic near landslide of 2008 could never have foretold the thumping Democrats took in 2010. Nor did the Republican tsunami of 2010 tell us very much about the eventual outcome in 2012, and so on. Everybody has an opinion, freely expressed. But only a fool would bet much on election results so distant in the future.

The past is worth analyzing at length because retrospective judgment grounded in hard data is fascinating and illuminating. But the future is endlessly unknowable, and we should be hesitant to project a reality beyond our knowledge. Events not in anyone's immediate control (economy, war, scandal, terrorism, the identity of the Democrats' nominee—and perhaps even the Republican choice) can only be guessed at now.

Table 1.10   Exit Polls, 2018

Vote by gender

(Percentage of Total)	Democrat	Republican
Male (48%)	47% [41%]*	51% [52%]**
Female (52%)	59% [54%]	40% [41%]

Vote by age

(Percentage of Total)	Democrat	Republican
18–29 (13%)	67% [55%]	32% [36%]
30–44 (22%)	58% [51%]	39% [41%]
45–64 (39%)	49% [44%]	50% [52%]
65 + (26%)	48% [45%]	50% [52%]

Vote by age

(Percentage of Total)	Democrat	Republican
18–24 (7%)	68% [56%]	31% [35%]
25–29 (6%)	66% [53%]	33% [39%]
30–39 (15%)	59% [51%]	37% [40%]
40–49 (16%)	52% [46%]	46% [50%]
50–64 (30%)	49% [44%]	50% [53%]
65 + (26%)	48% [45%]	50% [53%]

Vote by age

(Percentage of Total)	Democrat	Republican
18–44 (35%)	61% [52%]	36% [40%]
45 + (65%)	49% [44%]	50% [53%]

Vote by race

(Percentage of Total)	Democrat	Republican
White (72%)	44% [37%]	54% [58%]
African American (11%)	90% [88%]	9% [8%]
Latino (11%)	69% [65%]	29% [29%]
Asian (3%)	77% [65%]	23% [29%]
Other (3%)	54% [56%]	42% [37%]

Table 1.10   (Continued)

Vote by race

	Democrat	Republican
(Percentage of Total)		
White (72%)	44% [37%]	54% [58%]
Nonwhite (28%)	76% [74%]	22% [21%]

Vote by gender and race

	Democrat	Republican
(Percentage of Total)		
White men (35%)	39% [31%]	60% [63%]
White women (37%)	49% [43%]	49% [53%]
Black men (5%)	88% [80%]	12% [13%]
Black women (6%)	92% [94%]	7% [4%]
Latino men (5%)	63% [62%]	34% [33%]
Latino women (6%)	73% [68%]	26% [26%]
All other races (6%)	66% [61%]	32% [32%]

Vote by age and race

	Democrat	Republican
(Percentage of Total)		
White 18–29 (8%)	56% [43%]	43% [48%]
White 30–44 (15%)	48% [37%]	48% [55%]
White 45–64 (29%)	40% [34%]	59% [63%]
White 65 + (22%)	43% [39%]	56% [58%]
Black 18–29 (2%)	92% [83%]	7% [9%]
Black 30–44 (3%)	92% [87%]	7% [7%]
Black 45–64 (5%)	88% [90%]	11% [9%]
Black 65 + (2%)	88% [90%]	11% [9%]
Latino 18–29 (2%)	81% [70%]	17% [24%]
Latino 30–44 (2%)	74% [71%]	25% [22%]
Latino 45–64 (3%)	63% [67%]	35% [29%]
Latino 65 + (2%)	71% [71%]	25% [24%]
All others (6%)	65% [60%]	33% [34%]

Vote by education

	Democrat	Republican
(Percentage of Total)		
High school or less (23%)	48%	51%
Some college (25%)	52%	47%
Associate's degree (11%)	47%	50%
Bachelor's degree (24%)	55%	43%
Advanced degree (17%)	65%	34%

Table 1.10 (Continued)

Are you a college graduate?

	Democrat	Republican
(Percentage of Total)		
Yes (41%)	59% [52%]	39% [43%]
No (59%)	49% [44%]	49% [52%]

Education and race

	Democrat	Republican
(Percentage of Total)		
White college graduates (31%)	53% [45%]	45% [49%]
White no degree (41%)	37% [28%]	61% [67%]
Nonwhite college graduates (10%)	77% [71%]	22% [23%]
Nonwhite no degree (18%)	76% [75%]	22% [20%]

Whites by education and gender

	Democrat	Republican
(Percentage of Total)		
White college women (16%)	59%	39%
White non-college women (21%)	42%	56%
White college men (15%)	47%	51%
White non-college men (20%)	32%	66%
All nonwhites (28%)	76%	22%

Vote by income

	Democrat	Republican
(Percentage of Total)		
Under $30,000 (17%)	63%	34%
$30,000–$49,999 (21%)	57%	41%
$50,000–$99,999 (29%)	52%	47%
$100,000–$199,999 (25%)	47%	51%
Over $200,000 (9%)	47%	52%

Vote by income

	Democrat	Republican
(Percentage of Total)		
Under $100K (67%)	56% [49%]	42% [45%]
$100K or more (33%)	47% [47%]	52% [48%]

Table 1.10　(Continued)

Vote by income

	Democrat	Republican
(Percentage of Total)		
Less than $50K (38%)	59% [52%]	38% [41%]
$50K or more (62%)	49% [47%]	50% [49%]

Vote by income

	Democrat	Republican
(Percentage of Total)		
Under $50K (38%)	59% [52%]	38% [41%]
$50K–$100K (29%)	52% [46%]	47% [50%]
$100K or more (33%)	47% [47%]	52% [48%]

Vote by party ID

	Democrat	Republican
(Percentage of Total)		
Democrats (37%)	95% [89%]	4% [9%]
Republicans (33%)	6% [7%]	94% [90%]
Independents (30%)	54% [42%]	42% [48%]

Vote by gender and party

	Democrat	Republican
(Percentage of Total)		
Democratic men (14%)	94% [87%]	5% [10%]
Democratic women (23%)	96% [90%]	3% [8%]
Republican men (17%)	6% [6%]	94% [90%]
Republican women (16%)	6% [8%]	93% [89%]
Independent men (16%)	51% [37%]	44% [51%]
Independent women (13%)	56% [47%]	39% [43%]

Vote by ideology

	Democrat	Republican
(Percentage of Total)		
Liberal (27%)	91% [84%]	8% [10%]
Moderate (37%)	62% [52%]	36% [41%]
Conservative (36%)	16% [15%]	83% [81%]

Table 1.10 (Continued)

Vote by marital status

	Democrat	Republican
(Percentage of Total)		
Married (59%)	51% [43%]	47% [53%]
Unmarried (41%)	61% [55%]	37% [38%]

Vote by gender and marital status

	Democrat	Republican
(Percentage of Total)		
Married men (30%)	48% [37%]	51% [58%]
Married women (29%)	54% [49%]	44% [47%]
Unmarried men (18%)	54% [46%]	44% [45%]
Unmarried women (23%)	66% [62%]	31% [33%]

Are you a parent?

	Democrat	Republican
(Percentage of Total)		
Yes (30%)	54%	44%
No (70%)	55%	43%

Children under 18

	Democrat	Republican
(Percentage of Total)		
Only boys (11%)	59%	39%
Only girls (8%)	54%	45%
Both boys and girls (11%)	50%	48%
No children under 18 (70%)	55%	43%

Parents

	Democrat	Republican
(Percentage of Total)		
Fathers (14%)	48%	50%
Mothers (16%)	60%	39%
Men without children (34%)	51%	47%
Women without children (36%)	59%	39%

Table 1.10   (Continued)

Does anyone in your household own a gun?

	Democrat	Republican
(Percentage of Total)		
Yes (46%)	36%	61%
No (53%)	72%	26%

Served in the U.S. military

	Democrat	Republican
(Percentage of Total)		
Veterans (14%)	41% [34%]	58% [61%]
Non-veterans (86%)	56% [50%]	43% [45%]

Vote by religion

	Democrat	Republican
(Percentage of Total)		
Protestant (25%)	38%	61%
Catholic (26%)	50%	49%
Other Christian (23%)	47%	52%
Jewish (2%)	79%	17%
Muslim (1%)	N/A	N/A
Other religion (6%)	70%	28%
No religious belief (17%)	70%	28%

Religion, combined Protestant and other Christian

	Democrat	Republican
(Percentage of Total)		
Protestant/Other Christian (47%)	42% [39%]	56% [58%]
Catholic (26%)	50% [45%]	49% [52%]
Jewish (2%)	79% [71%]	17% [24%]
Other (8%)	73% [62%]	25% [29%]
No religion (17%)	70% [68%]	28% [26%]

How often do you attend religious services?

	Democrat	Republican
(Percentage of Total)		
Weekly or more (32%)	40% [40%]	58% [56%]
A few times a month (13%)	52% [46%]	46% [49%]
A few times a year (27%)	61% [48%]	37% [47%]
Never (27%)	68% [62%]	30% [31%]

Table 1.10   (Continued)

How often do you attend religious services?

	Democrat	Republican
(Percentage of Total)		
Monthly or more (46%)	44% [42%]	55% [54%]
Less than that (54%)	65% [54%]	34% [40%]

White born-again or evangelical Christian?

	Democrat	Republican
(Percentage of Total)		
Yes (26%)	22% [16%]	75% [81%]
No (74%)	66% [59%]	32% [35%]

First-time midterm election voter?

	Democrat	Republican
(Percentage of Total)		
Yes (16%)	62%	36%
No (84%)	53%	46%

2016 presidential vote

	Democrat	Republican
(Percentage of Total)		
Clinton (43%)	94%	5%
Trump (40%)	8%	91%
Other (8%)	54%	41%
Did not vote (8%)	70%	28%

Views of Donald Trump as president

	Democrat	Republican
(Percentage of Total)		
Strongly approve (31%)	5%	94%
Somewhat approve (14%)	24%	74%
Somewhat disapprove (8%)	63%	34%
Strongly disapprove (46%)	95%	4%

Views of Donald Trump as president

	Democrat	Republican
(Percentage of Total)		
Approve (45%)	11%	88%
Disapprove (54%)	90%	8%

Table 1.10   (Continued)

Was your vote for U.S. House today to:

	Democrat	*Republican*
(Percentage of Total)		
Support Trump (26%)	4%	95%
Oppose Trump (38%)	94%	4%
Trump not a factor (33%)	44%	52%

Opinion of the Democratic Party

	Democrat	*Republican*
(Percentage of Total)		
Favorable (48%)	92% [88%]	6% [8%]
Unfavorable (47%)	13% [9%]	86% [85%]

Opinion of the Republican Party

	Democrat	*Republican*
(Percentage of Total)		
Favorable (44%)	12% [11%]	87% [86%]
Unfavorable (52%)	87% [73%]	11% [20%]

Favorable opinion of:

	Democrat	*Republican*
(Percentage of Total)		
Both parties (6%)	66%	30%
Only Democrats (41%)	96%	2%
Only Republicans (37%)	3%	96%
Neither party (10%)	48%	47%

Opinion of Nancy Pelosi

	Democrat	*Republican*
(Percentage of Total)		
Favorable (31%)	89%	10%
Unfavorable (56%)	24%	75%

Which party should control the U.S. House?

	Democrat	*Republican*
(Percentage of Total)		
The Democrats (52%)	96%	3%
The Republicans (44%)	5%	94%

Table 1.10 (Continued)

Should Congress impeach Donald Trump

	Democrat	Republican
(Percentage of Total)		
Yes (39%)	92%	7%
No (56%)	19%	78%

Direction of the country

	Democrat	Republican
(Percentage of Total)		
Right direction (42%)	13% [90%]	86% [8%]
Wrong track (54%)	85% [25%]	13% [69%]

Politically, do you think Americans are:

	Democrat	Republican
(Percentage of Total)		
Becoming more united (9%)	28%	70%
Becoming more divided (76%)	60%	39%
Staying about the same (13%)	32%	66%

Time of decision in U.S. House election

	Democrat	Republican
(Percentage of Total)		
Last few days (8%)	53%	41%
Last week (8%)	49%	48%
Last month (19%)	51%	46%
Earlier than that (63%)	52%	47%

Time of decision in U.S. House election

	Democrat	Republican
(Percentage of Total)		
In last month (35%)	51%	46%
Before that (63%)	52%	47%

Time of decision in U.S. House election

	Democrat	Republican
(Percentage of Total)		
In last week (16%)	51%	45%
Before that (82%)	52%	47%

Table 1.10   (Continued)

Most important issue facing the country

	Democrat	Republican
(Percentage of Total)		
Health care (41%)	75%	23%
Immigration (23%)	23%	75%
Economy (22%)	34%	63%
Gun policy (10%)	70%	29%

Condition of national economy

	Democrat	Republican
(Percentage of Total)		
Excellent (17%)	12% [83%]	87% [16%]
Good (51%)	47% [76%]	51% [19%]
Not so good (23%)	83% [39%]	15% [55%]
Poor (7%)	85% [15%]	8% [79%]

Condition of national economy

	Democrat	Republican
(Percentage of Total)		
Good (68%)	39% [77%]	60% [18%]
Poor (31%)	83% [31%]	14% [63%]

Family's financial situation vs. two years ago

	Democrat	Republican
(Percentage of Total)		
Better today (36%)	21%	77%
Worse today (14%)	80%	18%
About the same (49%)	69%	29%

Effect of Trump's trade policies on local economy

	Democrat	Republican
(Percentage of Total)		
Helped (25%)	9%	91%
Hurt (29%)	89%	8%
Had no impact (37%)	53%	45%

Table 1.10 (Continued)

Effect of new tax laws on your personal finances

	Democrat	Republican
(Percentage of Total)		
Helped (29%)	15%	84%
Hurt (22%)	83%	15%
Had no impact (45%)	62%	36%

Health care in the U.S. needs:

	Democrat	Republican
(Percentage of Total)		
Major changes (69%)	55%	43%
Minor changes (24%)	41%	57%
No changes (4%)	40%	60%

Who would better protect preexisting conditions?

	Democrat	Republican
(Percentage of Total)		
Democrats (57%)	89%	9%
Republicans (35%)	4%	94%

Are Donald Trump's immigration policies:

	Democrat	Republican
(Percentage of Total)		
Too tough (46%)	90%	8%
Not tough enough (17%)	14%	86%
About right (33%)	13%	85%

Views on stricter gun control measures

	Democrat	Republican
(Percentage of Total)		
Support (59%)	76%	22%
Oppose (37%)	22%	76%

View of the Russia investigation

	Democrat	Republican
(Percentage of Total)		
Mostly justified (41%)	85%	14%
Politically motivated (54%)	25%	73%

Table 1.10   (Continued)

View of Mueller's handling of Russia investigation

	Democrat	Republican
(Percentage of Total)		
Approve (41%)	79%	19%
Disapprove (46%)	28%	71%

Does Trump's foreign policy make the U.S.:

	Democrat	Republican
(Percentage of Total)		
Safer (38%)	8%	91%
Less safe (46%)	90%	9%
No difference (13%)	60%	38%

View of Kavanaugh's Supreme Court appointment

	Democrat	Republican
(Percentage of Total)		
Support (43%)	12%	87%
Oppose (47%)	90%	9%

How should the Supreme Court handle Roe vs. Wade?

	Democrat	Republican
(Percentage of Total)		
Keep as is (66%)	69%	30%
Overturn it (25%)	21%	79%

In the U.S. today:

	Democrat	Republican
(Percentage of Total)		
Whites are favored (41%)	87%	11%
Minorities are favored (19%)	12%	85%
No group is favored (33%)	29%	69%

Importance of electing racial/ethnic minorities

	Democrat	Republican
(Percentage of Total)		
Very important (43%)	79%	20%
Somewhat important (29%)	44%	55%
Not too important (10%)	20%	79%
Not at all important (13%)	12%	84%

Table 1.10   (Continued)

Importance of electing racial/ethnic minorities

	Democrat	*Republican*
(Percentage of Total)		
Important (72%)	65%	34%
Not important (24%)	16%	82%

Importance of electing more women to public office

	Democrat	*Republican*
(Percentage of Total)		
Very important (45%)	82%	17%
Somewhat important (33%)	45%	52%
Not too important (12%)	17%	80%
Not at all important (8%)	8%	90%

Importance of electing more women to public office

	Democrat	*Republican*
(Percentage of Total)		
Important (78%)	66%	32%
Not important (20%)	13%	84%

Sexual harassment in this country today is:

	Democrat	*Republican*
(Percentage of Total)		
A very serious problem (46%)	72%	26%
A somewhat serious problem (38%)	48%	50%
Not too serious a problem (11%)	20%	79%
Not a serious problem (3%)	N/A	N/A

Sexual harassment in this country today is:

	Democrat	*Republican*
(Percentage of Total)		
A serious problem (84%)	61%	37%
Not a serious problem (14%)	20%	79%

Has government done enough to protect this election?

	Democrat	*Republican*
(Percentage of Total)		
Yes (38%)	27%	71%
No (50%)	75%	24%

Table 1.10   (Continued)

Which concerns you more? Some people will:

	Democrat	Republican
(Percentage of Total)		
Cast illegitimate votes (36%)	21%	78%
Be prevented from voting (53%)	80%	18%

Are you gay, lesbian, bisexual, or transgender?

	Democrat	Republican
(Percentage of Total)		
Yes (6%)	82% [78%]	17% [14%]
No (94%)	51% [47%]	47% [48%]

In your vote today, was recent extremist violence:

	Democrat	Republican
(Percentage of Total)		
The most important factor (23%)	62%	37%
An important factor (51%)	51%	48%
A minor factor (9%)	38%	60%
Not a factor at all (9%)	36%	61%

Was recent extremist violence important to vote?

	Democrat	Republican
(Percentage of Total)		
Yes (74%)	54%	44%
No (18%)	37%	61%

Was recent extremist violence a factor in vote?

	Democrat	Republican
(Percentage of Total)		
Yes (83%)	53%	46%
No (9%)	36%	61%

Area type

	Democrat	Republican
(Percentage of Total)		
Urban area (32%)	65% [59%]	32% [35%]
Suburban area (51%)	49% [45%]	49% [50%]
Rural area (17%)	42% [34%]	56.% [62%]

Source: "Exit Polls," CNN, https://www.cnn.com/election/2018/exit-polls
*Bracketed percentages in "Democrat" column indicate percentages received by Hillary Clinton in 2016.
**Bracketed percentages in "Republican" column indicate percentages received by Donald Trump in 2016.

NOTES

1. Glenn Kessler, Salvador Rizzo, and Meg Kelly, "President Trump has made 6,420 false or misleading claims over 649 days," *Washington Post*, November 2, 2018, https://www.washingtonpost.com/politics/2018/11/02/president-trump-has-made-false-or-mis leading-claims-over-days/?utm_term = .7bcc793ec63a.

2. Parts of the remainder of this chapter are drawn from previous volumes of the continuing Center for Politics series on national elections, published every two years since 2000.

3. The averages collected by RealClearPolitics do not gauge different approval levels for the president. Thus, the numbers that follow come from a poll taken by *Reuters*/Ipsos from 11/7/2018 to 11/13/2018.

4. 1950, 1966, and 1974 are not technically true "six-year itch" elections. The presidents serving during those times, Harry S. Truman, Lyndon B. Johnson, and Gerald R. Ford respectively, were not in their second terms. I have included them, however, as they all succeeded presidents of the same party and were effectively serving out their predecessors' terms.

2

The Trump Effect

The 2018 Midterm Election as a Referendum on a Polarizing President

Alan I. Abramowitz

Over 118 million Americans went to the polls in 2018—by far the largest number ever in a midterm election. They chose 435 members of the House of Representatives, 35 U.S. Senators, 36 governors, and thousands of members of state legislatures. The candidates spent vast sums of money and countless hours trying to influence voters. A small army of volunteers rang doorbells and distributed campaign literature. The airwaves were flooded with campaign ads and millions of citizens spread information, and sometimes misinformation, about the candidates via Facebook, Twitter, and other social media platforms. Yet, despite all of the money and effort expended by candidates and their supporters, in the end, the results of these elections were shaped largely by one man. The 2018 midterm election was, to an extraordinary degree, a referendum on the presidency of Donald Trump. President Trump would not have had it any other way.

Every midterm election is, to some extent, a referendum on the incumbent president's performance.[1] While the president's party almost always loses seats in the House of Representatives and usually loses seats in the Senate, the magnitude of those losses depends on the president's popularity. In the 18 midterm elections between 1946 and 2014, the president's party lost an average of 26 seats in the House and four seats in the Senate. However, in the nine elections in which the president's approval rating was 50 percent or higher, the average losses were only 14 seats in the House and two seats in the Senate. In contrast, in the nine elections in which the president's approval rating was under 50 percent, the average losses were 37 seats in the House and six seats in the Senate.

Three factors help to explain why the 2018 midterm election, more than most other midterms in the post-World War II era, became a referendum on the performance of the incumbent president: the growing nationalization of congressional elections since the 1970s, the intensity of voters' opinions about Donald Trump, and the president's unusually aggressive campaigning on behalf of Republican candidates.

Congressional elections have become increasingly nationalized over the past several decades in response to growing party polarization.[2] To a much greater extent than during the 1970s and 1980s, voters base their candidate choices in individual House and Senate contests on which party they want to control the chamber rather than which individual they want to represent their district or state. Thus, in a September 2018 Pew Research Center Survey, 75 percent of registered voters indicated that party control of Congress would be a factor in their vote: the highest percentage of voters citing party control of Congress as a factor in any midterm election since 1998.[3] This increased focus on party control of the chamber means that national issues, including opinions of the president, have a stronger influence on voting decisions than in the past. The late Democratic House Speaker Tip O'Neill famously stated that "all politics is local." Today, however, it would be more accurate to say that all politics is national.

The second reason why opinions of the president had an unusually powerful influence on the 2018 midterm elections is the intensity with which those opinions were held by voters. It is clear that Donald Trump inspires very strong reactions from the American people. Most Americans either love him or hate him. Relatively few have mixed opinions. However, while Trump inspires both strongly positive and strongly negative feelings among the public, throughout his presidency, those with strongly negative feelings have outnumbered those with strongly positive feelings by a fairly wide margin. This can be seen very clearly in the results of a CNN poll conducted on November 1–3, 2018, just days before the midterm election.[4] In this poll, Trump had an overall approval rating of 39 percent and an overall disapproval rating of 55 percent. Thirty percent of respondents approved strongly of his performance and 45 percent disapproved strongly. Only 9 percent of respondents approved moderately and only 10 percent disapproved moderately.

The ratio of strong to moderate opinions was even more striking among likely voters in the CNN survey. Among that more politically engaged group of respondents, 35 percent approved strongly and 52 percent disapproved strongly. Only 6 percent approved moderately and only 5 percent disapproved moderately. Thus, a remarkable 87 percent of likely voters had a strong opinion of the president's performance. This is important because voters with strong opinions are much more likely to vote on the basis of those opinions than those who feel less strongly. Thus, according to the 2018 national exit poll, 94 percent of those who strongly approved of the president voted for Republican House candidates while 95 percent of those who strongly disapproved voted for Democratic House candidates. In contrast, only 74 percent of those who somewhat approved voted for Republican House candidates and only 63 percent of those who somewhat disapproved voted for Democratic House candidates.[5]

The final reason why the presidential referendum effect was so pronounced in 2018 is that President Trump did everything in his power to turn the election into a referendum on his performance. To a much greater extent than other recent presidents, Trump campaigned aggressively for his party's candidates, especially his party's Senate candidates. Overall, Trump campaigned with GOP candidates in 16 of the 33 states with Senate contests. He held two or three rallies with six Republican candidates and four rallies with three candidates. At almost every one of these campaign events, many of which were covered on national news broadcasts, the president explained that even though he was not a candidate in 2018, his presidency was "on the ticket," urging voters to show their support for his policies by voting for GOP candidates.[6]

All of this campaigning on behalf of Republican candidates might seem surprising given the president's upside-down poll numbers. According to a weighted average of polls computed by FiveThirtyEight, on the date of the midterm election, President Trump had an approval rating of 42 percent and a disapproval rating of 53 percent. This suggests that for many GOP candidates, an appearance with the president might do more harm than good. And indeed, many Republican candidates tried to distance themselves from Trump during the campaign, especially those running in suburban House districts where the president was extremely unpopular.

Despite Trump's poor overall approval rating, however, his campaigning for GOP candidates may have had a rational purpose. By the summer of 2018, it was already apparent that Republicans were likely to lose their majority in the House of Representatives. Therefore, the focus of the White House and Republican campaign operatives was on holding, and perhaps expanding, the Republican majority in the Senate where the map was far more encouraging.[7] Of the 35 Senate seats up for grabs in 2018, 26 were held by Democrats, including 10 in states that Trump had carried in 2016.

Five of those Democratic seats—in Indiana, Missouri, Montana, North Dakota, and West Virginia—were in states that Trump had carried by a double-digit margin. In these states, holding a campaign rally with the president could have been helpful in turning out Republican base voters. At the same time, however, Trump's aggressive campaigning may have helped Democrats to run up their numbers in suburban House districts by increasing the salience of his performance as an issue in the minds of voters.

Whatever the president's intent may have been, it is clear that when they cast their ballots in the 2018 midterm election, voters, and especially Democratic voters, were very focused on his performance. According to a post-election survey conducted by the Pew Research Center, 64 percent of voters indicated that in casting their ballot in the congressional election, they were either voting for or against President Trump. Only 35 percent said that Trump was not much of a factor in their vote. However, those voting against the president greatly outnumbered those voting for the president: 39 percent of voters indicated that they were voting against Trump versus 25 percent who were voting for Trump. Among those voting for a Democratic candidate, 71 percent said they were voting against Trump. Among those voting for a Republican candidate, only 52 percent said they were voting for Trump.[8]

These findings reflect not only the growing nationalization of congressional elections but the prevalence of negative voting in midterm elections.[9] One of the main reasons why the president's party generally takes a hit in midterm elections is that opponents of the president are usually more motivated to express their dissatisfaction than supporters of the president are to express their satisfaction. That was clearly the case in 2018.

POLITICAL ENGAGEMENT AND TURNOUT

President Trump's impact on the 2018 election was also evident in another way—voter engagement and turnout. According to a September 18–24, 2018, Pew Research Center Survey, enthusiasm about voting was higher in 2018 than in any of the three previous midterm elections, including the 2010 midterm election in which Republicans made major gains. But the most striking feature of the rise in voter enthusiasm in 2018 is that it was concentrated mainly among those planning to vote for Democratic candidates. The percentage of Democratic voters indicating that they were more enthusiastic than usual about voting rose from 42 percent in 2010 and 36 percent in 2014 to a remarkable 67 percent in 2018. In contrast, the percentage of Republican voters indicating that they were more enthusiastic than usual was fairly stable, going from 57 percent in 2010 and 52 percent in 2014 to 59 percent in 2018. So while Republican voters were about as enthusiastic about voting as they had been in the two previous midterm elections, Democratic voters were far more enthusiastic.[10]

The unusually high level of voter enthusiasm recorded in the Pew Survey translated into a record level of voter turnout in the 2018 midterm election. According to data compiled by Michael McDonald's United States Elections Project, the total number of votes cast in the midterm election rose from 83 million in 2014 to an astonishing 118 million in 2018. In percentage terms, turnout rose from only 36.7 percent of eligible voters in 2014 to 50.3 percent of eligible voters in 2018. This was by far the largest increase in turnout from one midterm election to the next in the past century. Whereas the 2014 turnout was the lowest for any midterm election since 1942, the 2018 turnout was the highest for any midterm election since 1914.[11] There is little doubt that one person was largely responsible for the extraordinary surge in voter turnout that occurred in 2018—Donald Trump.

The surge in turnout in 2018 meant that the composition of the 2018 electorate was somewhat different from the composition of other recent midterm electorates. Specifically, the racial composition of the electorate was similar to that seen in recent presidential elections. According to the national exit poll, nonwhites made up 28 percent of the electorate in 2018, only slightly less than the 29 percent nonwhite share of the 2016 electorate and considerably larger than the 25 percent nonwhite share of the 2014 electorate. The Latino share of the electorate surged from only 8 percent in 2014 to 11 percent in 2018. Given the overall increase in turnout, this meant that the actual number of Latino voters nearly doubled. That higher Latino turnout contributed to Democratic victories in several competitive House districts in southern California, Arizona, and New Mexico as well as Democratic victories in the Arizona and Nevada Senate elections.

This increase in the nonwhite share of the electorate was partly responsible for a modest but significant swing in the partisan composition of the electorate. Whereas Republican identifiers outnumbered Democratic identifiers by one percentage point in 2014, Democratic identifiers outnumbered Republican identifiers by four percentage points in 2018. In the 2010 and 2014 midterm elections, Democrats suffered substantial setbacks because many of the voters making up their base were not as motivated to turn out as those making up the Republican base.[12] Thanks in large part to President Trump, however, that was not the case in 2018.

A DEEP POLICY DIVIDE

We have seen that Americans were sharply divided in their assessments of President Trump in 2018. The large majority of Republican voters not only approved but strongly approved of the president's performance. An even larger majority of Democrats not only disapproved but strongly disapproved of his performance. Moreover, these divisions over President Trump's performance reflected deep divisions over many of the president's major policy initiatives, and, just as in the case of opinions about the president himself, those who disapproved of his policies typically outnumbered those who approved. This was clearly the case with regard to two of the president's most significant domestic policy initiatives—the tax cut law passed by Trump and the Republican Congress in 2018 and billions of dollars in tariffs imposed by the administration on imports from China and other countries that the president accused of engaging in unfair trade practices.

According to a September 18–24, 2018, Pew Research Center Poll, only 36 percent of registered voters approved of the Republican tax law compared with 46 percent who disapproved. Seventy-two percent of Republicans approved compared with only 11 percent of Democrats. In the same survey, only 38 percent of registered voters felt that increased tariffs were good for the country, while 53 percent felt that they were bad for the country. Seventy percent of Republican voters felt that the higher tariffs were good for the country while 79 percent of Democratic voters felt that they were bad for the country.[13]

A similar pattern was evident when it came to perhaps the GOP's and Trump's most spectacular failed policy initiative during his first two years in office: the attempt to repeal and replace the Affordable Care Act (ACA; the law better known as Obamacare). With a Republican president in the White House and Republican majorities in the House and Senate, party leaders had good reason to believe that their long-held dream of repealing Obamacare would come to fruition. Instead, and despite Trump's repeated assurances that Republicans would pass a health care law that would not only expand coverage and protect individuals with preexisting conditions but lower health care costs to consumers, the GOP could never agree on anything other than repealing the Affordable Care Act. Even that attempt ultimately fell short with the party suffering a humiliating defeat on the floor of the Senate when Arizona's John McCain joined two other Republicans—Susan Collins of Maine and Lisa Murkowski of Alaska—to cast the decisive votes against repeal.[14]

The GOP's timing on this issue could not have been worse. Just as the president and congressional Republicans were moving to repeal the Affordable Care Act, polls showed that support for the law was at an all-time high. A February 7–12, 2017, Pew Research Center survey found, for the first time, a majority of the public approving of the law. Moreover, in addition to the 54 percent who approved of the ACA, among the 43 percent who disapproved, only 17 percent wanted to "get rid of the law entirely," while 25 percent wanted to keep it with modifications. Not surprisingly, there was a big partisan divide in opinions of the ACA. Eighty-five percent of Democrats, compared with only 10 percent of Republicans, approved of the law. But only 44 percent of Republicans favored repeal. Forty-two percent wanted to keep the law in place with modifications.[15]

Americans were also sharply divided over what was clearly the president's highest-profile policy proposal: building a wall along the U.S. border with Mexico. And just as with the tax law, tariffs, and repeal of the Affordable Care Act, opponents of the president's policy outnumbered supporters. According to a February 12–17, 2017, Pew Research Center Survey, 62 percent of Americans opposed building a wall along the border compared with only 35 percent who supported it. Republicans, including Independents leaning toward the Republican Party, favored building a wall by a margin of 74 percent to 24 percent. However, Democrats, including Independents leaning toward the Democratic Party, opposed building the wall by an even more lopsided margin of 89 percent to 8 percent.[16] It is clear from these data that discontent with President Trump prior to the midterm election was based not just on concerns about his personality and leadership style but on opposition to many of his major policy initiatives.

HOUSE AND SENATE RESULTS

The results of the 2018 midterm elections were a stinging setback for the president and his party. While the GOP did manage to increase its majority in the Senate by two seats thanks to an extremely favorable map, Democrats scored major gains on every other front. In the House elections, Democrats took back the majority by adding 40 seats and won the national popular vote for the House by a whopping 8.6 percentage points, or nearly 10 million votes. Meanwhile, Democrats scored major gains in state elections, picking up seven governorships and more than 300 seats in state legislatures.

There was an extremely close connection between the performance of Donald Trump in the 2016 presidential election and the performance of Republican candidates in the 2018 Senate and House elections. Figures 2.1 and 2.2 display scatterplots of the relationship between Trump's margin

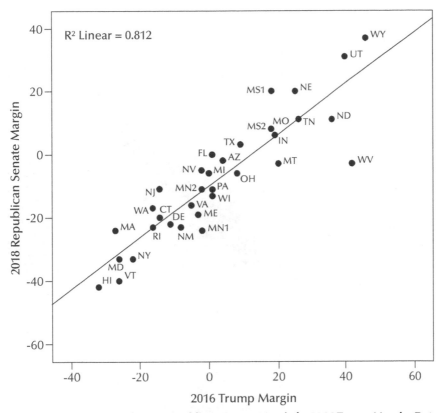

Figure 2.1   Scatterplot of 2018 Republican Senate Margin by 2016 Trump Margin. Data compiled by author.

against Hillary Clinton in 2016 and the margins of Republican Senate and House candidates in 2018. In the case of the Senate elections, the correlation between the 2016 Trump vote and the 2018 Republican Senate vote was .90, which means that the 2016 Trump margin explains over 80 percent of the variance in the 2018 GOP Senate margin. An examination of Figure 2.1 shows that only one Senate result was very far from what was predicted based on the presidential result. Democratic incumbent Joe Manchin managed to hold onto his seat by a margin of three points in West Virginia—a state that Donald Trump carried by 42 points in 2016.

Republicans defeated four Democratic incumbents in states won by Trump in 2016: Florida, Indiana, Missouri, and North Dakota. However, Democrats defeated a Republican incumbent in Nevada, a state won by Hillary Clinton in 2016, and won an open Republican seat in Arizona, a state won narrowly

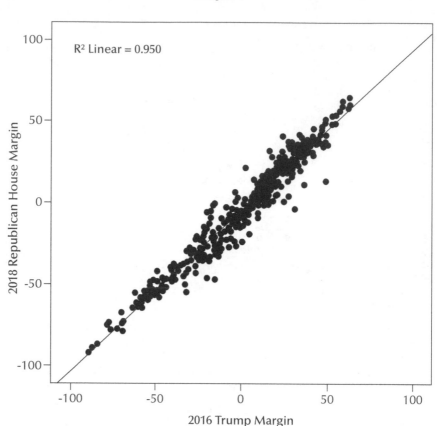

Figure 2.2   Scatterplot of 2018 Republican House Margin by 2016 Trump Margin. Data compiled by author.

by Trump two years earlier. Republicans did not win a single seat in a state carried by Hillary Clinton in 2016 while Democrats won seven seats in states carried by Trump: Arizona, Michigan, Montana, Pennsylvania, Ohio, West Virginia, and Wisconsin.

In the House elections, the 2016 presidential vote was an even stronger predictor of the results. The correlation between the Trump margin in 2016 and the GOP margin in 2018 was an astonishing .98, the highest for any election in at least 70 years. This means that the 2016 Trump margin explains 95 percent of the variation in the 2018 Republican House margin. Democratic challengers defeated 30 Republican incumbents in 2018. Not one Republican challenger defeated a Democratic incumbent.

Table 2.1   Outcomes of 2018 House Races in Republican Districts by 2016 Trump Margin

	2016 Trump Margin				
Winning Party	LT 0.00	0.0–4.99	5.00–9.99	10.00 +	Total
Republican	3	2	17	174	196
Democratic	20	8	6	5	39
Total	23	10	23	179	235

Source: Data compiled by author.

Table 2.1 displays the relationship between the Trump margin in 2016 and the results of 2018 House elections in districts previously held by Republicans. The data in this table show that Democratic gains in the House elections were heavily concentrated in districts that Donald Trump either lost in 2016 or won by less than five percentage points. Democrats flipped 20 of 23 seats in districts won by Clinton, including 14 of 17 seats with running Republican incumbents. They also flipped eight of 10 seats in districts that Trump won by less than five points, including six of eight seats with running Republican incumbents. In contrast, they flipped only six of 23 seats in districts that Trump won by between five and 10 points and only five of 179 seats in districts that Trump won by more than 10 points.

While the 2016 Trump vote was highly predictive of the 2018 Republican Senate and House vote, large majorities of Republican Senate and House candidates ran behind Trump. As a result, Democrats were able to win many contests in states and districts carried by Trump two years earlier, especially states and districts where his margin was under five points. In the Senate elections, Republicans ran behind Trump in 31 out of 34 contested races (there was no Republican candidate in California), including five of six contests with running Republican incumbents. In the House elections, Republicans ran behind Trump in 307 out of 392 contested races, including 142 out of 194 contested races with running Republican incumbents and 57 of 61 open-seat contests.

One question that the data on 2018 Senate elections makes it possible to address is the impact of President Trump's aggressive campaigning on behalf of Republican Senate candidates. Table 2.2 displays the results of a regression analysis of the 2018 Republican margin in 34 contested Senate elections on three predictors: the 2016 Trump margin in the state, the incumbency status of the race (coded as $+1$ for contests with running Republican incumbents, 0 for open seat contests, and -1 for contests with running Democratic

Table 2.2   Regression Analysis of 2018 Republican Senate Margin with 2016 Trump
Margin, Incumbency Status of Race, and Trump Campaign Rallies in State

Independent Variable	B (St. Error)	Beta	t-ratio	Sig. (1-tailed)
Constant	−4.844			
Trump Margin	.725 (.071)	.800	10.14	.001
Incumbency	6.973 (1.70)	.290	4.11	.001
Rallies	−.955 (0.97)	−.070	−0.99	N.S.

Source: Data compiled by author.

incumbents), and the number of campaign rallies in which the president appeared with the Republican Senate candidate.

The results show that the 2016 Trump margin was by far the strongest predictor of the 2018 Republican Senate margin. For each additional one point of margin for Trump, Republican Senate candidates gained an additional 0.725 points of margin. Incumbency also mattered. After controlling for the presidential results, incumbents gained about seven points of margin compared with what would be expected in an open-seat contest. However, these results indicate that the president's campaigning did not help Republican Senate candidates. In fact, the estimated coefficient for the campaign visits variable is negative although it is not close to statistical significance.

Republican candidates consistently ran behind Trump's 2016 margin in their state regardless of how many campaign rallies the president held on their behalf. In fact, by this metric, the 16 GOP candidates Trump campaigned for did slightly worse than the 18 candidates he did not campaign for, running an average of 13 points behind Trump in terms of margin compared with only 8.6 points for those he did not campaign for. Thus, it appears that whatever benefit Republican candidates received from a GOP base that was energized by Trump's campaigning was offset by a Democratic base that was also energized by Trump's campaigning.

IMPLICATIONS FOR 2020 AND BEYOND

Historically, the outcomes of midterm elections have not predicted the outcomes of either the presidential or the congressional elections that occur two years later. Indeed, recent history is full of examples of parties that suffered major setbacks in midterm elections but came back to win big victories two years later. In 1994, two years after Bill Clinton was elected president, Democrats suffered a defeat of historic proportions, losing control of both chambers of Congress for the first time in 40 years. Two years later, Clinton was easily reelected although Republicans did keep control of the House and Senate. Likewise, in 2010, two years after Barack Obama's landmark election, Republicans scored major gains in the midterm elections, taking back control of the House and picking up six seats in the Senate. Two years later, Obama won a second term in the White House. So there is no reason to assume that just because Republicans fared poorly in the 2018 midterm elections, President Trump cannot be reelected in 2020 or Republicans cannot make gains in the House and Senate elections.

Nevertheless, some aspects of the 2018 results probably should cause concern for the president and his supporters and for congressional Republicans. One is the remarkable surge in political engagement in the electorate as a whole but especially among Democrats. As long as Donald Trump is in the White House, there is no reason to think that will not continue through November 2020. Supercharged partisan polarization is a major problem for a political system based on checks and balances in which little can be accomplished without some degree of bipartisan cooperation and compromise. But one clear benefit of the intensified partisan divisions of the Trump era is heightened political engagement among the public and especially among supporters of the opposition party. Based on the turnout in 2018, it will not be surprising if voter turnout reaches record levels, at least for the modern era, in 2020. That is probably not good news for Republicans because it means that young people and racial minorities are likely to make up a larger share of the electorate and Donald Trump's approval ratings among groups such as millennials, African Americans, and Hispanics are extraordinarily low even for a Republican. Just as importantly, Trump seems to have little or no interest in doing anything that might improve his standing with these groups.

Every presidential election is, to some extent, a referendum on the performance of the incumbent. However, that is especially true when the incumbent is seeking a second term in the White House. Thus, for the 11 elections since World War II in which an incumbent was running for reelection, the correlation between the president's net approval rating and his share of the major party is a striking .92. In contrast, for the seven open-seat elections, the correlation is only .74. This means that when an incumbent is running, approval rating explains 85 percent of the variance in vote share; when the incumbent is not running, approval rating explains only 55 percent of the variance in vote share.

Of the 11 incumbents who have run for a second term in the White House since World War II, only three were unsuccessful: Gerald Ford in 1976, Jimmy Carter in 1980, and George H. W. Bush in 1992. Both Carter and Bush had approval ratings that were deep in negative territory at the time they were seeking a second term. Ford's approval rating in 1976 was barely in positive territory but his situation was rather unusual. Not only was Ford the only incumbent president who had never been elected to either the presidency or the vice presidency, he was also burdened by the deep unpopularity of his predecessor, Richard Nixon, the man who had appointed him to the vice presidency. If we remove Ford from the list of 11 incumbents seeking reelection, the correlation between approval rating and vote share jumps to .95.

These results suggest that Donald Trump's chances of winning a second term in the White House will be minimal if his approval numbers are anywhere near as bad as they were in late 2018 and early 2019. Even if the economy remains fairly strong, winning a second term would probably depend on getting his approval rating up considerably closer to the point where as many voters approve as disapprove of his performance. Certainly other presidents have been able to turn their approval ratings around during their third and fourth years in office. This was true of Bill Clinton and Barack Obama. It was also true of Ronald Reagan, who saw his net approval rating fall far below zero during 1982 but who won reelection in a landslide based on a strongly positive rating in the fall of 1984.

In contrast to the earlier presidents, however, Donald Trump has shown little ability or even interest in expanding his support in the American electorate beyond his hard-core party base. Since his first few weeks in office, his approval rating has remained consistently under water in almost every poll by every reputable polling organization. In late 2018 and early 2019 he continued to maintain solid ratings from Republicans but very poor ratings from Independents as well as Democrats. That pattern of support might be enough to protect him from a strong primary challenge, but it probably would not be enough to win him a second term in the White House, especially given the intensity of the disapproval. Indeed, in a January 21–24, 2019, *Washington Post*/ABC News poll, 56 percent of Americans including 59 percent of Independents, 64 percent of women, and 56 percent of suburbanites indicated that they definitely would vote against Trump in 2020 while only 28 percent indicated that they definitely would vote for him. In contrast, the percentage of Americans who indicated that would definitely vote against Barack Obama in six polls conducted during his first term ranged between 41 percent and 46 percent.[17]

Of course, it is possible that in 2020, Donald Trump could again eke out a victory in the Electoral College despite losing the popular vote. After all, it has happened twice in the last five presidential elections, after not happening once between 1888 and 2000. The key to Trump's Electoral College victory in 2016 was his extremely narrow wins in three swing states: Michigan, Pennsylvania, and Wisconsin. Trump carried each state by less than one percentage point. He also carried Florida with its trove of 29 electoral votes by a margin of just over one percentage point. If the popular vote margin in 2020 is again quite close there is at least a small chance of another Electoral College "misfire." And as in 2000 and 2016, a misfire would be more likely to favor the Republican candidate than the Democratic candidate because the swing states tilt slightly more Republican than the nation as a whole. But the chance of a misfire diminishes rapidly when the popular vote margin grows beyond two points. So while a misfire cannot be ruled out, it is clearly not something that President Trump can count on to save his candidacy.

An unpopular president running for a second term would also make it very difficult for Republicans to take back control of the House of Representatives and could even cost them control of the Senate. Given the extremely close connection between presidential and House voting patterns, a Trump defeat could well cost Republicans additional seats in the House. And the 2020 Senate map is much less favorable for the GOP than the 2018 map. In 2020, Democrats will need to gain at least four seats to take control of the Senate, and 22 Republican seats will be up for grabs compared with only 12 Democratic seats. It won't be easy—Democrats might well lose Doug Jones's seat in Alabama (unless Republicans nominate Roy Moore again), but six GOP seats could well be in play: Arizona, Colorado, Georgia, Iowa, Maine, and North Carolina.

Beyond 2020, it is very difficult to gauge the long-term effects of Trump's presidency on the party system and the electorate. Much obviously depends on the results of the 2020 elections and what direction the GOP takes after Donald Trump leaves the scene. However, there are some clear warning signs for Republicans in the results of the 2018 and other recent elections.

Republicans have lost the national popular vote in six of the last seven presidential elections. Losing in 2020 would make it seven of eight—an unprecedented string of losses for a major party in U.S. history. More ominously, the Trump's presidency and the subservience of Republicans in Congress to Trump may be doing long-term damage to the GOP brand among women, who already make up a majority of the electorate, and several other groups that will form a larger share of the electorate in the future—college graduates, millennials, and nonwhites, especially Hispanics. Meanwhile, non-college whites, the group that makes up a disproportionate share of Trump's core supporters, will continue to shrink as a share of the electorate. These trends began long before Donald Trump descended the golden escalator in Trump Tower to announce his candidacy for the White House, but the

Trump presidency appears to be exacerbating them in ways that pose a danger to the GOP's continued viability in national elections. Counting on a shrinking base of supporters, gerrymandered districts, and Electoral College misfires does not seem like a smart long-term business plan for a 21st century political party.

NOTES

1. James E. Campbell, "Presidential Losses in Midterm Congressional Elections," *The Journal of Politics*, Vol. 47, No. 4 (November 1985): 1140–1157. See also, Alan I. Abramowitz, "Economic Conditions, Presidential Popularity and Voting Behavior in Midterm Congressional Elections," *The Journal of Politics*, Vol. 47, No. 1 (Feb. 1985): 31–43.

2. Alan I. Abramowitz and Steven Webster, "The Rise of Negative Partisanship and the Nationalization of U.S. Elections in the 21st Century," *Electoral Studies*, Vol. 41 (2016): 12–22.

3. Pew Research Center, "Voter Enthusiasm at Record High in Nationalized Midterm Environment," September 26, 2018, http://www.people-press.org/2018/06/20/2-the-2018-congressional-election/.

4. Jennifer Agiesta, "CNN Poll: In Final Days, Democrats Maintain Advantage," November 5, 2018, https://www.cnn.com/2018/11/05/politics/cnn-poll-midterms-democrats-advantage/index.html.

5. Results of 2018 exit polls can be found at: https://www.cnn.com/election/2018/exit-polls.

6. Ashley Parker and John Dawsey, " 'I Am on the Ticket': Trump Seeks to Make the Election about Him, Even if Some Don't Want It to Be," *Washington Post*, October 18, 2018, https://www.washingtonpost.com/politics/i-am-on-the-ticket-trump-seeks-to-make-the-election-about-him-even-if-some-dont-want-it-to-be/2018/10/17/069406f6-d0bc-11e8-a275-81c671a50422_story.html?utm_term = .d320b1181535.

7. See Sean Sullivan, "GOP Increasingly Fears Loss of House, Focuses on Saving Senate Majority," *Washington Post*, April 9, 2018, https://www.washingtonpost.com/politics/gop-increasingly-fears-loss-of-house-focuses-on-saving-senate-majority/2018/04/08/6483ffc0-39bb-11e8-acd5-35eac230e514_story.html?utm_term = .45c6de6dc339.

8. Pew Research Center, "Public Expects Gridlock, Deeper Divisions with Changed Political Landscape," November 15, 2018, http://www.people-press.org/2018/11/15/public-expects-gridlock-deeper-divisions-with-changed-political-landscape/.

9. Samuel Kernell, "Presidential Popularity and Negative Voting: An Alternative Explanation of the Midterm Congressional Decline of the President's Party," *The American Political Science Review*, Vol. 77, No. 1 (March 1977): 44–66.

10. Pew Research Center, "Voter Enthusiasm at Record High in Nationalized Midterm Environment," September 26, 2018, http://www.people-press.org/2018/09/26/voter-enthusiasm-at-record-high-in-nationalized-midterm-environment/.

11. Turnout data for midterm and presidential elections can be found at the United States Elections Project website: http://www.electproject.org/home/voter-turnout/voter-turnout-data.

12. Ron Brownstein, "Can the Democrats Convince Millennials to Vote in 2018?" *The Atlantic*, May 4, 2017, https://www.theatlantic.com/politics/archive/2017/05/millennials -vote-democratic-party-minorities/525273/.

13. Pew Research Center, "2018 Midterm Voters: Issues and Political Values," Oct. 4, 2018, http://www.people-press.org/2018/10/04/2018-midterm-voters-issues-and-political -values/.

14. Robert Pear and Thomas Kaplan, "Senate Rejects Slimmed-Down Obamacare Repeal as McCain Votes No," *New York Times*, July 27, 2017, https://www.nytimes.com/ 2017/07/27/us/politics/obamacare-partial-repeal-senate-republicans-revolt.html.

15. Hannah Fingerhut, "Support for 2010 Health Care Law Reaches New High," Pew Research Center, February 23, 2017, http://www.pewresearch.org/fact-tank/2017/02/23/ support-for-2010-health-care-law-reaches-new-high/.

16. Rob Suls, "Most Americans Continue to Oppose Border Wall, Doubt Mexico Would Pay for It," Pew Research Center, February 24, 2017, http://www.pewresearch.org/ fact-tank/2017/02/24/most-americans-continue-to-oppose-u-s-border-wall-doubt-mexico -would-pay-for-it/.

17. Michael Scherer and Scott Clement, "Democrats' 2020 Presidential Contest Is Wide Open as Danger Mounts for Trump, New Washington Post-ABC News Poll Shows," *Washington Post*, January 29, 2019, https://www.washingtonpost.com/politics/democrats -2020-presidential-contest-is-wide-open-as-danger-mounts-for-trump-new-washington -post-abc-news-poll-shows/2019/01/28/88a3fd16–227b-11e9–90cd-dedb0c92dc17_story .html?utm_term = .207 67e642585.

3

The Primaries of 2018

Democrats Shine in the Era of Trump

Rhodes Cook

The primary elections of 2018 were some of the most unusual and consequential in modern American history. They featured an outsized role by President Donald Trump, who threw himself into the Republican primaries with a gusto unseen by any previous president. There, he enjoyed almost uninterrupted success in fashioning a field of GOP candidates that were defined by their loyalty to Trump.

The Democratic contests often showed sharper fault lines with a passion generated by sharp antipathy to the president. Fissures between progressives in the tradition of Bernie Sanders and a more benign party establishment may turn dark in 2020. But in 2018, Trump provided the glue for Democratic unity.

The headlines instead from the Democratic side were about making history, with a record number of women and candidates of racial, ethnic, and sexual diversity entering the electoral process. They participated mainly in the Democratic primaries, and by winning a considerable number of nominations and then elections in 2018, they opened a whole new era in American politics.

Midterm primaries in the past have often been defined by the more mundane manner of anti-incumbency, as measured by the number of sitting senators, representatives, and governors that were defeated for renomination by their party's voters. In the 2018 election cycle, the combined total numbered only six. Four casualties were House members (two Republicans and two Democrats). One was an appointed senator, Republican Luther Strange of Alabama, who lost the GOP nomination in a 2017 special primary election runoff. And one casualty was an unelected governor, Republican Jeff Colyer of Kansas, who was narrowly beaten in his primary by a favorite of Trump.

All in all, it was a modest number of defeated incumbents in the 2018 primaries that paled in comparison to some years past. Thirteen House members, for instance, lost primaries in the post-redistricting year of 2012; three senators were denied renomination in 2010; two governors were primary losers in 2004. The 2018 primaries did not come close to matching those levels of political volatility.[1]

And for that matter, Trump's level of involvement in the elections had at best a mixed effect. Throughout 2018, there was a perceptible "enthusiasm gap" between the two parties, with the Democrats showing an advantage because of their engrained antipathy to Trump that extended back to his successful "rock 'em, sock 'em, anything goes" presidential campaign against Hillary Rodham Clinton in 2016. Trump's efforts to arouse the Republican base did appear to generate some badly needed fervor on the GOP side in 2018. Yet in both the primaries and general election that year, far more Democratic than Republican votes were cast.

In the general election, a compilation by David Wasserman of the *Cook Political Report* showed that the aggregate nationwide vote for Democratic House candidates in November 2018 was nearly 10 million votes higher than the tally for Republicans: 60.7 million to 51 million. The Democratic total represented a record number of congressional votes in a midterm election for either party, and it is safe to say produced a record margin of victory in the overall vote. The payoff: Democrats scored a net gain of 40 House seats and flipped Congress's lower chamber.[2]

Meanwhile, voting in the 2018 primaries gave a strong clue that it would be a good year for the Democrats. The aggregate nationwide tally of primary votes favored them by almost 3 million—nearly 19.8 million to 17 million—using the total two-party vote for Senate or gubernatorial candidates, whichever was highest in a particular state. The tally was based on results from 43 states where both parties held primary contests for either Senate or governor and votes for candidates of both parties were tallied.[3]

TRUMP DOMINATES THE REPUBLICAN PRIMARIES

It is safe to say that no president in the nation's history threw himself into a midterm election as fully and forcefully as Donald Trump. He campaigned

Table 3.1   Incumbent Senate, House, Gubernatorial Primary Losers since 2000

In terms of the number of incumbents defeated, the 2018 election cycle's Senate, House, and gubernatorial primaries were quiet ones. The incumbent casualty list totaled just four House members, one senator, and one governor, with the latter two—Republican Sen. Luther Strange of Alabama and Republican Gov. Jeff Colyer of Kansas—unelected, having assumed office after the 2016 election. The House casualties were Republicans Robert Pittenger of North Carolina and Mark Sanford of South Carolina, and Democrats Michael Capuano of Massachusetts and Joe Crowley of New York. The latter was the most highly positioned of the four, serving as chairman of the Democratic Caucus in the House at the time of his primary defeat. Alabama's Strange, the lone senator to lose an intraparty contest this election cycle, was appointed to his seat in early 2017 upon the resignation of Senator Jeff Sessions to become attorney general in the Trump administration. Strange lost his bid to hold the seat later in the year by losing a Republican runoff to Roy Moore.

Election cycle	House	Senate	Governors	Senators	Governors
2000	3	0	0	—	—
2002	8	1	0	Bob Smith (R-N.H.) (lost to John E. Sununu)	—
2004	2	0	2	—	Bob Holden (D-Mo.) (lost to Claire McCaskill); Olene Walker (R-Utah)# (lost to Jon Huntsman)
2006	2	1	1	Joe Lieberman (D-Conn.)* (lost to Ned Lamont)	Frank Murkowski (R-Alaska) (lost to Sarah Palin)
2008	4	0	0	—	—
2010	4	3	1	Robert Bennett (R-Utah)# (lost to Mike Lee); Lisa Murkowski (R-Alaska)* (lost to Joe Miller); Arlen Specter (D-Pa.) (lost to Joe Sestak)	Jim Gibbons (R-Nev.) (lost to Brian Sandoval)
2012	13	1	0	Richard Lugar (R-Ind.) (lost to Richard Mourdock)	—
2014	4	0	1	—	Neil Abercrombie (D-Hawaii) (lost to David Ige)

Table 3.1   (Continued)

Election cycle	House	Senate	Governors	Senators	Governors
2016	5	0	0	—	—
2018	4	1 (S)	1	Luther Strange (R-Ala.) (lost to Roy Moore)	Jeff Colyer (R-Kan.) (lost to Kris Kobach)

Notes: "(S)" indicates a special election that was held in 2017. An asterisk (*) denotes that the incumbent was reelected on a third-party ballot line or as a write-in candidate. A pound sign (#) indicates that the incumbent was denied renomination at the Republican state convention.
Sources: Editions of *America Votes* (CQ Press, an Imprint of SAGE) for incumbent congressional and gubernatorial primary or convention losers from 2000 through 2016.

extensively throughout the fall of 2018 to rouse the Republican base. Yet it was during the 2018 primaries—with virtually unanimous support from GOP voters—that he was able to use his political capital most effectively.

Tweets, campaign rallies, and recorded telephone messages were all used to promote Republican candidates he favored and attack those he opposed. His involvement contrasted with previous occupants of the White House, who basically kept out of their party's primaries in midterm years. They preferred not to be seen as a divisive force in their party, and any pre-Trump presidential involvement in the primaries was generally limited.

Trump, by contrast, flaunted a hands-on role in the 2018 primaries, endorsing Republican candidates across the country and up and down the ballot—at the Senate, House, and gubernatorial levels as well as for some lesser elective offices. His active role in the primaries was made possible by his strong backing among Republican voters.

Throughout his presidency, Trump's approval ratings have reflected consistently high numbers among Republicans, infinitesimal approval ratings among Democrats, and a score among Independents that has usually been closer to the Democrats than the Republicans. Case in point: the July 16–22, 2018, Gallup Poll, taken in the midst of the primary season, which showed the president with 85 percent job approval among Republicans, 37 percent among Independents, and 11 percent among Democrats.[4]

Sometimes, Trump forcefully opposed a candidate who he viewed as either unfriendly or unelectable. Much more often he directly backed a candidate who he saw as both friendly to himself and electable in November. By and large, his efforts in the primaries were crowned with success.

After his ill-starred endorsement of interim Senator Luther Strange in the 2017 Alabama special Senate election, a seat Republicans ultimately lost, Trump had one success after another in the 2018 Republican primaries with

Table 3.2   Trump Presidential Approval Rating by Party: Republicans Stay Loyal

Through the first two years of his presidency, Donald Trump's job approval rating stayed tepid among independents and nearly infinitesimal among Democrats. But support for Trump among the Republican rank and file remained very strong. That helped to keep nearly all of the GOP members of Congress publicly in lockstep with the president, while enabling Trump to think, talk, and act outside the box that his presidential predecessors have normally stayed within. Trump exercised an outsized role in the 2018 Republican primaries, favoring some candidates, opposing others, and generally shaping his party's field of candidates more than any previous president. The Gallup Poll is used here because of its long track record in measuring presidential approval ratings back to the 1930s. Trump's approval ratings are presented here at six-month intervals among Republicans, Democrats, and independents, starting after his inauguration in January 2017 to July 2018, in the midst of the primary season.

Group	Post-Inauguration (January 2017)	6 months (July 2017)	12 months (January 2018)	18 months (July 2018)	Change (January 2017– July 2018)
Overall	45%	37%	36%	42%	−3%
Republicans	89%	86%	81%	85%	−4%
Independents	42%	31%	31%	37%	−5%
Democrats	13%	8%	5%	11%	−2%

Note: Donald Trump's presidential job approval ratings featured in Table 3.2 are from weekly Gallup Polls covering the following dates: January 20–29, 2017; July 17–23, 2017; Jan. 15–21, 2018; and July 16–22, 2018.
Source: "Trump Job Approval," Gallup, https://news.gallup.com/poll/203207/trump-job-approval-weekly.aspx.

rarely a setback. Two high-riding candidates he forcefully opposed both lost. The first, controversial former coal baron Don Blankenship, advertised himself in the May 8 West Virginia GOP Senate primary as "Trumpier than Trump." But Blankenship was dismissed by the president as unelectable with two words, "Remember Alabama," and finished a distant third.[5]

Another candidate that ended up on Trump's bad side, Representative Mark Sanford of South Carolina, was the victim of a hostile tweet by Trump just hours before the polls closed for the June 12 Republican primary for his Charleston-area seat. The tweet disparaged Sanford and elevated his opponent, state legislator Katie Arrington, who won the primary.

And then there were the Trump primary endorsements that appeared to have a guileful quality to them. In advance of the March 6 primary in Texas, he tweeted his support of state Land Commissioner George P. Bush, a son of Trump's foil from the 2016 Republican presidential campaign, Jeb Bush, and the Bush family's leading hope for national office in the next generation.

In Utah, Trump threw his backing behind one-time critic Mitt Romney, the 2012 GOP presidential nominee, after he entered the Senate race to succeed the retiring Orrin Hatch. Back in 2016, Romney had intimated that Trump was unfit for office, saying: "Think of Donald Trump's personal qualities, the bullying, the greed, the showing off, the misogyny, the absurd third-grade theatrics."[6]

And in Alabama, Trump endorsed another critic from two years earlier, Representative Martha Roby, before her July 17 Republican runoff against a former Democratic congressman, Bobby Bright. In 2016, she had lambasted Trump after release of the *Access Hollywood* tapes, saying that his language was "unacceptable" and that she could not vote for him. "I cannot look my children in the eye and justify my vote for a man who promotes and boasts about sexually assaulting women."[7]

After the 2016 election, both Roby and Romney toned down their criticism of Trump, with Romney even being publicly considered for secretary of state in the Trump administration. Romney's warmer relationship with the president did not last, as following the former's 2018 election he resumed his role as Trump critic. Nonetheless, all three candidates—George P. Bush, Roby, and Romney—won their nominating contests in 2018 with ease, and were elected by decisive margins in the fall.

These results tended to reinforce a basic theme of the 2018 Republican primaries: support Trump and win, oppose him and run the risk of losing. Few GOP candidates took the latter option, as Republican candidates tripped over themselves to win a Trump endorsement or at least to identify themselves as closely as they could with the president.

Meanwhile, two Republican senators who had been openly critical of Trump during his presidency, Bob Corker of Tennessee and Jeff Flake of Arizona, opted to retire rather than to slog through GOP primaries that they were seen as very likely to lose.

An irony of the 2018 primary season was that many of Trump's endorsements went to incumbents in spite of his sometimes heated anti-establishment rhetoric. Case in point: Senator Dean Heller in Nevada. Heller was the only Republican senator up for reelection in 2018 in a state won by Clinton two years earlier. And he faced the prospect of a primary challenge from Danny Tarkanian, the son of the legendary former University of Nevada-Las Vegas (UNLV) basketball coach. But the Trump White House weighed in to clear the primary field for Heller by nudging Tarkanian out of the Senate race and into a House contest.

Not surprisingly, Trump was at the height of his political effectiveness in 2018 when influencing the Republican primaries. In the fall campaign, he proved of value in rallying the Republican base but was also a lightning rod for the Democratic opposition. The latter was already well energized and turned out in far larger numbers in 2018 than Republicans.

Ultimately, Heller lost his Senate race in Nevada. Sanford's House seat in South Carolina went to the Democrats, and Representative Dan Donovan of New York, the recipient of a Trump endorsement in his June 26 primary against former Representative Michael Grimm, lost his Staten Island-based seat in November, leaving Republicans without a member of Congress in New York City. To be sure, plenty of Republicans with Trump endorsements in the general election were elected. But at best, his effectiveness in the general election was mixed.

PAST PRESIDENTIAL INVOLVEMENT IN MIDTERM PRIMARIES

Before Trump, the president most engaged in trying to reshape his party in the primaries was Franklin D. Roosevelt. After his landslide reelection victory in 1936, FDR felt emboldened to attack Democratic opposition within Congress, who resisted aspects of his New Deal agenda as well as his controversial 1937 effort to enlarge the Supreme Court. Roosevelt decided to seek the defeat of unfriendly Democrats in both houses in the midterm election of 1938.

Nine senators and three representatives were targeted by FDR for purging, with the manner and degree of presidential intervention varying. Direct and open opposition was reserved for a few special targets, such as Senator Walter F. George of Georgia, a powerful player among the large bloc of Southern Democrats in Congress that opposed much of the New Deal agenda.

Appearing on the same platform with George in a small town in central Georgia, FDR threw down the gauntlet. He felt "impelled," he said, "to make it clear that on most public questions he (George) and I do not speak the same language." And he urged support for one of George's primary challengers.

George, though, prevailed in the primary while Roosevelt's choice finished a distant third. Of the entire group targeted by FDR, only Representative John J. O'Connor of New York, the chairman of the House Rules Committee, was a primary loser.

Such a poor track record served as a powerful warning to FDR's successors not to get too engaged in congressional or gubernatorial primaries.

President Dwight D. Eisenhower was adamant about keeping an arms-length from intraparty contests. "I have always refused in advance of any primary or any selection of (a) Republican candidate for any office to intervene in any way," said Ike in 1958, "and I wouldn't want to be used directly or indirectly in such a campaign."[8]

Nearly a quarter century later, Ronald Reagan was just as adamant. He

Table 3.3 Selected 2018 Trump Primary Endorsements and Electoral Outcomes

Over the years, presidents have rarely ventured very far into the realm of congressional and gubernatorial primaries. There has often been concern that such involvement may not look presidential or could cost the occupant of the White House political capital if his candidates should lose. Until Donald Trump, Democrat Franklin D. Roosevelt had been the most proactive president in trying to reshape the nature of his party through the primary process. In the midterm election of 1938, he sought to purge a dozen Democratic members of Congress but succeeded in denying renomination to only one of them. Such a poor track record served as a powerful warning to FDR's successors not to get too engaged in congressional or gubernatorial primaries. That is, until 2018, when Trump jumped into the Republican nominating process with gusto. He opposed a few big-name candidates—Representative Mark Sanford of South Carolina and controversial West Virginia Senate entry Don Blankenship come quickly to mind—but Trump mainly offered friendly candidates his endorsement. To be sure, the list below is a selective one. But in basically every race cited, Trump got the result he wanted. One exception: the Republican gubernatorial primary in Wyoming, where Trump tweeted a primary day endorsement of wealthy GOP campaign contributor Foster Friess. He lost.

Senate candidate	Office/occupation	State	Trump Position in Primary	Primary outcome	General outcome
Lou Barletta	U.S. Representative	Pa.	For	Won	Lost
John Barrasso	Incumbent	Wyo.	For	Won	Won
Marsha Blackburn	U.S. Representative	Tenn.	For	Won	Won
Don Blankenship	Former coal baron	W.Va.	Against	Lost	(Reps. lost)
Deb Fischer	Incumbent	Neb.	For	Won	Won
Dean Heller	Incumbent	Nev.	For	Won	Lost
Jim Renacci	U.S. Representative	Ohio	For	Won	Lost
Roger Wicker	Incumbent	Miss.	For	Won	Won

Gubernatorial candidate	Office	State	Trump Position in Primary	Primary outcome	General outcome
John Cox	Businessman	Calif.	For	Qualified for Nov.#	Lost
Ron DeSantis	U.S. Representative	Fla.	For	Won	Won
Foster Friess	GOP campaign donor	Wyo.	For	Lost	(Reps. won)
Brian Kemp	GA Secretary of State	Ga.	For	Won Runoff	Won
Henry McMaster	Incumbent@	S.C.	For	Won Runoff	Won
Bill Schuette	MI Attorney Genral	Mich.	For	Won	Lost

Table 3.3   (Continued)

House candidate	Office	State	Trump Position in Primary	Primary outcome	General outcome
Dan Donovan	Incumbent	N.Y. 11	For	Won	Lost
Martha Roby	Incumbent	Ala. 2	For	Won Runoff	Won
Mark Sanford	Incumbent	S.C. 1	Against	Lost	(Reps. lost)

Note: A pound sign (#) indicates that Republican John Cox finished second in California's "top two" primary and qualified for the November gubernatorial election. The icon "@" denotes that Henry McMaster was an unelected incumbent, taking office in early 2017 when Republican South Carolina Governor Nikki Haley left to become ambassador to the United Nations.
Sources: This selective list of 2018 Republican primary endorsements by President Donald Trump was compiled from articles in the *New York Times*, the *Washington Post*, and other reliable news sources.

"literally would not support his own daughter in a primary because he felt so strongly that the party and president should not take sides," former Republican National Committee Chairman Haley Barbour once observed.[9] Maureen Reagan finished fifth in the 1982 California GOP Senate primary.

On the Democratic side, presidential involvement in congressional primaries was by and large similarly limited. In his lone midterm election in 1962, John F. Kennedy made a controversial endorsement of the embattled chairman of the House Public Works Committee, Charles A. Buckley of New York. Kennedy announced his support for Buckley in a letter, putting himself at odds with New York City Mayor Robert Wagner, Eleanor Roosevelt, and the reform wing of the state Democratic Party. With JFK's help, Buckley narrowly won renomination for a fifteenth term. Fortunately for Democrats, the primary did not leave lasting scars, as it was widely understood that it would be Buckley's last term.[10]

Yet the one race where Kennedy might have been expected to get visibly involved but did not was in the campaign of his 30-year-old brother, Edward M. Kennedy, for the president's former Senate seat. The younger Kennedy's greatest asset by far was his famous name, which drew a notable riposte from his Democratic opponent, state Attorney General Edward McCormack, at the close of their first debate: "If his name was Edward Moore, with his qualifications . . . (his) candidacy would be a joke," said McCormack, "but nobody's laughing because his name is not Edward Moore. It's Edward Moore Kennedy."[11]

Although the president was careful to take a hands-off attitude toward his brother's campaign in public, JFK and his allies provided Teddy with plenty of help behind the scenes. It paid off, as the younger Kennedy swamped

McCormack, a nephew of House Speaker John McCormack (a longtime rival of the Kennedys in Massachusetts politics) by a margin of more than two to one. In the general election, the younger Kennedy defeated Republican George C. Lodge, a son of former Senator Henry Cabot Lodge Jr. (whom JFK had unseated in 1952), by more than a dozen percentage points.

THE DEMOCRATIC PRIMARIES: ABOUT MORE THAN TRUMP

The most widely covered Democratic primaries of 2018 featured a basic cross current: establishment types (generally men) against progressive activists in the mold of Bernie Sanders (frequently women and/or people of color). Often young, the latter promoted themselves as agents of change—liberal agents to be sure—that featured agendas favoring a $15 per hour minimum wage, immigration reform, and Medicare for all.

Some of the individual Democratic contests were heated. But by and large, the stress on the party was far lower than a half century earlier, when divisions over the Vietnam War, law and order, and cultural values rent the party from local contests to presidential campaigns. And in 2018, Democrats were basically united in their hostility to Trump.

Where possible, Democratic leaders sought to clear primaries in competitive states and districts for candidates that they felt were a good fit for the constituency. Often that was a woman with national security credentials. In Virginia, women candidates unseated three Republican incumbents, with one of the Democrats a former CIA operative and another a former Navy commander.[12]

That is not to say there were not some sharp jabs thrown in the 2018 Democratic primaries that reflected ideological overtones. One such contest came in the Illinois primary on March 20, when Chicago-area Representative Dan Lipinski barely survived a challenge from his left from marketing consultant Marie Newman. Lipinski was pro-life on abortion; Newman, pro-choice. Lipinski was backed by large swaths of organized labor; Newman was supported by Bernie Sanders, Gloria Steinem, and an array of progressive groups. Lipinski said his challenger had a "tea party of the left" agenda; Newman called the incumbent a "Trump Democrat."

And at times, her attacks were much sharper than that. "I know what's in his heart, and it's called hate," Newman said at one point during her primary campaign. On primary night, she refused to concede the race, saying: "I would like Mr. Lipinski to have a very painful evening." The incumbent narrowly prevailed by a margin of two percentage points.[13]

Ideological infighting may increase in Democratic primaries in 2020, when the whole House, one-third of the Senate, *and* the presidency itself are all up for grabs.

In 2018, though, there were two House contests that tended to define the party's primary season. In them, a pair of feisty progressive women—Alexandria Ocasio-Cortez and Ayanna Pressley—took down veteran male Democratic House members. Ocasio-Cortez launched her campaign as the most unlikely of candidates. She was an unknown, twenty-something Latina from the Bronx, who skillfully wove together social media with endorsements from progressive organizations to upset a member of the party's House leadership (Caucus chairman Joseph Crowley).

She was arguably the beneficiary of an extremely light primary turnout in which less than 30,000 votes were cast. Still, with her victory, Ocasio-Cortez became an instant star of the Democratic left, and within weeks of her surprise triumph she was offering endorsements of her own.

Her primary triumph came in late June, Pressley's in early September. A Boston city council member of African-American descent, Pressley's primary victory over a longtime liberal congressman (Michael Capuano) added an exclamation point to the historic nature of the year. Both Ocasio-Cortez and Pressley won in urban Democratic districts, particularly favorable ground for female candidates of color. Yet taken together, their triumphs placed them in the vanguard of women and candidates of racial, ethnic, and sexual diversity that flourished in 2018.

As the year unfolded, the media began referring to it as "the year of the woman," or maybe more accurately, "the year of the woman, part two." The first such year to draw that title accompanied Bill Clinton's initial presidential election in 1992 and featured Democratic Senate victories by Barbara Boxer and Dianne Feinstein in California, Carol Moseley Braun in Illinois, and Patty Murray in Washington.

But the showing by women candidates in 1992 looked like a modest preamble compared to 2018. Altogether, a record 256 women won nominations for seats in Congress—197 Democrats and 59 Republicans. A record 127 were elected to House and Senate seats in the 116th Congress: 106 Democrats and 21 Republicans.[14]

2018 also was a "year of diversity," particularly on the Democratic side. Nominated and elected to Congress were the first Native American women (Democrats Deb Haaland of New Mexico and Sharice Davids of Kansas), the first Muslim women (Rashida Tlaib of Michigan and Ilhan Omar of Minnesota), and the first openly gay male governor (Jared Polis of Colorado).[15]

ble 3.4   2018 Primaries: Incumbent Losers and Close Calls

e number of congressional and gubernatorial incumbents that were defeated by their party's primary
ters could be counted on one hand plus one finger. But there were three senators, eight governors, and
ighly two dozen House members who had to break a sweat to win renomination—defined here as a
nning percentage of two-thirds or less of their party's primary vote. Most of this action took place in one-
rty districts, which were safely Democratic or Republican as the case may be. Meanwhile, the Democrats
d sharper fault lines in their primaries. There, progressives in the tradition of Bernie Sanders faced off with
re establishment types in a number of contests, with the former scoring some high-profile victories in the
ngressional primaries. There, two women—one a twenty-something political unknown from the Bronx,
xandria Ocasio-Cortez, the other a Boston city councilwoman of African-American descent, Ayanna
ssley—took down veteran white male Democratic House members. Running in urban Democratic dis-
ts, both women were elected easily to the 116th Congress in November. Among Republicans, the basic
sure—if you can call it that—was between candidates who tried to outdo themselves in proclaiming their
port for President Trump.

OVERNORS

feated

cumbent	Term	% of Primary (Runoff) Vote	Margin	2016 pres. vote in state
ff Colyer (R-Kan.)	@	40.5%	Lost to Kris Kobach by 0.1%	Trump by 21%

table challenges

cumbent	Term	% of Primary (Runoff) Vote	Margin	2016 pres. vote in state
enry McMaster (R-S.C.)	@	42.3% (53.6%)	Beat John Warren in run-off by 7%	Trump by 14%
avid Ige (D-Hawaii)	1	51.4%	Beat Colleen Hanabusa by 7%	Clinton by 32%
ruce Rauner (R-Ill.)	1	51.5%	Beat Jeanne Ives by 3%	Clinton by 17%
ay Ivey (R-Ala.)	@	56.1%	Beat Tommy Battle by 31%	Trump by 28%
ina Raimondo (D-R.I.)	1	57.2%	Beat Matt Brown by 24%	Clinton by 16%
harlie Baker (R-Mass.)	1	63.8%	Beat Scott Lively by 28%	Clinton by 27%
ndrew Cuomo (D-N.Y.)	2	65.5%	Beat Cynthia Nixon by 31%	Clinton by 22%
hil Scott (R-Vt.)	1	66.7%	Beat Keith Stern by 34%	Clinton by 26%

Table 3.4   (Continued)

SENATE

Defeated

Incumbent	Term	% of Primary (Runoff) Vote	Margin	2016 pres. vote in district
Luther Strange (R-Ala.)#	@	32.8% (45.4%)	Lost to Roy Moore in runoff by 9%	Trump by 28%

Notable challenges

Incumbent	Term	% of Primary (Runoff) Vote	Margin	2016 pres. vote in district
Bob Menendez (D-N.J.)	2	62.3%	Beat Lisa McCormick by 25%	Clinton by 14%
Tom Carper (D-Del.)	3	64.6%	Beat Kerri Harris by 29%	Clinton by 11%
John Barrasso (R-Wyo.)	2	64.8%	Beat Dave Dodson by 36%	Trump by 46%

REPRESENTATIVES

Defeated

Incumbent	Term	% of Primary (Runoff) Vote	Margin	2016 pres. vote in district
Michael Capuano (D-Mass. 7)	10	41.3%	Lost to Ayanna Pressley by 17%	Clinton by 72%
Joseph Crowley (D-N.Y. 14)	10	43.3%	Lost to Alexandria Ocasio-Cortez by 13%	Clinton by 58%
Robert Pittenger (R-N.C. 9)	3	46.2%	Lost to Mark Harris by 2%	Trump by 12%
Mark Sanford (R-S.C. 1)	5	46.5%	Lost to Katie Arrington by 4%	Trump by 13%

le 3.4 (Continued)

table challenges

umbent	Term	% of Primary (Runoff) Vote	Margin	2016 pres. vote in district
rtha Roby (R-Ala. 2)	4	39.0% (68.0%)	Beat Bobby Bright in runoff by 36%	Trump by 32%
alter B. Jones (R-N.C. 3)	12	43.0%	Beat Phil Law by 14%	Trump by 24%
n Lipinski (D-Ill. 3)	7	51.1%	Beat Marie Newman by 2%	Clinton by 15%
ug Lamborn (R-Colo. 5)	6	52.2%	Beat Darryl Glenn by 32%	Trump by 24%
ette Clarke (D-N.Y. 9)	6	53.0%	Beat Adem Bunkeddeko by 6%	Clinton by 69%
rkwayne Mullin -Okla. 2)	3	54.1%	Beat Jarrin Jackson by 29%	Trump by 50%
vid Kustoff (R-Tenn. 8)	1	56.0%	Beat George Flinn by 16%	Trump by 36%
cy Clay (D-Mo. 1)	9	56.7%	Beat Cori Bush by 20%	Clinton by 58%
yd Smucker (R-Pa. 11)	1	58.5%	Beat Chester Beiler by 17%	–
rolyn Maloney (D-N.Y.)	13	59.6%	Beat Suraj Patel by 19%	Clinton by 70%
Lawson (D-Fla. 5)	1	60.3%	Beat Alvin Brown by 21%	Clinton by 25%
rbara Comstock (R-Va.)	2	60.7%	Beat Shak Hill by 21%	Clinton by 10%
o Brooks (R-Ala. 5)	4	61.3%	Beat Clayton Hinchman by 23%	Trump by 33%
ke Quigley (D-Ill. 5)	4	62.5%	Beat Sameena Mustafa by 38%	Clinton by 47%
n Donovan (R-N.Y. 11)	1	62.9%	Beat Michael Grimm by 26%	Trump by 10%
rry Bucshon (R-Ind. 8)	4	63.0%	Beat Richard Moss by 38%	Trump by 34%
die Bernice Johnson -Texas 30)	13	63.6%	Beat Barbara Caraway by 41%	Clinton by 61%
endan F. Boyle (D-Pa. 2)	2	64.6%	Beat Michele Lawrence by 29%	–
m Cole (R-Okla. 4)	8	64.7%	Beat James Taylor by 29%	Trump by 37%

Table 3.4 **(Continued)**

Incumbent	Term	% of Primary (Runoff) Vote	Margin	2016 pres. v[] in district
Matt Gaetz (R-Fla. 1)	1	64.8%	Beat Cris Dosev by 35%	Trump by 39%
Billy Long (R-Mo. 7)	4	65.1%	Beat Jim Evans by 48%	Trump by 46%
John Carter (R-Texas 31)	8	65.5%	Beat Mike Sweeney by 31%	Trump by 13%
Adrian Smith (R-Neb. 3)	6	65.7%	Beat Kirk Penner by 40%	Trump by 55%
Darren Soto (D-Fla. 9)	1	66.4%	Beat Alan Grayson by 33%	Clinton by 13

Note: The icon "@" denotes an unelected incumbent. A pound sign (#) indicates that Luther Strange of Alabama lost a Repub[] runoff in September 2017 as part of a special election to fill the final years of the Senate term vacated by Jeff Sessions (R). The [] had left the Senate in early 2017 to become attorney general in the Trump administration. Strange had been appointed at the [] to fill the vacancy. An asterisk (*) indicates that the congressional district lines were changed in Pennsylvania before the 2[] election. Presidential vote results were not readily available to reflect the revised district lines.
Sources: The 2018 primary vote percentages are based on official returns posted on state election websites. The current ter[] each incumbent is as of the 2018 primary season and is from the *Almanac of American Politics 2018* (National Journal/Colu[] Books & Information Services). The 2016 presidential vote by congressional district is from Daily Kos Elections.

In two major Southern states, Florida and Georgia, Democratic primary voters selected African Americans to run for governor—former state House Minority Leader Stacey Abrams in the latter, Tallahassee Mayor Andrew Gillum in the former. Abrams glided to an easy primary victory over a former white state legislator; Gillum upset former Representative Gwen Graham, a daughter of former Florida governor and senator Bob Graham, by a margin of three percentage points.

Along with Ocasio-Cortez and Pressley, Abrams and Gillum—plus Democratic Senate nominee Beto O'Rourke in Texas—became the face of a new generation of Democrats in 2018. They were young (in their late 20s, 30s, and 40s), aspirational in their rhetoric, and able to draw national attention to their campaigns. Given the favorable nature of their districts, Ocasio-Cortez and Pressley won their November elections easily. Having to run on tougher turf, Abrams, Gillum, and O'Rourke all lost close races, but they are widely viewed to have bright futures in Democratic politics.

These candidacies and the history made in 2018 for women and for different racial groups are explored further and in more depth later in this volume.

ODDS AND ENDS

Several candidates with famous names won nomination and election in 2018. Among them were Mitt Romney, the GOP's 2012 presidential standard-bearer, who was elected in Utah to the Senate seat vacated by Republican

Orrin Hatch. It was his first election to office since winning the governorship of Massachusetts in 2002.

Meanwhile, Greg Pence, the older brother of Vice President Mike Pence, won an open House seat in Indiana, while Donna Shalala, a former Secretary of Health and Human Services in the Clinton administration and former president of the University of Miami, won a South Florida House seat. It is the first elected office for both.

But not every candidate with a modicum of celebrity made it through the primaries, let alone the general election. Levi Sanders, the son of Bernie, finished a distant seventh in the Democratic primary in the eastern New Hampshire congressional district with 2 percent of the vote. For whatever reason, the younger Sanders did not receive an endorsement from his famous father.

Then there was Richard Painter, an ethics lawyer in the George W. Bush administration, who since the 2016 election had emerged as a tough critic of Trump and his perceived ethical lapses on cable news networks such as MSNBC. In 2018, Painter ran in the Democratic Senate primary in Minnesota against interim incumbent Tina Smith, finishing a distant second with 14 percent of the vote.

But when it comes to the unusual, it is tough to top Roque "Rocky" De La Fuente and H. Brooke Paige. The former, a California businessman, showed an acumen in 2016 for getting on primary ballots. He appeared on roughly two dozen Democratic presidential primary ballots and about 20 state presidential ballots in the fall. Yet vote getting was not his forte, as De La Fuente collected less than 70,000 votes in the primaries and barely 30,000 votes in the general election.

De La Fuente switched to the Republicans in 2018, performing the unusual feat of running in nine Senate primaries from California to Florida and Vermont to Washington. His best showings: Rhode Island, 12 percent of the Republican primary vote; Florida and Hawaii, 11 percent; Minnesota, 6 percent; and Delaware, 5 percent. Altogether. De La Fuente's total vote in the primaries was roughly 350,000, with more than half of his vote coming from Florida, where he was the only Republican Senate challenger to Governor Rick Scott.[16]

A Vermont Republican with a penchant for straw hats, Paige ran in the state's August 14 GOP primary for six statewide offices at once—Senate, House, state treasurer, secretary of state, state auditor, and state attorney general. Paige won the GOP nomination for all six offices, four of them without opposition. He said that he did so to keep Democratic candidates from crossing over and poaching the Republican nomination. Ultimately, he was replaced on the November ballot by other Republicans for five of the six offices. He stayed in the race for secretary of state, which he lost to his Democratic opponent by a margin in excess of two to one.[17]

BATTLE OF THE PRIMARY BALLOTS

The nationwide tally of primary votes is not something that is closely watched, especially in a midterm election year. Yet maybe it should be. The aggregate nationwide count of Democratic and Republican primary ballots in recent elections has been a fairly accurate harbinger of the general election to come.

Higher turnouts in the primaries are considered a reflection of which party has the greater enthusiasm and whose voters are most likely to turn out in the fall. In 2010 and 2014, the Republicans drew the most primary votes, then went on to capture the House of Representatives in 2010 and the House and Senate in 2014.

In 2018, Democrats won the most primary votes, based on the number of ballots cast in each party's Senate or gubernatorial contest (whichever office produced the highest number of votes in a particular state). In the fall, Democrats reclaimed the House for the first time in nearly a decade.

Democrats drew more primary votes than Republicans in such populous states as California, Illinois, and New Jersey. For good measure, Democrats also outpolled the Republicans in 2018 primary balloting in the trifecta of industrial states that were so critical to Donald Trump's election as president in 2016: Michigan, Pennsylvania, and Wisconsin. Democrats also had the edge in the midterm primary vote in the battleground state of Iowa, which Trump carried in 2016, and bright red West Virginia, where Democrats still hold a sizable voter registration advantage.

But there was a caveat or two. Take away bright blue California, where the Democrats registered a primary turnout advantage in 2018 over the Republicans of more than 1.8 million votes, and the Democrats' overall edge was reduced to less than 1 million votes for the year. Republicans outpolled the Democrats in primary balloting in such large electoral prizes as Florida, Ohio, and Texas. In short, there were signs in the primary voting that Democrats could do well in the fall, as they ultimately did. But their advantage was not written in stone. That is something that has to be earned each election.

ble 3.5   Democrats Win Battle of the Primary Ballots

recent midterm election cycles, the party that won the most votes in the primaries tended to dominate
e voting in the fall. In both 2010 and 2014, Republicans won "the battle of the primary ballots." In the
10 general election, the GOP went on to capture the Senate; in 2014, they took both the House and the
nate. In 2018, Democrats won the most primary ballots, a precursor, it turned out, of their takeover of
e House in November. By and large, Democrats collected the most primary votes in 2018 in states that
d backed Hillary Clinton for president two years earlier, and Republicans drew the most midterm primary
tes in states that had been carried by Donald Trump, though with several exceptions. The 2018 results
low reflect the Democratic and Republican gubernatorial or Senate primary vote, depending on which
:e had the highest combined vote. Altogether, comparative partisan primary results were available in 2018
43 states. In three states (Kentucky, Louisiana, and North Carolina), there was neither a gubernatorial or
nate primary. In four states (New York, South Dakota, Utah, and Virginia), there was neither a gubernato-
 or Senate primary held by both parties, leaving nothing to compare.

ite	High race	Primary turnout	Democrat	Republican	Plurality	Edge	Dem share	Rep share
abama	Governor	874,904	283,705	591,199	R	307,494	32%	68%
aska	Governor	104,646	33,451	71,195	R	37,744	32%	68%
izona	Senator	1,165,268	509,970	655,298	R	145,328	44%	56%
kansas	Governor	312,324	105,919	206,405	R	100,486	34%	66%
ilifornia	Governor	6,869,649	4,350,513	2,519,136	D	1,831,377	63%	37%
olorado	Governor	1,140,207	637,002	503,205	D	133,797	56%	44%
onnecticut	Governor	355,401	212,543	142,858	D	69,685	60%	40%
elaware	Senator	120,908	83,039	37,869	D	45,170	69%	31%
orida	Governor	3,141,616	1,519,492	1,622,124	R	102,632	48%	52%
eorgia	Governor	1,162,530	555,089	607,441	R	52,352	48%	52%
awaii	Governor	273,670	242,514	31,156	D	211,358	89%	11%
aho	Governor	260,418	65,882	194,536	R	128,654	25%	75%
inois	Governor	2,046,710	1,324,548	722,162	D	602,386	65%	35%
diana	Senator	791,321	284,621	506,700	R	222,079	36%	64%
wa	Governor	274,549	179,124	95,425	D	83,699	65%	35%
ansas	Governor	473,438	156,273	317,165	R	160,892	33%	67%
aine	Governor	220,521	126,139	94,382	D	31,757	57%	43%
aryland	Governor	796,624	585,689	210,935	D	374,754	74%	26%
assachusetts	Senator	863,563	602,393	261,170	D	341,223	70%	30%
ichigan	Governor	2,121,023	1,131,447	989,576	D	141,871	53%	47%
innesota	Governor	904,649	583,735	320,914	D	262,821	65%	35%
ississippi	Senator	245,101	87,931	157,170	R	69,239	36%	64%
issouri	Senator	1,272,466	607,577	664,889	R	57,312	48%	52%

Table 3.5   (Continued)

State	High race	Primary turnout	Democrat	Republican	Plurality	Edge	Dem share	Rep share
Montana	Senator	268,294	114,948	153,346	R	38,398	43%	57%
Nebraska	Senator	261,854	92,760	169,094	R	76,334	35%	65%
Nevada	Governor	287,604	145,420	142,184	D	3,236	51%	49%
New Hampshire	Governor	215,549	122,966	92,583	D	30,383	57%	43%
New Jersey	Senator	645,151	421,475	223,676	D	197,799	65%	35%
New Mexico	Governor	251,060	175,898	75,162	D	100,736	70%	30%
North Dakota	Senator	107,016	36,883	70,133	D	33,250	34%	66%
Ohio	Governor	1,523,755	688,788	834,967	R	146,179	45%	55%
Oklahoma	Governor	848,100	395,494	452,606	R	57,112	47%	53%
Oregon	Governor	709,921	395,937	313,984	D	81,953	56%	44%
Pennsylvania	Governor	1,487,124	749,812	737,312	D	12,500	50.4%	49.6%
Rhode Island	Governor	150,962	117,875	33,087	D	84,788	78%	22%
South Carolina	Governor	608,451	240,468	367,983	R	127,515	40%	60%
Tennessee	Governor	1,166,278	373,3907	92,888	R	419,498	32%	68%
Texas	Senator	2,592,487	1,042,914	1,549,573	R	506,659	40%	60%
Vermont	Governor	97,606	61,391	36,215	D	25,176	63%	37%
Washington	Senator	1,623,652	989,462	634,190	D	355,272	61%	39%
West Virginia	Senator	298,825	161,252	137,573	D	23,679	54%	46%
Wisconsin	Governor	994,687	538,857	455,830	D	83,027	54%	46%
Wyoming	Governor	134,862	18,076	116,786	R	98,710	13%	87%
TOTAL		36,790,377	19,768,603	17,021,774	D	2,746,829	54%	46%

Notes: California and Washington held "top two" primaries featuring candidates from all parties running together on a single primary ballot. The vote totals for each state are based on the vote for all Democratic and all Republican candidates, but not votes cast Independent or third-party candidates. In California, the latter totaled 91,605 votes, producing a grand total of 6,961,254 primary votes cast for governor. In Washington, third-party and Independent candidates drew 77,188 votes, producing a grand total 1,700,840 primary votes cast for senator.

Sources: Official 2018 primary results from state election websites.

NOTES

1. Harold W. Stanley and Richard G. Niemi, *Vital Statistics on American Politics 2015–2016* (Los Angeles: CQ Press, an imprint of SAGE Publications Inc., 2015), 43–44.

2. David Wasserman and Ally Flinn, "2018 House Popular Vote Tracker," Cook Political Report. @Redistrict/@CookPolitical. (as of January 24, 2019).

3. The 2018 primary vote was tallied by the author. The Democratic advantage would have been even wider in the 2018 primaries if votes from New York were included. There, more than 1.5 million ballots were cast in the Democratic gubernatorial primary, where incumbent Andrew Cuomo fended off a lively challenge from his left by actress Cynthia Nixon. With no corresponding vote on the Republican side, though, the Democratic ballots were not included in the overall national tally cited here.

4. Gallup Poll online, Presidential Approval Ratings—Donald Trump, https://news.gallup.com/poll/203198/presidential-approval-ratings-donald-trump.aspx.

5. "The Rhodes Cook Letter," July 2018, 6.

6. "The Rhodes Cook Letter," July 2018, 4.

7. Richard E. Cohen with James A. Barnes, *The Almanac of American Politics 2018* (Columbia Books & Information Services/National Journal, 2017), 35.

8. Rhodes Cook, "President Bucks Tradition with Role in Primaries," *Congressional Quarterly Weekly Report*, March 19, 1994, 684.

9. Ibid.

10. Ibid.

11. Murray B. Levin, *Kennedy Campaigning: The System and the Style as Practiced by Senator Edward Kennedy* (Boston: Beacon Press, 1966), 182.

12. Jenna Portnoy, "Congresswomen-elect Who Made History Now Prepare to Serve," *The Washington Post*, November 13, 2018, B-1.

13. John Byrne, Annie Sweeney, and Michael Hawthorne, "Newman Concedes, Saying She Put Lipinski on Notice to Do 'Better for All of the People in Our District,'" *Chicago Tribune*, March 21, 2018, https://www.chicagotribune.com/news/local/politics/ct-met-illinois-primary-dan-lipinski-marie-newman-20180319-story.html.

14. Grace Sparks and Annie Grayer, "256 Women Won House and Senate Primaries, a Huge New Record," CNN, September 17, 2018, https://www.cnn.com/2018/09/16/politics/house-women-update-september/index.html; Current Numbers, Center for American Women and Politics at Rutgers University (as of January 22, 2019), http://cawp.rutgers.edu/current-numbers.

15. Grace Panetta, Shayanne Gal, and Michelle Mark, "12 Records the 2018 Midterm Elections Smashed," *Business Insider*, November 7, 2018, https://www.businessinsider.com/2018-midterm-election-records-early-voting-women-lgbt-candidates-2018-11.

16. Reuben Fischer-Baum, "This Underdog Candidate Ran in Nine Senate Primaries and Lost Them All," *The Washington Post,* Sept. 25, 2018, https://www.washingtonpost.com/graphics/2018/politics/rocky-de-la-fuente/?utm_term = .3c8bf3bb8930.

17. Emily Alfin Johnson, Bob Kinzel, and Sam Gale Rosen, "Campaign 2018: This Vermonter Is Running for 6 Statewide Offices. Here's Why," Vermont Public Radio, June 8, 2018, http://digital.vpr.net/post/campaign-2018-vermonter-running-6-statewide-offices-heres-why.

4

Humpty-Dumpty's Fall

How Trump's Winning Presidential Coalition Broke Down in 2018

David Byler

In every presidential election, somebody builds a winning coalition—that is, they find a way to get the votes they need to win the Electoral College (and often but not always the popular vote)—and become president. In 2016, Donald Trump did this in an odd way—he ran (to put it mildly) an unconventional campaign, picked up blue-collar white voters in swing states, forfeited traditionally Republican college-educated whites, and put together an Electoral College majority while losing the popular vote.[1] At the same time, down-ballot Republicans managed to outperform him in key races, and the GOP held the House and Senate, albeit with slightly reduced majorities.

In the aftermath of this unexpected outcome, the wonkier side of the elections analysis world started to ask two questions: Will this new alignment hold? And, if it does, will the GOP be able to maintain its majority?

For most of the last two years, our answers to that question have been speculative. But now that the 2018 election is over, we finally have House, Senate, and other results that can help us answer these questions.

Obviously we don't yet *know* whether the Trumpian alignment is permanent or if the GOP's current Electoral College majority will endure—we have no clue how 2020, 2024, or other elections are going to pan out. But the 2018 election suggests that while the Trumpian *alignment* may have some staying

80

power, a Trumpian *majority* is far from invincible. On top of that, there's a lot of variation in how the midterms panned out in different regions—and examining those more local results gives us important insights about how Trump has changed politics, who switched their votes from Republican to Democratic in the last two years, and where politics might be heading in the future.

THE NATIONAL TOPLINE: THE ALIGNMENT STUCK, BUT THE REPUBLICAN ADVANTAGE FROM IT DID NOT

The national results tell a simple story—that the general contours of the Trumpian alignment of 2016 stuck (even through Trump was technically not on the ballot) but the GOP's winning coalition fell apart. You can see that in the topline numbers, the demographic breakdown, and the race-by-race results.

The topline numbers show that the GOP took a hit in 2018. House Democrats won the overall popular vote by an 8.6-point margin[2]—a significant leftward shift from both the 2016 presidential popular vote (which Trump lost by two) and the 2016 House popular vote (which Republicans won by a point). The House popular vote isn't a perfect statistic. It combines the results of 435 different races with different candidates, and it can be thrown off by uncontested races and other idiosyncratic conditions. Accounting for these oddities might diminish Democratic margins some (e.g., using regression analysis to replace the vote totals in uncontested races with hypothetical vote totals for a contested race lowers the overall Democratic margin to seven points). But fidgeting with the data doesn't change the basic story: The topline numbers clearly show that public opinion strongly favored Democrats in 2018, while 2016 was a relatively close election.

Trump and the Republicans lost support between 2016 and 2018, but the new Trumpian alignment (namely a GOP that's more dependent on blue-collar whites and a Democratic Party that traded those same blue-collar voters for college-educated suburbanites) appears to have some staying power. Catalist, a Democratic data firm that uses voter lists in its analysis, found that House Democrats performed better with white college-educated voters, young voters, and suburbanites in 2018 than in 2016.[3] Republicans still did well among non-college-educated white voters, though they lost some ground with rural voters (though it's worth noting that not all rural voters are white). On the whole, this represents a continuation of the trends we saw in 2016—a Republican Party that's majority white and increasingly blue collar and a

Democratic Party that is adding well-educated whites, losing blue-collar whites, and holding its nonwhite base.

These two changes—further Trump-ification of politics and a GOP loss of support between 2016 and 2018—show up when you look at race-by-race data as well. Just look at Figures 4.1 and 4.2.

Figure 4.1 compares each Republican House candidate's margin of loss/ victory to Trump's margin in that district in 2016. There's obviously a strong relationship here (highly Republican districts tended to like both Trump and the GOP House candidate, and the opposite was true in Democratic districts) but many House Republicans managed to outperform Trump. Some even won their races while Hillary Clinton carried their district.

But in 2018 that all fell apart. Figure 4.2 compares the 2018 House results to the 2016 results. And, as Republican strategist Patrick Ruffini and others

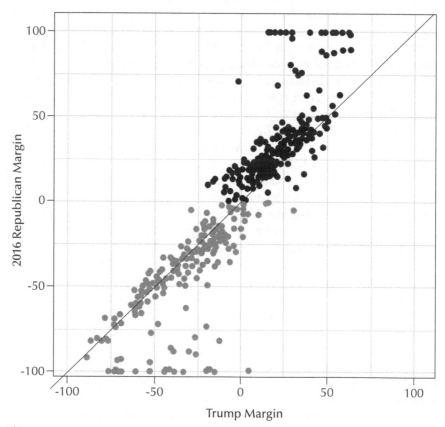

Figure 4.1   2016 House versus 2016 president.

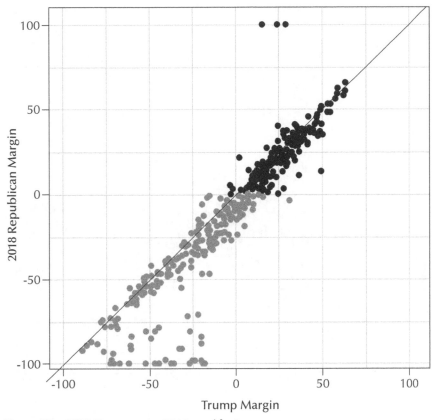

Figure 4.2 2018 House versus 2016 president.

have pointed out,[4] two things happened: the 2018 results were Trump-ier *and* worse for the GOP.

You can see the Trump-ification in the spread of points—the cloud of Republicans who outperformed Trump's margin is almost wholly gone, as those Republicans (some of whom represented suburbia) became more identified with the current iteration of the GOP. You can also see the GOP's decline in popularity by looking at where the points are positioned—most points fall beneath the black line, indicating that most 2018 GOP House candidates underperformed Trump's 2016 margin.

The Senate results show a similar pattern.

Figure 4.3 compares the GOP's win/loss margin in each 2018 Senate race (with the exception of California because two Democrats made it to the runoff) to Trump's margin in those states in 2016. Just like the 2018 House

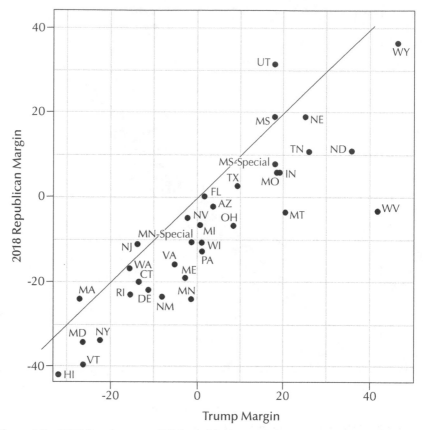

Figure 4.3   2018 Senate versus 2016 president.

results, the Senate results were strongly correlated with Trump's 2016 show-ing (Senate Republicans tended to perform better in states where Trump did well). And, like in 2018, most points fall below the black "break-even" line—indicating that most GOP Senate candidates underperformed Trump.

There are some obvious outliers and exceptions here. Democratic Senators Joe Manchin and Jon Tester won by wildly outperforming Hillary Clinton's 2016 margin in West Virginia and Montana. Republican Rick Scott managed to barely win against incumbent Bill Nelson (which is quite a feat in a swing state in a blue year), and Mitt Romney posted a sky-high margin in Utah (a heavily Mormon state[5] where Independent Evan McMullin likely cut into Trump's margin in 2016). But those races are outliers and most of the races followed the pattern of a Trumpified contest where the GOP lost ground.

These national results tell a helpful, bird's-eye-view story about the midterms and what changed between 2016 and 2018, but they don't give us much detail on *who* changed their vote and where politics might be *going* from here. For that, we have to turn to the local data—which I've decided to look at on a region-by-region basis.

THE NORTHEAST: PENNSYLVANIA, NEW JERSEY, AND TRUMP'S TWO-FRONT WAR

The Census Bureau defines the Northeast as New Jersey, Pennsylvania, New York, Connecticut, Rhode Island, Massachusetts, Vermont, New Hampshire, and Maine, and labels New York, New Jersey, and Pennsylvania "Middle Atlantic" while calling the rest New England.[6] Not too much of note happened in New England in 2018, but the Middle Atlantic results revealed some serious problems for the Trump coalition. To see exactly what those problems were, take a look at Map 4.1.[7]

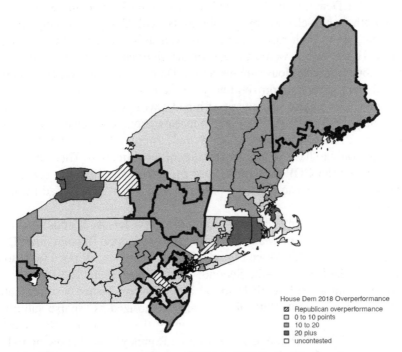

House Dem 2018 Overperformance
- ▨ Republican overperformance
- ☐ 0 to 10 points
- ■ 10 to 20
- ■ 20 plus
- ☐ uncontested

Map 4.1   Change in House results from 2016 to 2018 in the Northeast.

Map 4.1 (and the rest of the maps in this chapter) chart the changes in House districts between 2016 and 2018. The color of each district represents the difference between the Democratic win/loss margin in the 2016 presidential election and the 2018 House elections. The darker districts represent places where Democrats outran Hillary Clinton by the largest margins, the cross-hatched districts represent places where the Republican outran Trump (all in terms of margin of victory), and the white districts are uncontested. The districts with a dark outline represent districts that Democrats flipped.

Map 4.1 shows that New England didn't change too much. Democrats flipped Maine's Second District (an Obama-to-Trump district where a Republican won in 2016), but little of interest happened in Massachusetts, Vermont, New Hampshire, Connecticut, or Rhode Island (except for progressive Ayanna Pressley's primary victory in Massachusetts's Seventh District[8]).

Nobody expected the Trumpian iteration of the GOP to do particularly well in New England, so these results weren't too much of a surprise. But Democrats made big inroads in the Middle Atlantic.

Pennsylvania is probably the GOP's worst result on the map. Trump barely won the state in 2016 and probably needs to win it again if he wants to be re-elected. But Democratic Governor Tom Wolf and Democratic Senator Bob Casey both won re-election by double digits, with Casey improving on Clinton's margins in both rural counties as well as some key suburban areas.[9] And the House results weren't great for the GOP either. The combination of a new court-ordered House map[10] and a Democratic national environment allowed Democrats to improve greatly on their 2016 performance.

In the Empire State, Democrats flipped two upstate districts (the Nineteenth and the Twenty-second) and one New York City district (the Eleventh). In all three districts, Trump had improved on Romney's 2012 showing—only to have Democrats retake all three in 2018. This isn't a terrible result for the GOP (not much else of note changed in the state, aside from Alexandria Ocasio-Cortez's primary win), but it's not a bad result for Democrats either.

Republicans had a much rougher night in New Jersey. Scandal-plagued[11] Democratic Senator Bob Menendez cruised to reelection (though other Democrats outperformed him—see Figure 4.3), and Democrats flipped four House seats in the Garden State—the Second, Third, Seventh, and Eleventh.

The Seventh and Eleventh Districts arguably represented a solidification of Trumpian alignment. Both districts are categorized as "sparse suburban" by David Montgomery at CityLab—meaning that they're mostly suburban and exurban[12]—and Trump underperformed Romney's 2012 showing in both districts (Clinton won the Seventh and Trump only barely won the Eleventh in 2016). In short, these are exactly the sort of districts one might except

Democrats to flip if future elections followed the Trump verses Clinton battle lines.

But the Second and the Third districts are more troubling for the GOP. Both South Jersey districts went from voting for Obama in 2012 to Trump in 2016, yet Democrats flipped them in 2018. These results, like those in Pennsylvania's senate and governor contests and in the New York districts, suggest that areas that flipped to Trump in 2016 are not permanently red. These aggregate results don't tell us whether Democrats won these districts by running up the score with college-educated suburbanites or if Trump converts came back into the Democratic fold. But either way, losses here are not a great sign for the GOP. These numbers suggest that Democrats could both regain some of the ground they lost to Trump while holding onto Romney voters that Hillary Clinton converted.

The basic lesson here is that it's possible for the Democrats to, under the right circumstances, get the best of both worlds. They won in districts and states where Trump made big gains in 2016 without surrendering the new territory that Clinton took over. If that general pattern reappears in 2020, Republicans will be in deep trouble.

THE SOUTH: REPUBLICANS HOLD THE BASE BUT LOSE IN THE SUBURBS

But things looked somewhat different in the South. Republicans managed to hold onto much of their base—just as Trump did in 2016. But Democrats capitalized on the new Trumpian alignment, took over suburbs, and made important gains in states like Texas and Virginia (though the GOP did well in Florida).

The most obvious visual feature of Map 4.2 is the amount of cross-hatching. In the states of Texas, Arkansas, Mississippi, Georgia, Florida, and South Carolina, many Republicans managed to do as well or better than Trump. Moreover, some other Republican-held districts are only lightly shaded—meaning Democrats improved on Clinton's margin, but not by much. The story varies from district to district, but many of these places were Republican before Trump entered the political scene and will probably stay in the GOP fold after he's exited. The GOP can't win on the base alone, but the fact that they managed to keep them around is a positive sign for Republicans.

There are also real Democratic gains on this map. Democrats flipped two Miami-area districts, Georgia's Sixth District (right near Atlanta), Oklahoma's Fifth District (Oklahoma City), two Texas districts (one in the Dallas

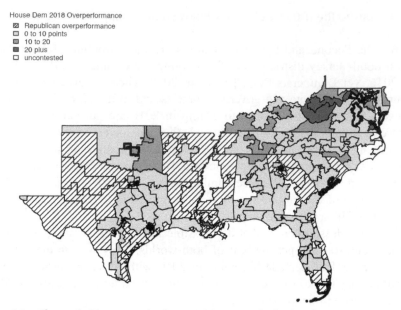

House Dem 2018 Overperformance
- ▨ Republican overperformance
- ☐ 0 to 10 points
- ▦ 10 to 20
- ■ 20 plus
- ☐ uncontested

Map 4.2 Change in House results from 2016 to 2018 in the South.

area, another in the Houston area), South Carolina's First (near Charleston), and three Virginia districts (Northern Virginia, Richmond, and Virginia Beach). In other districts, Democrats came close but didn't quite get there. Georgia's Seventh District (also the Atlanta area) was decided by less than half a point, and Democrats got within three points in Texas's Twenty-first District, which went for Trump by 10 points in 2016. It's hard to see most of these gains on the map because the urban/suburban districts are physically small in comparison to the similarly populated, sprawling rural and small-town districts of the South. But they're there, and they have big implications for the future of the electoral landscape.

These suburban losses were particularly significant in two states: Virginia and Texas.

Over the last few decades, Virginia has drifted from being reliably red to a swing state to an (arguably) slightly light blue state,[13] and 2018 looks like another step in that direction. Barbara Comstock, the Northern Virginia (read: DC suburbs) Republican, lost her race despite being able to attract a considerable number of ticket-splitters in 2016. Democrat Elaine Luria won Virginia's Second District—a slightly red but still marginal coastal district that CityLab labels as "Dense Suburban." And Democrat Abigail Spanberger beat Republican Dave Brat in Virginia's Seventh District (a GOP-leaning district that includes Richmond suburbs). Democratic Senator Tim Kaine also won re-election with 57 percent of the vote.

Spanberger likely wouldn't have won in a more neutral political environment (her district is fairly red) and Kaine's margin would have been at least a bit smaller if he wasn't running against Corey Stewart (who has done things like praise secession and defend Confederate symbols[14]). But on the whole, the Trump-ification of the map (along with the pro-Democratic national environment) helped Democrats gain ground in increasingly suburban Virginia.[15]

Democrats also improved their position in Texas. Contrary to conventional wisdom, Texas isn't really a rural state. Houston, Dallas, San Antonio, and Austin are all large metro areas (El Paso isn't so small either), and the areas outside of them are sparsely populated. Put simply, most Texas don't live in towns like the one from *Friday Night Lights*—they live in big metro areas.[16]

That urban-ness helped make Texas ground zero for some big Democratic gains: Beto O'Rourke lost to Ted Cruz by three points in a state that went for Trump by nine and Romney by 16, and House Democrats took two seats. Texas isn't a problem for the GOP yet—Republicans still won the marquee race in a year when House Democrats won the overall House vote by almost nine points. But it could become a worry down the line if our current political divides deepen.

Interestingly, this pattern doesn't extend to every Southern state with major cities: Florida, unlike Texas and Virginia, showed some encouraging signs for the GOP.

Republicans lost two south Florida seats (though GOP candidates in both races outperformed Trump by a solid amount) but won both a Senate seat and the governor's race. That's quite a feat—in some other swing states (e.g., Pennsylvania, Michigan), Republicans lost both the Senate and governor race by a sizable margin.

There are a couple possible explanations for these results. Republican Governor Rick Scott, the Senate candidate, had solid approval ratings[17] when he was running and Democratic Senator Bill Nelson was arguably a below-replacement-level candidate. At the same time, it's possible that Andrew Gillum, the Tallahassee mayor and governor candidate, was too far to the left[18] for Florida and that canceled out Ron DeSantis's Trump sycophancy[19] and racialized comments.[20] This combination of good luck on the GOP side (i.e., Scott running when he's popular) and not-so-great candidates on the Democratic side might have allowed the Republicans to simply get lucky twice.

But it's also possible that Florida is moving to the right or becoming less swingy. Florida has historically leaned slightly to the right of other swing states—meaning that it's winnable for Democrats in the right year, but is just a little bit more favorable to the GOP. But the results in the Senate and gubernatorial races could mean that Floridians have moved right over the last two years, or that the politics of the state have become more rigid (i.e., politics are divided such that a large national swing in public opinion doesn't cause much of a swing in Florida).

I don't know which version of the Florida story is correct, and we probably won't get any more helpful data until the 2020 election. But Florida is a critical state in the current electoral map, and a rightward move or an increase in rigidity would be a very positive development for the Republicans.

On the whole, the news from the South was still very good for Democrats—they won suburban House seats and performed well statewide in some of the big states. But the strong GOP showing in Florida and the resilience of the base make the results slightly more mixed than what we saw in the Northeast.

THE MIDWEST: DEMOCRATIC DOMINATION OR REPUBLICAN RESILIENCE?

The Midwest might be the most confusing and intriguing region because it holds some of the best signs for both parties.

The Democrats got two pieces of good news from the 2018 elections.

First, they performed very well in swing states where Trump won. Trump won Ohio, Wisconsin, and Michigan and came close to winning Minnesota. But Democrats won Senate races in each of these states, and they took the governorship in all of them except for Ohio. None of the Senate races were particularly close, and some of them were outright beatdowns (e.g., Amy Klobuchar won reelection in Minnesota by 24.1 points). Republicans did somewhat better in the gubernatorial races (they won in Ohio and Iowa), but Democrats managed to take down one of their most high-value targets of the cycle—conservative Wisconsin Governor Scott Walker.

Second, they won a variety of House races (as they did in the Northeast). They took over some suburban seats that shifted to the left between 2012 and 2016 (e.g., Illinois's Sixth, Illinois's Fourteenth, and Kansas's Third). But they also took over some seats that shifted strongly to the right (such as Iowa's First and Third) between 2012 and 2016. Not all the House news was great for the blue team: Minnesota Democrats lost races in the First and Eighth Districts, which were previously Democratically held Obama-to-Trump districts. But they made up for those losses by taking over Minnesota's Second and Third Districts, which are categorized by CityLab as "Sparse Suburban."

Put simply, the topline was good for Democrats. If the 2020 Democratic

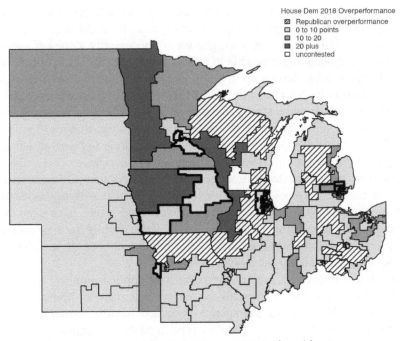

House Dem 2018 Overperformance
- ▨ Republican overperformance
- ☐ 0 to 10 points
- ◫ 10 to 20
- ■ 20 plus
- ☐ uncontested

Map 4.3   Change in House results from 2016 to 2018 in the Midwest.

presidential candidate repeats a performance like that in the Midwest, then the election is almost assuredly over.

But if you look underneath the topline, there are some real signs of life for the GOP.

First, there's the obvious resilience of the GOP in some parts of the Midwest. In a number of districts in Ohio, Michigan, Wisconsin, and Illinois, the GOP managed to meet or exceed Trump's margin despite facing considerable headwinds. Republicans also won governor races in Iowa and Ohio and took two Minnesota House seats.

Second, the GOP posted good *margins* in some of the states where they lost.

In Michigan's Senate race, Republican John James lost to Democratic Senator Debbie Stabenow by 6.5 points while Democrats won the national popular vote by more than eight points. If we adjust for uncontested districts, that national margin goes down to about seven points—meaning that James performed about as well as national Republicans did in 2018.

That's a big deal because it suggests that Michigan—longtime home of the industrial blue-collar Democrat—is no more red or blue than the country and that Michigan *might* be moving to the center of the political map in a more lasting way. James's margin suggests (though far from definitively proves) that Trump's 2016 victory in Michigan wasn't necessarily a one-off and that another Republican might be able to repeat it under the right circumstances.

A similar pattern showed up in Ohio. Democratic Senator Sherrod Brown won re-election by 6.8 points in 2018. Brown is widely considered to be an effective politician and a strong incumbent. If we subtract out some incumbent advantage and account for the national environment, that result suggests that Trump's gains in Ohio (which made the state look light red rather than swingy) might have shifted the state's baseline to the right.

Not every state exhibited this pattern. Neither the Minnesota Senate special election nor the Wisconsin Senate results suggested that those states were moving to the right in a more permanent way. And some states were more vague—Iowa elected three Democrats to the House (it only has four districts) while electing a Republican governor. (For more details on these points, see my November article for the *Weekly Standard*.[21])

But that vagueness is exactly the point—the topline numbers look good for the Democrats, and the beneath-the-surface calculations show some good signs for the Republicans. Democrats benefited from a favorable national environment and would win big if they replicated these margins in 2020. But in a more Trump-y version of politics—where the GOP is increasingly reliant on blue-collar white voters—Republicans might be able to keep Ohio or win Michigan more easily.

THE WEST: DEMOCRATIC GOLD RUSH?

The West is, in my view, the best overall region for Democrats—and the one Republicans should be most worried about. In the South, the GOP was able to hold onto the base while Democrats hacked away at the suburbs. In the Midwest, Democrats dominated the topline but the Republicans showed signs of life under the surface. In the Northeast, the Middle Atlantic subregion was rough for Republicans but the New England results were predictably uneventful.

But the West offers little good news to the GOP.

The key to understanding the West is understanding that many of the big western states are (as it is with Texas) mostly urban. There are large expanses of rural land in the West, but the people in those expanses are often far outnumbered by the people in major cities. That gives Democrats a lot of room to grow in the suburbs.

With that in mind, we'll generally move from east to west.

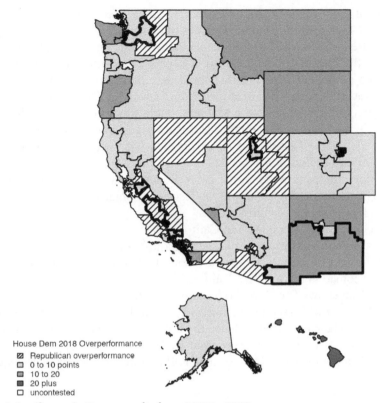

Map 4.4   Change in House results from 2016 to 2018.

Democrats took Colorado's Sixth District (Denver area) and retained the governorship (Democrat Jared Polis won by 10.6 points). Democrats also won the governorship of New Mexico and took the Second District. Republicans held Idaho and Wyoming (very rural states), but they failed to unseat Democratic Senator Jon Tester in Montana (Tester won by four points after Trump won by 20 in 2016).

Republican House candidates generally outperformed Trump in Utah, but Trump isn't a high bar there. His personal style played poorly in heavily Mormon Utah, which allowed Independent Evan McMullin to siphon votes and diminish Trump's overall margins there. The GOP's biggest bright spot in Utah was Mitt Romney—he cruised to a victory in the Senate race. But there was also a Democratic bright spot—Republican Representative Mia Love lost a close race to Ben McAdams in Utah's Fourth District (in/around Salt Lake City).

Two of the biggest Democratic triumphs came from Arizona and Nevada. Arizona—a state dominated by the cities of Phoenix and Tucson—gave Democratic Representative Kyrsten Sinema the win over Republican Representative Martha McSally. Arizona is still a Republican-leaning state (Trump won it by 3.5 points in 2016) but this could be a potential growth area for the Democrats. It's possible to imagine a future where the GOP takes a Trumpist strategy, performs better in the Midwest, but lets more urban states like Arizona slip out from under them. One could argue that's already happened in Nevada, where Democratic Representative Jacky Rosen beat Republican Senator Dean Heller by five points.

By now, the pattern should be clear. Republicans generally won in rural areas (though they did fail to unseat Tester in Montana), but Democrats did well in key urban and suburban areas.

And that pattern extended into California.

It's a little tough to see all of California in Map 4.4 (you can see Democratic flips in California's Tenth and Twenty-first Districts but not much else), so I've zoomed in on Southern California in Map 4.5.

This map shows five Democratic flips—California's Twenty-fifth, Thirty-ninth, Forty-fifth, Forty-eighth, and Forty-ninth districts. Every one of these districts is labeled as either "Dense Suburban" or "Urban-suburban mix" by CityLab and each of them were won by both Mitt Romney in 2012 and Hillary Clinton in 2016. Some of the GOP candidates in these districts were

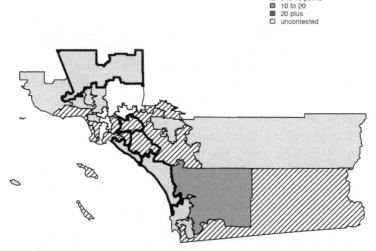

Map 4.5   Change in House results from 2016 to 2018 in Southern California.

able to appeal to Romney-Clinton voters and outperform Trump, but none of them won. These losses are particularly interesting (and probably painful to traditional Republicans) because of the historic anti-tax attitudes of parts of Southern California.[22] But Trump's style (which may have helped him in the Midwest) is likely a disadvantage among the affluent suburbanites of Los Angeles and Orange County, and Democrats have been more than happy to pick up these unhappy former Republicans.

Simply put, politics is often a set of actions and reactions (or maybe just actions and unforeseen consequences). Republicans might be gaining some underlying strength in the Midwest, but they're likely paying for it by losing strength in the Southwest and West Coast.

WHAT DOES IT ALL MEAN?

The 2018 election doesn't tell us much about 2020. As I've previously written, midterm election results just aren't a good predictor of the next presidential election. Sometimes a party has a great election right after a terrible one (see Democratic results in 2010 verses 2012). Sometimes a party has a terrible midterm followed by a terrible presidential election (see Republican results in 2006 and 2008). And sometimes a terrible midterm is followed up by a mediocre general election (see Republicans in 1974 verses 1976).[23] There's really no way to use this midterm to extrapolate outwards and figure out what's going to happen next time around.

But this midterm does suggest that Trumpian voting patterns—a more blue-collar GOP, a more suburbanized Democratic Party—apply to politicians that aren't named Donald Trump or Hillary Clinton. After the Trump Era is over, parts of this era may stick and politics likely won't snap to fights between Mitt Romney Republicans and Barack Obama Democrats.

And this midterm proves definitively that the laws of political gravity really do apply to Trump. During the 2016 election cycle, there were countless versions of the same "Trump Can't Win Because [Fill In The Blank]" takes—and his victory proved those to be wrong. After the election, a cottage industry of "Trump and the GOP Are Invincible and the Media Doesn't Get It" takes appeared, and the GOP's 2018 loss proved that that idea was wrong too. *Trump is different but he's not special*—he's capable of winning if his strategy is better than his opponent's, and he's capable of losing if he's unpopular.

Nobody knows what's going to happen in 2020, and nobody knows exactly what our politics are going to look like afterwards. But the difference between the 2018 and 2016 results suggest that Trump's influence may not immediately disappear and that politics will (as always) remain chaotic, unpredictable, and competitive.

NOTES

1. David Byler, "How Trump Picked the Democratic Lock and Won the Presidency," RealClearPolitics, April 12, 2017, https://www.realclearpolitics.com/articles/2017/04/12/how_trump_picked_the_democratic_lock_and_won_the_presidency_133571.html.

2. David Wasserman and Ally Flinn, "2018 House Popular Vote Tracker," Cook Political Report, https://docs.google.com/spreadsheets/d/1WxDaxD5az6kdOjJncmGph37z0BPNhV1fNAH_g7IkpC0/edit?ouid = 109462525920565658329&usp = sheets_home&ths = true.

3. Yair Ghitza, "What Happened Last Tuesday: Part 2—Who Did They Vote For?" Medium, November 14, 2018, https://medium.com/@yghitza_48326/what-happened-last-tuesday-part-2-who-did-they-vote-for-e3a2a63a5ef2.

4. "The 2018 Election, Explained in 13 Charts," Echelon Insights, November 2018, http://echeloninsights.com/wp-content/uploads/EchelonInsights-2018InCharts.pdf.

5. Jahnabi Barooah, "Most and Least Mormon States In America," *Huffington Post*, December 6, 2017, https://www.huffingtonpost.com/2012/05/21/most-and-least-mormon-states_n_1533973.html.

6. https://www.census.gov/geo/reference/gtc/gtc_census_divreg.html.

7. Results from Daily Kos Elections, Dave Wasserman, and *New York Times*. Shapefile from Daily Kos Elections (https://drive.google.com/drive/folders/0Bz_uFI8VY7xLbVRlZC1RMnRGODQ).

8. Ella Nilsen, "Ayanna Pressley Wins the Massachusetts 7th Congressional District Primary in an Upset," *Vox*, September 4, 2018, https://www.vox.com/2018/9/4/17820720/ayanna-pressley-massachusetts-seventh-congressional-district-primary-michael-capuano.

9. David Byler, "Are Republicans Blowing It in the Midwest?" *Weekly Standard*, November 12, 2018, https://www.weeklystandard.com/david-byler/are-republicans-blowing-it-in-the-midwest.

10. Nate Cohn, Matthew Bloch, and Kevin Quealy, "The New Pennsylvania Congressional Map, District by District," *New York Times*, February 19, 2018, https://www.nytimes.com/interactive/2018/02/19/upshot/pennsylvania-new-house-districts-gerrymandering.html.

11. Mike DeBonis, "Democratic Sen. Robert Menendez Is 'Severely Admonished' by Ethics Committee, Ordered to Repay Gifts," *Washington Post*, April 26, 2018, https://www.washingtonpost.com/powerpost/democratic-sen-robert-menendez-is-severely-admonished-by-ethics-committee-ordered-to-repay-gifts/2018/04/26/2bff0dc6–4978–11e8–9072-f6d4bc32f223_story.html.

12. David Montgomery and Richard Florida, "How the Suburbs Will Swing the Midterm Election," CityLab, October 5, 2018, https://www.citylab.com/equity/2018/10/midterm-election-data-suburban-voters/572137/. Montgomery data cited throughout available at: https://github.com/theatlantic/citylab-data/blob/master/citylab-congress/citylab_cdi.csv.

13. David Byler, "Is Virginia Permanently Blue Now?" *Weekly Standard*, November 21, 2017, https://www.weeklystandard.com/david-byler/is-virginia-permanently-blue-now.

14. Andrew Kaczynski and Nathan McDermott, "Corey Stewart Praised Southern Secession in 2017 Campaign Appearance," CNN, August 8, 2018, https://www.cnn.com/2018/08/08/politics/kfile-corey-stewart-southern-secession/index.html?no-st = 1547408 096.

15. Byler, "Is Virginia Permanently Blue Now?"

16. David Byler, "Blue Texas? It's Way More Complicated than You Think," *Weekly Standard*, February 21, 2018, https://www.weeklystandard.com/david-byler/blue-texas-its-way-more-complicated-than-you-think.

17. Cameron Easley, "Q3 2018 Rankings: America's Most and Least Popular Governors," Morning Consult, October 10, 2018, https://morningconsult.com/2018/10/10/americas-most-and-least-popular-governors-q3–2018/.

18. Max Greenwood, "Sanders-backed Andrew Gillum Wins Major Upset in Florida Dem Gov Primary," The Hill, August 28, 2018, https://thehill.com/homenews/campaign/404097-andrew-gillum-wins-florida-democratic-gubernatorial-race-in-stunning-upset.

19. "Ron DeSantis Teaches His Kids to Love Trump in Campaign Ad for Florida Governor," RealClearPolitics, July 31, 2018, https://www.realclearpolitics.com/video/2018/07/31/ron_desantis_goes_all_in_with_trump_endorsement_in_florida_governor_race.html.

20. Julia Jacobs, "DeSantis Warns Florida Not to 'Monkey This Up,' and Many Hear a Racist Dog Whistle," *New York Times*, August 29, 2018, https://www.nytimes.com/2018/08/29/us/politics/desantis-monkey-up-gillum.html.

21. Byler, "Are Republicans Blowing It in the Midwest?"

22. Guy Mazorati, "Republicans Hope Orange County's Historic Anti-Tax Sentiments Can Hold Off Blue Wave," KQED, October 12, 2018, https://www.kqed.org/news/11698068/republicans-hope-orange-countys-historic-anti-tax-sentiments-can-hold-off-blue-wave.

23. David Byler, "What Would a Democratic Takeover in the House Mean for 2020?" *Weekly Standard*, October 15, 2018, https://www.weeklystandard.com/david-byler/what-would-a-democratic-takeover-in-the-house-mean-for-2020.

5

The House

Where the Blue Wave Hit the Hardest

Kyle Kondik

It may well be that the outcome of the 2018 midterm elections for the U.S. House of Representatives was preordained the instant that 2016's upset victory by Donald Trump in the presidential race became official.

That's because simply holding the White House typically incurs significant down-ballot penalties.

Since World War II, there have been eight presidential administrations, including some combined administrations when vice presidents took over mid-term. Over the course of those eight presidential administrations, each administration saw their party lose an average of 40 net House seats from the beginning of their administration to the start of the next administration.[1]

Over a longer time frame (going back to the start of the Civil War), and looking at individual midterm elections, the president's party had lost ground in the House in 36 of 39 midterm elections, with an average loss of 33 seats. In the post-World War II time frame, the average seat loss was 26.

Democrats started the 2018 election cycle at a 241–194 disadvantage in the House, meaning that they needed to net 24 seats over the course of the cycle to win the majority. History did not guarantee such a gain, but it did suggest such a gain was plausible, if not outright likely, particularly given that Trump entered office as a divisive figure with a low approval rating that remained stuck in roughly the low 40s in averages of national opinion polls throughout the course of his first two years in office.

By the time Election Day arrived in November 2018, the Democrats needed to net 23 seats to win the majority—they had already picked up a seat courtesy of a special election in Pennsylvania earlier that year (more on that and other special elections below)—and they ended up blowing past that goal, netting an impressive 40 seats and electing 235 members of the 435-member body.

Speaking in early 2019, Republican National Committee Chairwoman Ronna McDaniel reportedly told some of her colleagues that "We minimized our losses in the House."[2] A fair-minded assessment of the results argues the opposite, particularly compared to other categories of races. Republicans actually could point to some encouraging signs in the two other major categories of races—netting two seats in the Senate and holding important governorships in Florida, Georgia, and Ohio in the midst of Democratic gubernatorial gains. In state legislative races, Democrats made gains but actually performed a bit behind the recent average in terms of both net seats gained and net chambers flipped.

Meanwhile, Democrats notched their biggest House gain in terms of raw seats since the 1974 midterm, when the Watergate scandal that forced President Nixon out of office contributed to a Democratic midterm triumph. They also exceeded the average midterm seat gain by the presidential out-party, winning a House majority that was not that much smaller than the one Republicans captured in their own 2010 wave (Republicans won 242 seats that year, seven more than the Democratic tally eight years later).

If 2018 truly was a "blue wave," it's the House results that represent the best argument in favor of that assertion. This was not the Republicans *minimizing* losses; the better assessment is that Democrats *maximized* their gains, especially given some of the surprising Election Night results that ended up breaking in favor of the Democrats.

What follows is a description of how the cycle progressed and how the Democrats ended up winning the House with seats to spare.

THE HOUSE AT THE START OF THE 2018 CYCLE

Trump's middling 2016 victory, in which he won the Electoral College despite losing the national popular vote by about two points, came without coattails in the race for the House. Democrats ended up netting six seats in 2016, reducing the GOP's majority from 247 (the biggest GOP House majority since 1928) to a more modest but still impressive 241. Democrats had hoped that Trump would go down in flames in the presidential race, and thus endanger the Republican House majority, but such a backlash obviously never developed. In fact, Republican House losses may have been even smaller if not for court-ordered redistricting that created new House district maps in Florida and Virginia; these changes alone likely accounted for a two-seat net Democratic gain in the former and a one-seat net Democratic gain in the latter, or half (three) of the Democrats' modest half-dozen seat overall gain. As of Election Day 2018, the median House seat by 2016 presidential performance was Nebraska's Second District, which Trump won by about two percentage points while losing the national popular vote by two points, meaning that the median district was situated about four points to the right of the national average. That demonstrated the generic lean of the House map and gave Republicans some hope that the House map could withstand a Democratic surge.

That Trump had been elected without prompting a broader GOP wave could have actually been an encouraging sign for House Republicans as they assessed their odds in 2018. The political science theory of "surge and decline," as explained right before the 2018 election by political scientists Daron Shaw and John R. Petrocik, suggested "a straightforward Off-Year Rule: The more you won, the more you will lose."[3]

In other words, perhaps Republicans might be insulated from big House losses because Trump had no surge in 2016 and did not elect with him a large number of House Republicans who would obviously be vulnerable in the absence of a "Trump surge"—because there was no Trump surge in the House.

That said, it turned out that the GOP position in the House was weaker than it seemed in the 2016 results. One reason *may* have been that many voters in 2016 did not get the outcome they expected that year.

Instead of prompting a backlash, perceptions of Trump as a general election underdog may have actually aided Republican House efforts. Writing in advance of the 2016 presidential election, veteran political scientist Robert Erikson found that in post-World War II presidential elections, a small but important group of well-informed voters may vote against the party of the candidate they perceive will win the White House as a way of providing a check on the president in the presidential year, as opposed to waiting for the midterm two years later to provide that balance. Betting markets, pundits, and the general public all saw Clinton as the favorite in the presidential election.[4] Writing in the leadup to the 2018 midterm, Erikson speculated that these perceptions may have hurt Democratic House performance: "Plausibly, many who thought Hillary Clinton would win voted Republican for Congress to block, thus accounting for the Democrats' surprisingly feeble performance at the congressional level in 2016."[5] While the differences were subtle, Trump lost the popular presidential vote by two points while House Republicans won the overall House vote by about a point. But in several Clinton-won, affluent, highly educated House districts—the kinds of places one might expect to find some of the very sophisticated voters Erikson identified as potential presidential-year ticket-splitters—Republican House incumbents such as Mike Coffman in suburban Denver's Sixth Congressional District, Barbara Comstock in Northern Virginia's Tenth Congressional District, and Erik Paulsen in the suburban Third Congressional District covering greater Minneapolis–St. Paul all ran at least 15 percentage points in terms of margin in their districts ahead of Trump.

Had Clinton actually won the White House, they all may have been fine in 2018. Clinton's approval, just like Trump's, could have been bad, and the usual out-party midterm trend would have been working against the Democrats, not the Republicans. But Trump winning put many of these seemingly strong incumbents in much more serious danger than their impressive 2016 victories would have otherwise suggested.

SIGNS AND PORTENTS: THE SPECIAL
AND OFF-YEAR ELECTIONS

To fill out his administration, Trump elevated several sitting Republican members of the House to high positions in the government. Representatives Mike Pompeo of Kansas's Fourth Congressional District, Tom Price of Georgia's Sixth, Ryan Zinke of Montana's at-large district, and Mick Mulvaney of South Carolina's Fifth all quickly joined the administration, leaving their seats to be filled in special elections held in the first half of 2017.

Political watchers carefully monitored these special elections for clues about the mood of the electorate. Just like midterm elections, "special elections show a consistent bias against the administration party" and can "serve as bellwethers for media interpretation of national trends," Andrew E. Busch observed in his study of midterm elections.[6] Famous examples include a string of Democratic special election victories in the first half of 1974 that may have helped Republicans break ranks with Richard Nixon, who resigned in August over the Watergate scandal. One of the Democratic wins in 1974 came in a historically very Republican Grand Rapids, Michigan-based seat that Gerald Ford left behind after Nixon picked him as his new vice president in 1973. However, special elections are not always perfectly predictive of the future: Democrats won three closely watched House special elections on GOP-leaning turf in upstate New York and western Pennsylvania in 2009 and early 2010. The Republicans then smashed the Democratic House majority in November 2010, netting 63 seats overall.

Furthermore, the districts that would host special elections in early 2017 did not profile as places that should be all that competitive. Trump had won Kansas's Fourth, Montana's at large, and South Carolina's Fifth by 27, 20, and 19 points, respectively. Republicans did end up holding all three districts in special elections contested in the first half of the 2017 calendar year, but the GOP margins were only in the single digits in each race. In other words, Democrats ended up running about 15 to 20 points ahead of Hillary Clinton's losing margin in each race.

But the highlight of the early special election season was in Georgia's Sixth. And the end result actually could have been seen as discouraging for Democrats.

Unlike the other three aforementioned House districts, Georgia's Sixth had been much closer in the 2016 presidential race, as Trump had won it by less than two points in 2016, but it had been much more Republican both down the ballot and in 2012, when it had voted for Republican presidential-nominee Mitt Romney by 23 percentage points.

Analysts wondered which statistic was more meaningful in districts like Georgia's Sixth, a suburban Atlanta district with much higher-than-average levels of four-year college attainment: the Trump underperformance, or the usual Republican showings for recent non-Trump Republicans.

All the candidates would run together in an April 18, 2017, election, with a runoff coming June 20 if none of the candidates received a majority. The Republican field was crowded, although Karen Handel, a former Georgia secretary of state who had lost high-profile statewide primaries for governor and Senate, seemed like the GOP frontrunner. Meanwhile, Democrats rallied around Jon Ossoff, a documentary filmmaker and former congressional aide. Ossoff almost assuredly benefited from a national political void in which Democrats, still shell-shocked over Trump's victory in 2016, had precious few opportunities to strike back. Ossoff became a vessel for this frustration, and a precursor of what was to come: He ended up raising an eye-popping $31.6 million, and the combined spending on both sides made it the priciest House race ever.

Ossoff ended up almost winning in the first round of voting, winning about 48 percent of the vote, with Handel winning a clear plurality among the Republicans. The two candidates slogged it out for two more months, yet Ossoff couldn't move his support beyond his first-round support, losing to Handel 51.8 percent to 48.2 percent.

Still, two facts stood out: First, even though Ossoff's margin in the district was actually a little worse than Clinton's, the results much more clearly mir-rored the close presidential contest as opposed to the other GOP blowouts in the district for other recent races; and, second, the total number of votes cast in the runoff, 260,316, was about 50,000 more votes than had been cast in the district in the 2014 midterm election. Granted, 2014 was generally a weak turnout year, but the huge interest in the Georgia Six race was a precursor for a high-turnout midterm in 2018.

While they weren't special elections, Democrats were encouraged by the November results in Virginia's odd-year statewide elections, in which they swept all three statewide elected executive offices by bigger-than-expected margins and netted a surprisingly large 15 seats in the lower house of the state legislature. The following month, Democrats scored their most impressive victory of 2017 when Democrat Doug Jones narrowly defeated Republican Roy Moore in the Alabama Senate special election. The Democratic success continued into 2018, when Democrat Conor Lamb narrowly won a special election in western Pennsylvania's Eighteenth District, which Trump had carried by nearly 20 points. Over the summer, Republicans had to sweat out another seemingly safe seat, this time in Central Ohio, as Republican Troy Balderson carried Ohio's Twelfth District by less than a point over Democrat Danny O'Connor.

Table 5.1 shows the results of the federal special elections held in 2017 and in 2018 in advance of the November general election. While Democrats did not overperform Clinton's 2016 margin in every single race, they did so in the lion's share of them, offering what turned out to be something of a fall preview. On average, the Democratic margin in these nine races improved about 15 points from the 2016 presidential race. Analysts also watched the larger universe of state legislative specials as mini-portents of the fall. In

Table 5.1   Democratic Performance in 2017–2018 Federal Special Elections

Date	Race	Dem Margin	2016 Dem Presidential Margin	Dem Improvement
4/11/2017	Kansas 4	− 6.20%	− 27.20%	21.00%
5/25/2017	Montana at large	− 5.60%	− 20.50%	14.90%
6/20/2017	Georgia 6 runoff	− 3.60%	− 1.50%	− 2.10%
6/20/2017	South Carolina 5	− 3.10%	− 18.50%	15.40%
11/7/2017	Utah 3	− 32.50%	− 23.90%	− 8.60%
12/12/2017	Alabama Senate	1.60%	− 27.70%	29.30%
3/13/2018	Pennsylvania 18	0.30%	− 19.50%	19.90%
4/24/2018	Arizona 8	− 4.70%	− 21.10%	16.40%
8/7/2018	Ohio 12	− 0.80%	− 11.30%	10.50%
Average change		− 6.83%	− 21.40%	14.59%

Source: "Special elections for Congress and state legislatures since Trump's election," compiled by Geoffrey Skelley *of FiveThirtyEight*, https://docs.google.com/spreadsheets/d/1vfNAc0DQWRQEudDnqO6hPaIPcDoo0 MpLWuyV04fl3RY/edit#gid = 864853559.

roughly 120 state and federal special elections prior to the midterm, Democrats on average improved a little more than 10 points over Clinton's 2016 margin. The special election improvement also ended up mirroring the change in the total U.S. House popular vote from 2016, which Republicans carried by about a point, to 2018, when Democrats won by about 8.5 points, or roughly a 9.5-point improvement.

Another sign of Democratic enthusiasm as the House picture crystalized was the high number of Democratic challengers in seats held by Republicans. Overall, Democrats fielded a candidate in all but three GOP-held districts, while Republicans did not field a candidate in 38 Democratic districts.[7] Many of these challengers couldn't put up much of a fight—the lion's share of the districts on both sides really are not competitive at all on paper—but fielding as full a slate of candidates as possible can be a sign of grassroots intensity. Over the last four decades, there have only been three times when a party left only a single-digit total of the opposing party's House seats unopposed: the Democrats in 2006 and 2018 and the Republicans in 2010. The House flipped each year. Again, this is not an argument about how fielding a large slate of candidates causes the House to flip; rather, it's a more modest suggestion that fielding challengers nearly everywhere is a positive sign of a party's energy in a given year.

Even though it is addressed in more depth in Michael Toner and Karen Trainer's chapter on money in the 2018 elections within this volume, Democrats' tremendous House fundraising was one other sign of grassroots enthusiasm. One way to illustrate the money edge Democrats enjoyed is as follows: Analyst Noah Rudnick found that in the closest House races—the ones decided by less than 10 points—the median Democratic House challenger spent $4.2 million in these races while the median Republican incumbent spent only $3.1 million, meaning that many Democratic House challengers were outraising and outspending Republican incumbents at will. Typically, one generally would expect incumbents to have a resource edge.[8]

THE OPEN SEATS AND PENNSYLVANIA REDRISTRICING

Ultimately, only individual members of Congress and maybe their families and closest advisers know the real reasons they decide to run or not run for another term, but it is not much of a leap to think that some members of the House had an inkling of the bad environment awaiting them in November, given both the history of midterm elections and the pro-Democratic special election results that were occurring as they were making their decisions about their futures. Some veteran members may have been worried about losing their reelection bids; others likely feared being in the minority; and still others were nudged out the door by term limits for committee chairmanships.

As it turned out, a significant slice of the GOP House caucus decided not to run for reelection to the House. Overall, 60 of the 435 House seats contested in 2018 did not feature an incumbent running for reelection. This was the second-highest total of open seats in the post-World War II era, eclipsed only by 1992, which was a redistricting year (naturally prompting more turnover) that also featured a House banking scandal that also contributed to a high level of turnover.

Of those 60 open seats, 39 were Republican-held seats and 21 were Democratic-held seats. Most notably, Speaker of the House Paul Ryan of Wisconsin's First District decided not to run, but he was not the only prominent House Republican to head for the exits: Nine of the party's 21 committee chairs opted against running for reelection to the House. Open seats historically are harder for the incumbent party to defend, particularly in a trying national environment, and in recent midterms the president's party's candidates in open seats saw very sharp declines in vote share from the performance of the incumbent in the preceding election.[9]

Veteran GOP retirees included Representatives Rodney Frelinghuysen and Frank LoBiondo of New Jersey, Darrell Issa and Ed Royce of California, and Ileana Ros-Lehtinen of Florida. Democrats would end up winning all five of these districts, and several more open seats.

Democrats also benefited from court-ordered redistricting in Pennsylvania that prompted at least one additional retirement.

In February 2018, the Pennsylvania Supreme Court, controlled by Democrats, threw out the state's Republican-drawn U.S. House map and replaced it with a map that, while not necessarily a Democratic gerrymander, "consistently makes subtle choices that nudge districts in the direction of Democrats," according to an analysis by the *New York Times*'s Nate Cohn.[10] The court altered the entire state's map, turning a map that Republicans drew to elect 13 Republicans and five Democrats to the House into one in which Democrats seemed guaranteed to make significant gains. It radically reconfigured a Southeast Pennsylvania seat held by Republican Representative Pat Meehan, turning it from a heavily gerrymandered swing seat into a district that Clinton would've won by about 30 points in 2016. Meehan had already announced his retirement in part because of a sexual harassment scandal, but no Republican could practically hold this seat. Charlie Dent, a Republican who represented a Republican-leaning seat that contained most of the Lehigh Valley, had also already decided to retire, but his seat went from one that Trump won by eight points to a more compact district that Clinton won by a point. Another Southeast Pennsylvania seat, held by Republican Representative Ryan Costello, also became significantly more Democratic, prompting Costello to retire. In Western Pennsylvania, special-election victor Lamb got a much better district to run in, one that Trump had won by less than three points as opposed to nearly 20, and he ran there against Republican Representative Keith Rothfus.

All told, Democrats went from holding five seats in Pennsylvania at the start of the cycle to forcing a nine-to-nine tie with Republicans. What's interesting to consider, though, is the possibility that Democrats could have netted four seats on the old, gerrymandered Republican map, too. We know that Lamb was capable of winning the old Pennsylvania Eighteen, because he won it in a March special election under the old lines. Additionally, because Dent and Meehan both eventually resigned, special elections were held in November for their old seats to fill their unexpired terms along with regular elections for the new districts. Democrats ended up winning the districts under the old lines as well as the new, although by much reduced margins in the old districts. Had his district not been altered, Costello may very well have run for reelection, and he conceivably could have held his seat against Chrissy Houlahan, the Democratic Air Force veteran who otherwise waltzed to victory in the reconfigured Sixth District after Costello left. Meanwhile, Democrats fell short in their bids to win three other GOP-held Pennsylvania seats, narrowly losing to incumbent Republican Representatives Brian Fitzpatrick in Bucks County's First District, Scott Perry in the reconfigured Tenth District around Harrisburg, and Mike Kelly in Western Pennsylvania's Sixteenth District.

Ultimately, the net change in Pennsylvania may have been the same without the new map, but the Democratic victories there under less favorable lines probably would have required significantly more investment from national outside groups. As it was, all four of the Democratic pickups in Pennsylvania came by at least double-digit margins.

Overall, 12 of the 43 GOP-held seats that the Democrats captured in November 2018 came in seats where no incumbent was on the ballot, and that tally increases to 13 if one counts as an open seat South Carolina's First District, which Democrat Joe Cunningham captured in a surprising upset after Katie Arrington beat Representative Mark Sanford in the Republican primary.

Republicans ended up picking up just three previously Democratic seats in 2018 and, perhaps unsurprisingly, all three of them were open seats in Republican-leaning turf. One of those was Pennsylvania's redesigned Fourteenth District, which was an even more Republican-leaning version of the district Lamb won in the special election and then left behind; the other two,

Minnesota's First and Eighth Districts, both voted for Trump by about 15 points in 2016 and were two of the relatively few remaining largely white and rural districts that Democrats held anywhere in the country. Both flipped to Republicans, although the First District was exceedingly close as Republican Jim Hagedorn, whose father served in the House and who himself had lost races for the district in 2014 and 2016, only beat Democrat Dan Feehan by less than half a point.

Democrats played defense in some other Trump-won open seats, winning clear victories in Nevada's Third District in the Las Vegas area and New Hampshire's perpetually competitive First District.

THE REPUBLICANS' POLICY PROBLEMS

In addition to midterm years often featuring a backlash against an unpopular president, midterm electorates can often use these elections to change the course of policy in Washington. It would be wrong to suggest that the election was *entirely* about Donald Trump, although his presence clearly opened the door to Democrats winning the House. But on two key issues Republicans found themselves arguably on the wrong side of the electorate—or, at very least, not on the right side.

During Barack Obama's presidency, Republicans railed against the Affordable Care Act, otherwise known as "Obamacare," which was the signature achievement stemming from Obama and the Democrats' brief, two-year unified control of Washington from 2009–2010. Republicans, and Trump, vowed to "repeal and replace" the ACA. However, when given the opportunity, Republicans failed to pass an alternative. The GOP spent much of the first half of 2017 trying to get a repeal through the House, initially failing but then succeeding. That bill narrowly died in the GOP-controlled Senate, though, meaning that several vulnerable Republicans found themselves compelled to cast a difficult vote on a bill that didn't even become law (It was reminiscent to a "cap and trade" climate change bill that was a tough vote for many moderate Democrats in 2009. That bill never even got a vote in the Democratic-controlled Senate after passing the House). Meanwhile, public sentiment about the ACA became more positive throughout 2017 and 2018, and the RealClearPolitics national polling average showed net favorability for the ACA improving from being net negative before Trump took office to net positive after.

That a liberal policy became more popular after a conservative government took over is very much in keeping with the rhythms of public opinion. James Stimson has noted how the public's policy preferences can oscillate between the two parties depending on which one of them is in power: "Preferences 'zig' upward (toward liberalism) when Republicans control the White House and 'zag' downward when Democrats are in charge."[11] Not only did Republicans not achieve the policy objective they desired—doing away with the ACA—they also found themselves open to Democratic attacks on the health care issue as Democratic candidates emphasized issues like maintaining the ACA's popular insurance protections for people with preexisting medical conditions. The Wesleyan Media Project found that health care messaging dominated Democratic advertising throughout the campaign season, with the issue coming up in 57 percent of all the pro-Democratic ads aired on broadcast television in October 2018.[12] An ABC News/*Washington Post* poll released a couple of days before the election found that Democrats enjoyed a 16-point edge over Republicans on health care.[13] Nine of the 20 Republican House members who voted no on the GOP ACA alternative did not return to the House in 2019, either because they retired or lost. It was somewhat reminiscent of what happened when the Democrats passed the ACA in early 2010: There were 34 members who voted no, and half lost anyway in November 2010. And just three of those Democrats remain in the House as of this writing: Collin Peterson of Minnesota's Seventh District (where Trump won by a little more than 30 points in 2016, making him a true outlier in an era not known for as much ticket-splitting in the past) as well as Dan Lipinski of Illinois's Third District and Stephen Lynch of Massachusetts's Eighth District. Lipinski barely hung on against a liberal challenger in the 2018 primary and Lynch is one of the least liberal members of the House Democratic caucus.

In other words, strategic voting on health care—both for Democrats in the 2010 cycle and Republicans in the 2018 cycle—was not enough to save many vulnerable members.

While failing to repeal the ACA, Republican did pass a tax cut package that Democrats would attack as a giveaway to the rich. Democrats also pointed to a cap on state and local tax deductions included in the tax cuts as harmful to taxpayers in states with high taxes, like California, New Jersey, and New York (Democrats would end up netting 14 House seats alone from just these three states combined, although it's hard to draw a straight line from the questions over the tax bill to those gains). Polling on the tax bill generally showed perceptions to be either split or a bit negative.

While there is always nuance in public opinion, it's hard to say that these two issues helped Republicans in 2018; in fact, it's easier to argue the opposite, and that the combination of the president's unpopularity and a policy agenda that also was not popular further contributed to the large Democratic House wave.

WHERE THE HAMMER FELL

Following the Pennsylvania redistricting, Republicans controlled 25 districts that Hillary Clinton had won in 2016, and Democrats controlled 13 districts that Donald Trump had carried. These were the naturally most vulnerable seats on both sides. As noted above, Republicans ended up winning three of those Trump-won Democratic seats, all of which did not feature a Democratic incumbent running for reelection.

Meanwhile, Democrats ended up winning all *but* three of the Clinton-Republican districts.

Many of the Democratic victories came in well-to-do suburban areas with higher-than-average rates of four-year college attainment. Coffman, Comstock, and Paulsen—three of the 2016 Republicans mentioned earlier in this chapter that ran well ahead of Trump in 2016—all lost in relative blowout fashion, falling by double digits to well-heeled Democratic challengers. The suburban voters who shifted to Clinton in 2016—but not to Democratic House candidates—could not vote against Trump in 2018, so they did what for them was the next best way to register their disapproval: vote against their congressional Republican representatives. Figure 1.4 in the opening chapter shows a map of where the Democratic and Republican flips came; the seats themselves that changed hands are listed in Tables 5.2 and 5.3.

The Democratic near sweep in Clinton districts stood out, but in addition to winning 22 of those 25 districts, the Democrats made similar gains among the Trump-won districts, picking off 21 in total. About half of them, 10, were only marginal Trump districts, though, ones he won by less than five points. One of those was a district made famous in the earlier special election: Georgia's Sixth, in the Atlanta suburbs, where Lucy McBath, an African-American Democrat who ran for office after losing a son to gun violence, succeeded in beating Karen Handel after Jon Ossoff had failed the previous year. McBath, among many other Democratic candidates, emphasized gun control as part of her platform; unlike in 2006, when Democrats won the House in part because of culturally conservative candidates running in right-of-center districts, it was hard to classify many if any of this new crop of Democrats as being consistently conservative on hot-button social issues such as gun control, abortion, and same-sex marriage. That said, there were some Democrats elected in 2018 who did run as pro-gun candidates: examples include Lamb in Western Pennsylvania, Jeff Van Drew in New Jersey's Second District, and Jared Golden in Maine's Second District. Golden merits mention as an unusual winner: He finished very narrowly behind Republican Representative Bruce Poliquin, but because Poliquin did not receive a majority of the vote, the state's new ranked-choice voting system kicked in and

Chapter 5

Table 5.2   Seats that Flipped from Republican to Democrat in 2018 House Elections

State	District	Winner	Democrat Percentage	Republican Percentage	Clinton 2016 Margin	Beat Incumbent?
AZ	2	Ann Kirkpatrick	54.70%	45.20%	4.80%	No
CA	10	Josh Harder	52.30%	47.70%	3.00%	Yes
CA	21	T.J. Cox	50.40%	49.60%	15.40%	Yes
CA	25	Katie Hill	54.40%	45.60%	6.60%	Yes
CA	39	Gil Cisneros	51.60%	48.40%	8.50%	No
CA	45	Katie Porter	52.10%	47.90%	5.40%	Yes
CA	48	Harley Rouda	53.60%	46.40%	1.70%	Yes
CA	49	Mike Levin	56.40%	43.60%	7.50%	No
CO	6	Jason Crow	54.10%	42.90%	8.90%	Yes
FL	26	Debbie Mucarsel-Powell	50.90%	49.10%	16.30%	Yes
FL	27	Donna Shalala	51.80%	45.80%	19.70%	No
GA	6	Lucy McBath	50.50%	49.50%	−1.50%	Yes
IL	6	Sean Casten	53.60%	46.40%	6.80%	Yes
IL	14	Lauren Underwood	52.50%	47.50%	−4.00%	Yes
IA	1	Abby Finkenauer	51.00%	45.90%	−3.50%	Yes
IA	3	Cindy Axne	49.30%	47.10%	−3.50%	Yes
KS	3	Sharice Davids	53.60%	43.90%	1.20%	Yes
ME	2	Jared Golden	50.60%	49.40%	−10.30%	Yes
MI	8	Elissa Slotkin	50.60%	46.80%	−6.70%	Yes
MI	11	Haley Stevens	51.80%	45.20%	−4.40%	No
MN	2	Angie Craig	52.70%	47.10%	−1.20%	Yes
MN	3	Dean Phillips	55.60%	44.20%	9.40%	Yes
NJ	2	Jeff Van Drew	52.90%	45.20%	−4.60%	No
NJ	3	Andy Kim	50.00%	48.70%	−6.20%	Yes
NJ	7	Tom Malinowski	51.70%	46.70%	1.10%	Yes
NJ	11	Mikie Sherrill	56.80%	42.10%	−0.90%	No
NM	2	Xochitl Torres Small	50.90%	49.10%	−10.20%	No
NY	11	Max Rose	53.00%	46.60%	−9.80%	Yes
NY	19	Antonio Delgado	51.40%	46.20%	−6.80%	Yes
NY	22	Anthony Brindisi	50.90%	49.10%	−15.30%	Yes
OK	5	Kendra Horn	50.70%	49.30%	−13.70%	Yes
PA	5	Mary Gay Scanlon	65.20%	34.80%	28.20%	No
PA	6	Chrissy Houlahan	58.90%	41.10%	9.30%	No
PA	7	Susan Wild	53.50%	43.50%	1.10%	No
PA	17	Conor Lamb	56.30%	43.70%	−2.50%	Yes
SC	1	Joe Cunningham	50.60%	49.20%	−12.70%	No
TX	7	Lizzie Fletcher	52.50%	47.50%	1.40%	Yes
TX	32	Colin Allred	52.30%	45.80%	1.90%	Yes
UT	4	Ben McAdams	50.10%	49.90%	−6.70%	Yes
VA	2	Elaine Luria	51.10%	48.80%	−3.40%	Yes
VA	7	Abigail Spanberger	50.30%	48.40%	−6.50%	Yes
VA	10	Jennifer Wexton	56.10%	43.70%	9.80%	Yes
WA	8	Kim Schrier	52.40%	47.60%	3.00%	No

Table 5.3   Seats that Flipped from Democrat to Republican in 2018 House Elections

State	District	Winner	Democrat Percentage	Republican Percentage	Clinton 2016 Margin	Beat Incumbent?
MN	1	Jim Hagedorn	49.70	50.10	−14.80	No
MN	8	Pete Stauber	45.20	50.70	−15.50	No
PA	14	Guy Reschenthaler	42.10	57.90	−29.00	No

Source: Research by the author; David Wasserman & Ally Flinn, "2018 House Popular Vote Tracker," *Cook Political Report*, https://docs.google.com/spreadsheets/d/1WxDaxD5az6kdOjJncmGph37z0BPNhV1fNAH_g7lkpC0/edit#gid=0.

allowed Golden to win because he had gotten a larger number of second-place votes.

Democrats also won a handful of districts that went to Trump by double-digit margins. Perhaps the two biggest surprises came in the Southern cities of Charleston and Oklahoma City, where Democrats Joe Cunningham and Kendra Horn won victories that few saw coming.

All told, Democrats ended up winning a 235–199 majority. That only adds up to 434 seats, though, because as of this writing, there was still one House contest that had not been resolved. In North Carolina's Ninth Congressional District, Republican Representative Robert Pittenger lost a primary to Mark Harris, a former pastor who had nearly beaten Pittenger in a 2016 primary. Harris faced Democrat Dan McCready in the general election in a GOP-leaning district that covers part of the Charlotte suburbs while sprawling east along the South Carolina border. On Election Night, it appeared that Harris won by just about 900 votes, but there was a catch: The state refused to certify the results because of emerging, and credible, accusations of fraud involving absentee ballots. There would be a new election for the seat in 2019 after this book was published.

LOOKING AHEAD

By netting 40 seats—and not just the 23 they needed for a bare 218-seat majority—Democrats gave themselves some breathing room as they seek to defend their majority in 2020. Republicans will need to net at least 18 seats to win back the House majority, depending on what happens in North Carolina's Ninth District.

Assuming Donald Trump is renominated, history suggests that even if he wins, his coattails could be limited. Since World War II, six presidents have been reelected to second full terms: Dwight Eisenhower (1956), Richard

Nixon (1972), Ronald Reagan (1984), Bill Clinton (1996), George W. Bush (2004), and Barack Obama (2012). On average, their parties netted only seven House seats in those elections. In other words, reelected presidents often don't provide much of a lift down the ballot. Additionally, 2018 showed once again that it's typically the midterm election, not the presidential, that changes the House majority. Since the start of the 20th century, the House has flipped party control eleven times. Nine of those 11 changes (1910, 1918, 1930, 1946, 1954, 1994, 2006, 2010, and now 2018) came in midterm years, while only two of them (1948 and 1952) came in presidential election years.

However, the sample sizes on both of these trends is small, and in a time of political polarization and less ticket-splitting, Republicans could win back the House without winning back a single one of the Clinton-won districts they lost in 2018. The Democrats will be defending 31 districts that Trump won, while Republicans will be defending just three Clinton-won districts. Those districts, which will help determine the majority in 2020, are listed in Tables 5.4 and 5.5. The Democrats will have chances to pick up seats, too: One state both sides were watching as the 2020 House campaign began was Texas, where Democrats picked up two typically Republican, highly educated suburban districts that voted for Clinton in 2016. Democrats came close to winning several other districts with similar demographic profiles that Trump had carried, which makes Texas a likely focus of Democrats' 2020 efforts.

Table 5.4   Democratic House Members from Districts Carried by Donald Trump in the 2016 Presidential Election

Democratic House Member	2018 Result	2016 Trump Performance	First Elected
Tom O'Halleran (AZ-1)	53.8%-46.2%	47.7%-46.6%	2016
Lucy McBath (GA-6)	50.5%-49.5%	48.3%-46.8%	2018
Abby Finkenauer (IA-1)	51.0%-45.9%	48.7%-45.2%	2018
Dave Loebsack (IA-2)	54.8%-42.6%	49.1%-45.0%	2006
Cindy Axne (IA-3)	49.3%-47.1%	48.5%-45.0%	2018
Cheri Bustos (IL-17)	61.8%-38.2%	47.4%-46.7%	2012
Lauren Underwood (IL-14)	52.5%-47.5%	48.7%-44.8%	2018
Jared Golden (ME-2)	50.6%-49.4%	51.4%-41.1%	2018
Elissa Slotkin (MI-8)	50.6%-46.8%	50.6%-43.9%	2018
Haley Stevens (MI-11)	51.8%-45.2%	49.7%-45.3%	2018
Angie Craig (MN-2)	52.7%-47.2%	46.5%-45.3%	2018
Collin Peterson (MN-7)	52.1%-47.8%	61.8%-31.0%	1990
Chris Pappas (NH-1)	53.6%-45.0%	48.2%-46.6%	2018
Josh Gottheimer (NJ-5)	57.9%-40.9%	48.8%-47.7%	2016
Andy Kim (NJ-3)	50.0%-48.7%	51.4%-45.2%	2018
Mikie Sherrill (NJ-11)	56.8%-42.2%	48.8%-47.9%	2018
Jeff Van Drew (NJ-2)	53.0%-45.3%	50.6%-46.0%	2018
Xochitl Torres Small (NM-2)	50.9%-49.1%	50.1%-39.9%	2018
Susie Lee (NV-3)	51.9%-42.8%	47.5%-46.5%	2018
Anthony Brindisi (NY-22)	50.6%-49.4%	54.8%-39.3%	2018
Antonio Delgado (NY-19)	50.2%-47.3%	50.8%-44.0%	2018
Sean Patrick Maloney (NY-18)	55.1%-44.9%	49.0%-47.1%	2012
Max Rose (NY-11)	52.8%-46.8%	53.6%-43.8%	2018
Kendra Horn (OK-5)	50.7%-49.3%	53.2%-39.8%	2018
Matt Cartwright (PA-8)	54.6%-45.4%	53.3%-43.7%	2012
Conor Lamb (PA-17)	56.3%-43.7%	49.4%-46.8%	2018
Joe Cunningham (SC-1)	50.6%-49.2%	53.5%-40.4%	2018
Ben McAdams (UT-4)	50.1%-49.9%	39.1%-32.4%	2018
Elaine Luria (VA-2)	51.1%-48.8%	48.8%-45.4%	2018
Abigail Spanberger (VA-7)	50.3%-48.4%	50.5%-44.0%	2018
Ron Kind (WI-3)	59.7%-40.3%	49.3%-44.8%	1996

Table 5.5   Republican House Members from Districts Carried by Hillary Clinton in the 2016 Presidential Election

Republican House Member	2018 Result	2016 Clinton Performance	First Elected
John Katko (NY-24)	53.1%-46.9%4	8.9%-45.3%	2014
Brian Fitzpatrick (PA-1)	51.3%-48.7%	49.1%-47.1%	2016
Will Hurd (TX-23)	49.2%-48.7%	49.8%-46.4%	2014

NOTES

1. Larry J. Sabato, Kyle Kondik, and Geoffrey Skelley, "16 for '16," *Sabato's Crystal Ball*, November 17, 2016, http://crystalball.centerforpolitics.org/crystalball/articles/16 -for-16/. Specifically, this counts as a single administration the combined terms of Franklin Roosevelt and Harry S. Truman (1945–1953), John F. Kennedy and Lyndon B. Johnson (1961–1969), and Richard M. Nixon and Gerald R. Ford (1969–1977).

2. S. V. Date, "RNC Chief's Message: Don't Worry, Everything Is Fine," *Huffington Post*, January 25, 2019, https://www.huffingtonpost.com/entry/republican-national-com mittee-trump-roger-stone_us_5c4b4bdbe4b06ba6d3bca589.

3. John R. Petrocik and Daron R. Shaw, "How Republicans Could Hold the House," *Sabato's Crystal Ball*, November 1, 2018, http://crystalball.centerforpolitics.org/crystal ball/articles/how-republicans-could-hold-the-house/.

4. Robert Erikson, "Congressional Elections in Presidential Years: Presidential Coattails and Strategic Voting," *Legislative Studies Quarterly* 41, no. 3 (August 2016), 551–74.

5. Andrew Gelman, "Bob Erikson on the 2018 Midterms," Statistical Modeling, Causal Inference, and Social Science, October 1, 2018, https://statmodeling.stat.columbia .edu/2018/10/01/the-2018-midterms/.

6. Andrew E. Busch, *Horses in Midstream* (Pittsburgh: University of Pittsburgh Press, 1999), 34.

7. Theodore S. Arrington, "The Seats/Votes Relationship in the U.S. House, 1972–2018," *Sabato's Crystal Ball*, January 31, 2019, http://crystalball.centerforpolitics.org/ crystalball/articles/the-seats-votes-relationship-in-the-u-s-house-1972-2018/.

8. Noah Rudnick, "The Year of the Green Wave," *Sabato's Crystal Ball*, January 31, 2019, http://crystalball.centerforpolitics.org/crystalball/articles/the-year-of-the-green -wave/.

9. Kyle Kondik, "For House Republicans, Past Performance Is No Guarantee of Future Results," *Sabato's Crystal Ball*, July 20, 2017, http://crystalball.centerforpolitics.org/ crystalball/articles/for-house-republicans-past-performance-is-no-guarantee-of-future -results/.

10. Nate Cohn, "Democrats Didn't Even Dream of This Pennsylvania Map. How Did It Happen?" *New York Times*, February 21, 2018, https://www.nytimes.com/2018/02/21/ upshot/gerrymandering-pennsylvania-democrats-republicans-court.html.

11. James A. Stimson, *Tides of Consent* (New York: Cambridge University Press, 2015), 70.

12. "Advertising Issue Spotlight (10/1/18–10/31/18)," Wesleyan Media Project, November 5, 2018, http://mediaproject.wesleyan.edu/releases/issues-110518/.

13. "Q: (Among Registered Voters) Which Political Party, the (Democrats) or the (Republicans), Do You Trust to Do a Better Job Handling Health Care?" *Washington Post*–ABC News Poll October 29–November 1, 2018, *Washington Post*, November 3, 2018, https://www.washingtonpost.com/page/2010-2019/WashingtonPost/2018/11/04/ National-Politics/Polling/question_20878.xml?uuid = rr_9cN_lEeiLrL_gH83Dpg.

6

How Republicans Picked up Senate Seats during a Blue Wave

James Hohmann

The 2018 midterm elections were a referendum on Donald Trump. This allowed Democrats to net 40 seats in the House, but it is also why Republicans managed to pick up two Senate seats in the face of a blue wave. The upper chamber was a rare bright spot for the party in power during an otherwise abysmal Election Night.

The GOP triumphed over strong national headwinds in the Senate because the battles played out on one of the most hospitable maps a party has ever faced, thanks to the random luck that comes with staggered elections and the nature of a political realignment that the disruptive president has accelerated. Democrats needed to defend 10 seats in states Trump carried in 2016. There was a lot of low-hanging fruit, states represented by Democratic senators where Trump had won by double digits, and Republicans picked it. While Democrats seized GOP-held seats in Nevada and Arizona, their incumbents were defeated in North Dakota, Indiana, Missouri, and Florida.

Trump all but put himself on the ballot in the fall with an aggressive travel schedule. He stayed away from most competitive congressional districts because he was unpopular in the suburbs, where the battle for the House played out. But he was eager to hit the hustings. That meant more focus on Senate races. An 11-rally, six-day campaign swing in the homestretch helped galvanize the Trump coalition, especially voters who don't typically participate in off-year elections.

Senate elections have become increasingly parliamentary and nationalized, which makes it much harder to defy political gravity than it used to be—even for talented politicians.[1]

In 2016, for the first time in American history, the same party won the presidential and senatorial vote in all 34 states with Senate contests.[2] In 2019, the number of states with a split Senate delegation dropped from 14 to 10. That's the fourth election in a row this number of divided delegations declined. This reflects how states are becoming more polarized with less split-ticket voting.[3] The national sorting out continues.

This dynamic was also on display in House races. As noted in the last chapter, Republicans needed to defend 25 seats in November 2018 in districts that Hillary Clinton carried. They lost 22 of them.[4]

Across the Senate races of 2018, with few exceptions, results tracked remarkably closely with the level of local support for Trump. The president's job approval among people who voted in North Dakota was 59 percent, for example, according to exit polls, and Republican Representative Kevin Cramer defeated Democratic Senator Heidi Heitkamp (D) with 56 percent of the vote. Trump's job approval rating in Nevada was 45 percent, meanwhile, and Senator Dean Heller (R) lost with exactly 45 percent of the vote to Representative Jacky Rosen (D).[5]

In Arizona, Trump's approval rating was 49 percent and Republican Representative Martha McSally got 48 percent of the vote. She won nine in 10 Trump supporters, but Democratic Representative Kyrsten Sinema won narrowly because she got nine in 10 of the 51 percent who disapproved of Trump in the Grand Canyon State. Exit polls showed 37 percent of Arizona voters said they cast their ballot primarily to express opposition for Trump while 30 percent voted mainly to show support for Trump.[6] Sinema became the first Democrat to win an Arizona Senate seat in 30 years. Afterward, McSally was appointed to fill the late John McCain's open seat.[7]

REALIGNMENT

Trump's numbers hint at an ongoing realignment that just might be the biggest political story of our time. The Rust Belt has gotten redder. The Sun Belt has become bluer.

The Rust Belt includes the states along the Great Lakes and has become shorthand for the Midwest more broadly. Trump's sweep of Pennsylvania, Ohio, Indiana, Michigan, Wisconsin—and a near upset in Minnesota that no one saw coming—put an exclamation on long-term trends. His protectionist, nativist, and isolationist rhetoric excited white working-class Democrats who in many cases voted for Barack Obama in 2008 and 2012 or hadn't voted at all. Many other members of the Obama coalition, specifically African Americans, were unenthusiastic about Clinton and their Democratic options.[8]

The Sun Belt stretches from Florida to California and includes the Southern and Southwestern states where many people emigrated from the Rust Belt during the decades after World War II in search of jobs, warmth, and a lower cost of living. Even though Republicans continue to win in places like Texas, every election brings demographic changes—namely thanks to Latinos—that make them slightly more competitive. Clinton lost Iowa and Ohio in 2016 by about the same margins that she lost Texas (eight to nine points). But she won Nevada and lost Arizona by only four points. New Mexico was a presidential battleground as recently as 2004 but has become solidly blue, and Colorado has trended blue. Both of those moves can be chalked up to Latinos and the rising American electorate.

These dynamics all came into play during the 2018 Senate races. Republican Senator Ted Cruz ultimately got reelected in Texas, but Democratic Representative Beto O'Rourke lost by fewer than three points. In the heartland states where Trump won in the single digits, Democratic incumbents managed to survive in Pennsylvania, Michigan, Ohio, and Wisconsin. (Democrats also picked up the governorships in Michigan and Wisconsin.) The historical trends, after all, say that a president's party is almost certain to lose seats during his first midterms as his popularity slips. The 2002 midterms after the September 11 attacks were an exception to the rule, and Democrats almost certainly would have struggled had Clinton prevailed in the Electoral College.[9]

But Republicans knocked off Democratic senators in all three of the Midwestern states with races in 2018 that Trump carried by more than 10 points in 2016: Missouri, North Dakota, and Indiana. Each state opted for what would be unified Republican Senate representation. Most of all, they won by promising loyalty to Trump.

THE SHOW ME STATE SHOWS WHAT HAPPENED

Missouri tells the story of the cycle in miniature.[10] This was the third-most expensive Senate race of 2018, behind only the mega-states of Florida and Texas, but the TV ads wound up being noise and seemed to cancel each other out.[11] Trump's disapproval rating in the state was 46 percent on Election Day, and Democratic Senator Claire McCaskill garnered 46 percent of the vote. The president's approval rating was 53 percent, and the state's young attorney general, Republican Josh Hawley, won 89 percent of those Trump approvers. That was good for 51.4 percent of the vote.

McCaskill, a moderate who had held elected office almost as long as Hawley had been alive, was holding her own among Trump voters until after Labor Day, which is why many handicappers thought she'd survive. She was talented at retail campaigning, kept a relentless schedule around the state with oodles of town hall meetings, proved herself a prodigious fundraiser, and carved out niches on issues her constituents care about, such as veteran health care. But it didn't matter. Voters who approved of Trump defected from McCaskill as the race became more nationalized, even if they had supported her in 2012 over Republican Todd Akin after his comment about "legitimate rape" and in 2006 when she was able to surf another blue wave.

"The Republican Party is the party of Donald Trump right now," McCaskill said after her defeat. "Now, that really helped him in Missouri. And it helped him in Indiana. And it helped him in North Dakota. But it hurt him in a whole lot of other places."[12]

Hawley agreed with that assessment. "My own view is that we're in the middle of a political realignment," he said during an interview in the rural town of Boonville, on the banks of the Missouri River. "It's comparable to a century ago when you had a complete change in political coalitions, and I think President Trump is driving much of that. We're seeing that happen. We're right in the midst of it."

The 38-year-old highlighted how much the state has changed politically since he grew up, especially in rural areas. "Places that used to be home to what I call Harry Truman Democrats, now they're Donald Trump Republicans," Hawley said. "Donald Trump speaks to those folks, and I think if the Republican Party is going to have a future as a party they're going to have to do the same. Meanwhile, you see a sorting out where you have folks who have advanced degrees and so forth, who live in suburbs, who once tended to vote Republican now shifting more toward Democrats. I think that there's a real worldview shifting, or sifting, that's going on."

Trump won Missouri by 19 points in 2016, which is remarkable because the state voted for the winner of all but one presidential election for a century between 1904 and 2004. George W. Bush carried the Show Me State by three points in 2000 and then seven points in 2004. John McCain barely won it over Obama by a few thousand voters, but Mitt Romney won handily by nine points.

Hawley, a Stanford-educated historian who attended Yale Law School and clerked for Supreme Court Chief Justice John Roberts, clearly had many disagreements with Trump. But he kept all of them to himself until after securing a six-year term. Instead, he insisted that there was no daylight between him and the president. And Hawley praised Trump for doing better than Romney, McCain, and Bush at tapping viscerally into the fear among

Missourians that their way of life is profoundly at risk due to cultural transformation.

"It's at risk from folks who are taking jobs and taking them overseas," Hawley said. "It's at risk from falling wages. It's at risk from an immigration system that does not work well for workers in this country. The president said a lot of things that folks have thought for a long time but nobody else had been willing to say. He faced 16 Republicans or whatever it was. The other 15 sounded a lot like each other . . . but he was the one who sounded completely different. I think that's why he's redrawing political coalitions."

McCaskill tacked to the right as her numbers slipped during the final weeks of the contest. The Democratic senators went on Fox News to criticize "crazy Democrats" who "walk in restaurants and scream" at elected officials. "Claire's not one of those crazy Democrats," a narrator said in a radio commercial that aired heavily through rural Missouri. "She works right in the middle." McCaskill also said she would support Trump "100 percent" on whatever he decided to do to "stop" the caravan of migrants at the border. Trump mocked her for this during a rally. The president noted correctly that McCaskill almost never backed him up until she needed votes from his supporters on the eve of the election.

McCaskill dated Missouri's transformation from swing state to red state to 1960, when Democrats nominated the Catholic John F. Kennedy for president. "Dad was a Democratic committeeman, and somebody threw a rock through the window of the county Democratic headquarters. It was bigotry," she said before the election. "There was a cataclysmic shifting when we decided that civil rights was the cause of our party. Missouri, along with the traditional Democratic Southern states, began to shift."[13]

McCaskill said a lot of rural whites believed through the 1980s that Democrats cared about their economic condition more than Republicans. "No more," she complained. "A lot of people gave up on me. They gave up on us. . . . There used to be a way to work your way up from the mailroom. Now there's no more mailroom. Donald Trump gave voters a place to put their anger."

Hawley's strategists marveled at a consistent pattern in their private polling all year. The Republican fared worse among likely voters over age 65 than any other age group, including those under 35 years old. This is very unusual for any GOP nominee. But it's because many seniors still identify with the party they grew up with. African Americans who vote in Missouri also tend to be older. And it is not a very transient state. Few new people move in. That means younger voters tend to be natives and thus more inclined to vote for the conservative candidates their parents support than transplants from elsewhere.

Hawley himself said Trump is as much the product of the realignment as the cause of it. "This concern about what I call the heartland way of life . . . has become more acute," he said. "In the last 10 to 15 years, it's really come to a head. People have said we just can't go on like this," he said. "If you want to know where Claire's positions are . . . just ask yourself: How would an East Coast donor vote on this? That's where she'll be."

Bigger picture, the midterms became a base election. And intensity was off the charts on both sides. Voters who hated Trump and loved Trump felt like the stakes were especially high. Turnout rates nationally were the highest for any midterm election since 1914, when people turned out to directly elect their senators for the first time thanks to the Seventeenth Amendment. The 2018 numbers broke previous high watermarks set in 1966. "[That] is the middle of the civil rights movement," said University of Florida professor Michael McDonald, who tracks turnout through the United States Elections Project. "We had Vietnam going on. It's a tumultuous time in our politics. If you look at 2018, that's your parallel. The country's doing well economically, but Trump is really driving the conversation. He's impassioned people both for and against him."[14]

Exit polls showed that eight in 10 Americans in November 2018 believed the country was more divided at that moment than ever before. In fact, thankfully, that's not true. America is less divided than during Vietnam, and certainly less than during the Civil War, but the fact it feels this way to the overwhelming majority of the electorate spoke volumes about the polity.[15]

McCaskill said Trump's two visits to the state in the final five days hurt her by ginning up enthusiasm for Hawley among lower-propensity Trump voters, and Missouri has no early voting so she couldn't lock in her own base support.[16] "People need to realize my problem wasn't getting Democrats to vote for me," McCaskill said. "I hope that no one thinks that because some of the red-state Democrat moderates lost that means we have to nominate a progressive" in 2020.[17]

THE KAVANAUGH EFFECT

North Dakota is another case study to illustrate the growing partisan polarization and how hard it is for a Democrat to survive in a red state. Heitkamp said her loss had nothing to do with who her own challenger was and everything to do with Donald J. Trump. She knew Trump was popular in her state, but she portrayed herself as an independent voice who could work with both sides and stand up to the president on something like tariffs, which hurt many farmers in her state. Kevin Cramer, her opponent, avoided criticizing Trump even when the president said trade wars are good and easy to win.

"I made a simple gamble that people in North Dakota were not going to vote with somebody who is going to vote with the president 100 percent of the time," Heitkamp said after leaving office. "I honestly believed that was a good judgment on my part. It proved not to be true. He gambled the other way that people desperately wanted somebody who was going to vote with Donald Trump 100 percent of the time. . . . That kind of was the theory of the case to begin with: Are you going to be an independent voice or are you going to be a partisan voice? Cramer promised to be a partisan voice. . . . If you couldn't stand with the farmers in this tariff fight, then there's nothing that would shake my belief that he won't stand with the president over North Dakota's interests on anything."

Heitkamp noted that there was a 12-point increase in North Dakotans identifying as Republican between when she got elected in 2012, with Barack Obama at the top of the ticket no less, and lost in 2018. She assumed she'd be able to get about 20 percent of Republicans to cast a ballot for her, which is in line with what former Democratic senators Kent Conrad and Byron Dorgan had been able to do. "Those numbers now, even nationally because we've become so tribal, are only four percent," Heitkamp said. "So if only four percent of Republicans were willing to cross over and vote for me, we couldn't win. It was impossible to win."

She blamed the rise of big agribusinesses for the decline of family farmers, who used to be part of the Democratic coalition. Heitkamp noted that she ran up her score with professionals and college-educated people in the cities of North Dakota. "When I started off in 1984, do you know who my political base was? High school-educated, working-class people and seniors," she said. "And that's just flipped!"[18]

As far as Heitkamp is concerned, however, the key moment that sealed her defeat was voting in October against confirming Brett Kavanaugh, Trump's nominee to the Supreme Court, after Christine Blasey Ford and other women accused him of sexual misconduct when they were in high school and college. Kavanaugh denied everything after his accuser, an academic, testified under oath at a televised hearing.[19]

It brought flashbacks for many women to Anita Hill's testimony about Clarence Thomas in 1991, but it also played out against the backdrop of the #MeToo movement, which grew out of sexual abuse allegations against film producer Harvey Weinstein. Many women came forward to tell stories for the first time about their run-ins with powerful men. This led to the resignation of Democratic Senator Al Franken of Minnesota, who would have questioned Kavanaugh had he resisted calls to step down from fellow Democrats. More

importantly, Trump himself mocked Ford and the #MeToo movement generally at campaign rallies. Republicans, especially men, tended to take the side
of the accused and downplayed the seriousness of the allegations. Conservative media pushed a narrative that Kavanaugh was being mistreated by Senate
Democrats.[20]

"We lost by a bigger margin than I thought we'd lose by, but I think that
was . . . the Kavanaugh vote," Heitkamp said after the election. "I will go to
my grave believing it was the right vote. It's interesting because there was a
public opinion poll after the confirmation. Only 21 percent of the people in
this country believed he was telling the truth. I guess that's still okay to put
people who lie in the White House and put people who lie on the Supreme
Court. That's a whole brave new world for me. I've always believed two
things in politics: You can't lie and that you can't be a hypocrite. I think
we've kind of proven that's not true anymore in politics. . . . And I knew
when I made it, I told my colleagues, 'This is kind of the defining moment
whether people in my state are going to decide which way they are going to
go.' "

Heitkamp raised millions of dollars in small-dollar contributions from progressive grassroots activists around the country when she took her stand on
principle, but the money flowed in so late that she couldn't spend all of it in
such a sparsely populated state with media markets that are inexpensive to
advertise in. Some number of Trump supporters opted against voting for her
as a result of the vote.[21]

The Kavanaugh effect cut both ways, however. Backlash to the way that
Ford was treated almost certainly cost Republicans House seats, contributing
to a historic gender gap. In a base election, it also had an impact on partisans.
Democrat Phil Bredesen was a popular former governor of Tennessee, known
as a moderate, who ran for the seat that opened up with the retirement of
Republican Senator Bob Corker. He was a top recruit of national Democrats,
and he even nabbed a rare endorsement of pop star Taylor Swift. But Trump's
endorsement mattered far more in the Volunteer State; his approval rating
was 57 percent in exit polling. And when Bredesen said he would vote for
Kavanaugh if he was in the Senate, many of his volunteers—especially
women—stopped showing up to help. The enthusiasm for his campaign, and
donations, dried up.

RISING TRIBALISM

The willingness of Republican voters to rally around Kavanaugh in the wake
of the allegations against him was one of many striking examples during

the 2018 election cycle of tribalism becoming a more prominent feature of American politics, rather than a bug.

The best illustration of this reflexive partisanship is Roy Moore, who only lost the Alabama special Senate election in December 2017 by 22,000 votes out of more than 1.3 million cast despite a cascade of credible allegations of sexual misconduct. The Republican, who refused to concede defeat, had been removed from the state Supreme Court twice for refusing to obey lawful court orders. Ultimately, eight women accused Moore of pursuing them when they were teenagers. The series of allegations began with a *Washington Post* report in November 2017, a month before the election, headlined: "Woman Says Roy Moore Initiated Sexual Encounter When She Was 14, He Was 32." He denied everything.[22]

During the GOP primary, Moore was a deeply polarizing figure. Establishment conservative leaders warned, including in attack ads, that he couldn't win a general election because he was too extreme. But they rallied behind him when Moore defeated Senator Luther Strange, who had been appointed by the governor to fill the seat when Jeff Sessions stepped down to become attorney general. Initially, the national party apparatus ditched Moore when the stories about his past first came to light, concluding that he had no chance to win. But the Republican National Committee and the Senate GOP election arm returned to supporting him at the direction of Trump himself.[23]

In another Southern special election, in Mississippi, Cindy Hyde-Smith won by eight points in a late November runoff despite a rash of gaffes and racially insensitive comments because the state was red enough and the president was popular enough to get her across the finish line. Hyde-Smith was appointed to replace Republican Thad Cochran, who resigned because of ailing health, but she had to stand for election to complete the remainder of his term. Hyde-Smith declared in the weeks leading up the runoff that she'd proudly sit with a supporter in the front row of a "public hanging." That dredged up dark memories of the state's history as the site of more lynchings than any other between the Civil War and the civil rights movement. Her botched response made the situation worse. Several large companies demanded that their corporate donations be refunded, but none of those businesses got to vote.[24]

Republican voters also disregarded a stream of local stories that Hyde-Smith attended and graduated from a segregation academy that was set up so that white parents could avoid having to send their children to schools with black students. She was pictured in a high school yearbook as a cheerleader next to the school's mascot, who was dressed as a Confederate general and waving a Confederate flag. A photo the senator had posted on Facebook in 2014 resurfaced, showing her wearing a Confederate cap as she toured former

Confederate President Jefferson Davis's house. She had proposed legislation in 2001 to rename a stretch of highway with the title it had during the 1930s, Jefferson Davis Memorial Highway, but her bill died in committee. Trump carried Mississippi by 18 points in 2016. Polls showed his approval rating at the end of 2018 was still in the high 50s. That mattered more.[25]

To be sure, tribalism helped both parties. Democratic Senator Robert Menendez got reelected in New Jersey over a wealthy Republican self-funder despite years of serious legal trouble. He was indicted in 2015 for using his official position to help a donor—who took Menendez on lavish trips aboard his private jet—bypass regulatory scrutiny. A mistrial was declared in 2017 after the jury deadlocked. In April 2018, the Senate Ethics Committee—after a judge acquitted him on the most serious charges—found Menendez guilty of breaking federal law, formally admonished him, and ordered that he pay back all the gifts he received. But no Republican has won a New Jersey Senate seat in 46 years, Trump had lost the state by 14 points, and state Democratic leaders stayed loyal to Menendez. He won despite facing a Republican challenger who was willing to spend millions of his own money on attack ads highlighting the scandals.[26]

In contrast, none of the four Democratic senators who lost reelection were mired in personal scandals during the election. They just had the letter "D" after their names on the ballot in places where Trump generally was more popular than unpopular.

This tribalism dynamic was even more evident on the House side, however. Despite being indicted for serious crimes, which they denied, Republican Representatives Chris Collins of New York and Duncan Hunter Jr. of California both got reelected in November 2018. And Democratic Representative Keith Ellison of Minnesota got elected as his state's attorney general even after an ex-girlfriend stepped forward with claims of emotional and physical abuse. Ellison denied the allegation.[27]

Almost entirely because he was a Republican in a red state, Greg Gianforte won a May 2017 special congressional election in Montana to replace Ryan Zinke—who had been named Interior secretary—despite physically assaulting a reporter. There were witnesses, and it was on tape, but Gianforte prevailed by six points.[28]

THE TRUMP TAKEOVER OF THE GOP

Nevada has become a bluish-purple state because of a large Latino population and an influx of Californians to Las Vegas. Politically, the state has become much less rural over the past few decades. Trying to keep up with the Silver

State, Republican Senator Dean Heller repudiated Trump in 2016. He said that he "vehemently" opposed his party's nominee that fall. He made a show of returning a campaign contribution he'd received from Trump.

Heller started 2017 by positioning himself as a moderate maverick and a critic of the GOP's approach to repealing Obamacare. He was the only GOP incumbent up for reelection in a state Trump lost, compared to 10 Democrats who had to run in states Trump won. Nevada's outgoing Republican governor, Brian Sandoval, had expanded Medicaid, and it was popular. The state's Medicaid recipients stood to suffer significantly from the plan being considered in Congress, Heller warned at a news conference.

But suddenly Heller changed his tune. He freaked out about a primary challenge from Danny Tarkanian, an outspoken Trump supporter, and worried supporters of the president wouldn't turn out for him in a general election. So he flip-flopped. He voted for cloture on the legislation he had earlier said would hurt Nevada and wholeheartedly embraced the president. This prompted the White House political operation to push Tarkanian out of the Senate race. When Trump flew to Elko for a rally two weeks before the election, the senator literally hugged him. "Mr. President," Heller said, "everything you touch turns to gold." Not quite. Heller lost to Democrat Jacky Rosen by five points.[29]

Trump blamed Heller's defeat on his disloyalty in 2016. "What happened with Dean Heller is I tried for him, but my base did not believe him," Trump told the *Nevada Independent* in February 2019. "They wouldn't go for him because Dean Heller was really hostile in my race. . . . [He] was hostile beyond normal politics and the hostility carried over, unfortunately."[30]

What happened in Nevada played out across the country. Republican candidates cozied up to Trump to varying degrees or they decided not to run for reelection. That's what happened in Arizona, a neighbor of Nevada. Republican Senator Jeff Flake, a principled conservative, was an outspoken critic of the president and refused to board the Trump Train. He even wrote an entire book contrasting his vision of conservatism to Trumpism. Trump responded in kind, routinely attacking him in public. Flake's numbers tanked among GOP voters, and polls suggested he might lose a primary. Rather than try to make amends with Trump, he decided not to seek a second term. In other words, Flake retired at 55.[31]

Senator Bob Corker, a Tennessee Republican and chairman of the Foreign Relations Committee, also opted to retire after criticizing the president and drawing his ire. He was replaced by Marsha Blackburn, a House Republican who had staked a claim as one of the more pro-Trump Republicans in the House. By closely linking herself to the president, she avoided what could have been a bruising primary fight with a congressional colleague.

In the open primary to replace Flake, the GOP establishment rallied behind McSally because party leaders perceived her to be the most electable option. She faced Kelli Ward, a former state senator who had unsuccessfully challenged John McCain in a 2016 primary, and former Maricopa County Sheriff Joe Arpaio, who both claimed Trump's mantle. Like Heller, McSally broke with Trump in October 2016 after the *Access Hollywood* tape emerged from 2005, in which he could be heard boasting about groping women and getting away with it because he was a star. "Trump's comments are disgusting," she tweeted at the time. "Joking about sexual assault is unacceptable. I'm appalled."

As her rivals criticized her for this, McSally refused to say whether she had voted for Trump. "Not your business," she snapped at a reporter who asked during an event in Phoenix. "I made a couple of, a very small number of, statements about particular statements that were made, and on the spectrum of things, it was very measured compared with a lot of other Republicans."

McSally sought to make up for this past apostasy by changing her position on immigration and going out of her way on the stump to link herself with Trump. She talked constantly about the face time she had with him. "Like our president, I'm tired of PC politicians and their BS excuses," she said in one commercial. McSally ultimately won her primary, but her hard-line posturing on immigration in a border state and strategic decision to tie herself to Trump at the hip hurt her in the general.[32]

The Trump loyalty test also took center stage in other competitive GOP primaries where the candidates had not split with him in 2016. Everyone seemed to be trying to outdo everyone else on who was more pro-Trump. Indiana Representative Todd Rokita released a video attacking his opponent, Representative Luke Messer, as a "Never Trump lobbyist." The narrator described Rokita as "a pro-Trump conservative." They were vying to take on Senator Joe Donnelly (D) in a state Trump carried by 19 points. Ultimately, the two congressmen lost to former state representative and businessman Mike Braun, who prevailed in the fall campaign. Like Trump, Braun ran against the system and tied both of his opponents to D.C. He also promised to be a reliable pro-Trump vote.[33]

Even Mitt Romney was not immune from the pressure to make nice with Trump. Romney ran for the seat that opened with Republican Senator Orrin Hatch's retirement in Utah. Not only had he been the Republican standard-bearer in 2012, Romney is revered in his adopted state for saving the 2002 Winter Olympics and as a leader of the Mormon church. Battling a primary challenge from a no-name state legislator, the former governor of Massachusetts nonetheless felt compelled to emphasize his desire to work with Trump on areas of common ground and to highlight positions, like tax cuts, where they were on the same page. After winning the primary, Romney distanced himself again from Trump. After the general election, he went further and criticized the president—drawing Trump's ire. But at that point, the then-71-year-old really didn't have anything to worry about. If he runs again, he won't be on the ballot until 2024.[34]

Meanwhile, Democrats avoided Senate primaries that could have been a problem. One of the biggest political stories of 2018 was Alexandria Ocasio-Cortez's defeat of Representative Joe Crowley, the No. 4 in House Democratic leadership, in a June primary. She was a 28-year-old activist who got engaged in the Democratic socialist movement during the Bernie Sanders campaign. She had been a bartender just a few months before. Crowley was considered a favorite to replace Nancy Pelosi as the potential next speaker of the House; instead, Ocasio-Cortez instantly became a star of the left.[35]

But leaders of the far left made a calculated decision to take a much more pragmatic approach toward Senate races. They did not target moderate senators like Joe Manchin in West Virginia, even though he had a record that unsettled them on most issues, because they recognized that it would be self-defeating. It was a smart strategy that got them a big batch of liberals in the House from safe districts.[36]

THE RED STATE SURVIVORS

Manchin in West Virginia and Jon Tester in Montana defied political gravity. They were the only two Democratic senators to get reelected in states Trump won by double digits. Both had brands and political identities that were established many years before Trump announced his campaign in 2015. Manchin had been a governor. Tester had been in the Senate for 12 years.[37]

Both senators also played up their ties to Trump and emphasized a willingness to work with the White House, even if it wasn't always totally matched by reality. Manchin liked to talk about being offered a Cabinet posting by Trump; he also did vote to confirm both Kavanaugh and Neil Gorsuch, Trump's other Supreme Court nominee. Tester's first ad highlighted bills he co-sponsored that Trump had signed into law. They both localized the race as much as possible and focused on health care; they steadfastly avoided talking about special counsel Bob Mueller and impeachment. They knew from the get-go that they'd have tough races and planned accordingly.[38]

Manchin and Tester also benefited from weak Republican challengers, a reminder that candidate quality matters. It's hard to imagine now because he was later forced to resign as Interior secretary under an ethical cloud and amid a swirl of investigations, but national GOP strategists saw Ryan Zinke—who held the state's at-large House seat—as the best recruit to take on Tester. Mitch McConnell was angry at Trump for appointing him. The GOP wound up instead with Matt Rosendale, the state auditor who was born in Maryland and had an accent to match.[39] The winner of a contentious GOP primary in West Virginia was state Attorney General Patrick Morrisey, who had spent eight years as a lobbyist in Washington representing big pharmaceutical companies. That was a potent line of attack in a state that has been ravaged as hard by the opioid crisis as any other.[40]

Donnelly, the Indiana Democratic senator who lost reelection, blamed the national Democratic Party's leftward drift. "The talk on the coasts just doesn't get it done in the middle," he said during his final week in office. "We have not made enough of a connection—I worked like a dog nonstop to make that connection—that the people of my state understand culturally, we want to make sure you succeed. But when you talk 'Medicare for all,' you start losing the people in my state. When we start talking about, 'Hey, we're going to work together with the insurance companies to lower premiums,' that's what connects. People want to make sure they have a good job, decent healthcare, that they can retire with dignity and that they know that the future is better for their children and grandchildren. When we talk about those things, we have success."[41] Manchin and Tester were able to do just that in a way Donnelly was not.

FLORIDA, FLORIDA, FLORIDA

The Sunshine State was somewhat anomalous. Outgoing Republican Governor Rick Scott defeated Democratic Senator Bill Nelson, although he was declared the victor by only 10,000 votes out of several million cast. Nelson ran a lackluster campaign devoid of energy. He was outspent by Scott, who benefited from strong leadership after a hurricane that became a sort of October surprise.

The Republican also reached out aggressively to Hispanic voters in ways others in his party did not. Scott aired intensive Spanish-language television ads, made eight trips to Puerto Rico after a hurricane ravaged the island, and distanced himself from Trump's harsh rhetoric about immigrants. Scott lost among Hispanic voters, but his standing was much stronger than the president's, and that arguably made the difference in the tight race.[42]

"We showed up," Scott said in an interview as he prepared to join the Senate. "Hispanics have the same issues as everybody else has. And so, I showed up and tried to solve their problems."[43]

The governor also figured out how to thread the needle on Trump, who carried Florida in 2016 and whose reelection in 2020 would require winning it again. While Scott kept some distance during the campaign, he stood by Trump's side during a rally on the eve of the election. He was not as chummy with the president as Republican gubernatorial candidate Ron DeSantis, who won by a slightly larger margin. But Scott dined with Trump several times, from the Trump hotel in D.C. to the Mar-a-Lago Club in Palm Beach. "My experience in life has been that if you go build relationships with people, and you don't ask for things that are foolish, you get things done," Scott said after the election.[44]

It certainly helped that Scott put more than $64 million of his personal fortune into this Senate campaign, starting with an early ad blitz that successfully drove up Nelson's negatives. His net worth, including assets in his wife's name, is estimated at around $500 million, though it's hard to know for sure because the ranges in the disclosure reports are so broad. He spent $75 million to win the 2010 governor's race and $15 million on his 2014 reelection, which means people have been exposed to positive messages about him before. As a result, Florida was the most expensive Senate race in the country, with a total of $204 million in spending. It's a reminder that money matters.[45]

LOOKING AHEAD TO 2020

Republicans started the next election cycle with 53 seats, but the GOP was expected to have a harder time in 2020 than 2018. Republicans must defend 22 seats, including McSally's in Arizona, while Democrats only need to defend a dozen. But one of those dozen is Doug Jones in Alabama, who few in either party expect to win a full term. Another Democrat who could have a tough fight is New Hampshire Senator Jeanne Shaheen, who narrowly beat Scott Brown, the former short-term Massachusetts senator, in 2014.

But Senate Republican incumbents could face tough reelection fights in Colorado, Iowa, North Carolina, and Georgia. In Maine, Republican Senator Susan Collins cruised to an easy reelection in 2014. She is now the only New England Republican who remains in either chamber of Congress. If she runs again, Collins will face a much more spirited challenge. Her decisive vote for Kavanaugh galvanized abortion rights activists and undercut her moderate credentials.[46]

Meanwhile, more old bulls continue to retire. In addition to Flake and Corker, two senators who joined the Senate during the 1970s also retired in

2018: Orrin Hatch from Utah, who was replaced by Romney, and Thad Cochran from Mississippi, who was replaced by Hyde-Smith. In December 2018, Tennessee Republican Senator Lamar Alexander—who has been a national figure since the 1970s—announced plans to retire, prompting speculation that he might feel liberated during his final two years in office. In January 2019, Kansas Republican Senator Pat Roberts—first elected to the House in 1980 and the Senate in 1996—also said he wouldn't run again. Republicans will need to defend both open seats, but their departure will continue to change the culture of the Senate.[47]

Senate Majority Leader Mitch McConnell, a Kentucky Republican who joined the chamber in 1985 and is now the longest-serving GOP leader ever, does not want to go anywhere. He is up for reelection in a red state in 2020, but he could still have a competitive race. Polls at the start of the cycle showed Trump is significantly more popular in Kentucky than McConnell, which creates a strong incentive for the majority leader to tie himself to Trump, just as so many of his members did in 2018.[48]

Trump found himself trying to adjust to divided government as 2019 began. Nancy Pelosi was now the speaker of the House, and the president was counting on McConnell to be a bulwark against the Democratic agenda. During the months after the midterms, Trump often cited the GOP's Senate gains to minimize the impact of divided government. When Senate Minority Leader Chuck Schumer, a New York Democrat, criticized comments Trump made in February 2019, the president replied on his favorite medium: Twitter. "He's just upset that he didn't win the Senate, after spending a fortune, like he thought he would," Trump wrote of Schumer, three months after the elections. "Too bad we weren't given more credit for the Senate win by the media!"[49]

NOTES

1. James Hohmann, "House Races Become More Nationalized in Trump-era Midterms," *Washington Post*, October 31, 2018, https://www.washingtonpost.com/news/powerpost/paloma/daily-202/2018/10/31/daily-202-house-races-become-more-nationalized-in-trump-era-midterms/ 5bd9245e1b326 b37e00b5a31/.

2. Geoffrey Skelley, "Straight Tickets for Senate, Split Tickets for Governor: The 2016 Senate and Gubernatorial Elections," *Trumped*, ed. Larry Sabato, Kyle Kondik, and Geoffrey Skelley (Lanham, MD: Rowman & Littlefield, 2017), 53.

3. Drew DeSilver, "Split U.S. Senate Delegations Have Become Less Common in Recent Years," Pew Research Center, January 4, 2018, http://www.pewresearch.org/fact-tank/2018/01/04/split-u-s-senate-delegations-have-become-less-common-in-recent-years/.

4. The three GOP holdouts in Clinton districts were Will Hurd in Texas, Brian Fitzpatrick in Pennsylvania, and John Katko in New York. James Hohmann, "Late Gains in California Vindicate DCCC's Intervention in House Primaries," *Washington Post*, November 28, 2018, https://www.washingtonpost.com/news/powerpost/paloma/daily-202/2018/11/28/daily-202-late-gains-in-california-vindicate-dccc-s-intervention-in-house-primaries/5bfe0ce61b326b60d128006d/.

5. Exit poll numbers are all from AP VoteCast, a survey of the American electorate in all 50 states conducted by NORC at the University of Chicago for the Associated Press and Fox News. The survey of voters was conducted Oct. 29 to Nov. 6, concluding as polls close on Election Day. AP VoteCast combines interviews with a random sample of registered voters drawn from state voter files; interviews with self-identified registered voters conducted using NORC's probability-based AmeriSpeak panel, which is designed to be representative of the U.S. population; and interviews with self-identified registered voters selected from non-probability online panels. Interviews are conducted in English and Spanish. Respondents receive a small monetary incentive for completing the survey. Participants selected from state voter files are contacted by phone and mail and have the opportunity to take the survey by phone or online. All surveys are subject to multiple sources of error, including from sampling, question wording and order, and nonresponse. All the exit polls and results are accessible through: https://www.washingtonpost.com/graphics/2018/politics/voter-polls/north-dakota.html.

6. Elise Viebeck, "Sinema Wins in Arizona as Democrats Capture a Longtime GOP Senate Seat," *Washington Post*, November 12, 2018, https://www.washingtonpost.com/politics/sinema-wins-in-arizona-as-democrats-capture-a-longtime-gop-senate-seat/2018/11/12/96805254-e44b-11e8-8f5f-a55347f48762_story.html.

7. McSally could face Democrat Mark Kelly, the husband of former Representative Gabby Giffords, in 2020.

8. James Hohmann, "Joe Biden Appeals to Working-Class Whites Who Defected to Trump. Is That How Democrats Will Win Again?" *Washington Post*, October 15, 2018, https://www.washingtonpost.com/news/powerpost/paloma/daily-202/2018/10/15/daily-202-joe-biden-appeals-to-working-class-whites-who-defected-to-trump-is-that-how-democrats-win-again/5bc396dc1b326b7c8a8d19a1/.

9. James Hohmann, "Generic Democrats in Midwest Faring Better Than More Fiery Liberals in the Sun Belt," *Washington Post*, October 22, 2018, https://www.washingtonpost.com/news/powerpost/paloma/daily-202/2018/10/22/daily-202-generic-democrats-in-midwest-faring-better-than-more-fiery-liberals-in-sun-belt/5bccea5e1b326b7c8a8d1ab8/.

10. James Hohmann, "Republican Senate Gains Would Show That Trump Accelerated a Political Realignment," *Washington Post*, November 5, 2018, https://www.washingtonpost.com/news/powerpost/paloma/daily-202/2018/11/05/daily-202-republican-senate-gains-would-show-that-trump-accelerated-a-political-realignment/5bdfce231b326b39290545c5/.

11. "Most Expensive Races," Center for Responsive Politics, November 2018, https://www.opensecrets.org/overview/topraces.php?cycle=2018&display=allcandsout.

12. Peter Granitz, "McCaskill Blames Senate Defeat on Democratic 'Failure' with Rural America," National Public Radio, November 30, 2018, https://www.npr.org/2018/11/30/671988738/mccaskill-blames-senate-defeat-on-democratic-failure-with-rural-america.

13. Nicholas Lemann, "Claire McCaskill's Toughest Fight," *New Yorker*, October 29, 2018, https://www.newyorker.com/magazine/2018/10/29/claire-mccaskills-toughest -fight.

14. Michael McDonald, "2018 November General Election Turnout Rates," United States Election Project, December 14, 2018, http://www.electproject.org/2018g; Emily Stewart, "2018's Record-Setting Voter Turnout, in One Chart; It's the Highest Level in a Century for a Midterm Election," Vox, November 19, 2018, https://www.vox.com/policy -and-politics/2018/11/19/18103110/2018-midterm-elections-turnout.

15. James Hohmann, "10 Midterm Takeaways," *Washington Post*, November 7, 2018, https://www.washingtonpost.com/news/powerpost/paloma/daily-202/2018/11/07/daily -202-10-midterm-takeaways/5be20c681b326b3929054634/.

16. Susan Glasser, "Before She Leaves the Senate, Claire McCaskill Gives an Exit Interview," *New Yorker*, December 11, 2018, https://www.newyorker.com/news/the-new -yorker-interview/before-she-leaves-the-senate-claire-mccaskill-gives-an-exit-interview.

17. Jonathan Martin and Alexander Burns, "Democrats Have Two Paths for 2020," *New York Times*, November 10, 2018, https://www.nytimes.com/2018/11/10/us/politics/ democrats-2020-president.html.

18. Mike McFeely, "Heitkamp Says There Is 'Great Irony' the Way Some in N.D. Voted. Former U.S. Senator Says Her Work on Behalf of Certain Groups Didn't Matter in Election Loss," *Fargo Forum*, January 28, 2019, https://www.inforum.com/opinion/ columns/958452-McFeely-Heitkamp-says-there-is-great-irony-the-way-some-in-N.D. -voted.

19. Seung Min Kim and John Wagner, "Kavanaugh Sworn in as Supreme Court Justice after Divided Senate Votes for Confirmation," *Washington Post*, October 6, 2018, https:// www.washingtonpost.com/politics/kavanaugh-vote-divided-senate-poised-to-confirm -trumps-nominee/2018/10/06/64bf69fa-c969-11e8-b2b5-79270f9cce17_story.html.

20. James Hohmann, "Tribalism Fuels GOP Embrace of Kavanaugh," *Washington Post*, September 27, 2018, https://www.washingtonpost.com/news/powerpost/paloma/ daily-202/2018/09/27/daily-202-tribalism-fuels-gop-embrace-of-kavanaugh/5bac 1c5f1b326b7c8a8d16b8/; James Hohmann, "Conservatives Divided over Kavanaugh Alle- gations, Mostly Along Gender Lines," *Washington Post*, September 21, 2018, https://www .washingtonpost.com/news/powerpost/paloma/daily-202/2018/09/21/daily-202 -conservatives-divided-over-kavanaugh-allegations-mostly-along-gender-lines/ 5ba3e1ab1b326b7c8a8d1586/; James Hohmann, "Trump's Mockery of Christine Blasey Ford Underscores His Scorn for the Me Too Movement," *Washington Post*, October 3, 2018, https://www.washingtonpost.com/news/powerpost/paloma/daily-202/2018/10/03/ daily-202-trump-s-mockery-of-christine-blasey-ford-underscores-his-scorn-for-the-metoo -movement/5bb3e6031b326b7c8a8d17d8/; James Hohmann, "How Senate Republicans Could Win the Battle and the War on Kavanaugh," *Washington Post*, October 4, 2018, https://www.washingtonpost.com/news/powerpost/paloma/daily-202/2018/10/04/daily -202-how-senate-republicans-could-win-the-battle-and-the-war-on-kavanaugh/5bb 50b311b326b7c8a8d17f3/; Michelle Ye Hee Lee, "Democratic Senate Candidate in Ten- nessee Phil Bredesen Says He Would Support Kavanaugh's Confirmation," *Washington Post*, October 5, 2018, https://www.washingtonpost.com/politics/tennessee-democratic -senate-candidate-phil-bredesen-says-he-would-support-kavanaugh-nomination/2018/10/ 05/efd3130e-c8c7-11e8-b1ed-1d2d65b86d0c_story.html; James Hohmann, "Trump's

Attacks on Kavanaugh's Second Accuser Shows Why the GOP Hired a Woman to Question Ford," *Washington Post*, September 26, 2018, https://www.washingtonpost.com/news/powerpost/paloma/daily-202/2018/09/26/daily-202-trump-s-attacks-on-kavanaugh-s-second-accuser-show-why-the-gop-hired-a-woman-to-question-ford/5ba aae991b326b7c8a8d168c/; James Hohmann, "Polarization Poses Problems for Kavanaugh as He Prepares to Testify in His Defense," *Washington Post*, September 18, 2018, https://www.washingtonpost.com/news/powerpost/paloma/daily-202/2018/09/18/daily-202-polarization-poses-problems-for-kavanaugh-as-he-prepares-to-testify-in-his-defense/5ba064af1b326b47ec9596bc/.

21. Kevin Robillard, "Heidi Heitkamp Flooded with Donations after Voting against Brett Kavanaugh; Donors Gave More Than $12 Million in 17 days," *HuffPost*, October 25, 2018, https://www.huffingtonpost.com/entry/heidi-heitkamp-donations-brett-kavanaugh_us_5bd2726fe4b0a8f17ef5fdc5.

22. James Hohmann, "Six Takeaways from Doug Jones's Stunning Win in Alabama's Senate Race," *Washington Post*, December 13, 2017, https://www.washingtonpost.com/news/powerpost/paloma/daily-202/2017/12/13/daily-202-six-takeaways-from-doug-jones-s-stunning-win-in-alabama-s-senate-race/5a30733c30fb0469e883fb64/; James Hohmann, "Why So Many Women Are Still Supporting Roy Moore in the Alabama Senate Race," *Washington Post*, December 6, 2017, https://www.washingtonpost.com/news/powerpost/paloma/daily-202/2017/12/06/daily-202-why-so-many-women-are-still-supporting-roy-moore-in-the-alabama-senate-race/5a27303f30fb0469e883fa40/.

23. James Hohmann, "Trump Solidifies Control of GOP with RNC Reversal on Roy Moore," *Washington Post*, December 5, 2017, https://www.washingtonpost.com/news/powerpost/paloma/daily-202/2017/12/05/daily-202-trump-solidifies-control-of-gop-with-rnc-reversal-on-roy-moore/5a259bfb30fb0469e883f9e0/; James Hohmann, "As Roy Moore Declines to Step Aside, a Tale of Two Parties Emerges," *Washington Post*, November 10, 2017, https://www.washingtonpost.com/news/powerpost/paloma/daily-202/2017/11/10/daily-202-as-roy-moore-declines-to-step-aside-a-tale-of-two-republican-parties-emerges/5a04e1dd30fb045a2e002f77/; James Hohmann, "Whether Roy Moore Wins or Loses, There Is No Good Outcome for Senate Republicans," *Washington Post*, November 14, 2017, https://www.washingtonpost.com/news/powerpost/paloma/daily-202/2017/11/14/daily-202-whether-roy-moore-wins-or-loses-there-is-no-good-outcome-for-senate-republicans/5a0a00fe30fb045a2e002fe5/.

24. James Hohmann, "Trump's Rescue Mission to Mississippi May Drag Cindy Hyde-Smith across the Finish Line," *Washington Post*, November 26, 2018, https://www.washingtonpost.com/news/powerpost/paloma/daily-202/2018/11/26/daily-202-trump-s-rescue-mission-to-mississippi-may-drag-cindy-hyde-smith-across-the-finish-line/5bf b669c1b326b60d128001d/.

25. Ashton Pittman, "Hyde-Smith Attended All-White 'Seg Academy' to Avoid Integration," *Jackson Free Press*, November 23, 2018, http://www.jacksonfreepress.com/news/2018/nov/23/hyde-smith-attended-all-white-seg-academy-avoid-in/; James Hohmann, "Trump Voters Stay Loyal because They Feel Disrespected," *Washington Post*, May 14, 2018, https://www.washingtonpost.com/news/powerpost/paloma/daily-202/2018/05/14/daily-202-trump-voters-stay-loyal-because-they-feel-disrespected/5af8 aac530fb0425887994cc/; Matt Viser, "Cindy Hyde-Smith Has Embraced Confederate History More than Once in Her Political Career," *Washington Post*, November 22, 2018,

https://www.washingtonpost.com/politics/cindy-hyde-smith-has-embraced-confederate
-history-more-than-once-in-her-political-career/2018/11/22/2d8ac440-ed0c-11e8-baac
-2a674e91502b_story.html; Eric Bradner and Andrew Kaczynski, "Mississippi Sen.
Cindy Hyde-Smith Pushed Resolution Praising Confederate Soldier's Effort to 'Defend
His Homeland,'" *CNN*, November 24, 2018, https://www.cnn.com/2018/11/24/politics/
cindy-hyde-smith-confederacy-mississippi-senate-race/index.html.

    26. Colby Itkowitz, "What Is Going on with Bob Menendez's New Jersey Senate
Race?," *Washington Post*, October 30, 2018, https://www.washingtonpost.com/politics/
2018/10/30/what-is-going-with-bob-menendezs-new-jersey-senate-race/?utm
_term=.1f8608273391.

    27. Stephen Montgomery, "Keith Ellison Elected Minnesota Attorney General over
Doug Wardlow," *Star Tribune*, November 7, 2018, http://www.startribune.com/keith
-ellison-elected-minnesota-attorney-general-over-doug-wardlow/499701441/; James Hohmann, "Duncan Hunter Embraces the Smash-Mouth Tactics Trump Learned from Roy
Cohn," August 23, 2018, *Washington Post*, https://www.washingtonpost.com/news/power
post/paloma/daily-202/2018/08/23/daily-202-duncan-hunter-embraces-the-smash-mouth
-tactics-trump-learned-from-roy-cohn/5b7dda0d1b326b3f31919d14/; James Hohmann,
"The Chris Collins Indictment Ensures Ethics Will be a Major Issue in the Midterms,"
Washington Post, August, 9, 2018, https://www.washingtonpost.com/news/powerpost/
paloma/daily-202/2018/08/09/daily-202-the-chris-collins-indictment-ensures-ethics-will
-be-a-major-issue-in-the-midterms/5b6bb0041b326b020795600e/; Sean Sullivan, "Rep.
Keith Ellison Denies Abuse Allegations," *Washington Post*, August 12, 2018, http://www
.washingtonpost.com/news/powerpost/wp/2018/08/12/rep-keith-ellison-denies-abuse
-allegations/.

    28. James Hohmann, "Gianforte's Victory after Assaulting Reporter Reflects Rising
Tribalism in American Politics," *Washington Post*, May 26, 2017, https://www.washing
tonpost.com/news/powerpost/paloma/daily-202/2017/05/26/daily-202-gianforte-s
-victory-after-assaulting-reporter-reflects-rising-tribalism-in-american-politics/59275c2ae
9b69b2fb981dba2/.

    29. Seung Min Kim, "President Campaigns for Former Foe at Nevada Rally," *Washing-
ton Post*, October 20, 2018, https://www.washingtonpost.com/politics/trump-campaigns
-for-former-gop-foe-at-nevada-rally/2018/10/20/7ebab6a0-d483-11e8-a275-81c671
a50422_story.html?utm_term=.4ecc0f768a51.

    30. Humberto Sanchez, "Trump: Heller's Lukewarm Support for Him Cost Ex-Senator
the GOP Base and His Seat," *Nevada Independent*, February 6, 2019, https://thenevada
independent.com/article/trump-hellers-lukewarm-support-for-trump-cost-heller-the-gop
-base-and-his-seat.

    31. James Hohmann, "Sen. Jeff Flake's Flame-Throwing Polemic Takes Aim at
Trump," *Washington Post*, August 3, 2017, https://www.washingtonpost.com/opinions/
sen-jeff-flakes-flame-throwing-polemic-takes-aim-at-trump/2017/08/03/dec886e0-77d6
-11e7-8f39-eeb7d3a2d304_story.html; James Hohmann, "Flake and Corker Feel Liberated to Speak Their Minds. That Should Terrify Trump," *Washington Post*, October 25,
2017, https://www.washingtonpost.com/news/powerpost/paloma/daily-202/2017/10/25/
daily-202-flake-and-corker-feel-liberated-to-speak-their-minds-that-should-terrify-trump/
59efd11030fb045cba000a28/; James Hohmann, "Roy Moore's Victory and Bob Corker's
Retirement Are Fresh Indicators of a Senate That's Coming Apart," *Washington Post*,

September 27, 2017, https://www.washingtonpost.com/news/powerpost/paloma/daily -202/2017/09/27/daily-202-roy-moore-s-victory-and-bob-corker-s-retirement-are-fresh -indicators-of-a-senate-that-s-coming-apart/59cb0b0e30fb0468cea81c04/; James Hohmann, "Jeff Flake Delivers the Most Courageous Conservative Rebuttal of Trumpism Yet," *Washington Post*, August 2, 2017, https://www.washingtonpost.com/news/powerpost/ paloma/daily-202/2017/08/02/daily-202-jeff-flake-delivers-the-most-courageous -conservative-rebuttal-of-trumpism-yet/59812c9b30fb045fdaef10a8/; James Hohmann, "Bob Corker's Tirade Encapsulates Five Reasons Why Trump Has Failed at Governing," *Washington Post*, October 9, 2018, https://www.washingtonpost.com/news/powerpost/ paloma/daily-202/2017/10/09/daily-202-bob-corker-tirade-encapsulates-five-reasons -why-trump-has-failed-at-governing/59dae42b30fb0468cea81dff/.

32. James Hohmann, "Trump's Warped View of Loyalty and the Conceit of the October 8th Coalition," *Washington Post*, July 31, 2017, https://www.washingtonpost.com/ news/powerpost/paloma/daily-202/2017/07/31/daily-202-trump-s-warped-view-of -loyalty-and-the-conceit-of-the-oct-8th-coalition/597ea60230fb045fdaef100e/; Michael Finnegan, "Arizona Exposes Danger for GOP in 2018 Primaries: Embracing Trump Could Backfire," *Los Angeles Times*, January 20, 2018, http://www.latimes.com/politics/la-na -arizona-senate-trump-20180130-story.html.

33. James Hohmann, "Loyalty to Trump Emerges as a Top Issue in Republican Primary Campaign Commercials," *Washington Post*, March 29, 2018, https://www.washingtonpost .com/news/powerpost/paloma/daily-202/2018/03/29/daily-202-loyalty-to-trump-emerges -as-a-top-issue-in-republican-primary-campaign-commercials/5abc494530fb 042a378a2f32/?utm_term = .b56ecb324975; James Hohmann, "Primary Results Confirm 2018 Is a Terrible Year to Be a House Republican," *Washington Post*, May 9, 2018, https:// www.washingtonpost.com/news/powerpost/paloma/daily-202/2018/05/09/daily-202 -primary-results-confirm-2018-is-a-terrible-year-to-be-a-house-republican/5af24 14530fb042db5797400/.

34. James Hohmann, "Mitt Romney Threads the Needle on Trump in Utah Senate Race," *Washington Post*, May 30, 2018, https://www.washingtonpost.com/news/power post/paloma/daily-202/2018/05/30/daily-202-romney-threads-the-needle-on-trump-in -utah-senate-debate/5b0dbfbc30fb0425887996ac/; James Hohmann, "Is Mitt Romney the Future or the Past of the Republican Party?," *Washington Post*, February 2, 2018, https:// www.washingtonpost.com/news/powerpost/paloma/daily-202/2018/02/02/daily-202-is -mitt-romney-the-future-or-the-past-of-the-republican-party/5a7384aa30fb04 1c3c7d75d9/; James Hohmann, "Paul Ryan's Party Is Over," *Washington Post*, April 12, 2018, https://www.washingtonpost.com/news/powerpost/paloma/daily-202/2018/04/12/ daily-202-paul-ryan-s-party-is-over/5acec10f30fb0406a5a12341/.

35. James Hohmann, "Crowley Going Down Spotlights the Looming Democratic Identity Crisis," *Washington Post*, June 27, 2018, https://www.washingtonpost.com/news/ powerpost/paloma/daily-202/2018/06/27/daily-202-crowley-going-down-spotlights-the -looming-democratic-identity-crisis/5b32e96b30fb046c468e6f54/.

36. David Weigel, "Red State Democrats Face Down Progressives Who Want Primary Challenges," *Washington Post*, February 28, 2017, https://www.washingtonpost.com/ news/powerpost/wp/2017/02/28/red-state-democrats-face-down-progressives-who-want -primary-challenges/?utm_term = .2ae8876e036b.

37. Michael Kruse, "How the Most Endangered Democrat in America Survived," *Politico Magazine*, November 6, 2018, https://www.politico.com/magazine/story/2018/11/06/

manchin-win-west-virginia-senate-2018-elections-midterms-222226; James Hohmann, "Red State Democrats Are Proposing Lots of Ideas to Cut Taxes and Work with Trump," *Washington Post*, November 2, 2017, https://www.washingtonpost.com/news/powerpost/paloma/daily-202/2017/11/02/daily-202-red-state-democrats-are-proposing-lots-of-ideas-to-cut-taxes-and-work-with-trump/59fa201130fb0468e7654022/; James Hohmann, "Ohio Democrats Say Talking about Mueller's Probe Is Not the Way to Win in 2018," *Washington Post*, October 30, 2017, https://www.washingtonpost.com/news/powerpost/paloma/daily-202/2017/10/30/daily-202-ohio-democrats-say-talking-about-mueller-s-probe-is-not-the-way-to-win-in-2018/59f6932230fb0468e7653e5a/; James Hohmann, "Tom Steyer Rips Democratic Establishment for Resisting Trump Impeachment," *Washington Post*, August 3, 2018, https://www.washingtonpost.com/news/powerpost/paloma/daily-202/2018/08/03/daily-202-tom-steyer-rips-democratic-establishment-for-resisting-trump-impeachment/5b63ba061b326b0207955ee7/.

38. James Hohmann, "Red State Democratic Senator Highlights Bills Signed by Trump in First Election Ad," *Washington Post*, March 12, 2018, https://www.washingtonpost.com/news/powerpost/paloma/daily-202/2018/03/12/daily-202-red-state-democratic-senator-highlights-bills-signed-by-trump-in-first-reelection-ad/5aa5f23930fb047655a06c01/; James Hohmann, "VA's Nominees Struggles Are a Consequence of Trump's Vetting Failures," *Washington Post*, April 24, 2018, https://www.washingtonpost.com/news/powerpost/paloma/daily-202/2018/04/24/daily-202-va-nominee-s-struggles-are-a-consequence-of-trump-s-vetting-failures/5adea75530fb04371192683a/.

39. Kevin Robillard, "Jon Tester Was Donald Trump's Top Target. Here's How He Survived," *HuffPost*, November 27, 2018, https://www.huffingtonpost.com/entry/jon-tester-2018-midterms_us_5bf48044e4b0eb6d9309508e.

40. Theodoric Meyer, "Morrisey under Fire in West Virginia over Lobbyist Past," *Politico*, May 3, 2018, https://www.politico.com/story/2018/05/03/patrick-morrisey-west-virginia-senate-race-511801.

41. Naomi Lim, "Joe Donnelly: Democrats 'Start Losing the People' in the Midwest When They Talk about 'Medicare for All,'" *Washington Examiner*, December 29, 2018, https://www.washingtonexaminer.com/news/joe-donnelly-democrats-start-losing-the-people-in-the-midwest-when-they-talk-about-medicare-for-all.

42. James Hohmann, "Rick Scott Prepares to Join the Senate as Florida Recount Continues," *Washington Post*, November 12, 2018, https://www.washingtonpost.com/news/powerpost/paloma/daily-202/2018/11/12/daily-202-rick-scott-prepares-to-join-the-senate-as-florida-recount-continues/5be906601b326b3929054733/.

43. Sean Sullivan, "Rick Scott's Standing among Hispanics Faces Test with Trump's Demand for Wall Money," *Washington Post*, January 7, 2019, https://www.washingtonpost.com/powerpost/scotts-standing-among-hispanics-faces-test-with-trumps-demand-for-wall-money/2019/01/07/02294dbe-1294-11e9-803c-4ef28312c8b9_story.html.

44. Tim Craig, "Florida Republicans Split on Trump: Scott Wants Distance, DeSantis a Hug," *Washington Post*, October 1, 2018, https://www.washingtonpost.com/national/florida-republicans-split-on-trump-scott-wants-distance-desantis-a-hug/2018/10/01/d4cb41d4-c337-11e8-97a5-ab1e46bb3bc7_story.html.

45. Amber Phillips, "No, Beto O'Rourke's Insane $38 Million Fundraising Haul Does Not Mean He Can Win Texas," *Washington Post*, October 12, 2018, https://www.washingtonpost.com/politics/2018/10/12/no-beto-orourkes-insane-million-fundraising-haul-does-not-mean-he-can-win-texas/.

46. James Hohmann, "Only One New England Republican Remains in Congress—and She Could Lose or Retire in 2020," *Washington Post*, November 16, 2018, https://www.washingtonpost.com/news/powerpost/paloma/daily-202/2018/11/16/daily-202-only-one-new-england-republican-remains-in-congress-and-she-could-lose-or-retire-in-2020/5bee2cd21b326b3929054888/.

47. David Weigel and Sean Sullivan, "Sen. Pat Roberts of Kansas Announces He Won't Seek Reelection in 2020," *Washington Post*, January 4, 2018, http://www.washingtonpost.com/powerpost/kansas-sen-pat-roberts-announces-he-wont-seek-reelection-in-2020/2019/01/04/569b7bf4-0a1c-11e9-a3f0-71c95106d96a_story.html; James Hohmann, "Retirement Could Liberate Lamar Alexander during His Final Two Years in the Senate," *Washington Post*, December 18, 2018, https://www.washingtonpost.com/news/powerpost/paloma/daily-202/2018/12/18/daily-202-retirement-could-liberate-lamar-alexander-during-his-final-two-years-in-the-senate/5c1889631b326b2d6629d4d8/.

48. James Hohmann, "The Legislative Filibuster Will Be at Risk as Soon as the Senate Goes Nuclear," *Washington Post*, April 6, 2017, https://www.washingtonpost.com/news/powerpost/paloma/daily-202/2017/04/06/daily-202-the-legislative-filibuster-will-be-at-risk-as-soon-as-the-senate-goes-nuclear/58e5c0afe9b69b3a72331e4f/?utm_term=.960e474f3611.

49. Donald Trump tweet, February 5, 2019, https://twitter.com/realdonaldtrump/status/1092807525102247938.

7

The Governors

Democratic Wave Falls Short of a Wipeout

Madelaine Pisani

Gubernatorial elections rose to higher prominence in 2018 than they otherwise might in the national psyche because of the role they had in determining whether 2018 was really a "blue wave" year. It was likely that neither party would capture both the House and the Senate, and Republicans were at the party's high water mark for control of governorships going into the election cycle. The map of 36 governor elections offered significantly more offensive opportunities to Democrats, especially in the first midterm election of a controversial, opposing-party president. Additionally, the frequency and length of government shutdowns combined with President Trump's adversarial relationship with the Congress resulted in a prospect of more governing happening at the state level. Governors had the opportunity to make a big impact by aligning with or standing up to Trump's policy as executives in their own right.

The 2018 cycle did not deliver the huge shift in power that seemed possible with such an open map for Democrats and the buzz about backlash against the president. There is no question, though, that Democrats made a dent in the GOP majority. They matched the net change Republicans achieved in their 2010 wave year that launched them toward their 2016 high point. After Republicans reached their high water mark of 33 governorships to Democrats' 16, the GOP seemed to have reached a ceiling. Democrats began chipping away at the majority by capitalizing on anti-Trump energy, picking up seven seats in 2018, while the GOP held on in a handful of contests that had drawn national attention. Republicans also picked up one Independent-held seat in Alaska. This resulted in a six-seat net loss for Republicans, the same net loss Democrats suffered in 2010 after President Obama came into power. Though it should be noted that in 2010 Republicans started with control of 24 seats as opposed to the 16 seats Democrats started with in 2018.[1]

This is why some opposing-party operatives argue that Democrats should have put up a better performance this cycle (when they had fewer races to defend than Republicans did in 2010), if they want to make equally significant state-level gains as Republicans did during Obama's tenure. According to the previous edition of this book, *Trumped*, Democrats suffered a net loss of 13 governorships and around 950 state legislative seats from Barack Obama's first presidential victory in 2008 to 2016. Since the post–World War II period, the president's party has lost an average of 20 percent of governorships by the president's second midterm. As shown in table 7.1, Republicans have already gone from holding 66 percent to 54 percent in the two years President Trump has been in power.

Republicans held 26 of the 36 state governorships up for election in 2018, forcing the party to spend most of its energy playing defense. Additionally, unlike in 2014, half of the Republican-held seats (13 of 26) were open seats. In 2014, only three of 22 Republican-held seats were incumbent-less.[2] Thus in addition to a less favorable political atmosphere, Republicans also had

Table 7.1   Post–World War II Change in President's Party's Share of Governorships after Sixth-Year Election

Presidency	Total State Governors	Pres. Party Governors at Start of Term	Starting % Held	Pres. Party Governors after 6th Year	6th Year % Held	Change
FDR/Truman (D)	48	25	52%	23	48%	−4%
Eisenhower (R)	48/49	30	63%	14	29%	−34%
JFK/LBJ (D)	50	34	68%	25	50%	−18%
Nixon/Ford (R)	50	31	62%	13	26%	−36%
Reagan (R)	50	24	48%	24	48%	0%
Clinton (D)	50	30	60%	17	34%	−26%
G.W. Bush (R)	50	29	58%	22	44%	−14%
Obama (D)	50	29*	58%	18	36%	−22%
Trump (R)	50	33	66%	N/A	N/A	N/A
Average	N/A	29.4	59%	19.5	39%	−19%

Note: *Includes Gov. Janet Napolitano (D-AZ), who was appointed secretary of homeland security in January 2009. Percentages are rounded post-arithmetic.
Sources: *CQ Guide to U.S. Elections*, vol. ii, 6th ed., 1558; *Sabato's Crystal Ball*.

fewer states where they could rely on incumbent advantage. In 2018, Democrats only had four incumbent-less states of their nine and managed to protect them all as well as all of their incumbents. Three of the four incumbents who did not win reelection in 2018 were Republican. However, Illinois Governor Bruce Rauner is the only one who enjoyed the standard incumbent advantage: that is, an incumbent running for a second straight elected term. Wisconsin Governor Scott Walker was seeking a third term, which is historically much harder considering former Wisconsin Governor Tommy Thompson is the only person to have won more than two terms as the state's governor. Then there was Kansas Governor Jeff Colyer, who was not elected to his position. He held the position for about a year after Governor Sam Brownback resigned to take a federal post, making Colyer a successor incumbent. The fourth incumbent to fail in his quest for reelection was Alaska's Independent Governor Bill Walker, who withdrew from the race at the last minute in an effort to boost the Democratic Party challenger. As table 7.2 shows, at least 70 percent of incumbent governors in 24 of the 37 cycles since 1946 have had success in their bids for reelection.

Another unique factor at play in 2018 was President Trump's early involvement in many races. Trump broke with tradition by endorsing candidates during the primary season, something past presidents have largely avoided doing. He boosted outsider candidates over the state party establishment's pick in several states, including four of the most competitive governor races: Florida, Georgia, Kansas, and Michigan. Trump held rallies for Kris Kobach in Kansas, Brian Kemp in Georgia, and Ron DeSantis in Florida, where he stressed victories on tax reform and the Brett Kavanaugh Supreme Court nomination and warned against Democrats' immigration policies. Though after his primary endorsement, he largely stayed out of Michigan as Bill Schuette's performance in polling went from bad to worse. The outcomes for this foursome were mixed. Schuette and Kobach were both met with hostility from their respective state's party establishments and had trouble uniting their bases. Meanwhile, the Florida and Georgia state Republican parties rallied behind DeSantis and Kemp after Trump signaled his chosen favorite. Both carried around 90 percent favorability among Republicans in statewide polling. Trump also lifted his ally, South Carolina Governor Henry McMaster, who had replaced Nikki Haley when she became U.S. ambassador to the United Nations, with a rally and enthusiastic endorsement during the state's contentious Republican primary runoff. Like many things about Trump, his unconventional influence on the party's overall strategy did not always yield consistent results, but he did prove his base could be powerful, toppling well-connected and well-funded candidates, when his chosen candidates were able to harness the base's enthusiasm.

Table 7.2 Post–World War II Election Performance by Incumbent Governors

Year	Inc. Running Again	Lost Primary	Lost General	Won	Inc. Success Rate	General Election Rate
1946	20	3	3	14	70.0%	82.4%
1948	24	4	8	12	50.0%	60.0%
1950	20	1	4	15	75.0%	78.9%
1952	21	2	3	16	76.2%	84.2%
1954	19	3	4	12	63.2%	75.0%
1956	20	2	4*	15	75.0%	78.9%
1958	20	0	9	11	55.0%	55.0%
1960	14	0	6	8	57.1%	57.1%
1962	28	2	11	15	53.6%	57.7%
1964	15	1	2	12	80.0%	85.7%
1966	24	2	7	15	62.5%	68.2%
1968	14	0	4	10	71.4%	71.4%
1970	25	1	7	17	68.0%	70.8%
1972	11	2	2	7	63.6%	77.8%
1974	21	0	5	16	76.2%	76.2%
1976	8	1	2	5	62.5%	71.4%
1978	23	2	5	16	69.6%	76.2%
1980	11	1	3	7	63.6%	70.0%
1982	25	1	5	19	76.0%	79.2%
1984	6	0	2	4	66.7%	66.7%
1986	18	1	2	15	83.3%	88.2%
1988	9	0	1	8	88.9%	88.9%
1990	23	0	6	17	73.9%	73.9%
1992	4	0	0	4	100.0%	100.0%
1994	23	2	4	17	73.9%	81.0%
1996	7	0	0	7	100.0%	100.0%
1998	25	0	2	23	92.0%	92.0%
2000	6	0	1	5	83.3%	83.3%
2002	16	0	4	12	75.0%	75.0%
2004	7	1	2	4	57.1%	66.7%
2006	27	1	1	25	92.6%	96.2%
2008	8	0	0	8	100.0%	100.0%
2010	14	1	2	11	78.6%	84.6%
2012	6	0	0	6	100.0%	100.0%
2014	29	1	3	25	86.2%	89.3%
2016	5	0	1	4	80.0%	80.0%
2018	20	1	3	16	80.0%	84.2%
Total	616	36	128	453	73.5%	78.1%

Note: *In 1956, Gov. J. Bracken Lee (R-UT) lost renomination in the GOP primary but then ran as an Independent in the general election, which he also lost.
Sources: *CQ Guide to U.S. Elections*, vol. ii, 6th ed., 1558; *Sabato's Crystal Ball*.

UNCERTAIN CONTESTS

In their final pre-election projections, University of Virginia Center for Politics' *Crystal Ball* newsletter rated 16 gubernatorial races as "leaning" toward one candidate. These lean races were the most competitive, indicating a high level of uncertainty. The *Crystal Ball* also handicapped Georgia as "toss-up/ lean runoff" because of the likelihood of that contest being too close to call and going to a December runoff. This resulted in a total of 17 highly competitive races. Democrats won nine of the 17, including five of their seven pickups. Republicans won eight competitive seats, including the party's lone pickup in Alaska. Those races—Alaska, Colorado, Connecticut, Florida, Georgia, Iowa, Kansas, Maine, Minnesota, New Hampshire, New Mexico, Nevada, Ohio, Oklahoma, Oregon, South Dakota, and Wisconsin—are described in this section.

Democrats did their best to take advantage of the favorable map, rife with open-seat elections in red states, but, in terms of the competitive races, they split about even with Republicans. Democrats picked up key open seats in Nevada, New Mexico, and Maine but missed opportunities in Florida, Ohio, and Georgia. The biggest upset of the night was Democrats' victory in Kansas, which seemed further out of reach than other more purple states.

Republicans recaptured Kansas in the 2010 wave election when Sam Brownback took office, becoming the state's most conservative executive in 50 years.[3] The seat did not appear to be among those most at risk of swinging back to the blue column even after Brownback resigned as governor to become President Trump's Ambassador-at-Large for International Religious Freedom. Brownback's tenure was not all smooth sailing. His tax reduction initiative, in particular, led to severe budget problems and caused a dip in his approval ratings. By 2017, lawmakers had reversed many of his tax cuts.[4] Lieutenant Governor Jeff Colyer took over for Brownback in January 2018. The first electoral shock delivered by Kansas came when Colyer, despite being a successor incumbent, lost to Kansas Secretary of State Kris Kobach in the primary, making him the only incumbent not to win his party's nomination in 2018.[5] Colyer's primary defeat was an early sign that voters were eager to reject a perceived extension of the Brownback years. Additionally, Kobach received a last-minute endorsement from President Trump that may have boosted him on Election Day. Trump did so against the wishes of national Republicans who worried Kobach would be more vulnerable in a general election.[6]

Meanwhile, Laura Kelly, a state senator, kept her campaign focused on fiscal responsibility and preventing a return to the Brownback years. As Kobach promised more tax reductions, Kelly highlighted school funding and government transparency.[7] She backed up her reputation for working across the aisle by earning endorsements from every living ex-governor of Kansas except Brownback, who did not endorse.[8] Kelly also avoided attacking the president, instead keeping her focus on state-specific issues. The race was tied in most public polling, with third-party-candidate Greg Orman pulling around 10 percent of the vote. The final poll from *Reuters*/Ipsos/UVA Center for Politics showed Kelly ahead by two points[9] and came out just as Orman's campaign manager resigned and endorsed Kelly. However, President Trump and Vice President Pence had visited Kansas at least twice on Kobach's behalf and a Democrat prevailing in a state Trump won by over 20 points still seemed like a long shot. Trump's cache did not end up transferring to Kobach and Kelly won by 4.5 points, within the margin of error in the final poll.

Perhaps the most-watched race of the night occurred in Florida, where Republican Ron DeSantis, a congressman who resigned to focus on his campaign, faced off against Tallahassee's Democratic Mayor Andrew Gillum. Democrats saw the race as their chance to break a 20-year drought, considering the last time a Democrat occupied the governor's mansion was 1999. But the party also had to defend its vulnerable Senate seat held by Bill Nelson, which Florida's outgoing Republican Governor Rick Scott had put in his crosshairs. DeSantis, like Kobach, was not the party's first pick but got a hefty boost from President Trump in the primary that drew voters and fundraising.[10] Gillum also sent shock waves through the state when he won his party's nomination. He had been trailing two other heavyweight Florida Democrats in a crowded primary field and was viewed as running to the left of most of his opponents. He was backed by Vermont Senator Bernie Sanders as well as liberal financiers George Soros and Tom Steyer. When he won the primary, Gillum became Florida's first African-American major party candidate for governor.[11]

Already a high-profile race, the general election contest dominated headlines when DeSantis said voters should not "monkey this up" by choosing Gillum during an interview with Fox News the day after the primary. DeSantis had a lot of ground to recover after that point and eventually brought on veteran GOP campaign manager Susie Wiles for a campaign overhaul. He began highlighting his Ivy League and military experience, contrasting that with attacks against Gillum's economic and criminal justice policies.[12] DeSantis trailed in the polls leading up to Election Day and major party surrogates including President Trump, President Obama, and Hillary Clinton were crisscrossing the state to drive turnout for their chosen candidate. DeSantis won the election by a 0.4-point margin, which took 11 days and a statewide recount to confirm.[13] The hard-fought race reflected national tensions and sent a message that Trump's base is still incredibly powerful in the bellwether state.

A similar phenomenon gripped the race in Georgia, where Republican Secretary of State Brian Kemp, Trump's primary pick, battled Stacey Abrams, who would have been the first black female governor in the United States and who drew national headlines and celebrity star power. Georgia is more solidly red than Florida at the presidential level, though Democrats had held the governor's mansion since 1872 until Sonny Perdue unseated Roy Barnes in 2002. Republicans have helmed the governorship since then. Abrams won her primary handily, but Kemp spent eight weeks in a contentious runoff against Lieutenant Governor Casey Cagle, the establishment candidate and primary frontrunner. Kemp caught up with a strong ground game and ran attention-grabbing ads in which he loaded guns, revved chainsaws, and drove his pickup truck "just in case I need to round up criminal illegals and take 'em home myself." President Trump endorsed Kemp in a tweet just two weeks before the runoff, which gave him a huge boost in a state where Trump held an 80 percent approval rating among Republicans.[14] Kemp pivoted to slightly more moderate messaging in the general and framed Abrams as a far-left liberal who would not manage state finances well, attacking Abrams's personal debt.[15] Abrams, the former state House minority leader, called on Kemp to resign as secretary of state, citing claims his office suppressed minority votes.[16] Despite visits from President Obama, Oprah Winfrey, and Will Ferrell, Kemp defeated Abrams by 1.4 points, meeting the 50 percent threshold to avoid a runoff by a slim margin.

Republicans also defended a competitive open seat in Ohio. Longtime rivals Mike DeWine, the state's attorney general, and Richard Cordray, the former Consumer Financial Protection Bureau director under President Obama, engaged in a rematch of their 2010 state attorney general election fight, this time aiming at the governorship. DeWine narrowly unseated Cordray as attorney general in 2010, attacking Cordray on untested drug and rape kits piling up in police departments. That issue resurfaced in 2018, with both candidates attacking each other on his record as top cop.[17] Cordray also hoped protecting Medicaid expansion would be a wedge issue that could give him the edge over DeWine. DeWine, however, changed his stance in July, vowing to protect the provision of the Affordable Care Act, which he previously opposed.[18] The race contrasted with other toss-up governor contests because both campaigns kept their messaging state focused, rarely drawing national attention. Polls were neck and neck, more often showing Cordray ahead by a few points than DeWine in the closing weeks. Outgoing Republican Governor John Kasich largely avoided the race but seemed to warm up to DeWine after he changed his tune on Medicaid expansion. Just a week before Election Day, Kasich held a rally for DeWine in an effort to provide a last-minute boost.[19] DeWine outspent Cordray by a whopping $16.1 million margin, and on his own broke Ohio's record on total spending in a governor's race.[20] The effort paid off: DeWine once again defeated Cordray, this time winning by nearly four points.

The open-seat race in Nevada delivered a late-night gain for Democrats and reminded Republicans of the power of the Democrats' grassroots infrastructure in the state. In 2014, Democrats put up a pitiful fight against popular Republican Governor Brian Sandoval, who won with over 70 percent of the vote. Sandoval's departure and the prospect of blue wave energy attracted stronger candidates in 2018. Clark County Commissioner Steve Sisolak emerged bruised from a bitterly fought Democratic primary as Republican state Attorney General Adam Laxalt easily claimed his party's nomination.[21] Though Laxalt had a head start on the airwaves after the primary, the Democratic Governors Association stepped in with attack ads on Sisolak's behalf. The group spent $9.5 million to boost its candidate. The Republican Governors Association was close behind, totaling $8.9 million for Laxalt.[22] While Sisolak left the attacks to outside groups, he maintained consistent messaging to appeal to Independent voters on three priorities: health care, jobs, and education. Sisolak vowed to protect Medicaid expansion and Sandoval's commerce tax, both policies Laxalt had criticized in the past. Laxalt's platform was less disciplined and his attacks on Sisolak's character, calling him a "shady dealer," ultimately did not resonate with voters. Laxalt also failed to secure an endorsement from Sandoval, which made it difficult to capitalize on the outgoing governor's popularity.[23] Sisolak topped Laxalt by four points, putting a Democrat back in the governor's mansion for the first time since 1999.

After failing twice to defeat Maine's outspoken Republican Governor Paul LePage, Democrats were determined to bring the state back to the blue column. Democratic state Attorney General Janet Mills led most polls and capitalized on her history of going to bat against LePage, especially on the issue of Medicaid expansion. Her Republican opponent, Shawn Moody, a businessman billed as a political outsider, did not do much to differentiate himself from LePage, hiring former LePage staffers, including LePage's daughter. In the weeks before Election Day, he shifted his position from outright opposition to Medicaid expansion and said he would implement the law if funding was there.[24] Two Independent candidates, Alan Caron and Terry Hayes, added an element of unpredictability to the race, allowing for a lower threshold for victory. However, Caron withdrew at the end of October and urged his supporters to vote for Mills. He was under pressure not to split the Democratic vote, causing an outcome like the 2010 election when LePage won with just 38 percent of the vote.[25] Hayes, the state treasurer, stayed in the race, but she appeared to be more of a spoiler for Republicans because the state GOP began running ads targeting her in October.[26] Mills outraised Moody by $1.2 million and benefited from more outside spending on her behalf by nearly a 2.5 to 1 ratio.[27] Mills won the race handily with a little more than 50 percent of the vote, becoming the state's first female governor.

The race in New Mexico was a top target for Democrats from the start because of term-limited Republican Governor Susana Martinez's unpopularity. Republican Steve Pearce and Democrat Michelle Lujan Grisham both entered the race as House Representatives jockeying to leave Washington D.C. for the governor's mansion. Lujan Grisham centered her campaign on criminal justice and infrastructure, focusing less on health care than Democrats in other states likely because Pearce was mounting heavy attacks related to the profits her own health care company made under the Affordable Care Act.[28] Pearce and the Republican Governors Association hammered Lujan Grisham with ads attacking her company and previous state-government service. However, Pearce overplayed his hand with an ad that attacked a former attorney for Lujan Grisham's company as "corrupt." It turned out the attorney had been battling pancreatic cancer for two years and was in hospice by the time the ad came out.[29] The headline in the *Santa Fe New Mexican* read: *Pearce Campaign Attacks Terminally Ill Man*. It was not a good look. Despite the gaffe, Lujan Grisham still had to spend heavily to trounce Pearce as handily as she did. She spent a total of $9.5 million, while Pearce spent just $4.9 million.[30] Lujan Grisham topped Pearce 57 percent to 43 percent.

The race in Wisconsin was the biggest incumbent takedown of the night for Democrats, in which battle-tested Republican Governor Scott Walker faced off against state schools Superintendent Tony Evers, who emerged from a huge primary field. Walker was initially elected in the Tea Party wave of 2010 and survived a recall election in 2012 sparked by cuts he made to union benefits and collective bargaining power that enraged labor groups.[31] Walker had a significant fundraising advantage throughout the campaign and released over 30 TV ads across the state. His aggressive ad strategy hinged on highlighting taxes and jobs, while churning out quick rebuttals to attacks from Evers and the Democratic Governors Association.[32] Despite the meticulous campaign strategy and active ground game, Walker had a large target on his back from making enemies like labor unions as governor, turning Wisconsinites off with his 2016 presidential bid, and energizing Democrats with a fourth chance to defeat him at the ballot box.[33] For Evers, the main hurdle was boosting his name ID and overcoming the perception that he was boring. Evers, a former schoolteacher, focused heavily on education and health care, and he leaned on visits from high-profile Democratic surrogates like

President Obama, Vice President Joe Biden, and Vermont Senator Bernie Sanders.[34] Polls showed Walker and Evers neck and neck in the final months, but Evers ultimately won the day, beating Walker by just over one percentage point.

Iowa Governor Kim Reynolds did not have the same advantage as most incumbents, ascending to the position only about a year and a half before Election Day. She faced Democrat Fred Hubbell, a former state economic development official and formidable self-funder. She kept her platform closely tied to the legacy of former Republican Governor Terry Branstad, who resigned to become the ambassador to China under President Trump. Hubbell, a former board member of Planned Parenthood, and Reynolds clashed on the issue of abortion. Hubbell took particular issue with a bill Reynolds signed that would be the most restrictive abortion law in the country if it does not get struck down in the courts.[35] Hubbell contributed $7 million of his own money to his total of $20.4 million in fundraising as of Election Day. Reynolds didn't quite raise as much, totaling $14.5 million.[36] Polls showed Hubbell and Reynolds within the margin of error as Election Day approached, and they were largely accurate. Top female Republican voices like First Daughter Ivanka Trump and White House spokeswoman Sarah Huckabee Sanders traveled to Iowa to help boost the GOP incumbent over the finish line. Reynolds beat Hubbell by the smallest margin Iowa has seen in a governor's race in 62 years.[37] She also made history by becoming the first female governor elected in Iowa.

The Republican Party's lone pickup of 2018 came from Alaska after a series of dramatic political shake-ups throughout the race. Incumbent Governor Bill Walker, an Independent, initially expected Democrats to offer their party's nomination to him uncontested, thus avoiding a three-way situation that would pave an easy road for Republicans. However, just hours before the candidate filing deadline, former Democratic Senator Mark Begich filed his candidacy. This left Walker with little choice but to run as a third-party candidate because he would not be able to defeat an actual Democrat for the party's nomination. Meanwhile, former state Senator Mike Dunleavy clinched the Republican nomination in part by criticizing government cuts to the annual payout Alaskans receive from the state's oil-wealth fund and calling for reduced spending.[38] The Republican Governors Association was on the air early in the race backing Dunleavy while Democrats waited to see what would happen between Walker and Begich. Walker suspended his campaign less than three weeks before Election Day, following the sudden resignation of his lieutenant governor.[39] With Walker out and endorsing Begich, the Democratic Governors Association launched a Hail Mary, six-figure TV ad buy against Dunleavy to boost the party's candidate. However, the ground-work put down by Republicans prevailed and Dunleavy won by seven points.

Democrats defended each open seat the party held in 2018, shutting Republicans out of even the most competitive states: Minnesota, Colorado, and Connecticut. They also fended off a challenge to their most vulnerable incumbent, Governor Kate Brown of Oregon. Brown faced moderate Republican state Representative Knute Buehler in a surprisingly competitive race that had the two close in polls. Her campaign kept a steady focus on continuing to prioritize gun control and access to health care.[40] As the race tightened and Buehler got a financial boost from Nike founder Phil Knight to the tune of $2.5 million, Independent candidate Patrick Starnes decided to withdraw from the race and endorse Brown to avoid becoming a spoiler for the Democrat.[41] Brown spent nearly $16.4 million in her race and ended with over $1 million cash on hand. Buehler raised $19.3 million and spent nearly all of it, though he came up short in the end.[42] Brown held her seat with a six-point margin. Republicans had hoped Minnesota's open-seat race would give them an opportunity to retake the state with a strong candidate like former Republican Governor Tim Pawlenty. However, Pawlenty lost the primary to Hennepin County Commissioner Jeff Johnson despite being the heavy favorite to win. Democratic groups spent heavily on ads attacking Pawlenty. His early defeat and Johnson's poor poll numbers caused the Republican Governors Association and other GOP donors to turn their attention to more winnable states.[43] Democratic Representative Tim Walz's campaign theme of being a unifier focused on improving education and infrastructure paid off, and he won the governorship by more than 10 points. Colorado Democrat Jared Polis, a wealthy Congressman, made history when he became the first openly gay man elected governor in the United States.[44] He replaced outgoing Democratic Governor John Hickenlooper, who may run for president in 2020. He did not shy away from setting down a liberal platform including expanding access to health care, pursuing government-funded preschool, and prioritizing environmental protection. Despite backing from Denver Broncos general manager John Elway and a family connection to President George W. Bush, Republican state Treasurer Walker Stapleton failed to gain steam against Polis. He trailed in the polls and had a hard time competing with the $22 million Polis personally invested in his campaign.[45] Finally in Connecticut, Democrat Ned Lamont secured the governorship despite the low approval ratings of outgoing Democratic Governor Dannel Malloy. Lamont, a former cable executive, squared off against Republican former UBS executive Bob Stefanowski in a battle of the businessmen. Polls showed a close race and Stefanowski nearly challenged the validity of some precincts' same-day voter registration.[46] By the morning after Election Day, with Lamont driving up his margin thanks to a strong showing in Bridgeport, Stefanowski conceded and Lamont prevailed with a roughly three-point margin.

Republicans had to put up a surprisingly strong defense in the deep red states of Oklahoma and South Dakota to ensure the party didn't lose out in those stronghold territories. In Oklahoma, Democrat Drew Edmondson, a former state Attorney General, tried to capitalize on the intense unpopularity of term-limited Republican Governor Mary Fallin by focusing a lot of his campaign on education and tying his opponent, Republican businessman Kevin Stitt, to her record. However, Stitt's strong base among rural voters and his profile as a political outsider protected him from the weight of Fallin's legacy.[47] While polls prompted some handicappers to rate Oklahoma as a toss-up, Stitt defeated Edmondson by a little over 12 points. South Dakota's Republican Representative Kristi Noem had to bring in extra support to beat back a challenge from state Senate Minority Leader Billie Sutton, a former rodeo star who was paralyzed from the waist down after being bucked from his horse. While Noem emerged from a bruising primary, Sutton went uncontested and spent that time fundraising to build a hefty war chest. Republican Governor Dennis Daugaard realized Noem could be in trouble and called in reinforcements from the Republican Governors Association, and even President Trump traveled to the state to hold a fundraiser for her. Despite the boost, Sutton was still gaining in some polls, which prompted more national Republicans to come rally for Noem, including Vice President Mike Pence, South Carolina Senator Lindsey Graham, and Colorado Senator Cory Gardner in the days before the election.[48] The strategy worked and, though Sutton did better than any Democrat in decades, Noem was able to continue the GOP's 40-year hold on the governor's mansion by a little more than three points. Noem also made history as the state's first female governor.

Republican Governor Chris Sununu also faced a surprisingly competitive race in New Hampshire against Democratic candidate Molly Kelly, a former state senator. Kelly took Sununu to task on bread-and-butter issues for Democrats, particularly focusing on paid family leave. Sununu initially appeared secure thanks to his incumbency advantage and lead in the polls. However, after a series of visits and endorsements from high-profile Democrats, including New York Senator Kirsten Gillibrand and Hillary Clinton, who even held a fundraiser for Kelly,[49] she surged in the polls, prompting the Republican Governors Association to make a late-stage ad buy protecting Sununu.[50] Sununu ultimately held his seat with a seven-point margin.

OTHER GUBERNATORIAL ELECTIONS

The other 19 gubernatorial races, which were viewed by *Crystal Ball* as "likely" or "safe," played out largely as expected. Though Democrats' takeover of Michigan and Illinois certainly merit a closer look. The election results for these other races—Alabama, Arizona, Arkansas, California, Hawaii, Idaho, Illinois, Maryland, Massachusetts, Michigan, Nebraska, New York, Pennsylvania, Rhode Island, South Carolina, Tennessee, Texas, Vermont, and Wyoming—are described below.

Democrats toppled an additional incumbent in Illinois Republican Governor Bruce Rauner, though he was in a much more vulnerable position than Walker in Wisconsin. Rauner went down in a bitter fight against Democrat J. B. Pritzker, a billionaire venture capitalist. Illinois's identity as a blue state and Rauner's inability to appeal to Independent voters without further infuriating his own party base made him consistently one of the most vulnerable incumbents of 2018. Rauner spent a whopping $78.6 million on the race, but that was no match for Pritzker, who sunk $173 million of his own money into the contest. Sam McCann, whose Conservative Party bid further pulled voters from Rauner, spent $4.5 million on the race. Overall the Illinois governor race broke California's 2010 spending record and became the country's most expensive governor race in history.[51] Pritzker, thanks to his estimated $3.2 billion net worth, became the country's wealthiest elected official, winning the governor's seat by roughly 16 points. Michigan's open governor race featured another female-led victory in which Democrat Gretchen Whitmer, a former state Senate Minority Leader, defeated the Trump-endorsed Republican state Attorney General Bill Schuette. Term-limited Republican Governor Rick Snyder never endorsed Schuette, exposing a hint of the deep fractures within Michigan's Republican base at the state level.[52] Meanwhile, Whitmer was able to unite progressives and moderates with her mantra of "fix the damn roads" and her focus on health care without isolating Trump voters. Whitmer won the election with a nine-point margin.

Republicans protected nine incumbents in races considered "likely" or "solid" prospects. The most impressive from this list are the two popular GOP incumbents in deep blue states: Charlie Baker of Massachusetts and Larry Hogan of Maryland. Both Baker and Hogan regularly top lists of the most popular governors in the country.[53] Democrats hoped to topple Hogan in Maryland, but Ben Jealous, the Democratic candidate and former NAACP president, had a hard time shaking the narrative that he was a radical leftist, despite his background as a venture capitalist. He was especially touchy about being called a socialist and slipped up by dropping an expletive when a reporter asked him about it.[54] Other predictably victorious Republican incumbents were Doug Ducey of Arizona, Henry McMaster of South Carolina, Kay Ivey of Alabama, Asa Hutchinson of Arkansas, Pete Ricketts of Nebraska (who was also elected chairman of the Republican Governors Association), Greg Abbott of Texas, and Phil Scott of Vermont. Republicans also elected newcomers to GOP-held open seats, including Bill Lee of Tennessee, Brad

Little of Idaho, and Mark Gordon of Wyoming. On the Democratic side, Rhode Island Governor Gina Raimondo beat back a second challenge attempt from Republican Mayor of Cranston Allan Fung, who went down by a 16-point margin. Other Democratic incumbents who won reelection by wide margins were David Ige of Hawaii, Tom Wolf of Pennsylvania, and Andrew Cuomo of New York, though at one point Cuomo did have to work hard to deter actress Cynthia Nixon, his former Democratic primary challenger, from mounting a third-party bid against him.[55] Voters in California also promoted outgoing Democratic Governor Jerry Brown's Lieutenant Governor Gavin Newsom to the top spot by a 24 point margin.

2018 STATE LEGISLATIVE ELECTIONS SUMMARY

In 2018, state legislative elections reinforced the deep partisan trend spreading across the country. According to calculations by the National Conference of State Legislatures, more than 80 percent of all 7,383 state legislative seats were up for election in 2018 and just after the primaries 21 percent of those seats had already turned over. That's a higher turnover rate than analysts normally see in a full election cycle, which signaled early on that 2018 could see a lot of flipped seats.

Republicans went into 2018 with a historically high advantage in state legislatures: they had 32 states where they controlled both chambers. Democrats had 14 states where they held both and 3 states were divided. (Nebraska has a unicameral and nonpartisan body).[56] Following the election, both chambers of every legislature in the country, except Minnesota, will be under single-party control. This marks the first time in 104 years that just one state has split control in the legislature. Democrats only picked up control in seven state legislatures, which is underwhelming considering the turnover rate from the primary season. It does not measure up to the Republican wave of 2010, when the GOP picked up more than 20 statehouse chambers.[57] The GOP won bicameral control in 30 states, while Democrats won complete control in 18 states.

2019–2020 OUTLOOK

While both parties have new governorships in their crosshairs, Republicans are going back on offense in a big way in the upcoming cycle. Fourteen states will hold gubernatorial elections in 2019 and 2020. President Trump carried 10 of them and won 9 by over 15 points. While Democrats had an extremely

favorable map in 2018, their upcoming cycle requires infiltrating Trump territory for both protecting Democrat-held seats and angling to pick up others.
Republicans, on the other hand, see the next two years as a chance to again
reach 30 governorships if they can knock off Democratic incumbents in Louisiana and North Carolina, while picking up an open seat in Montana. Democrats have to hope they can make inroads in the states of Kentucky,
Mississippi, and West Virginia, as well as put up stronger fights in New
Hampshire and Vermont, two states Hillary Clinton won but that also
reelected Republican governors in 2018.

Trump carried all three states—Louisiana, Kentucky, and Mississippi—
holding governor elections in 2019. Louisiana's Democratic Governor John
Bel Edwards will try to maximize his incumbent advantage as he prepares to
protect Democrats' only governorship in the Deep South. He entered the race
with a war chest of $8.4 million and high job approval ratings.[58] Edwards
will face at least two Republican challengers, Ralph Abraham, a congressman
from Louisiana's Fifth District, and Eddie Rispone, a wealthy Baton Rouge
businessman. Both Abraham and Rispone came to the table with less name
ID than someone like Republican Senator John Kennedy of Louisiana, who
many expected to join the race before he decided against it in December of
2018. One man who would throw a wrench in things for Edwards is U.S.
House Minority Whip Steve Scalise. He has the name recognition and popularity to pose a significant threat to the governor, but he has denied on several
occasions any interest in challenging him in 2019.[59] If the field stays as is,
Edwards' incumbency advantage, fundraising chops, and popularity make
him a favorite to hold the seat.

Republicans will also have to worry about defending an incumbent in
2019. Kentucky Governor Matt Bevin will run for reelection, but the Blue-
grass State governor faced much more criticism from within his own party at
the outset than Edwards. Bevin already had two Republican challengers, state
Representative Robert Goforth and businessman William Woods. Additionally, his 2015 primary opponent, Representative James Comer took several
opportunities to attack Bevin in local media but decided not to challenge the
incumbent. Democrats for their part fielded three strong competitors in state
Attorney General Andy Beshear, the presumed frontrunner, state House
Minority Leader Rocky Adkins, and former state Auditor Adam Edelen.
Republicans must also defend Mississippi's governor seat, which will be left
open by term-limited Republican Governor Phil Bryant. The race will likely
be a matchup between Democratic Attorney General Jim Hood and Republican Lieutenant Governor Tate Reeves, though both face challengers from
within their own parties. While Hood is uniquely popular for a Democrat in
Mississippi, Reeves has been laying the foundations for this race throughout

his career. After eight years as the state's second in command, he managed to align himself both with Bryant and President Trump and hit the ground running with $5 million in the bank.

Democrats will have to defend another incumbent in a Trump state when North Carolina Governor Roy Cooper seeks reelection in 2020. Edwards and Cooper are similar in that they are both popular Democrats in Trump-friendly states, but their challenges are different. While Louisiana is a redder state than North Carolina, the bench of Republicans gearing up to challenge Cooper appears much more formidable than the slate lining up against Edwards. Republican Lieutenant Governor Dan Forest will be a likely front-runner and former Governor Pat McCrory, the Republican who lost to Cooper in 2016, may consider a rematch. An early poll showed Cooper leading five potential challengers, including Forest and McCrory.[60] The race will likely draw additional Republicans, but Cooper's formidable fundraising capability could be a deterrent. He outraised McCrory by $8 million in 2016. The race will be a slugfest no matter what because the state will be home to a presidential, Senate, and governor battleground. Money will flow.

Montana's open-seat race to replace outgoing Democratic Governor Steve Bullock will have Republicans clamoring to run in a state Trump won by 20 points. It will likely be the most challenging defense Democrats play in the 2019–2020 cycle. Montana's Republican Secretary of State Corey Stapleton announced his bid in the early days of 2019, kicking off the race nearly two years ahead of the election. Tim Fox, the state's Republican attorney general, joined the race a few weeks later, looking to position himself as the frontrunner. On the Democratic side, Lieutenant Governor Mike Cooney is a top prospect, but he could face competition from some fresh faces in the state Democratic party, including firearms executive Ryan Busse and Whitney Williams, a businesswoman and daughter of former U.S. Representative Pat Williams. The only other definite open seat in 2020 will be in Utah, where Republican Governor Gary Herbert has suggested he would not run again. It's a solid hold prospect for the party but will likely draw a wide field of GOP hopefuls, making for an exciting primary. Among the possible Republican contenders are former Utah Representative Jason Chaffetz and Lieutenant Governor Spencer Cox.[61] On the flip side, Washington State could see an open-seat race if Democratic Governor Jay Inslee runs for president. The two-term governor could run for a third term, but if he does not, Washington will be a similarly safe open seat for Democrats that Utah is for Republicans.

West Virginia has been helmed by Governor Jim Justice since he was elected in 2016, but its governorship only became a Republican-held seat when Justice switched parties because of his alignment with President Trump. He announced his 2020 candidacy in January 2019 with the backing of the state Republican Party. Democratic Senator Joe Manchin, a former governor himself, may decide to challenge his onetime ally. News leaked that Manchin was mulling the possibility around the same time Justice announced he would run again.[62] Democrats see the deep red state as a possible pickup, especially if Manchin steps up to the plate. Democrats also point to New Hampshire and Vermont as offensive opportunities where Trump is not as popular. Hillary Clinton won both states in 2016. New Hampshire's Republican Governor Chris Sununu, in particular, may have to distance himself from the president more than he has in past years because of his state's role as a battleground in the 2020 presidential election.[63]

The rest of the races in 2020 all feature incumbents who appear relatively safe. Democratic Governor John Carney will start as a strong favorite in Delaware, and likewise the Republican governors in Indiana, Missouri, and North Dakota will have the edge to hold their places as chief executive. Overall, Republicans have a good shot at reelecting all their incumbents and protecting open seats to deliver a similar shutout that Democrats did in 2018. If they succeed in doing that and picking up the party's three top targets, Louisiana, Montana, and North Carolina, they could hold 30 governorships again by 2021. However, Democrats hope to continue the success they had in 2018, and even in the most partisan states it's difficult to unseat an incumbent.

NOTES

1. "2009 Gubernatorial Election Results," National Governors Association, https://classic.nga.org/cms/home/governors/elections/col2-content/past-election-information/2009-gubernatorial-election-resu.default.html.

2. "2014 Gubernatorial Elections Quick Facts," National Governors Association, https://classic.nga.org/files/live/sites/NGA/files/pdf/2014ElectionsQuickFacts.pdf.

3. A. G. Sulzberger, "Kansas Governor's Race Seen Redefining G.O.P.," *New York Times*, October 21, 2010, https://www.nytimes.com/2010/10/22/us/politics/22brownback.html.

4. Christina A. Cassidy and Roxana Hegeman, "Moderates Are Key to Defeating Kobach in Kansas," AP, August 15, 2018, https://apnews.com/8097208e7e0a4ad5bbe047668ce09297.

5. Geoffrey Skelley, "A Failure to Launch? Kansas' Republican Gubernatorial Contest and the History of Incumbent Governor Primary Performance," *Sabato's Crystal Ball*, August 9, 2018, http://www.centerforpolitics.org/crystalball/articles/a-failure-to-launch-kansas-republican-gubernatorial-contest-and-the-history-of-incumbent-governor-primary-performance/.

6. Dion Lefler, Bryan Lowry, Hunter Woodall, and Jonathan Shorman, "Colyer Concedes, Handing Kobach the Republican Nomination for Kansas Governor," *Wichita Eagle*,

August 14, 2018, https://www.kansas.com/news/politics-government/election/article21 6687305.html.

7. Ariel Rothfield, Cat Reid, and Andres Gutierrez, "Laura Kelly Topples Kris Kobach in Kansas Gubernatorial Race," KSHB, November 7, 2018, https://www.kshb.com/news/ political/laura-kelly-topples-kris-kobach-in-kansas-gubernatorial-race.

8. Hunter Woodall, "Another Former GOP Governor of Kansas Just Endorsed Dem Laura Kelly over Kris Kobach," *Kansas City Star*, October 19, 2018, https://www.kansas city.com/news/politics-government/election/article220180385.html.

9. "Reuters/Ipsos/UVA Center for Politics State Poll: Kansas," Ipsos, October 31, 2018, https://www.ipsos.com/sites/default/files/ct/news/documents/2018–10/october_ 2018_state_topline_-_kansas_october.pdf.

10. Matt Dixon, "Putnam's Cash Dries Up as Gubernatorial Star Fades," *Politico*, August 13, 2018, https://www.politico.com/states/florida/story/2018/08/13/putnams-cash -dries-up-as-gubernatorial-star-fades-556139.

11. Steven Lemongello, Chabeli Herrera, Kyle Arnold, Gray Rohrer, and Gabrielle Russon, "Andrew Gillum Shocks Gwen Graham to Face Ron DeSantis in Florida Gover- nor's Race," *Orlando Sentinel*, August 28, 2018, https://www.orlandosentinel.com/news/ politics/political-pulse/os-florida-primary-florida-governor-20180828-story.html.

12. Emily L. Mahoney, "How Ron DeSantis Won Florida Governor," *Tampa Bay Times*, November 6, 2018, http://www.tampabay.com/florida-politics/buzz/2018/11/06/ how-ron-desantis-won-florida-governor/.

13. Dan Merica and Sophie Tatum, "Andrew Gillum Concedes Florida Governor's Race to Ron DeSantis," CNN, November 17, 2018, https://www.cnn.com/2018/11/17/poli tics/gillum-concedes-florida-governors-race-desantis/index.html.

14. Madelaine Pisani, "Late White House Support Gives Kemp Edge in Georgia Tues- day," *National Journal*, July 23, 2018, https://www.nationaljournal.com/s/670583/late -white-house-support-gives-kemp-edge-in-georgia-tuesday.

15. Greg Bluestein, "Georgia 2018: Kemp Takes Aim at Abrams' Finances," *Atlanta Journal-Constitution*, August 8, 2018, https://www.ajc.com/blog/politics/georgia-2018 -kemp-takes-aim-abrams-finances/v3JLxB8QDlbU5Ut4rmQDZK/.

16. Gregory Krieg, "Stacey Abrams Campaign Demands GOP's Kemp Resign as Georgia Secretary of State amid Voter Registration Uproar," CNN, October 12, 2018, https://www.cnn.com/2018/10/11/politics/georgia-governor-election-voter-registration -abrams-kemp/index.html.

17. Randy Ludlow, "Cordray vs. DeWine: Performance as Attorney General Key Issue for Each in Ohio Governor's Race," *Columbus Dispatch*, August 20, 2018, https://www .dispatch.com/news/20180820/cordray-vs-dewine-performance-as-attorney-general-key -issue-for-each-in-ohio-governors-race.

18. Amy Sherman, "Ohio Republican Mike DeWine Changed Position on Medicaid Expansion," *Politifact*, July 20th, 2018, https://www.politifact.com/ohio/statements/2018/ jul/20/mike-dewine/ohio-republican-mike-dewine-changed-medicaid/.

19. Seth A. Richardson, "John Kasich to Hit the Campaign Trail for Mike DeWine after Months of Staying Out of the Race," *Cleveland.com*, October 29, 2018, https:// www.cleveland.com/open/index.ssf/2018/10/john_kasich_to_hit_the_campaig.html.

20. Randy Ludlow, "DeWine Breaks Spending Record for Governor's Race—All by Himself—to Swamp Cordray," *Columbus Dispatch*, December 14, 2018, https://www

.dispatch.com/news/20181214/dewine-breaks-spending-record-for-governors-race---all
-by-himself---to-swamp-cordray.

21. James DeHaven, "It's Sisolak vs. Laxalt Following Brutal Democratic Primary for Nevada Governor," *Reno Gazette-Journal*, June 12, 2018, https://www.rgj.com/story/news/politics/2018/06/12/who-face-laxalt-tough-democratic-primary-comes-down-wire/696959002/.

22. Michelle L. Price, "Outside Spending on Nevada Governor, Other Races Topped $48M," Associated Press, November 26, 2018, https://www.usnews.com/news/best-states/nevada/articles/2018-11-26/outside-spending-on-nevada-governor-other-races-topped-48m.

23. Michelle Rindels, "How Democrat Steve Sisolak Defeated Conservative Rising Star Adam Laxalt in Bid for Governor's Mansion," *Nevada Independent*, November 14, 2018, https://thenevadaindependent.com/article/how-democrat-steve-sisolak-defeated-conservative-rising-star-adam-laxalt-in-bid-for-governors-mansion.

24. Paulina Firozi, "The Health 202: Maine's Race for Governor Could End Medicaid Standoff," *Washington Post*, October 15, 2018, https://www.washingtonpost.com/news/powerpost/paloma/the-health-202/2018/10/15/the-health-202-maine-s-race-for-governor-could-end-medicaid-standoff/5bc39a841b326b7c8a8d19a2/?utm_term = .27d470b0456f.

25. Noel K. Gallagher, "Independent Alan Caron Ends His Run for Governor, Endorses Janet Mills," *Portland Press Herald*, October 29, 2018, https://www.pressherald.com/2018/10/29/amid-speculation-independent-candidate-for-governor-alan-caron-plans-announcement/.

26. Darren Fishell, "Maine Republicans Give Unenrolled Terry Hayes Airtime in New Attack Ad," *Bangor Daily News*, October 9, 2018, https://bangordailynews.com/2018/10/09/politics/maine-republicans-give-unenrolled-terry-hayes-airtime-in-new-attack-ad.

27. Michael Shepherd, "Election Spending in Maine Topped $65 Million in 2018. Democrats Spent More Than Half of It." *Bangor Daily News*, December 28, 2018, https://bangordailynews.com/2018/12/28/politics/daily-brief/election-spending-in-maine-topped-65-million-in-2018-democrats-spent-more-than-half-of-it/.

28. Dan Boyd, "Pearce Takes Aim at Lujan Grisham in New Campaign Ad," *Albuquerque Journal*, September 14, 2018, https://www.abqjournal.com/1220864/pearce-takes-aim-at-lujan-grisham-in-new-campaign-ad.html.

29. Steve Terrell, "Pearce Campaign Attacks Terminally Ill Man," *Santa Fe New Mexican*, September 25, 2018, http://www.santafenewmexican.com/news/local_news/pearce-campaign-attacks-terminally-ill-man/article_f6a59810-60d0-5053-9ba9-a406047117df.html.

30. Andy Lyman, "2018 Top Stories #1: Lujan Grisham Wins Election," *NM Political Report*, December 28, 2018, http://nmpoliticalreport.com/2018/12/28/2018-top-stories-1-lujan-grisham-wins-election/.

31. Eyder Peralta, "Wisconsin Gov. Scott Walker Survives Recall," NPR, June 5, 2012, https://www.npr.org/sections/itsallpolitics/2012/06/05/154384654/live-blog-wisconsin-decides-governors-fate-in-recall-vote.

32. Madelaine Pisani and Kyle Trygstad, "Hotline's Governor Power Rankings," *National Journal*, November 1, 2018, https://www.nationaljournal.com/s/674316/hotlines-governor-power-rankings.

33. Mark Sommerhauser, "What Sank Scott Walker? His Ambition, His Record, Tony

Evers, and the Donald Trump Backlash," *Wisconsin State Journal*, November 11, 2018, https://madison.com/wsj/news/local/govt-and-politics/what-sank-scott-walker-his -ambition-his-record-tony-evers/article_38932b3b-1f7e-5e24-b61f-27f6e011d69 2.html.

34. "Obama, Biden Announce Wisconsin Visits," Associated Press, October 24, 2018, https://journaltimes.com/news/local/obama-biden-announce-wisconsin-visits/ article_b4a99260-1132-5f76-a878-5910da0ac5a5.html.

35. Rachana Pradhan, "Iowa Governor Signs Most Restrictive Abortion Ban in Country," *Politico*, May 5, 2018, https://www.politico.com/story/2018/05/04/iowa-abortion -ban-kim-reynolds-569680.

36. Brianne Pfannenstiel, Kim Norvell, and Kevin Hardy, "Iowa Election 2018: Kim Reynolds Wins Full Term, a Validation of the Republican Policies She Has Led," *Des Moines Register*, November 7, 2018, https://www.desmoinesregister.com/story/news/poli tics/elections/2018/11/05/iow a-election-2018-results-governor-republican-kim-reynolds -democrat -fred-hubbell-jake-porter-vote/1732343002/.

37. Kevin Hardy, Kim Norvell, and Brianne Pfannenstiel, "These Four Counties Show How Kim Reynolds Won the Historically Tight Iowa Governor Race," *Des Moines Register*, November 7, 2018, https://www.desmoinesregister.com/story/news/politics/2018/11/ 07/republican-kim-reynolds-iowa-governor-fred-hubbell-congress/1918899002/.

38. Becky Bohrer, "Alaska Primary Sets Stage for Three-Way Governor's Race," Associated Press, August 22, 2018, https://www.pbs.org/newshour/politics/alaska-pri mary-sets-stage-for-three-way-governors-race.

39. Annie Zak, Tegan Hanlon, Alex DeMarban, "Alaska Lt. Gov. Byron Mallott Abruptly Resigns following 'Inappropriate Comments,'" *Anchorage Daily News*, October 16, 2018, https://www.adn.com/politics/2018/10/16/alaska-lt-gov-byron-mallott-abruptly -resigns-followiing-inappropriate-comments/.

40. Connor Radnovich, "Kate Brown Wins Race for Oregon's Governor, Easily Defeating Knute Buehler," *Salem Statesman Journal*, November 7, 2018, https://www .statesmanjournal.com/story/news/politics/2018/11/06/kate-brown-knute-buehler -oregons-governor/1780303002/.

41. Connor Radnovich, "Independent Candidate Starnes Drops Out of Oregon Governor's Race, Endorses Kate Brown," *Salem Statesman Journal*, October 30, 2018, https:// www.statesmanjournal.com/story/news/politics/2018/10/30/oregon-election-governor -candidate-drops-out-endorses-kate-brown/1822196002/.

42. Hillary Borrud, "Political Spending in Oregon Governor's Race Tops $37 Million, Shatters Old record," *Oregonian*, November 20, 2018, https://www.oregonlive.com/poli tics/2018/11/political-spending-in-oregon-governors-race-tops-37-million-shatters-old -record.html.

43. Madelaine Pisani, "RGA Backs Out as Poll Shows Walz Leading," *National Journal*, September 17, 2018, https://www.nationaljournal.com/s/672538/rga-backs-out-as -poll-shows-walz-leading.

44. James Anderson and Colleen Slevin, "Colorado's Jared Polis Makes History as Gay Governor," Associated Press, January 8, 2019, https://www.tulsaworld.com/news/ government/ap/colorado-s-jared-polis-makes-history-as-gay-governor/ar ticle_3e5775d9-5e1e-5d17-b66d-51ac32c78365.html.

45. Nick Coltrain, "Colorado Governor: Jared Polis Is First Openly Gay Man Elected Governor in US," *Fort Collins Coloradoan*, November 6, 2018, https://www.coloradoan

.com/story/news/politics/elections/2018/11/06/colorado-governor-jared-polis-wins-2018
-race-against-walker-stapleton/1862928002/.

46. Harriet Jones, Ray Hardman, and Patrick Skahill, "Democrat Ned Lamont Wins
Connecticut Governor's Race," Connecticut Public Radio, November 7, 2018, https://
www.wbur.org/news/2018/11/07/democrat-ned-lamont-wins-connecticut-governors-race.

47. Alex Clearfield, "Oklahoma's Outgoing Governor Weighs on Race to Replace
Her," *National Journal*, August 20, 2018, https://www.nationaljournal.com/s/671647/
oklahomas-outgoing-governor-weighs-on-race-to-replace-her.

48. Jonathan Ellis, "Ellis: How a GOP Rescue Party Saved Kristi Noem's Campaign
for Governor," *Sioux Falls Argus Leader*, November 10, 2018, https://www.argusleader
.com/story/news/2018/11/10/kristi-noem-governor-won-election-results-2018/
1930329002/.

49. Adam Sexton, "She's with Her: @HillaryClinton to Headline Boston Fundraiser
for @NHMollyKelly Next Weekend," WMUR, https://twitter.com/AdamSextonWMUR/
status/1053363937079640069.

50. John DiStaso, "NH Primary Source: Democratic Poll Claims Dead Heat in Governor's Race as RGA Ups Its Anti-Kelly Buy," WMUR, November 2, 2018, https://www
.wmur.com/article/nh-primary-source-democratic-poll-claims-dead-heat-in-governors
-race-as-rga-ups-its-anti-kelly-buy/24576396.

51. Greg Bishop, "Illinois' Gubernatorial Race Sets National Spending Record," *Illinois News Network*, January 17, 2019, accessed on January 22, 2019, https://www.ilnews
.org/news/state_politics/illinois-gubernatorial-race-sets-national-spending-record/
article_81122c72-1a91-11e9-8ce1-438f59ef61ef.html.

52. Madelaine Pisani, "The GOP's Uphill Battle in Michigan," *National Journal*, September 30, 2018, https://www.nationaljournal.com/s/673042/the-gops-uphill-battle-in
-michigan.

53. Cameron Easley, "America's Most and Least Popular Governors," *Morning Consult*, January 10, 2019, https://morningconsult.com/2019/01/10/americas-most-and-least
-popular-governors-q4-2018/.

54. Baltimore Sun Editorial Board, "Ben Jealous Isn't a Socialist, but He's Sure
Touchy about Being Called One," *Baltimore Sun*, January 10, 2019, https://www.balti
moresun.com/news/opinion/editorial/bs-ed-0813-jealous-socialist-20180810-story.html.

55. Jesse McKinley and Shane Goldmacher, "Progressives Grudgingly Offer Ballot
Line to Gov. Cuomo after Backing Cynthia Nixon," *New York Times*, October 3, 2018,
https://www.nytimes.com/2018/10/03/nyregion/cynthia-nixon-andrew-cuomo-wfp-ballot
-election.html.

56. Tim Storey and Wendy Underhill, "A Wave or a Wash? Midterm Outcomes Will
Depend on How Voters Feel about Trump," National Council of State Legislatures, October 31, 2018, http://www.ncsl.org/research/elections-and-campaigns/midterm-legislative
-elections-a-wave-or-a-wash.aspx.

57. Adam Nagourney and Sydney Ember, "Election Consolidates One-Party Control
over State Legislatures," *New York Times*, November 7, 2018, https://www.nytimes.com/
2018/11/07/us/politics/statehouse-elections.html.

58. Cameron Easley, "America's Most and Least Popular Governors," *Morning Consult*, January 10, 2019, https://morningconsult.com/2019/01/10/americas-most-and-least
-popular-governors-q4-2018/.

59. Bryn Stole, "U.S. Rep. Steve Scalise, on Whirlwind Book Tour, Rejects Run for Governor and Returns to Congress," *New Orleans Advocate*, November 12, 2018, https://www.theadvocate.com/new_orleans/news/politics/article_73e92078-e6d4–11e8-ba3a-4f50baaa4d9f.html?utm_medium = social&utm_source;eqtwitter&utm_campaign = user-share.

60. "North Carolina Looks Like Battleground Once Again for 2020," Public Policy Polling, January 9, 2019, https://www.publicpolicypolling.com/polls/north-carolina-looks-like-battleground-once-again-for-2020/.

61. Benjamin Wood, "Gov. Chaffetz? Former Utah Congressman Leads Field of Potential 2020 Republican Candidates for Governor," *Salt Lake Tribune*, July 8, 2018, https://www.sltrib.com/news/politics/2018/07/02/gov-chaffetz-former-utah/.

62. Jeff Jenkins, "Manchin Says West Virginia Deserves, Needs 'Full-Time' Governor," *WV Metro* News, January 11, 2019, http://wvmetronews.com/2019/01/11/manchin-says-west-virginia-needs-full-time-governor/.

63. Madelaine Pisani, "Democrats Face Tougher Gubernatorial Terrain," *National Journal*, January 15, 2019, https://www.nationaljournal.com/s/675991/democrats-face-tougher-gubernatorial-terrain.

8

The Money Wars

Emerging Campaign Finance Trends and Their Impact on 2018 and Beyond

Michael E. Toner and Karen E. Trainer

Continuing a trend over the last few decades of ever-increasingly expensive election cycles, the 2018 election was the costliest midterm election in history, with approximately $5.2 billion raised and spent in total.[1] To put that aggregate figure in perspective, only approximately $4 billion[2] was spent overall on the last midterm election in 2014. The historic spending tally during the 2018 election cycle was fueled primarily by record-breaking fundraising by campaign committees and outside groups.

Although unprecedented amounts of funds were raised and spent on the 2018 midterm election overall, it is important to note that not all sectors of the campaign finance system shared equally in the money bounty. Notably, aggregate national political party fundraising increased only slightly during the 2018 election cycle compared with the 2014 cycle, and political party spending represented a much smaller share of total election-related spending in 2018. Increasingly, we are seeing a tale of two fundraising stories—one story for Super PACs and outside groups, which can accept unlimited contributions and which are thriving—and a very different landscape for political parties, which are forced to operate under strict contribution limits and prohibitions. Absent legislative action, this imbalance in the campaign finance system could become even more pronounced in future election cycles.

CONGRESSIONAL CAMPAIGNS RAISED
RECORD AMOUNTS IN 2018

Analysts project that the total cost of the 2018 midterm election was $5.2 billion,[3] which represents a 30 percent increase over 2014 midterm election spending. One major factor contributing to this surge in election spending in 2018 was a major increase in congressional campaign committee fundraising.[4] In particular, Democratic candidates, and especially Democratic House candidates, outraised their Republican counterparts by significant amounts. In total, House and Senate campaign committees raised $1 billion more than in 2016. Table 8.1 below outlines House and Senate campaign committee fundraising across time in 2018, 2016, and 2014.

As is noted in Table 8.1 below, Democratic candidates for the House and Senate raised a combined $1.6 billion in the 2018 election cycle, compared to $1.1 billion raised by their Republican counterparts. Through the end of the third quarter of 2018, Democratic candidates had outraised their Republican opponents in 53 out of 73 competitive races.[5] In the third quarter of 2018 alone, Democratic House candidates raised $250 million, compared to only $111 million raised by Republican House candidates.[6] Also in the third quarter, a remarkable 92 Democratic challengers outraised their Republican incumbent opponents.[7]

In one of the most expensive races of the election cycle, Senator Ted Cruz and Representative Beto O'Rourke set the record for the most ever spent collectively by candidates in a Senate election—$93 million total—in their marquee race in Texas. The previous record was $92 million in spending for the 2000 New York Senate race between Rick Lazio and Hillary Rodham Clinton.[8] In total, 89 percent of House races were won by the biggest spender, while 84 percent of Senate races were won by the biggest spender.[9]

Congressional Campaigns Raised Record Amounts in 2018

A significant amount of contributions to Democratic congressional candidates—including 55 percent of contributions made by individuals—were processed through ActBlue,[10] which describes itself as "a nonprofit, building fundraising technology for the left" with the goal of "help[ing] small-dollar donors make their voices heard in a real way."[11] ActBlue allows donors to save their credit card information when making a contribution, which makes additional contributions easier and allows candidates to raise funds for each other. For example, both Senators Elizabeth Warren and Kamala Harris used ActBlue to help raise funds for a number of Democratic

Table 8.1   Comparison of House and Senate Campaign Committee Fundraising

2018

Republican House Campaign Committees	$659 Million	Democratic House Campaign Committees	$1.0 Billion
Republican Senate Campaign Committees	$444 Million	Democratic Senate Campaign Committees	$587 Million
Republican Campaign Total	$1.1 Billion	Democratic Campaign Total	$1.6 Billion

2018 Total Campaign Fundraising: $2.7 Billion

2016

Republican House Campaign Committees	$558 Million	Democratic House Campaign Committees	$469 Million
Republican Senate Campaign Committees	$302 Million	Democratic Senate Campaign Committees	$363 Million
Republican Campaign Total	$861 Million	Democratic Campaign Total	$833 Million

2016 Total Campaign Fundraising (Not Including Presidential Campaigns): $1.7 Billion

2014

Republican House Campaign Committees	$587 Million	Democratic House Campaign Committees	$455 Million
Republican Senate Campaign Committees	$376 Million	Democratic Senate Campaign Committees	$337 Million
Republican Campaign Total	$963 Million	Democratic Campaign Total	$792 Million

2014 Total Campaign Fundraising: $1.77 Billion

Source: Center for Responsive Politics, https://www.opensecrets.org/overview/index.php?display = T&type = A&cycle = 2014, https://www.opensecrets.org/overview/index.php?display = T&type = A&cycle = 2016, https://www.opensecrets.org/overview/index.php?display = T&type = A&cycle = 2018.
2018 election cycle totals include fundraising data reported to the FEC through November 26, 2018. Election cycle totals for 2016 and 2014 include fundraising data reported to the FEC through December 31 of the election year. Campaign fundraising totals for the cycle may not add up exactly because of rounding.

House challengers across the country.[12] All told, ActBlue processed a total of $1.6 billion in contributions during the 2018 election cycle, which was double the amount ActBlue handled in the 2016 election cycle.[13] ActBlue also had more than three million new donors in 2017–2018, with an average contribution size of $40.[14]

By contrast, on the Republican side, there are multiple for-profit online fundraising firms that raise funds for campaigns and other political committees. The fragmentation between different vendors has limited the ability of the various vendors to provide conveniences such as saved credit card numbers and fundraising by one candidate for another. Many Republicans, including the Republican National Committee (RNC) chair, have voiced concerns over the lack of a Republican counterpart to ActBlue,[15] and creating an Act-Blue-like entity on the right is a major fundraising imperative for the Republican Party in the years ahead.

A Number of Candidates Did Not Accept Contributions from Corporate PACs

In 2008, under the direction of Barack Obama's presidential campaign, the Democratic National Committee (DNC) ceased accepting contributions from federally registered lobbyists. Although this prohibition was rescinded in 2016,[16] the DNC explored new restrictions on certain types of contributions during the 2018 cycle. For example, the DNC passed a resolution in June 2018 indicating it would reject contributions from fossil fuel industry PACs.[17] However, the resolution was reversed two months later.[18]

Following the trend of rejecting contributions from certain sources, a number of candidates also explored imposing restrictions on campaign contributions in 2018. A whopping 72 percent of so-called "Red to Blue" candidates[19]—which received national party funds and support—pledged not to accept corporate PAC money.[20] In total, 52 members of the new Congress rejected corporate PAC contributions at some point during the 2018 election cycle. Of these members, 50 are Democrats and 35 are newly elected members.[21]

The rejection of corporate PAC contributions by primarily Democratic candidates did not appear to have an impact on total PAC contributions to Democratic candidates. In fact, PACs overall actually increased their contributions to Democratic candidates in the 2018 election cycle, contributing $207.8 million compared to $191.8 million in the 2016 election cycle.[22] However, if the rejection of corporate PAC contributions continues to grow in future election cycles—particularly if it involves members almost exclusively from one side of the political aisle as is currently the case—it may ultimately erode the role and importance of corporate PACs in American politics. For example, if corporate PACs are only able to contribute a tiny fraction of their funds to Democratic candidates, the PACs may increasingly become perceived as partisan entities, which could make it more difficult for the PACs to raise funds from rank-and-file corporate employees. Some analysts predict that rejecting contributions from federal lobbyists—mirroring the DNC's ban on lobbyist contributions during the Obama administration—may be the next major fundraising development to take place in congressional elections.[23]

SPENDING BY OUTSIDE GROUPS ALSO
BROKE RECORDS IN 2018

The passage of the McCain-Feingold campaign finance law in 2002, combined with court decisions permitting unlimited corporate, union, and individual contributions to finance independent expenditures sponsored by outside organizations such as Super PACs and 501(c) organizations, has led to a proliferation of outside groups in recent years that are having a growing impact on federal elections. These outside groups, which have flourished on both the right and the left, are increasingly engaged in political activities that were once the province of political parties, such as voter registration drives, absentee ballot programs, GOTV, voter identification, and political advertising and issue advocacy efforts.

The McCain-Feingold law, which took effect during the 2004 presidential election cycle, prohibits the RNC, the DNC, and the other national political party committees from raising or spending soft-money funds for any purpose. "Soft money" is defined as funds raised outside of the prohibitions and limitations of federal law, including corporate and labor union general treasury funds and individual contributions in excess of federal limits. Funds raised in accordance with federal law come from individuals and from federally registered PACs and are harder to raise; hence, these funds are commonly referred to in campaign finance parlance as "hard money." Prior to McCain-Feingold, the national political parties were legally permitted to accept unlimited corporate, union, and individual soft-money contributions and could use these funds to help underwrite a wide variety of political and electoral activities, including voter registration efforts, absentee ballot drives, GOTV activities, slate cards, and similar ticket-wide political activities. The national political parties prior to McCain-Feingold were also able to use soft-money contributions to help finance issue advertisements supporting and opposing federal candidates. "Issue advertisements" are public communications that frequently attack or promote federal candidates and their records, but which refrain from expressly advocating the election or defeat of any candidate (which is referred to as "express advocacy").

In *Citizens United v. FEC*, the U.S. Supreme Court in 2010 struck down the long-standing prohibition on corporate independent expenditures in connection with federal elections. That same year, in *SpeechNow v. FEC*, a federal appeals court invalidated limits on contributions from individuals to political committees that fund only independent expenditures for or against federal candidates. In advisory opinions issued after the *SpeechNow* decision, the Federal Election Commission (FEC) concluded that political committees formed strictly to make independent expenditures supporting or opposing federal candidates could accept unlimited contributions from individuals, corporations, and labor organizations.[24] These new kinds of political committees, which are prohibited from making contributions to federal candidates and to other federal political committees, are commonly referred to as "Super PACs."

501(c) entities are organized and operate under Section 501(c) of the Internal Revenue Code and include social welfare organizations established under Section 501(c)(4) and trade associations and business leagues organized under Section 501(c)(6). Section 501(c)(4) and 501(c)(6) entities are permitted to accept unlimited corporate, union, and individual contributions and may engage in partisan political activities, provided such political activities are not their primary purpose. By contrast, Super PACs, as political committees registered with the FEC, are by definition partisan entities and may spend all of their funds on partisan political activities. Super PACs are required to publicly disclose their donors, whereas 501(c) organizations are generally not.

In the 2018 election cycle, outside group spending totaled an estimated $1.31 billion, which represented a remarkable 61 percent increase over outside spending in 2014.[25] During the 2018 election cycle, an estimated 38.4 percent of election-related advertisements were aired by outside organizations such as 501(c)(4) organizations, which are not legally required to publicly disclose their donors. An additional 42.2 percent of advertisements were reportedly aired by groups that are required to disclose their donors but which accepted contributions from entities that are not required to disclose their donors.[26]

Super PACs supporting Democratic candidates had a notable fundraising and spending edge over their Republican counterparts in 2018, mirroring the Democratic fundraising advantage on the candidate side. In the last week before the election, Super PACs supporting Democratic candidates spent $82.4 million compared with only $40.5 million by Super PACs supporting Republican candidates.[27] Table 8.2 lists the largest non-party outside spenders of the 2018 election cycle.

Because Super PACs and 501(c) organizations may not make contributions to federal campaign committees, traditional PACs—which can only accept donations subject to federal contribution limits and source prohibitions—remain an important vehicle for supporting federal candidates.[28] Table 8.3 below lists the 10 largest PACs based upon the total amounts contributed to candidates during the 2018 election cycle. Each of these PACs are "connected" PACs associated with corporations, trade associations, labor organizations, and membership organizations. A number of

Table 8.2   Largest Non-Party Outside Spenders (2018 Election Cycle)

Name	Entity Type	2017–2018 Disclosed Spending
Congressional Leadership Fund	Super PAC	$137,501,727
Senate Majority PAC	Super PAC	$112,847,349
Senate Leadership Fund	Super PAC	$95,054,956
House Majority PAC	Super PAC	$71,623,390
Majority Forward	501(c)	$45,862,781
Independence USA PAC	Super PAC	$37,506,875
America First	Super PAC/501(c)	$31,474,416
New Republican PAC	Super PAC	$30,508,059
Women Vote!	Super PAC	$28,022,551
Priorities USA Action	Hybrid PAC	$27,503,213

Source: Center for Responsive Politics, https://www.opensecrets.org/outsidespending/summ.php?cycle=2018&chrt=V&disp=O&type=P.

Table 8.3   Largest PACs by Total Contributions Made (2018 Election Cycle)

PAC Name	2017–2018 Total Contributions
National Beer Wholesalers Assn PAC	$3,038,500
AT&T Inc PAC	$2,858,700
Northrop Grumman PAC	$2,734,740
National Assn of Realtors PAC	$2,595,250
Sheet Metal, Air, Rail & Transportation Union PAC	$2,493,450
American Bankers Assn PAC	$2,462,130
National Air Traffic Controllers Assn PAC	$2,445,000
Operating Engineers Union PAC	$2,434,109
Credit Union National Assn PAC	$2,388,500
Lockheed Martin PAC	$2,340,500

Source: Center for Responsive Politics, https://www.opensecrets.org/pacs/toppacs.php.

connected PACs disseminated advertisements supporting or opposing federal candidates in addition to making direct contributions to candidates.

Spending by Outside Groups Also Broke Records in 2018

A number of Super PACs, which have come to be known as "pop-up PACs," structured their activities such that their donors were not publicly disclosed until after the election. While a limited number of Super PACs operated in this manner in 2016, a larger number did so in 2018. In the 2016 election cycle, approximately $9 million in primary election spending corresponded to incoming contributions disclosed after the election. In the 2018 election cycle, this total increased to $15.6 million in spending on primary and special elections with donor disclosure delayed until after the election.[29]

One strategy that a number of these pop-up Super PACs used to delay public disclosure of their donors was registering with the FEC after the close of books for the last disclosure report due before Election Day. These Super PACs were required to disclose information about certain independent expenditures within 24 hours of disseminating the independent expenditures, but were not required to disclose information concerning their donors until after the election. Specifically, Super PACs that followed this strategy for the 2018 general election registered on or after October 18, 2018, and were not required to disclose their donors until December 6, 2018, which was a month after Election Day.

For example, a Super PAC called Texas Forever registered with the FEC on October 19, 2018, and spent $2.3 million in connection with the Texas Senate race.[30] The PAC was not required to disclose that its funding came from the Super PAC Senate Majority Fund until December 6, 2018.[31] In total, 44 PACs formed between October 18 and November 2, 2018.[32]

Similarly, a number of Super PACs that were already registered with the FEC engaged in a significant amount of activity in connection with the 2018 general election on or after October 18, 2018. For example, a Super PAC called DefendArizona had approximately $300,000 cash on hand as of October 17, 2018, but spent $7.71 million in connection with the Arizona Senate race after that date. Although the PAC was required to disclose certain information concerning its expenditures within 24 hours, the source of the majority of the $7.71 million in funds that the PAC spent was not disclosed until after Election Day.[33]

Given that pop-up Super PACs became more prevalent during the 2018 election—and some of them raised many millions of dollars from donors that were not publicly disclosed until after Election Day—it is likely this phenomenon will become more widespread in future election cycles. Because the PAC strategies outlined above are compliant with the law and the FEC's reporting requirements, some campaign finance observers would like Congress to amend the law for future election cycles, but it appears highly doubtful that Congress will act in this area anytime soon.[34]

Individuals Contributed to Super PACs in Unprecedented Amounts

In April 2014, the Supreme Court in *McCutcheon v. FEC* invalidated the individual biennial aggregate limit on federal campaign contributions as unconstitutional under the First Amendment. Since the 1970s, federal law had capped the total amount of money that individuals could contribute to federal candidates and other federal political committees collectively during each two-year election cycle. Before this biennial aggregate contribution limit was struck down, individuals were prohibited from contributing more than $123,200 to all federal candidates and political committees combined during the 2014 election cycle. The aggregate contribution limit existed in addition to the per-recipient "base limit" that applies to particular campaign committees, political party committees, and other federal political committees.[35] With the aggregate contribution limit gone, individual donors now only need adhere to the base contribution limits and are free to contribute to an unlimited number of candidate committees and other political committees.

Since the *McCutcheon* decision, a number of individuals have made contributions to congressional candidates, political party committees and other political committees in excess of what was legally permissible when the aggregate contribution cap was in effect. Moreover, separate and apart from the *McCutcheon* decision, since 2010 an astounding 20 percent of all Super PAC receipts—totaling $1 billion—came from just 11 individuals.[36] Consistent with this multi-year trend, from the beginning of the 2018 election cycle through November 2, 2018, 56 individuals had each contributed in excess of $2 million to Super PACs. Contributions from these 56 individuals totaled almost $481 million and comprised 37 percent of total contributions to all Super PACs during the 2018 election cycle.[37]

Table 8.4 below lists the top 10 individual donors to Super PACs during the 2018 election cycle. Some of these individuals were also among the top 10 individual donors to Super PACs in the 2016 election cycle as well. The total contributed by Sheldon and Miriam Adelson represented the highest total contributions from a single household within an election cycle.[38]

POLITICAL PARTY EXPENDITURES REPRESENTED A SMALLER SHARE OF TOTAL OUTSIDE GROUP SPENDING

There are growing indications that national political party committees are struggling to remain as relevant as they once were in federal elections as spending increasingly shifts to Super PACs and other outside groups that are not subject to the hard-dollar fundraising requirements that apply to the national political parties.[39] As Figure 8.1 demonstrates, despite a slight increase in fundraising, total spending by national political party committees during the 2018 election cycle comprised a noticeably smaller proportion of

Table 8.4   Top Individual Super PAC Donors, 2017–2018 Election Cycle

Donor Name	Total Amount	Ideology
*Sheldon and Miriam Adelson	$112,250,000	100% Rep
*Michael Bloomberg	$59,234,421	100% Dem
*Thomas Steyer	$58,745,251	100% Dem
Richard Uihlein	$36,925,000	100% Rep
*James H and Marilyn H. Simons	$16,716,000	100% Dem
*S. Donald Sussman	$13,275,000	100% Dem
Stephen A. Scwarzman	$11,750,000	100% Rep
Kenneth C. Griffin	$10,250,000	100% Rep
Jeff Bezos	$10,129,170	**N/A
Timothy Mellon	$10,010,000	100% Rep

Source: Center for Responsive Politics, https://www.opensecrets.org/outsidespending/summ.php?cycle=2018&disp=D&type=V&superonly=S and https://www.opensecrets.org/outsidespending/summ.php?cycle=2016&disp=D&type=V&superonly=S.
* Denotes an individual who was also among the top 10 contributors to Super PACs during the 2016 election cycle.
** Jeff Bezos made a single contribution to a Super PAC that supported both Democratic and Republican candidates.

overall outside spending than was the case during the 2014 midterm election cycle. In 2014, spending by national political parties constituted 30 percent of total outside spending; in 2018, this percentage dropped to only 18 percent.

Because outside groups do not labor under the hard-dollar fundraising restrictions that apply to the national political parties, outside groups can raise large amounts of money from a small group of donors in a very short period of time. In addition, Super PACs, 501(c) organizations, and other types of outside groups are now spending more on independent expenditures and other election-related communications than are political party committees.

The biggest outside spenders in the 2018 election cycle included Super PACs associated with members of the House and Senate leadership, such as the Senate Majority PAC, House Majority PAC, Senate Leadership Fund, and Congressional Leadership Fund.[40] These Super PACs are frequently run by individuals who previously worked for congressional leadership or are otherwise known by senior members of Congress.[41] These four PACs raised over four times as much money in 2018 as they did in 2014, while national political party committee fundraising in 2018 only increased slightly over 2014.[42] Three of these four Super PACs outraised the corresponding political party committees and almost 90 percent of their funds came from donors contributing $100,000 or more.[43]

Through October 21, 2018, national political party committees and Super PACs tied to congressional leadership were responsible for 59 percent of general election independent expenditures during the 2018 election cycle.[44]

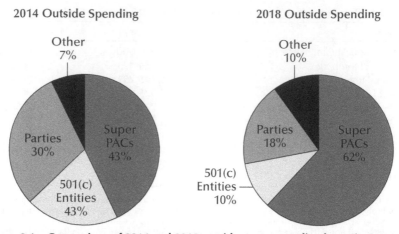

Figure 8.1   Comparison of 2014 and 2018 outside group spending by entity type.
Center for Responsive Politics. Created by Michael E. Toner and Karen E. Trainer. htps://
www.opensecrets.org/outsidespending/fes_summ.php?cycle=2014; htps://
www.opensecrets.org/outsidespending/fes_summ.php?cycle=2018.

In addition to this increase in spending on independent expenditures by outside groups, national political party committees decreased their spending on independent expenditures. In 2018, the national political parties spent $228 million on independent expenditures, compared to $243 million in 2014.[45]

Tables 8.5 and 8.6 and Figure 8.2 detail national party fundraising figures for the 2018 election cycle and as compared with the 2014 and 2010 election cycles.

One fascinating element of national political party fundraising in 2018 was the extraordinary fundraising advantage that the DCCC enjoyed over the NRCC, which was all the more remarkable given that Republicans controlled the House of Representatives. As was noted in Table 8.5 above, the DCCC raised $274,186,744 for the 2018 election, which was 67 percent more than the NRCC's $164,038,224. Analysis of DCCC and NRCC FEC reports

Table 8.5   2017–2018 National Political Party Committee Receipts

DNC	$142,297,947	RNC	$261,618,953
DSCC	$136,043,851	NRSC	$133,936,464
DCCC	$274,186,744	NRCC	$164,038,224
Total Democratic	$552,528,542	Total Republican	$559,593,641

Source: Federal Election Commission Data. Totals have been adjusted to exclude "Other Receipts," which include contributions to sub-accounts for recounts and other legal proceedings, party headquarters buildings, and conventions.

Table 8.6   Comparison of National Political Party Fundraising

Year	Party	Nominal Dollars	2018 Dollars
2018	Democratic Party Committees	$553 Million	$553 Million
2018	Republican Party Committees	$559.6 Million	$559.6 Million
	2018 Total	**1.112 Billion**	**1.112 Billion**
2014	Democratic Party Committees	$530.3 Million	$562.5 Million
2014	Republican Party Committees	$465.8 Million	$494.1 Million
	2014 Total	**$996.1 Million**	**$1.056 Billion**
2010	Democratic Party Committees	$518.3 Million	$596.83 Million
2010	Republican Party Committees	$444.7 Million	$512.08 Million
	2010 Total	**$963 Million**	**$1.108 Billion**

Source: Federal Election Commission Data. Totals in the "2018 Dollars" column have been adjusted for inflation. Totals for the 2018 election cycle have been adjusted to exclude "Other Receipts," which include contributions to sub-accounts for recounts and other legal proceedings, party headquarters buildings, and conventions. 2018 election cycle totals include fundraising data reported to the FEC through November 26, 2018. Election cycle totals for 2016 and 2014 include fundraising data reported to the FEC through December 31 of the election year.
Note: Dollar amounts have been adjusted for inflation.

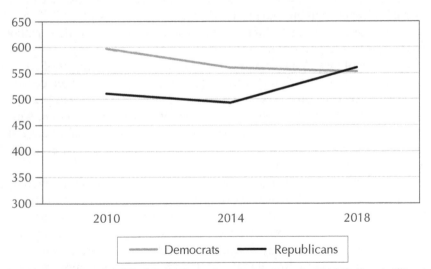

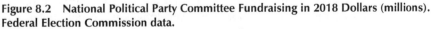

Figure 8.2   National Political Party Committee Fundraising in 2018 Dollars (millions). Federal Election Commission data.

reveals that the DCCC and NRCC each raised approximately $44 million from PACs. However, the DCCC raised $201,895,302 from individuals, compared to the NRCC's $61,327,615.[46]

EARLY VOTING LAWS CONTINUED TO HAVE A MAJOR IMPACT ON CAMPAIGN STRATEGY IN 2018

For many years, voters who expected to be absent from their home communities on Election Day could apply for an absentee ballot and could cast an absentee ballot prior to the election. However, in order to obtain an absentee ballot, many jurisdictions required voters to show cause or otherwise explain why they were not able to vote on Election Day in their local precincts, which reduced the number of people who voted absentee.[47] In 1980, California amended its laws to permit voters to cast ballots before Election Day without providing any excuse or showing any cause.[48] In succeeding decades, many more states changed their laws to permit voters to vote prior to Election Day without cause, either in person or by mail. Some states today allow voters to become permanent absentee voters and automatically receive absentee ballots for each election without having to submit a request. As of late 2018, 38 states and the District of Columbia had some form of early voting, without requiring voters to provide an excuse.[49]

As a result of these legal changes across the country, the number of Americans voting prior to Election Day has exploded during the last three decades, reaching 16 percent of voters in 2000 and 22 percent of voters by 2004.[50] Approximately 39 million votes were cast early in the 2008 election, which constituted 30 percent of the total votes cast.[51] As of the day before the 2018 election, an estimated 36 million people had voted early, compared to 27.2 million early voters in 2014.[52]

Some election analysts have concluded that it is unclear whether the rising popularity of early voting impacts voter turnout overall or has an effect on the outcome of elections.[53] However, the extraordinary increase in early voting has had a profound impact on the strategies and tactics employed by modern campaigns. For many years, the last 72 hours before Election Day were the primary focus for GOTV efforts, but now those campaign operations must be performed for a month or even longer in certain states. For example, in a special primary election held in Georgia in early 2017, Democrat Jon Ossoff's campaign released advertisements on the first day of early voting in several counties, while his main opponent did not. Ossoff won significantly more absentee and mail-in votes than in-person votes cast on Election Day.[54]

With some election scholars projecting that up to half the electorate will vote early in the years ahead, there is no question that future campaigns will closely track any changes in early voting laws and will continue to expand their GOTV and voter contact strategies accordingly. There is no longer a single Election Day in America but rather a multi-week election window, and maximizing early voting margins will increasingly be a key strategic priority of future campaigns.

LOOKING AHEAD TO 2020

President Donald J. Trump made history in 2016 by becoming the first presidential candidate in the modern era to win the presidency while being significantly outspent by both his Republican rivals during the primaries and by Hillary Rodham Clinton during the general election. Trump was able to achieve this notable feat in part by bypassing the traditional media and communicating directly with voters, excelling at social media, and attracting tremendous amounts of earned media coverage. In many ways, Trump's election called into question the long-standing assumption in campaign finance literature that a presidential candidate can never raise enough money and that those candidates who can afford to pay for huge campaign staffs and paid advertising programs have a major advantage in winning their party's nomination and in ultimately capturing the White House.

President Trump has continued to be a campaign finance innovator since the 2016 election, becoming the first president to actively fundraise for his reelection campaign during the first two years of his term. By the fall of 2018, Trump had already raised in excess of $100 million for his reelection campaign and associated fundraising committees,[55] and the president reportedly planned to continue raising tens of millions of dollars for his reelection campaign through the fall and winter of 2018–2019. Given that aggressive fundraising profile—and the many advantages of incumbency in modern presidential politics—it is difficult to envision any serious Republican primary challenger emerging against Trump in 2020.

On the Democratic side, as of this writing it appears that a large number of top-tier candidates will enter the race during the first quarter of 2019 and that a number of them—including Senators Kamala Harris, Cory Booker, and Elizabeth Warren—have the potential to be top-tier candidates and raise significant funds. One wild card is whether former Vice President Joseph Biden decides to run—if he does, he will be able to immediately draw upon an established, nationwide fundraising network. A second wild card is whether former New York City Mayor Michael Bloomberg—who has the ability to spend hundreds of millions of dollars of his own money on a campaign—enters the race; if Bloomberg does, it will place an even greater premium on fundraising in order to be a top-tier candidate in the Democratic primary.

All and all, the stage is set for the 2020 presidential contest to be as highly competitive as the 2016 race and to feature unexpected campaign finance developments and innovations.

NOTES

1. Center for Responsive Politics, "Blue Wave of Money Propels 2018 Election to Record-Breaking $5.2 Billion in Spending," October 29, 2018, https://www.opensecrets.org/news/2018/10/2018-midterm-record-breaking-5–2-billion/.

2. Rebecca Ballhous, "At $4 Billion, 2014 Is Most Expensive Midterm Ever," *Wall Street Journal,* October 23, 2014.

3. Unless otherwise noted, totals in this chapter are in nominal dollars that have not been adjusted for inflation. Totals that have been adjusted for inflation are listed in 2018 dollars.

4. Individuals could contribute up to $2,700 per election to congressional candidates for the 2018 election and federal multi-candidate PACs could contribute up to $5,000 per election, with the primary and general elections considered separate elections. The individual contribution limits are adjusted for inflation each election cycle.

5. Michelle Ye Hee Lee, "How Small Donations Gave Underdog Democrats a Fighting Chance for the House," *Washington Post,* November 4, 2018.

6. Karl Evers-Hillstrom, "Democratic House Candidates Raise $250 Million in Third Quarter, Double Up GOP," October 17, 2018, https://www.opensecrets.org/news/2018/10/dem-candidates-double-up-gop-third-quarter/.

7. Elena Schneider, "We're Getting Our Asses Kicked: Republicans Massively Out-Raised in Election Home Stretch," *Politico*, October 16, 2018.

8. Karl Evers-Hillstrom, "Cruz, O'Rourke Break Spending Record," October 29, 2018, https://www.opensecrets.org/news/2018/10/cruz-orourke-break-spending-record-texas-senate/.

9. Karl Evers-Hillstrom, "Democrats Ride Monster Fundraising to Take the House, GOP Successfully Picks Its Senate Battles," November 7, 2018, https://www.opensecrets.org/news/2018/11/2018-wrap-up-am/.

10. Carrie Levine and Chris Zubak-Skees, "How ActBlue Is Trying to Turn Small Donations into a Blue Wave," October 25, 2018, https://publicintegrity.org/federal-politics/how-actblue-is-trying-to-turn-small-donations-into-a-blue-wave/.

11. ActBlue, "Meet ActBlue: About Us," https://secure.actblue.com/about.

12. Julie Bykowicz, "GOP's Fundraising Problem: Democrats' One-Stop Online Platform," *Wall Street Journal,* December 25, 2018.

13. ActBlue, "2018 Election Cycle in Review," https://report.actblue.com/.

14. Lee, "How Small Donations Gave Underdog Democrats a Fighting Chance for the House."

15. Stephanie Saul and Rachel Shorey, "Republicans Seek to Boost Small Donations, but a Fragmented System Stymies Them," *New York Times,* January 4, 2019.

16. Tom Hamburger and Paul Kane, "DNC Rolls Back Obama Ban on Contributions from Federal Lobbyists," *Washington Post,* February 12, 2016.

17. Alexander C. Kaufman, "DNC Quietly Adopts Ban on Fossil Fuel Company Donations," June 12, 2018, https://www.huffingtonpost.com/entry/dnc-ban-fossil-fuel -donations_us_5b20116ae4b09d7a3d77d094.

18. Lisa Hagen and Timothy Kama, "DNC Reverses Ban on Fossil Fuel Donations," August 10, 2018, https://thehill.com/policy/energy-environment/401356-dnc-passes-reso lution-on-fossil-fuel-donations.

19. So-called "Red to Blue candidates" were part of a program for strong Democratic House candidates challenging Republican incumbents. Eric Garcia, "Democrats Announce New Red to Blue Candidates," *Roll Call,* August 1, 2018.

20. Simone Pathe, "How the 'No Corporate PAC' Pledge Caught on Fire," *Roll Call,* November 6, 2018.

21. Karl Evers-Hillstrom, "Democrats Are Rejecting Corporate PACs: Does It Mean Anything?," December 7, 2018, https://www.opensecrets.org/news/2018/12/democrats -say-no-pacs/.

22. Center for Responsive Politics, "Political Action Committees," https://www .opensecrets.org/pacs/index.php?chart = P.

23. Pathe, "How the 'No Corporate PAC' Pledge Caught on Fire."

24. FEC Advisory Opinions 2010–09 and 2010–11.

25. Andrew Mayersohn, "Most Expensive Midterms in History Set Several Spending Records," November 8, 2018, https://www.opensecrets.org/news/2018/11/2018-midterm -records-shatter/.

26. Wesleyan Media Project, "61% Increase in Volume of Negative Ads," October 30, 2018, http://mediaproject.wesleyan.edu/releases/103018/.

27. Campaign Finance Institute, "Democrats Outspending Republicans Two-to-One in Final Independent Spending Push," November 5, 2018, http://www.cfinst.org/Press/PRe leases/18–11–05/DEMOCRATS_OUTSPENDING_REPUBLICANS_TWO-TO -ONE_IN_FINAL_INDEPENDENT_SPENDING_PUSH.aspx.

28. Traditional PACs, unlike Super PACs, may make contributions to federal candidates and other federal political committees. Traditional PACs are prohibited from accepting corporate and labor union contributions and may accept contributions from individuals up to $5,000 per calendar year. Traditional PACs are referred to herein as "PACs."

29. Derek Willis and Maggie Severns, "The Hidden Money Funding the Midterms," *Politico,* October 15, 2018.

30. Campaign Legal Center, "Dodging Disclosure: How Super PACs Used Reporting Loopholes and Digital Disclaimer Gaps to Keep Voters in the Dark in the 2018 Midterms," November 2018, https://campaignlegal.org/document/dodging-disclosure-how-super -pacs-used-reporting-loopholes-and-digital-disclaimer-gaps.

31. Michelle Ye Hee Lee and Anu Narayanswamy, "Super PACs That Spent Millions in Final Weeks of Midterms Did Not Disclose Donors Until after Elections," *Washington Post,* December 7, 2018.

32. Ashley Balcerzak, "Pop-up PACs Are Spending Big in Election 2018's Final Days—But They're Hiding Their Bankrollers," November 2, 2018, https://archive.public

integrity.org/2018/11/02/22437/pop-pacs-are-spending-big-election-2018-s-final-days-theyre-hiding-their.

33. Campaign Legal Center, "Dodging Disclosure: How Super PACs Used Reporting Loopholes and Digital Disclaimer Gaps to Keep Voters in the Dark in the 2018 Midterms."

34. Campaign Legal Center, "Dodging Disclosure: How Super PACs Used Reporting Loopholes and Digital Disclaimer Gaps to Keep Voters in the Dark in the 2018 Midterms."

35. These "base limits" include a $2,700 per election limit on individual contributions to federal campaign committees and a $5,000 annual limit on individual contributions to federal PACs.

36. Michelle Ye Hee Lee, "One-Fifth of All Super-PAC Money, from Just 11 Pockets," *Washington Post*, October 27, 2018.

37. Alan Zibel, "Ultra-Rich Fund Huge Surge in Midterm Spending," November 2, 2018, https://www.citizen.org/sites/default/files/superpacs-november-2018.pdf.

38. Mayersohn, "Most Expensive Midterms in History Set Several Spending Records."

39. The Republican national party committees are the RNC, the National Republican Senatorial Committee (NRSC), and the National Republican Congressional Committee (NRCC). The Democratic national party committees are the DNC, the Democratic Senatorial Campaign Committee (DSCC), and the Democratic Congressional Campaign Committee (DCCC). National political party committees are prohibited from accepting corporate and labor union contributions and may accept contributions from individuals of up to $33,900 per calendar year. In late 2014, Congress passed an appropriations bill that included provisions allowing the national political parties to also receive contributions from individuals of up to $101,700 per year to additional sub-accounts for nominating conventions, election recounts and legal proceedings, and building funds.

40. Ken Doyle, "Shadow Parties Dominate Campaign Spending in Midterms," October 26, 2018, https://about.bgov.com/blog/shadow-parties-dominate/.

41. Ian Vandewalker, "The Rise of Shadow Parties," October 22, 2018, https://www.brennancenter.org/blog/rise-shadow-parties.

42. Maggie Severns, "Democratic, GOP Super PACs Quadruple Fundraising as Big-Money Groups' Influence Grows," *Politico*, December 7, 2018.

43. Vandewalker, "The Rise of Shadow Parties."

44. Campaign Finance Institute, "Independent Spending Continues Record Pace; Party Groups Lead the Way," October 23, 2018, http://www.cfinst.org/Press/PReleases/18–10–23/INDEPENDENT_SPENDING_CONTINUES_RECORD_PACE_PARTY_GROUPS_LEAD_THE_WAY.aspx.

45. Federal Election Commission data.

46. Federal Election Commission data. These figures do not include contributions received through joint fundraising committees.

47. For example, scholars estimate that only about 5 percent of the nation's voters cast absentee ballots in 1980. June Krunholz, "Forget Election Day—Early Voting for President Has Started," *Wall Street Journal*, September 23, 2008.

48. Michael P. McDonald, "Early Voting in 2012: What to Expect," http://www.huffingtonpost.com/michael-p-mcdonald/early-voting-in-2012-what_b_1773768.html.

49. National Conference of State Legislatures, "Absentee and Early Voting," http://www.ncsl.org/research/elections-and-campaigns/absentee-and-early-voting.aspx.

50. Stephen Ohlemacher and Julie Pace, "A Third of Electorate Could Vote Before Nov. 4," Associated Press, September 22, 2008.

51. Phillip Elliot and Jim Kuhnhenn, "Weeks Before Election Day, Early Voting Kicks Off." Associated Press, September 5, 2012.

52. Zach Montellaro, "A Staggering 36 Million People Have Voted Early, Setting the Stage for Big Midterm Turnout," *Politico*, November 5, 2018.

53. Adele Malpass, "Midterm Early Voting Is in Full Swing—Will It Matter?" September 28, 2018, https://www.realclearpolitics.com/articles/2018/09/28/mid term_early_voting_is_in_full_swing_--_will_it_matter.html.

54. Sean Miller, "Consultants Grapple with Early Vote Ad Strategy," May 22, 2017, https://www.campaignsandelections.com/campaign-insider/consultants-grapple-with -early-vote-ad-strategy.

55. Michelle Ye Hee Lee, "President Off to Huge Head Start for 2020," *Washington Post,* October 17, 2018.

9

Women Rule

2018 Midterms Bring Surge of Women to Congress

Emily C. Singer

The overarching theme of the 2018 midterm elections was the surge in anti-Trump enthusiasm that propelled Democrats into power in the House for the first time in eight years.

And it was women who carried Democrats to victory, both through the flood of women voters who broke heavily toward Democratic nominees, as well as the Democratic women who stepped up to run—winning primaries and then general elections to help make the 116th Congress the most female in history.

Of course, there's a long way to go before women hold a proportional amount of seats in both the House and the Senate. But women made huge headway in November, increasing their ranks by 15.5 percent.

When the 116th Congress was sworn in on January 3, 2019, a total of 127 women took their places in the legislative branch, with 102 in the House and 25 in the Senate, an increase from the 110 women who served in the previous Congress. That represents the largest single jump in the number of women in Congress since the 1992 midterms, when women saw their ranks skyrocket from 32 members to 54 members in what became known at the Year of the Woman.

To explain women's successes in the 2018 midterms, it is hard to avoid the striking parallels between the 2018 cycle and 1992's Year of the Woman. It

Table 9.1 Number of Women Elected to House and Senate, 102nd–116th Congresses

Congress	Years	Senate	House	Total
102nd	1991-1993	4 (3D, 1R)	28 (19D, 12R)	32 (22D, 10R)
103rd	1993-1995	7 (5D, 2R)	47 (35D, 12R)	54 (40D, 14R)
104th	1995-1997	9 (5D, 4R)	48 (31D, 17R)	57 (36D, 21R)
105th	1997-1999	9 (6D, 3R)	54 (37D, 17R)	63 (43D, 20R)
106th	1999-2001	9 (6D, 3R)	56 (39D, 17R)	65 (45D, 20R)
107th	2001-2003	13 (9D, 4R)	59 (41D, 18R)	73 (51D, 22R)
108th	2003-2005	14 (9D, 5R)	60 (39D, 21R)	74 (48D, 26R)
109th	2005-2007	14 (9D, 5R)	68 (43D, 25R)	82 (52D, 30R)
110th	2007-2009	16 (11D, 5R)	72 (52D, 20R)	88 (63D, 25R)
111th	2009-2011	17 (13D, 4R)	73 (56D, 17R)	90 (69D, 21R)
112th	2011-2013	17 (12D, 5R)	73 (49D, 24R)	90 (61D, 29R)
113th	2013-2015	20 (16D, 4R)	80 (61D, 19R)	100 (77D, 23R)
114th	2015-2017	20 (14D, 6R)	84 (62D, 22R)	104 (76D, 28R)
115th	2017-2019	23 (17D, 6R)	87 (64D, 23R)	110 (81D, 29R)
116th	2019-2021	25 (17D, 8R)	102 (89D, 13R)	127 (106D, 21R)

Source: Center for American Women and Politics.

all began with more women expressing interest in elected politics, which resulted in an influx of women choosing to run for Congress. Democratic women in particular saw sweeping victories in primary contests, paving their way to forming one of the most diverse freshman classes in Congress that the party has seen. On the other hand, the number of Republican women in the House dropped significantly, leaving Republicans soul searching for a way to make up ground in 2020.

THE YEAR OF THE WOMAN 2.0

In fact, there are many parallels between the 2018 midterms and 1992's Year of the Woman.

For one, anger at how women are subjected to sexual harassment in the workplace, and how they are treated once they report that harassment, motivated more women to run in both 1992 and 2018. And women voters responded positively to those female candidates, choosing them at the ballot box to help grow the ranks of women in both the House and Senate.

In 1992, women were motivated by the Anita Hill hearings, when an all-male Senate Judiciary Committee hurled insensitive questions at Hill, who had accused then-Supreme Court nominee Clarence Thomas of sexually harassing her when he was her supervisor at both the Department of Education and the Equal Employment Opportunity Commission, which ironically is the government organization that handles workplace harassment complaints, among other things. The image of Hill being dismissed by male lawmakers sparked women to want to run for office, including current Democratic Senators Patty Murray of Washington and Dianne Feinstein of California, who now serves as the ranking member on the Senate Judiciary Committee.

In 2018, similar anger about how women are still subjected to sexual harassment and sexual assault by powerful men who face little to no consequences for their actions helped spur another wave of women heading to the polls to elect more female representatives.

The story of the surge of women running for—and ultimately winning— seats in Congress in 2018 truly began on November 8, 2016, when President Donald Trump shocked the world by winning the Electoral College to defeat Hillary Clinton.

Trump's unexpected victory ignited a movement of hundreds of thousands of women, who wound up organizing women's marches to be held in cities across the country on January 21, 2017—the day after Trump's inauguration. The marches grew organically as a way for women to voice their discontent that a man who not only made offensive comments about how women looked but was also accused by more than a dozen women of sexual assault could ascend to the White House. In all, approximately four million people marched across the United States.[1]

The image of women filling the streets of major cities and smaller towns all across the country was the first real sign that women were going to be a force in November 2018.

Then, in October 2017, the #MeToo movement was born following bombshell reports from the *New York Times* and the *New Yorker* in which dozens of actresses and models came forward to accuse powerful film producer Harvey Weinstein of sexual harassment and sexual assault. Those reports led women in Hollywood and other industries to come forward with their own stories of being victims of sexual harassment and/or sexual assault in both their personal and professional lives, and this empowered women to use their voice to spark change, including deciding to run for Congress and other elected offices.

EMILY's List, a political action committee that helps propel Democratic women who support abortion rights into office at all political levels, said it saw a massive increase in women asking about running for office from the 2016 cycle to the 2018 midterms. EMILY's List President Stephanie Schriock told NPR that the group spoke to more than 30,000 women about running for office in 2018, up from 920 women in 2016.

"We've never seen anything like this," Schriock told NPR.[2]

In all, 53 women ran for the Senate and 476 ran for the House, according to Rutgers University's Center for American Women and Politics (CAWP).[3]

Those numbers blew the previous record of women running for Congress out of the water, according to the CAWP. The previous record for women running for Senate was set in 2016, when 40 women ran. The record in the House was set in 2012, when 298 women waged bids.

PRIMARIES

While getting more women to run for office is important, advancing through primaries to compete in general elections is a crucial step.

And Democrats have simply been better at getting women through primary contests,[4] especially in safe Democratic seats where the primary victor is virtually assured to win the general election, thus growing the number of women in Congress.

To be sure, more Democratic women ran for Congress in 2018 than Republican women. But Democrats had a higher percentage of their female candidates come out victorious in primaries than their GOP counterparts—putting Democrats in a better position to increase the number of women in their congressional delegation than the GOP.

Looking at the numbers, 51 percent of the 356 Democratic women who ran for the House won their primaries, as opposed to 43 percent of the 120 Republican women who ran in House primaries, according to the CAWP.

Why Democrats are better at advancing women through primaries can be chalked up to a few factors.

First, Democrats have a well-established machine in EMILY's List that has been successful at electing women at all levels of government. The group has a robust fundraising apparatus that directs donors to female candidates that the group has endorsed, which ensures that female candidates have the resources to compete. EMILY's List also has its own independent expenditure arm that spends money in primary contests to help boost women to victory.

Through its Super PAC, Women Vote!, EMILY's List spent more than $40 million in the 2018 midterms to propel female candidates the group endorsed to victory, according to the Center for Responsive Politics.

Republicans, try as they might to create an EMILY's List equivalent, simply do not have the same kind of infrastructure to help women candidates succeed. There are groups like Susan B. Anthony List, which backs female candidates who are anti-abortion rights (basically the opposite of EMILY's List, which backs women who support abortion rights). However, the group raised and spent a tiny fraction of what EMILY's List did in 2018, bringing in just $799,063 for the cycle, also according to the Center for Responsive Politics.

And while the Democratic Congressional Campaign Committee (DCCC) gets involved in primaries to help push the candidates the organization feels are best suited to a district—whether it be overt or more behind the scenes by pushing donors toward certain contenders—the National Republican Congressional Committee (NRCC) does not, which some Republican women say is a reason why it's harder for GOP women to succeed.

"It wasn't a recruitment failure last cycle, we successfully recruited over 100 women to file and run for office," Republican Representative Elise Stefanik of New York, who in 2014 was the youngest woman ever elected to Congress, told *Politico.* "They felt it was a challenge to raise that early funding."[5]

Aside from having strong infrastructure to help women win, Democrats also have a base that appears to value electing a diverse set of voices, with Democratic operatives saying that being a female candidate in 2018 Democratic primaries presented an inherent advantage.

"There is a trend where all things being equal, a woman candidate in a race is receiving a lift," Ian Russell, a former DCCC staffer, told *BuzzFeed* in May 2018.[6]

In fact, female Democratic candidates pulled off some unexpected primary wins in 2018, in some cases shocking the party establishment, which was backing other candidates.

For example, in Kentucky's Sixth District, the Democratic Congressional Campaign Committee had recruited Lexington Mayor Jim Gray to run for the seat, thinking he had a good chance to pick off the GOP incumbent, Andy Barr.[7] Gray had run for Senate the previous cycle, and while he lost, he had carried the district against Republican Senator Rand Paul. However, Amy McGrath, a political newbie who ran on her background as a trailblazing military veteran, defeated Gray in the primary by eight points. McGrath didn't end up winning her general election, but her personal story catapulted her into the national spotlight during the midterm cycle.

And then there were Alexandria Ocasio-Cortez and Ayanna Pressley, two women of color who picked off incumbent male lawmakers in primaries, instantly becoming rising stars within the Democratic Party.

Ocasio-Cortez defeated then-House Democratic Caucus Chair Joe Crowley in New York's Fourteenth District, which encompasses parts of the Bronx and Queens. Ocasio-Cortez's win was shocking, given Crowley was a potential successor to Nancy Pelosi as leader of the Democratic House caucus, and no public polls showed him at risk of defeat. She is now one of the most visible Democratic members of Congress, both because of her skills at social media and the Republican Party's attacks on her self-proclaimed Democratic-Socialist identity.

Pressley also handily defeated her Democratic incumbent opponent, Michael Capuano, a longtime elected official in this Boston-based district. Capuano was not plagued by scandal, but Pressley spoke to the changing demographics of her district, engaging people of color and talking about the need for diversity and new ideas among Democratic elected officials, on the road to victory.[8]

DIVERSITY

Increasing the number of women lawmakers on Capitol Hill helped diversify Congress in and of itself.

It is notable, however, how diverse the group of women who ran and won in 2018 actually are.

A number of the Democratic female freshman lawmakers represent historic firsts in the halls of Congress:

- There's Ocasio-Cortez, who at 29 is the youngest woman ever elected to the House.
- Pressley, along with Democratic Representative Jahana Hayes of Connecticut, are the first black women in their respective House delegations.
- Then there's Deb Haaland of New Mexico and Sharice Davids of Kansas, who together are the first Native-American women elected to Congress.
- Ilhan Omar of Minnesota and Rashida Tlaib of Michigan both share the title as the first Muslim women in Congress. Omar also holds the title of the first Somali refugee elected to Congress.
- Veronica Escobar and Sylvia Garcia became the first female Latinas elected to Congress in Texas.
- Lauren Underwood of Illinois is the youngest African-American female lawmaker in history at the age of 32.
- In Iowa, Cindy Axne and Abby Finkenauer became the first women elected to the House from the Hawkeye State.
- Angie Craig is the first LGBT member of Congress from Minnesota, while Kyrsten Sinema became the first bisexual senator and the first woman elected to the Senate from the Grand Canyon State.
- Lastly, there's Republican Marsha Blackburn, who became the first female senator from Tennessee.

A LOPSIDED VICTORY

While women made significant headway to growing their ranks in Congress, the increase was almost exclusively on the Democratic side.

In the House, Republicans saw the number of women in their conference fall from 23 after some special elections in 2018 to just 13 when the 116th Congress was sworn in. It's the fewest number of Republican women in the House since the 103rd Congress, when 12 GOP women served in the lower chamber.

The major setback for Republicans can be attributed to a number of factors—including that many of the women in the House GOP conference held districts based in the suburbs, where a revolt against Trump helped sink Republican lawmakers seeking reelection.

Five Republican women in total lost reelection to the House, many of whom held seats located in the suburbs of some of the country's largest cities. They are: Representatives Barbara Comstock of Virginia, Karen Handel of Georgia, Mia Love of Utah, Claudia Tenney of New York, and Mimi Walters of California.

Comstock could not overcome the anti-Trump sentiment in her Northern Virginia district and lost by a whopping 12 points to Democrat Jennifer Wexton, who became one of the 25 new Democratic women in the House. Comstock's district had a dramatic Democratic swing between 2012, when then-GOP presidential nominee Mitt Romney carried the seat by a two-point margin, to 2016, when Clinton bested Trump in the district by a 10-point spread.

Walters faced similar struggles in her Orange County-based district. Romney had carried Walters' district by a comfortable 12-point margin in 2012, however the district swung heavily toward Democrats in 2016, with Clinton carrying the seat by five points. And that shift almost perfectly aligns with the 2018 results, as Walters lost her ancestrally Republican House seat by four points to Democrat Katie Porter, yet another new Democratic woman elected to the House.

Handel—who had won a special election against Democrat Jon Ossoff in this well-educated suburban Atlanta district in late 2017—fell to yet another Democratic woman in Lucy McBath. McBath, a black woman who became a gun control activist after her son was shot and killed by a white man at a gas station, used her backstory to connect with voters in Georgia's Sixth District. It led her to pull off what Ossoff could not, a narrow victory in a seat Trump barely carried in 2016.

Love and Tenney are more interesting cases of GOP losses in 2018. Both represented districts Trump carried comfortably in 2016 (he carried Love's seat by seven points and Tenney's by 15), yet both could not hold on against

Democratic challengers. Love faced a campaign finance scandal, while Tenney's attempt to be a female version of Trump fell flat in her upstate New York district. Both lost to Democratic men.

GOP newcomer women who won primaries—even some in safe GOP seats—also fared poorly.

In South Carolina's First District, Katie Arrington ousted sitting GOP Representative Mark Sanford in a primary, successfully convincing Republican primary voters that Sanford was not sufficiently pro-Trump. But Arrington, who was injured in a severe car accident[9] after winning her primary, lost the general election to Democrat Joe Cunningham, a shocking result in a seat that Trump carried by 13 points in 2016.

Young Kim, a Korean-American Republican woman from Orange County, lost an open-seat race in California's Thirty-ninth District to Democrat Gil Cisneros. Kim had been ahead on Election Night, and some Republicans were celebrating what would have been a historic victory. (Had she won, Kim would have made history as the first Korean-American woman in Congress.) But as mail-in and provisional ballots were counted in the weeks after the election, her lead slowly evaporated and Cisneros pulled ahead, ultimately defeating her by a three-point spread.

Ultimately, in the House, there was just one woman in the incoming freshman Republican class: Carol Miller from West Virginia's Third District.

Another issue for Republicans was that a number of women in their conference chose to retire or run for higher office, and they were either replaced in the House by male candidates or Democratic lawmakers, helping lead to the decline in women in the GOP conference.

For example, GOP Representatives Lynn Jenkins of Kansas and Ileana Ros-Lehtinen of Florida announced their retirements from the House early in the midterm election cycle. Jenkins was ultimately replaced by a Republican man, while Ros-Lehtinen's Miami-based district flipped from red to blue, with Democrat Donna Shalala defeating a female GOP candidate in Maria Salazar, a Cuban American and popular Telemundo reporter who simply could not overcome the district's strong Democratic bent (Hillary Clinton carried it by 20 points in 2016).

A handful of House Republican women opted to run for higher office rather than seek reelection to their House seats—and all of them were either replaced by GOP men or Democratic women candidates, effectively lowering the number of Republican women in the House.

They include Republican Representatives Kristi Noem of South Dakota and Diane Black of Tennessee, both of whom ran for governor in their respective states (Noem was successful while Black lost the race in a primary to a male candidate). Both Noem and Black were replaced by Republican men in their respective House districts, further helping chip away at the number of GOP women in the House.

In Tennessee, Republican Marsha Blackburn successfully ran for Senate, helping raise the number of women in the upper chamber. She was replaced by a man in the House seat she vacated, though, again helping lower the number of GOP women in the House.

And in Arizona, Republican Martha McSally chose to run for Senate rather than reelection to her Second District House seat and ended up losing to now-Democratic Senator Kyrsten Sinema. McSally, however, wound up making it to the Senate, after the state's GOP governor appointed her to the Senate seat of the late Senator John McCain. Yet in her vacated House seat, she was replaced by a Democratic woman in Ann Kirkpatrick, once again lowering the number of women in the GOP's House ranks.

The decline in the number of Republican women in the House has left some of the remaining GOP women frustrated.

Stefanik has criticized GOP leadership for not putting enough resources into diversifying the overwhelmingly white and male Republican conference.[10]

Stefanik said at a summit hosted by *Politico* that she plans to use her leadership PAC to boost Republican women in primaries, and that Republican leadership needs to do the same. Backing women in primaries is something Democratic groups like EMILY's List—which stands for Early Money is Like Yeast, a nod to giving women financial backing early in the primary process—have been doing for years, helping grow the number of Democratic women in the House.

"If they care about what the future, not just of the Republican Conference but of Congress as a whole, looks like and that it's more reflective, we need to ensure that they are investing in those women early," Stefanik said at the December 2018 event.[11]

However, some of the men in Stefanik's conference have a different idea of why Republican women struggle to win congressional races.

GOP Whip Steve Scalise of Louisiana blamed Nancy Pelosi for the lack of diversity within the Republican conference, rather than his own party for not supporting female candidates earlier in the election cycle.

"I've noticed that when female members run on the Republican side, Nancy Pelosi will spend a lot more money in many cases twice as much more to defeat Republican female candidates," Scalise said at the launch of Stefanik's super PAC to elect more women.[12]

And Representative Tom Emmer of Minnesota, the newly elected chairman of the National Republican Congressional Committee—which has a mission of electing Republicans to the House—told the Capitol Hill publication *Roll Call* that it would be a "mistake" for the NRCC to get involved in primaries.[13]

"It shouldn't be just based on looking for a specific set of ingredients— gender, race, religion—and then we're going to play in the primary," Emmer told *Roll Call*.

LOOKING FORWARD

With the 2020 election season already underway, Democrats now face the daunting task of defending many of the women who won in 2018, as well as continue to grow the ranks of female lawmakers.

It won't be an easy task.

A number of the women who won in 2018 face re-election in competitive or downright tough seats. They include women like Kendra Horn in Oklahoma, who shocked the world when she picked off now-former Representative Steve Russell, a Republican who held a seat that Trump carried by 14 points in 2016.

Horn's race begins as a toss-up, according to *Sabato's Crystal Ball*, as do the reelection campaigns of two other freshmen Democrats: Finkenauer in Iowa and Xochitl Torres Small of New Mexico.

Even more, a number of Democratic women senators threw their hats into the ring in early 2019 for the 2020 presidential contest, including Elizabeth Warren of Massachusetts, Kirsten Gillibrand of New York, and Kamala Harris of California. This could potentially lead to open-seat Senate contests where men could ostensibly win and diminish the number of women in Congress.

Republicans, on the other hand, will try and come together to solve their problem with electing women to Congress, a task that won't be easy and will require buy-in from some skeptical wings of the party.

NOTES

1. Erica Chenoweth and Jeremy Pressman, "This Is What We Learned by Counting the Women's Marches," *Washington Post*, February 7, 2017, https://www.washingtonpost .com/news/monkey-cage/wp/2017/02/07/this-is-what-we-learned-by-counting-the -womens-marches/?utm_term = .50a415b9e928.

2. Danielle Kurtzleben, "More Than Twice as Many Women Are Running for Congress in 2018 Compared with 2016," NPR, February 20, 2018, https://www.npr.org/2018/ 02/20/585542531/more-than-twice-as-many-women-are-running-for-congress-in-2018 -compared-to-2016.

3. "2018 Summary of Women Candidates," Center for American Women and Politics,

updated November 14, 2018, http://cawp.rutgers.edu/potential-candidate-summary -2018#house.

4. Denise Lu and Kate Zernike, "Women Have Won More Primaries Than Ever Before. Will They Set a Record in November?" *New York Times*, September 17, 2018, https://www.nytimes.com/interactive/2018/09/14/us/women-primaries-house-senate -governor.html.

5. Zach Montellaro, "Stefanik Kicks Off Effort to Recruit More Republican Women," *Politico*, January 18, 2019, https://www.politico.com/newsletters/morning-score/2019/01/ 18/stefanik-kicks-off-effort-to-recruit-more-republican-women-484735.

6. Ruby Cramer, "In a 2018 Democratic Primary, It's Good to Be a Woman," *Buzz-Feed*, May 6, 2018, https://www.buzzfeednews.com/article/rubycramer/democratic -primary-women-candidates.

7. Ally Mutnick, "How Democrats Created a Pricey Primary in Kentucky," *National Journal*, December 7, 2017, https://www.nationaljournal.com/s/661600/how-democrats -created-pricey-primary-kentucky.

8. Anthony Brooks, "Capuano's Challenge from Pressley Is Called a Fight for 'The Soul of the Democratic Party,'" WBUR, June 14, 2018, https://www.wbur.org/news/ 2018/06/14/capuano-pressley-race-democrats.

9. Dartunorro Clark, "After Horrific car Crash, Katie Arrington, Trump-backed Congressional Hopeful, Released from Hospital," NBC News, July 6, 2018, https://www .nbcnews.com/politics/politics-news/katie-arrington-trump-backed-congressional -hopeful-released-hospital-after-car-n889446.

10. Juliegrace Brufke, "Stefanik: GOP Leaders Need to Step Up Their Female Recruitment Efforts," *The Hill*, December 11, 2018, https://thehill.com/homenews/house/420802 -stefanik-gop-leadership-needs-to-put-their-money-where-their-mouth-is-on.

11. Ibid.

12. Steve Benen, "GOP Leader: Pelosi Bears Responsibility for Party's Lack of Diversity," MSNBC, January 21, 2019, http://www.msnbc.com/rachel-maddow-show/gop -leader-pelosi-bears-responsibility-partys-lack-diversity.

13. Simone Pathé, "Elise Stefanik Wants to Play in Primaries to Help Republican Women," *Roll Call*, December 4, 2018, https://www.rollcall.com/news/politics/elise -stefanik-wants-to-play-in-primaries-to-help-republican-women.

10

Hindsight in 2020

Black Voting Behavior and the Next Presidential Election

Theodore R. Johnson

When the smoke cleared from Donald Trump's surprising 2016 presidential election win, it revealed a lot of fingers pointing at black voters. There was a sense in the election's immediate aftermath that the black electorate's reduced turnout was the primary contributor to Hillary Clinton's loss. The real revelation, however, was that black voters are not well understood by most politicians, campaign officials, or pundits; the myth of the black mono-lith still prevails in conventional thinking. For presidential candidates who aspire to occupy the White House, especially Democrats, they cannot afford to make the same mistake in the next election. Before they begin measuring the drapes, they will need to update their approach to black voters.

To be fair, the Monday morning quarterbacking about the 2016 black elec-torate was understandable. The durability of black voters' near-uniform parti-sanship in congressional and presidential elections is a defining phenomenon of contemporary American politics. And it is true that the black voting rate declined nationwide in 2016 for the first time in over two decades, hitting its lowest level for a presidential contest—59.6 percent—since the controversial 2000 election.[1] Hillary Clinton missed out on the presidency thanks to about 80,000 votes spread across Michigan, Pennsylvania, and Wisconsin—states Barack Obama won in 2008 and 2012. Wayne County (Detroit), Michigan; Philadelphia County, Pennsylvania; and Milwaukee County, Wisconsin, are each about 40 percent black, and turnout was down by 88,000 votes in just those three locales.[2] Indeed, nearly 1.6 million black voters who supported Barack Obama in 2012 stayed home in 2016.[3] Higher black turnout in the right three or four cities probably would have led to Trump's defeat.

But with just a little more distance from the election's outcome, the role of another segment of the electorate came into focus: the white working class. Data show that more white 2012 Obama voters stayed home in 2016 than black ones. The vast majority of 2012 Obama voters who supported Trump or third-party candidates in 2016 were white working class.[4] And since white voters made up 70 percent of the electorate, it is more than reasonable to suggest that white Obama-Trump voters, estimated to be between 6.7 million and 9.2 million, had more impact on the election's outcome than the black voters who stayed home.[5] Once this became evident, a debate emerged in the Democratic Party about whether its time and resources would be better spent on mobilizing black voters or winning back the white working-class voters that Trump won over.

No matter what electoral coalition the next Democratic nominee builds in 2020, one thing is clear: Black voters must be the crux of the strategy. They have played an outsized role in the last three presidential elections, recent state-level Democratic gubernatorial primaries, and select congressional races. This will not change. Further, since at least two black candidates will compete for the 2020 Democratic presidential nomination in a party primary process where one in four voters is black,[6] the road to the White House necessarily passes through black America. This is also true for Trump—or whomever the Republican nominee is—because increased black turnout, or losing as little as a third of a percent of his 2016 black vote total to the Democratic nominee, could lead to defeat. As such, it's important that we develop a deeper understanding of, and appreciation for, the nature and evolution of black voters' political and electoral behavior.

THE MYTH OF THE BLACK MONOLITH

When scholars—and everyday black citizens, for that matter—point out the extant political diversity within black America, the argument is often muted by the bloc's observed monolithic voting behavior. Over the last four decades, nearly 88 percent of black voters have cast a ballot for the Democratic nominee in presidential and congressional elections.[7] In the last decade, the number has only increased: more than 92 percent of black voters supported the Democratic nominees for president and 90 percent voted for Democrats in midterm elections.[8] This constitutes the largest, most enduring, and most uniform bloc in American politics—a veritable monolith indeed. Where exactly is the myth?

The myth is located in the suggestion that black voters' political ideologies and policy preferences are as monolithic as their voting behavior. That is, it asserts that because black voters exercise an apparent partisan loyalty, they must all be avid supporters of the Democratic Party's platform, policy agenda, and governing philosophies. It also implies that black politics are inherently more progressive than other racial groups. This mythical logic concludes that black voters' only relevance in elections is how many of them will show up to cast a vote for Democratic nominees and that policy appeals are immaterial except the extent to which they are symbolic gestures meant to mobilize the black electorate. In this way, the myth further compels Republicans to employ tactics that focus on inhibiting turnout to counter the Democrats' enormous advantage among black voters instead of making earnest petitions for their support. Finally, the myth suggests that the black electorate will automatically support black Democratic candidates or, when such a candidate isn't present, follow the cues of black political elites en masse.

The danger of such thinking is quickly apparent: It can cause the Democratic Party to take black votes for granted while disincentivizing the Republican Party from pursuing them at all. The result is *electoral capture*, a term that refers to a situation wherein a group is forced to align itself with one party, not because its interests are well-represented by that party, but because the other party makes no attempt at earning its votes and espouses views perceived as antithetical to the group's well-being.[9] The only choice the captured bloc has is to attempt to exert influence in a party that recognizes the group's only viable alternative is to dilute its voting power by supporting third-party candidates or exiting elections altogether—actions that only further undermine the power of its vote.

Contrary to the myth's premise, the black electorate contains just as much political diversity as any other bloc in the United States. Twenty-seven percent of black voters identify as Independents, nearly one in 10 lean Republican, and two out of three black voters identify as Democrats, a number that steadily declined throughout the course of the Obama presidency.[10] Of those who identify as Democrats, 40 percent characterize their views as moderate, 30 percent as conservative, and only 28 percent call themselves liberal.[11] Black political diversity briefly took center stage in the 2016 Democratic presidential primaries when candidates Clinton and Bernie Sanders split the under-30 black vote.[12] Large contingents of black voters express policy views that do not accord with the national Democratic party platform. For example, black voters are more conservative on marijuana legalization,[13] favor school choice,[14] and are less supportive of environmental regulations that are perceived to harm black employment opportunities.[15] On a range of state and local issues and ballot initiatives, black voters can be found across the ideological spectrum, often near-evenly divided between the liberal position and the conservative one.

What, then, explains the electoral monolithism amid this political diversity? The answer is simple: For black voters, presidential and congressional elections are akin to direct democracy referenda on civil rights. The questions of racial justice and racial inequality marshal the black electorate into a collection of single-issue voters. This is the product of the Democratic Party transforming itself in the mid-20th century into the champions of progressive civil rights policies while the Republican Party has chosen to court disaffected white voters that register higher levels of racial resentment.[16] The perception of extremely polarized positions between the parties on the civil rights issue is the single most important explanation for black vote choice.

With civil rights as the main electoral issue of concern, uniform black voting behavior is shaped by three pressures outlined in political science scholarship. The first is the *black utility heuristic*, more commonly referred to as linked fate. Introduced by political scientist Michael Dawson, the black utility heuristic states that "as long as African Americans' life chances are powerfully shaped by race, it is efficient for individual African Americans to use their perceptions of the interests of African Americans as a group as a proxy for their own interests."[17] In other words, black voters often place group interest over self-interest when making political choices because they understand what happens to black Americans generally is likely to affect them specifically. Since racial inequality still exists in the United States, black citizens know that their fates are inextricably linked to one another by virtue of little more than being part of the same racial group. As long as race is perceived as the primary determinant of black Americans' life chances, evinced in persistent racial socioeconomic disparities and stubborn racial injustices, salience of the group interest will characterize black political behavior.

The product of a second pressure is the identification of exactly what the group interest is. The theory of everyday talk, a concept articulated by political scientist Melissa Harris-Perry, helps explain how black group interest is shaped and formed through ordinary social interactions. This theory "posits that although none of the individuals engaging in the conversation will be instantly convinced by the argument of others, all will be affected by their participation in this conversation."[18] These conversations occur in black counterpublic arenas such as barbershops, beauty salons, churches, fraternal and sororal organizations, and in traditional and social media circles ("counterpublic" means an area where marginalized communities formulate their own worldviews outside of the larger public eye). The group interest is not dictated by elites and then spread via counterpublic conversations; rather, the group interest emerges from a vast and intricate network of dialogues and debates that meld, alter, and parse black political thought. This process is constant, always evolving, and determinant of political behavior. The black group interest is fashioned from dozens of millions of daily conversations, ranging from the scholarly to the mundane, and is an essential component of black Americans' lived experiences.

The third pressure is the policing of black Americans' voting behavior to ensure individuals are prioritizing the group interest over self-interest. After all, black electoral uniformity would not have solidified and endured if it was nothing more than an expedient and efficient way of understanding and advancing the group interest. The threat of social penalty is what gives the black electoral monolith its strength, rigidity, and resilience. Political scientists have found that *racialized social pressure*—the exacting of consequences on black voters who defect from group norms—"places significant constraints on black [Americans'] political behavior."[19] Reputational sanctions, especially in subjugated communities, can harm one's access to already limited social and economic prospects, thereby threatening overall personal well-being. This is a strong corrective that promotes compliance with group behavioral norms.[20] For example, the use of intraracial epithets—such as Uncle Tom, sellout, and coon—in black counterpublic spaces are linguistic evidence of such sanctions, used and received in a manner that shapes group members' behavior.[21] Because there is such political diversity within black America, the risk of facing social punishment or ostracization is an important factor in ensuring collective action. Besides, if race causes group members' fates to be linked, then the group cannot afford for too many members to pursue politics seen as inimical to the group interest lest it place other members at risk.

Taken together, black electoral behavior is defined by the formation of the group interest, members' prioritization of that interest, and penalization of those who defect from it. The myth of the black monolith accounts for none of this and suggests it's all of little importance because the end result is black citizens voting as a bloc based on deep-seated partisan loyalty. Choosing to ignore the black political diversity muted by the group's pragmatic partisanship, however, is done at the peril of Democratic candidates seeking the party's 2020 presidential nomination and of future Republican candidates whose electoral prospects are shakier as the party's base shrinks with the nation's changing demographics. Ascribing to the myth causes Democratic nominees to pursue facile and ineffective strategies, such as one pundit's recent advice about 2020: "For [Bernie] Sanders to espouse the most liberal list of policy positions early and often may be his best gambit to win over African-Americans."[22] And Republicans will bank on restrictive voting measures and fostering distrust of Democratic candidates as effective methods to reduce black turnout, only to be surprised when black voters defeat Republican candidates in party stronghold states like Alabama where historic black turnout defeated Trump-proxy senatorial candidate Roy Moore in 2017.

When it comes to black voters, the last decade of hindsight is 2020's key to a successful presidential campaign.

THE 2020 PRESIDENTIAL PRIMARIES

The state of the black electorate is strong and positioned to be a king- (or queen-) maker in 2020. The candidate that black voters coalesce behind in the Democratic primaries will have the inside track on the party nomination, particularly in a large field. And the outcome of the general election may hinge on the black voter participation rate and the extent to which the Republican nominee—or a third-party candidate—prevents the Democratic nominee from receiving 90 percent of the black vote.

The Democratic field is already the most diverse in history. As of this writing, the candidates who have either formally entered the fray or formed exploratory committees include no less than six people of color and six women (two of whom are of color). Once the field is complete, it will span the ideological spectrum from moderates who are elders of the party establishment to far-left progressives advocating for significant and fundamental societal reform. The age range will cover about four decades, from the 37-year-old Representative Tulsi Gabbard of Hawaii to potential candidates former Vice President Joe Biden and Senator Bernie Sanders, who will both be in their late 70s by Election Day 2020. And there are at least three black candidates: senators Kamala Harris of California and Cory Booker of New Jersey and Florida's Wayne Messam, the mayor of Miramar. Whatever primary voters are looking for in a candidate, they are likely to find some version of it.

The black electorate will, of course, be especially intrigued and interested in the black candidates. This is a natural reaction to such candidacies and not specific to black Americans—women, Hispanic voters, and the gay community, for example, react similarly to women, Hispanic, and gay candidates, respectively. Scholars agree that descriptive representation—the representation of a constituency by a person who sufficiently resembles it in appearance or lived experience—is important to groups, even when it is mostly symbolic and doesn't result in policy gains.[23] For this reason, Harris and Booker—maybe even the little-known Messam—will attract black voters' attention and will be immediately scrutinized through individual and group assessments. Black voters will get a sense of the candidates' policy histories and proposals, and, perhaps more importantly, determine the viability of each of their campaigns.

The size of the primary's black voting bloc will be of interest to most of the Democratic candidates. Black candidates understand quite well that their success is contingent on whether they can carry the black electorate. Past elections have proven that this is not a foregone conclusion. One need only recall that black voters preferred Clinton to Obama in the 2008 primary season until Obama won the Iowa caucuses. As Democratic strategist Donna Brazile said of black women at the end of 2007, "Most [of them] simply believe Clinton can win."[24] The notoriously pragmatic black electorate simply isn't willing to automatically devote the lion's share of its support to a black candidate based on race alone. This realization can provide a window of opportunity for white and non-black candidates of color, reminding them that they cannot afford to ignore black voters or tacitly surrender them to black competitors. But they will also need to be realistic about the extent to which they can compete for them. If they have not undertaken deep, consistent, and prolonged engagement, they cannot expect policy appeals alone to do the trick. The Clinton-Obama example demonstrates that established and well-known white candidates can effectively compete for black voters against black candidates. Should Biden decide to run, this should be encouraging news.

For candidates making new entreaties to black voters, a goal of placing alongside or just behind black and respected white party elder candidates is a sound strategy. It positions him or her to inherit black support should the frontrunners lose traction and be perceived as no longer competitive. Contrary to common logic, attempting to appeal to black voters by espousing a series of far-left policy proposals is unlikely to work for reasons already covered: the majority of black Democrats are not liberals. Besides, in a crowded field that will have multiple progressive candidates running to the left of the Democratic mainstream, such policy appeals will not provide a sufficient distinction. Further, engaging black political elites in hopes they signal who black voters should support is also insufficient. There are plenty of examples of this—Congressional Black Caucus members initially supported Clinton over Obama; advocated for the reelection of Representative Mike Capuano in 2018 over primary challenger Ayanna Pressley, a black Boston city councilwoman who won the primary and was elected to the U.S.

House of Representatives in 2018; and backed Representative Chris Van Hollen in Maryland's 2016 senatorial primary over CBC member Donna Edwards, who won the black vote by 20 points but lost the election.[25] Black voters tend not to take their cues from black political elites. Consistent engagement at the local level is the only way non-black candidates with low name recognition can make inroads with the black electorate.

The schedule of Democratic primaries will figure largely into the choices available to black primary voters. The first two are in Iowa and New Hampshire with black populations of 3.8 percent and 1.6 percent, respectively. In a change from previous election cycles, Nevada will be the third primary, and its population is just about 10 percent black. In 2016, black voters comprised 13 percent of the caucus, indicating that Nevada will provide the first look at who black voters may support in 2020.[26] The outcomes of these three contests will have a substantial effect on the South Carolina primary, where black voters were 61 percent of the primary electorate in 2016.[27] If history is any guide, black candidates that emerge from the preceding primaries in a strong position win South Carolina. Both Jesse Jackson and Barack Obama entered South Carolina as real contenders for the nomination, and black voters in South Carolina blazed a trail for their long-haul competitive campaigns. Thus, the 2020 South Carolina primary will determine the viability of a black candidate's campaign and foreshadow the black electorate's preferred candidate.

Here is where the black voters' pragmatism is on full display. They want to know that the presidential candidate who receives their support has a realistic shot at winning the nomination. Casting symbolic or ideological votes for black candidates in the name of racial solidarity has little place in the voting booth. In November 2007, Obama was trailing Clinton in South Carolina by 13 points.[28] He did not garner a plurality of black support there until after he won the 2008 Iowa caucus and effectively tied in the New Hampshire primary. Once black voters realized he could win white voters, thereby demonstrating a real opportunity to secure the nomination, his support skyrocketed. He won the South Carolina primary in January with over 55 percent of the vote in a three-person contest, garnering 82 percent of the black vote.[29] Winning white voters in Iowa and New Hampshire was a critical factor that permitted most South Carolina black voters to align their pragmatism with their desire for descriptive representation.

It is quite possible that no black candidates will emerge from the Iowa, New Hampshire, and Nevada primaries with a delegate count that places them in the top three or four of the primary field. A number of candidates are likely to withdraw if they are not competitive in those first three contests. In this case, the black vote choice is more difficult to discern. Black candidates may make the case that if black voters in Deep South states support their campaigns, they can emerge as a leading candidate, just as Jesse Jackson did in 1988 when he rode wins in six southern states to a second-place finish for the nomination. Leading white and non-black candidates are likely to lean on their engagement strategies to convince black voters that their campaigns are the safest and most rewarding bet to make for the protection and advancement of black group interests. Again, the candidate that can win the majority of black support has the inside track to the nomination.

One final word on the Democratic primary: If two black candidates enter South Carolina and the ensuing Deep South primaries with viable campaigns, black electoral behavior will likely hinge on other factors, such as gender, policy positions, and cultural markers. For example, should Senators Harris and Booker be in strong positions to secure the nomination, research suggests that there will be a discernible gender split in the black vote, with more men supporting Booker and more women supporting Harris.[30] The two senators are similar on social and economic policy, but Harris's moderate criminal justice record as California attorney general may help with older black voters who tend to be more conservative whereas Booker's more progressive stance may advantage him with the more liberal younger voters. Harris's cultural markers—she's a graduate of a historically black university and a member of the nation's oldest black sorority—communicate a shared black lived experience that Booker's biography is missing. This, too, could make a difference to voters attempting to ascertain authenticity. Finally, it simply isn't known the extent to which Booker's being unmarried or Harris's interracial marriage and immigrant parentage will influence black vote choice, if at all. What is certain, however, is that the black electorate perceives both candidates as black Americans, and the impact of race consciousness on political behavior indicates marital status and parentage will pale in comparison to the opportunity for descriptive representation. Most importantly, it remains to be seen how the candidates' gender, culture, and policy attributes are received and weighed in black counterpublic spaces where group members will have to balance the pull of each on their individual preferences.

What does this all mean for the party's nomination? The 2020 Democratic presidential primary will be the first in which most Democrats identify as liberal. The party's leftward drift is led by millennials (57 percent identify as liberal), those with postgraduate education (60 percent), and the doubling of liberal white voters from 28 percent in 2000 to 55 percent in 2017.[31] This evolution is reflected in the number of progressive candidates who have chosen to run for the party nomination and the policy proposals they're championing. Meanwhile, the number of black liberal voters has held steady for two decades at about one in four. Candidates will need to fashion campaigns that can balance the desire the majority of voters have for more progressive policies with the need to appeal to the more moderate and relatively conservative ideologies of black Democrats.

The Republican side is much more straightforward. Black voters only comprise about 2 percent of the party's primary electorate.[32] It is expected that Donald Trump will seek reelection, and no candidates have announced their intention to contest the primary. It stands to reason that black voters will play virtually no role in the GOP primary. There are, however, two small caveats to this. The first is if party elites decide to pull support for Trump in favor of a more moderate conservative, the ability of such a candidate to make palatable, if only symbolic, appeals to a more diverse contingent of voters may be a factor. And second, in the highly unlikely chance a black candidate competes for the party nomination—like former secretary of state and retired army general Colin Powell or perhaps Senator Tim Scott—black voter participation in one of the 22 states with open primaries could see a notable increase, particularly among black men.

THE GENERAL ELECTION

No matter which two nominees vie for the presidency in 2020, it will likely be a close election. In the last seven presidential elections, two resulted in the loser of the popular vote winning the Electoral College and four where the winner failed to secure 50 percent of the popular vote. The only ones decided by sizable margins were in 1996, when Bill Clinton bested Bob Dole by 8 million votes, and in both of Obama's campaigns won by 9.5 million and 5 million votes.

Progressives are fond of saying, "When voter turnout is high, Democrats win."[33] But such a blanket statement deserves some scrutiny. After all, voter turnout increased in 2004 and George Bush won, and white voter turnout increased in 2016 and Trump eked out a victory. There does appear to be some merit, though, in the idea that Democrats win when relative black turnout and black share of the electorate increases. In recent elections where Democrats won comfortably—1996, 2008, and 2012—the black share of the electorate increased by two points. Black voters made up 8 percent of the electorate in 1992 and 10 percent in 1996, and they comprised 11 percent in 2004 and 13 percent in 2008 and 2012.[34] The next presidential election is likely to conform to this trend—if black voter turnout rebounds to 60 percent or higher and share of the electorate increases from the 12 percent observed in 2016, the Democratic nominees' prospects look very good.

It is impossible to predict voter turnout accurately, either overall or of a specific group. However, we do know a few things that impact black voter participation rates. Though the extent is debated, descriptive representation does appear to have an impact on black turnout. Some studies suggest that black voter turnout increases when black candidates are on the ballot; others indicate black voters are more likely to participate as its share of the population increases in a given district, which is typically associated with a higher likelihood of having descriptive representatives.[35] Certainly, Barack Obama's campaigns in 2008 and 2012 led to the highest levels of black turnout in U.S. history and were responsible for the black voting rate exceeding the white rate for the first time.[36] And Stacey Abrams's historic 2018 gubernatorial campaign in Georgia contributed to a 43 percent increase in black turnout.[37] However, these effects appear to be limited—black Democratic candidates can increase black voter turnout, but black Republican candidates typically have no effect.[38] Overall, this behavior bodes well for black presidential candidates in 2020.

Recent elections also provide a data point for turnout expectations. Black turnout surged in special elections, primaries, and general elections in states like Alabama, Georgia, and Virginia, sometimes swinging the election outcomes.[39] The thing all these elections have in common is that the Republican candidates were running on messages similar to President Trump, which is anathema to black voters. Increased black turnout didn't occur in responses to the Democratic candidates or their policy appeals, but the opportunity to repudiate Trump, even if only by proxy, was sufficient to drive up turnout.[40] The polling suggests rejecting Trump is perceived to be squarely in the black group interest: 93 percent of black voters disapprove of President Trump, 77 percent believe the president is setting race relations back, the majority of black voters believe "Trump is a racist whose policies are intended to hurt," and a third voted in the 2018 midterms specifically to "stop Donald Trump and the Republican agenda."[41] Much to Republicans' chagrin and Democrats' delight, Trump has a positive effect on black turnout, at least now that he's president.

Overall, it is pretty safe bet that black voter turnout will rebound in 2020, though probably not to 2008 or 2012 levels. Should Harris secure the Democratic nomination, however, the potential for another historic candidacy could cause turnout to approach 2008 levels, though the share of the electorate is much more difficult to hypothesize. Not only does Abrams's campaign support this, but so does Andrew Gillum's 2018 campaign to be the first black governor of Florida, where black turnout increased by 33 percent.[42] And though restrictive voting measures do disproportionately impact black voters, whether they have significant effects on turnout is a hotly contested issue.[43]

Black candidates' chance at securing the nomination will depend as much on how they campaign as on the policy appeals they make. Beyond black voters, they will need to convince an increasingly liberal base of white voters of their progressive bona fides. This will make their party primary campaigns trickier propositions than the general election where differences are much starker, especially against an incumbent Trump. Here, three 2018 gubernatorial races are instructive: Georgia, Florida, and Maryland, where black candidates won the Democratic Party's primaries. Abrams in Georgia, Gillum in Florida, and Ben Jealous in Maryland all ran to the left of their primary competition in order to secure white liberals while cultivating the black vote through descriptive representation appeals.[44] Once Abrams and Gillum won the nomination, they employed more moderate rhetoric during the general election against white Republican men in an attempt to attract white centrists and disaffected voters. Conversely, Jealous maintained his far-left message in his race against a white Republican man, popular incumbent Republican Governor Larry Hogan. Both Abrams and Gillum won more than 90 percent of black voters, but Jealous only managed just over 70 percent. All three lost their general elections. Black 2020 presidential candidates can learn from each how to build a winning coalition in the party primary, but they will need to innovate methods to expand it for the general election.

The Obama coalition is likely to serve as the party model. Obama managed to align black voters and Northern white voters, including those in the Rust Belt states of Michigan, Ohio, Pennsylvania, and Wisconsin.[45] Harris and Booker will certainly attempt to woo the latter back into the party. But there is another development that may allow them to underperform Obama with white voters and still win: the rise of Hispanic voters. For the first time, Hispanic voters will be the largest racial or ethnic minority group in the electorate, projected to comprise 13.3 percent of voters compared to 12.5 percent for black voters.[46] More Hispanic Democratic voters identify as liberal—41 percent—than black voters, but still less than the 55 percent of white Democrats.[47] Obama won 71 percent of the Hispanic vote in 2012, and Clinton only won 66 percent in 2016.[48] In 2018, Abrams managed 62 percent of the Hispanic vote, and Gillum fared worse, only garnering 54 percent.[49] And Hispanic approval of Trump has remained fairly steady, hovering at around 25 percent.[50] All of this suggests that the Hispanic electorate offers an opportunity for Democratic candidates, but it will not be easy to triangulate the vote choice of the sizable racial and ethnic groups in the party. Appeals based on minority descriptive representation or attacking Trump's hard-line immigration policies will resonate differently, and perhaps unexpectedly, with Hispanic voters. Candidates, especially black candidates, will need to ensure their messaging and policy proposals account for this shift in the electorate.

When it comes to the black electorate, the Republican nominee, presumably Trump, is likely to pursue a turnout strategy that tamps down excitement for whichever Democratic nominee emerges. In 2016, 8 percent of black voters and 13 percent of black men supported Trump; it'll likely be a challenge to replicate that for 2020 given how his presidency has unfolded. Trump once claimed he'd get 95 percent of the black vote—that may prove to be correct in that he may get 95 percent of the black electorate to vote against him.[51] That would be disastrous for the party's chances of holding on to the White House.

In the 2020 presidential election, the black electorate will be what it has long been—an influential, practical bloc motivated by racial solidarity that throws nearly all of its weight behind the Democratic nominee for president. It will play an outsized role in the Democratic primary and effectively no role in the Republican process. Black candidates will jockey for position in the early primaries to prove the viability of their candidacies to pragmatic black voters. And Trump's presidency has crystallized the group interest and will probably mobilize black voters, to his detriment. It remains to be seen how the general election will unfold, but there is no doubt that the black electorate will be heard.

The myth of the black monolith will be dispelled, once again, during the long run-up to the parties' conventions next summer. But the electoral monolith will certainly reform once more the ensuing November. The best way to make sense of all the swirling that occurs aside from these two moments is to apply hindsight in 2020.

NOTES

1. Thom File, "Voting in America, a Look at the 2016 Presidential Election," United States Census Bureau, May 10, 2017, accessed January 28, 2019, https://www.census.gov/newsroom/blogs/random-samplings/2017/05/voting_in_america.html.

2. These figures are derived from the 2010 United States Census; Lauren Gibbons, "See How Voter Turnout Changed in Every Michigan County from 2012 to 2016," *Michigan Live*, November 11, 2016, accessed January 28, 2019, https://www.mlive.com/news/index.ssf/2016/11/see_how_every_michigan_county.html; Wisconsin Elections Commission; and the Pennsylvania Department of State.

3. Philip Bump, "4.4 million 2012 Obama Voters Stayed Home in 2016—More Than a Third of Them Black," *Washington Post*, March 12, 2018, accessed January 28, 2019, https://www.washingtonpost.com/news/politics/wp/2018/03/12/4-4-million-2012-obama-voters-stayed-home-in-2016-more-than-a-third-of-them-black/.

4. Ibid.

5. Geoffrey Skelley, "Just How Many Obama 2012-Trump 2016 Voters Were There?" *Sabato's Crystal Ball*, University of Virginia Center for Politics, June 1, 2017, accessed January 28, 2019, http://www.centerforpolitics.org/crystalball/articles/just-how-many-obama-2012-trump-2016-voters-were-there/.

6. See Bill McInturff and Gordon Price, "Democratic Primary Voter Demographic Shifts and Candidate Coalitions," Public Opinion Strategies, June 3, 2016, accessed January 29, 2018, https://pos.org/democratic-primary-voter-demographic-shifts-and-candidate-coalitions/; and Elaine Kamarck and Alexander R. Podkul, "The 2018 Primaries Project: The Demographics of Primary Voters," in Political Polarization and Voters in the 2018 Congressional Primaries, Brookings Institution, October 23, 2018, accessed January 29, 2018, https://www.brookings.edu/research/the-2018-primaries-project-the-demographics-of-primary-voters/. In 2008, black voters were 24 percent of the Democratic primary electorate. In 2016, that number rose to 27 percent. For the 2018 midterms, the figure was 24.1 percent.

7. Roper Center, "How Groups Voted," accessed January 28, 2019, https://ropercenter.cornell.edu/data-highlights/elections-and-presidents/how-groups-voted.

8. See David A. Bositis, *Blacks and the Democratic National Convention*, Joint Center for Political and Economic Studies, 2012, accessed January 28, 2019, https://jointcenter.org/sites/default/files/Blacks%20and%20the%202012%20Democratic%20National%20Convention.pdf; Nia-Malika Henderson, "Republicans Won 10 Percent of the Black Vote on Tuesday. That's Actually a Step in the Right Direction," *Washington Post*, November 6, 2014, accessed January 28, 2018, https://www.washingtonpost.com/news/the-fix/wp/2014/11/06/the-gop-moved-the-ball-forward-with-black-voters-but-progress-is-slow/; Alec Tyson, "The 2018 Midterm Vote: Divisions by Race, Gender, Education," Pew Research Center, November 8, 2018, accessed January 28, 2019, http://www.pewresearch.org/fact-tank/2018/11/08/the-2018-midterm-vote-divisions-by-race-gender-education/.

9. Paul Frymer, *Uneasy Alliances: Race and Party Competition in America* (Princeton, NJ: Princeton University Press, 1999).

10. Pew Research Center, "Wide Gender Gap, Growing Educational Divide in Voters' Party Identification," March 2018, accessed January 29, 2019, http://www.people-press.org/wp-content/uploads/sites/4/2018/03/03–20–18-Party-Identification-CORRECTED.pdf

11. Samantha Smith, "Democratic Voters Are Increasingly Likely to Call Their Views Liberal," Pew Research Center, September 7, 2017, accessed January 29, 2019, http://www.pewresearch.org/fact-tank/2017/09/07/democratic-voters-are-increasingly-likely-to-call-their-views-liberal/.

12. Perry Bacon Jr., "Huge Split between Older and Younger Blacks in the Democratic Primary," NBC News, May 28, 2016, accessed January 29, 2019, https://www.nbcnews.com/news/nbcblk/huge-split-between-older-younger-blacks-democratic-primary-n580996.

13. Hannah Hartig and Abigail Geiger, "About Six-in-Ten Americans Support Marijuana Legalization," Pew Research Center, October 8, 2018, accessed January 29, 2019, http://www.pewresearch.org/fact-tank/2018/10/08/americans-support-marijuana-legalization/.

14. Albert Cheng, Michael Henderson, Paul E. Peterson, and Martin R. West, "Public Support Climbs for Teacher Pay, School Expenditures, Charter Schools, and Universal Vouchers: Results from the 2018 EdNextPoll," *Education Next*, Vol. 19, no. 1, accessed January 29, 2019, https://www.educationnext.org/files/ednext_xix_1_ednext_poll.pdf.

15. See, for example, American Energy Alliance, "Black Leaders Fight Obama's Ozone Rule," September 14, 2015, accessed January 29, 2019, https://www.americanen ergyalliance.org/2015/09/black-leaders-fight-obamas-ozone-rule/.

16. See, for example, Kevin M. Kruse, *White Flight: Atlanta and the Making of Modern Conservatism* (Princeton, NJ: Princeton University Press, 2005); Jonathan Knuckey, "Racial Resentment and the Changing Partisanship of Southern Whites," *Party Politics*, Vol. 11, no. 1, 5–28; Stanley Feldman and Leonie Huddy, "Racial Resentment and White Opposition to Race-Conscious Programs: Principles or Prejudice?" *American Journal of Political Science*, Vol. 49, no. 1, 168–718; Aram Goudsouzian, "Why the Republican Party Is So Polarizing," *Washington Post*, November 6, 2018, accessed February 1, 2019, https://www.washingtonpost.com/outlook/2018/11/06/why-republican-party-is -so-polarizing/.

17. Michael C. Dawson, *Behind the Mule: Race and Class in African-American Politics*. (Princeton, NJ: Princeton University Press), 61.

18. Melissa Victoria Harris-Lacewell, *Barbershops, Bibles, and BET Everyday Talk and Black Political Thought* (Princeton, NJ: Princeton University Press, 2010), 12.

19. Ismail K. White, Chryl N. Laird, and Troy D. Allen, "Selling Out?: The Politics of Navigating Conflicts between Racial Group Interest and Self-Interest," *American Political Science Review*, Vol 108, no. 4, 783–800.

20. Dennis Chong, *Collective Action and the Civil Rights Movement* (Chicago, IL: University of Chicago Press, 1991).

21. White et al., "Selling Out?" 785.

22. David Catanese, "Can Bernie Sanders Bet on Black Voters?" *US News & World Report*, January 25, 2019, accessed January 29, 2019, https://www.usnews.com/news/the -report/articles/2019–01–25/can-bernie-sanders-bet-on-black-voters.

23. Hanna Fenichel Pitkin, *The Concept of Representation* (Berkeley, CA: University of California Press, 1967).

24. Michelle Peltier, "Why Black Women Prefer Clinton to Obama," CBS News, December 3, 2007, accessed January 30, 2019, https://www.cbsnews.com/news/why -black-women-prefer-clinton-to-obama/.

25. See Josephine Hearn, "Black Caucus Divided over Obama," *Politico*, January 17, 2008, accessed January 31, 2019, https://www.politico.com/story/2008/01/black-cau cus-divided-over-obama-007948; and Astead Herndon, "John Lewis and Other Black Leaders Spurn Black Challenger in Boston," *New York Times*, May 19, 2018, accessed January 31, 2019, https://www.nytimes.com/2018/05/19/us/politics/john-lewis -elections-black-caucus.html. Additionally, it should be noted that while black political elites cannot crown a victor, disapprovals by these figures work their way into political black dialogue and can severely damage a candidate's standing. This is the case for black and non-black candidates alike. For example, the Congressional Black Caucus's refusal to support Representative Donna Edwards' 2016 candidacy for a Maryland U.S. Senate seat contributed to her primary loss to fellow Maryland Democrat Representative Chris Van Hollen, who is white. See Rachel Bade, "Edwards Confronts Black Lawmakers over

Refusal to Back Her," *Politico*, April 21, 2016, accessed January 31, 2019, https://www
.politico.com/story/2016/04/donna-edwards-congressional-black-caucus-chris-van-hollen
-222169.

26. Samuel Granados, Ted Mellnik, and Kevin Schaul, "Why Minority Voters Matter
for Democrats in Nevada and Beyond," *The Washington Post*, February 20, 2016, accessed
January 30, 2019, https://www.washingtonpost.com/graphics/politics/2016-election/pri
maries/nevada-democratic-analysis/.

27. South Carolina Exit Polls, CNN, February 27, 2016, accessed January 30, 2019,
https://www.cnn.com/election/2016/primaries/polls/sc/Dem.

28. South Carolina Democratic Primary Polling, RealClearPolitics, January 26, 2008,
accessed January 31, 2019, https://www.realclearpolitics.com/epolls/2008/president/sc/
south_carolina_democratic_primary-234.html.

29. 2008 Democratic Primary Exit Poll Results, ABC News, https://abcnews.go.com/
images/PollingUnit/08DemPrimaryKeyGroups.pdf.

30. See Tasha S. Philpot and Hanes Walton Jr., "One of Our Own: Black Female Candidates and the Voters Who Support Them," *American Journal of Political Science*, Vol 51,
no. 1, 49–62; and Evelyn Simien and Rosalee A. Clawson, "The Intersection of Race and
Gender: An Examination of Black Feminist Consciousness, Race Consciousness, and Policy Attitudes," *Social Science Quarterly*, Vol. 85, no. 3, 793–810.

31. Smith, "Democratic Voters Are Increasingly Likely."

32. See Pew Research Center, "Republican Primary Voters: More Conservative than
GOP General Election Voters," January 2016, accessed January 31, 2019, http://www.pew
research.org/wp-content/uploads/sites/4/2016/01/1–28–16-Profile-of-2012-GOP-Pri
mary-Voters-release.pdf; and Kamarck and Podkul, "2018 Primaries Project."

33. See, for example, Chris Baker, "Bernie Sanders' Plan to Win New York: Get Highest Voter Turnout in Primary History," *Post-Standard*, April 12, 2016, accessed January
31, 2019, https://www.syracuse.com/politics/index.ssf/2016/04/bernie_sand
ers_syracus e.html; Progressive Turnout Project Press Release, June 4, 2018, accessed
January 31, 2019, https://www.turnoutpac.org/progressive-turnout-project-launches
-voter-turnout-program-in-virginias-seventh-congressional-district/.

34. Roper Center, "How Groups Voted."

35. For examples of these arguments, see Kenny J. Whitby, "The Effect of Black
Descriptive Representation on Black Electoral Turnout in the 2004 Elections," *Social Science Quarterly*, Vol. 88, no. 4, 1010–1023; and Bernard L. Fraga, "Candidates or Districts? Reevaluating the Role of Race in Voter Turnout," *American Journal of Political
Science* Vol. 60, no. 1, 97–122.

36. Rachel Weiner, "Black Voters Turnout at a Higher Rate than White Voters in 2012
and 2008," *Washington Post*, April 29, 2013, accessed January 30, 2019, https://www
.washingtonpost.com/news/the-fix/wp/2013/04/29/black-turnout-was-higher-than
-white-turnout-in-2012-and-2008/.

37. Mark Niesse and Greg Bluestein, "Black and Democratic voters gain on Republicans in Georgia," *Atlanta Journal-Constitution*, June 29, 2018, accessed February 1, 2019,
https://www.ajc.com/news/state--regional-govt--politics/black-and-democratic-vot
ers-gain-republicans-georgia/TCkvHmtpJ90NsGZTUMwJPK/.

38. Amir Shawn Fairdosi and Jon C. Rogowski, "Candidate Race, Partisanship, and
Political Participation: When Do Black Candidates Increase Black Turnout?" *Political
Research Quarterly* Vol. 68, no. 2, 337–49.

39. Christopher Parker and Henry Fernandez, "There's a Boost in Black Turnout, Especially among Black Women," *The Hill*, August 28, 2018, accessed February 1, 2019, https://thehill.com/opinion/campaign/403977-theres-a-boost-in-black-turnout-especially-among-black-women-voters.

40. Susan Milligan, "Trump Drove Black Voters to the Polls—to Choose Democrats," *U.S. News & World Report*, November 19, 2018, accessed February 1, 2019, https://www.usnews.com/news/politics/articles/2018–11–19/trump-drove-black-voters-to-the-polls-to-choose-democrats.

41. African American Research Collaborative, 2018 NAACP Mid-Term Election Survey, August 7, 2018, accessed February 1, 2019, https://docs.wixstatic.com/ugd/8b2f7d_311de9bd83524e9abdd220752d924797.pdf.

42. Based on CNN exit polls from 2014 and 2018, accessed February 1, 2019, http://www.cnn.com/election/2014/results/state/FL/governor/ and https://www.cnn.com/election/2018/results/florida/governor.

43. See Zoltan L. Hajnal, Nazita Lajevardi, and Lindsay Nielson, "Do Voter Identification Laws Suppress Minority Voting? Yes. We Did the Research." *Washington Post*, February 15, 2017, accessed February 1, 2019, https://www.washingtonpost.com/news/monkey-cage/wp/2017/02/15/do-voter-identification-laws-suppress-minority-voting-yes-we-did-the-research/; and German Lopez, "A Major Study Finding That Voter ID Laws Hurt Minorities Isn't Standing Up Well under Scrutiny," Vox, March 15, 2017, accessed February 1, 2019, https://www.vox.com/identities/2017/3/15/14909764/study-voter-id-racism.

44. For more on this idea, see Theodore R. Johnson, "How 2018 Became the 'Year of the Black Progressive,'" *Politico*, October 19, 2018, accessed February 1, 2019, https://www.politico.com/magazine/story/2018/10/19/black-democrats-progressives-primaries-abrams-gillum-pressley-2018–221610.

45. Nate Cohn, "How the Obama Coalition Crumbled, Leaving an Opening for Trump," *New York Times*, December 23, 2016, accessed February 1, 2019, https://www.nytimes.com/2016/12/23/upshot/how-the-obama-coalition-crumbled-leaving-an-opening-for-trump.html.

46. Anthony Cilluffo and Richard Fry, "An Early Look at the 2020 Electorate," Pew Research Center, January 30, 2019, accessed February 1, 2019, http://www.pewsocialtrends.org/essay/an-early-look-at-the-2020-electorate/.

47. Smith, "Democratic Voters Are Increasingly Likely."

48. CNN exit polls 2012, 2016; Smith, "Democratic Voters Are Increasingly Likely."

49. CNN exit polls 2018; Smith, "Democratic Voters Are Increasingly Likely."

50. Gabby Orr, "Is Trump Really Winning Over Hispanics?" *Politico*, January 29, 2019, accessed February 1, 2019, https://www.politico.com/story/2019/01/29/trump-hispanic-support-poll-2020–113 6373.

51. Theodore R. Johnson, "Trump Is Almost Right. He'll Get '95 Percent' of Black Voters—Voting against Him," *Washington Post*, January 19, 2018, accessed February 1, 2019, https://www.washingtonpost.com/news/posteverything/wp/2018/01/19/trump-is-almost-right-hell-get-95-percent-of-black-voters-voting-against-him/.

11

The Brown Tide and the Blue Wave in 2018

Matt Barreto, Gary Segura, and Albert Morales

In his groundbreaking book, *Brown Tide Rising*, Otto Santa Ana details how the media used negative and racist metaphors to describe immigrant and Latino population growth in the 1990s. Quoting a notorious media story, Santa Ana writes ". . . awash under a brown tide . . . the relentless flow of immigrants . . . like waves on a beach, these human flows are remaking the face of America. . . ."[1]

In 2018, the relentless brown tide was indeed like waves on a beach, blue waves that crested in historically red enclaves from Orange County, California, to the suburbs of Houston, Texas, to rural Arizona to Miami, Florida. Across nearly 30 competitive congressional districts, significant growth in the Latino vote helped propel Democrats to victory and retake the U.S. House. Beyond these marquee House seats, Latinos also demonstrated boosts in turnout that provided the margin of victory for U.S. Senate races in Nevada (Jacky Rosen) and Arizona (Kyrsten Sinema). Even in statewide contests where Latino-preferred candidates did not prevail, such as Texas Senate candidate Beto O'Rourke, the large gains in Latino votes cast significantly influenced down-ballot contests and may have forever changed Texas's electoral competitiveness.

Three main themes emerged in the Latino community in 2018 that we discuss in this chapter. First, voter anger was real: Latinos were tired of the relentless racialization of immigrants and attacks against Mexicans and Central Americans. Related to this, it became clear in 2018 that the Democrats—not President Trump—were winning on immigration, and not just with

Latinos. We argue that Trump and Republicans overplayed their hand, leading to record anger among Latinos, as well as the American electorate as a whole. Second, Latinos reported record high rates of participation for a midterm election, as a result of both campaign outreach as well as internal "self-mobilization" within the community. This participation was critical in swinging dozens of congressional seats to the Democrats and propelling the Blue Wave. Third, for the Latino community, the glass is only half-full, with even more potential for vote growth given the comparatively lower rate of voter registration of only 57 percent among those eligible. Leaving Latino votes on the table in Florida remains an issue for Democrats. As campaigns conduct outreach and invest in the Latino community, we expect to see further increases in voter registration and voter turnout across the country.

ANGER AND FRUSTRATION IN THE LATINO COMMUNITY: HOW THE DEMOCRATS STARTED WINNING ON IMMIGRATION

To no one's surprise, almost immediately after being sworn in to office, President Trump doubled down on his anti-immigrant rhetoric. In his 2018 State of the Union address, he drew parallels between the Central American gang MS-13 and law-abiding immigrants in the United States. The next week, he reiterated that "MS-13 killers" are "pouring into our country."[2]

This kind of language is a Trump trademark and has, for much of this last cycle, assumed the role of signature message for GOP candidates. This 2018 strategy was foreshadowed in 2017, in both Virginia and New Jersey, as GOP gubernatorial nominees Ed Gillespie and Kim Guadagno ran on explicitly anti-immigrant fearmongering. Despite the significant losses for both of those candidates, MS-13 and attempts to stir anti-immigrant fear and anger appeared early in the 2018 cycle and in diverse locations. This message had limited electoral effect, and polls of voters nationwide showed that immigration and its alleged dangers were not a significant driver of voter turnout or choice.

What has changed? For years, Democratic candidates chose to shy away from incorporating and welcoming immigrants into their own rhetoric. When Republicans would embark on mean-spirited immigrant bashing, Democrats often retreated into silence or half-hearted defenses coupled with border-security votes.

Beginning, however, with then-Senate Majority Leader Harry Reid's 2010 reelection victory in Nevada, and clearly demonstrated in the Democrats' 2017 gubernatorial win in Virginia, it has become increasingly clear that immigration is not an issue that largely cuts against Democrats. Part of this is the significant growth of the Latino electorate, about which we shall have more to say in a moment. And part of this is that the politics of immigration reform now clearly pits an outspoken and passionate minority—the immigration restrictionists—against a significant majority of Americans who don't find immigrants frightening and favor sensible reform to our processes.

Both Reid and Ralph Northam, the Democrat who won the Virginia governorship in 2017, rebuffed racially charged anti-immigrant campaigns, stood up for Dreamers, and in the process won over Latino voters alongside a coalition of progressive and moderate college-educated whites. Pro-immigration positions, and the willingness to call out racial scare tactics for what they are, have demonstrated the ability not just to mobilize growing Latino electorates, but also to appeal to the majority of non-Hispanic voters who overwhelmingly favor comprehensive immigration reform with a path to citizenship.

In 2010, Reid made a strong stand for the Dream Act while competing against a Republican, Sharron Angle, who ran a nativist campaign equating immigrants with gang members. Reid defied the polls and won reelection on the strength of very high Latino turnout—and no signs of a white working-class backlash.

According to the exit polls, Reid ran 11 percentage points ahead of Angle among white voters who earn less than $50,000 and, according to our data compiled by our firm, Latino Decisions, he won an estimated 90 percent of the Latino vote. In 2016, Nevada proved to be one of the bright spots for Democrats. Reid's strategy was embraced by his successor, Catherine Cortez Masto, who became the first Latina elected to the Senate.

In Virginia, polling data has made it clear that Gillespie's MS-13 rhetoric backfired among minority voters as well as, crucially, among many whites. Northam won a majority of white college-educated voters, who made up a larger share of the electorate in 2017 than they did in 2016. Gillespie matched Trump with non-college whites, but their turnout was down. And minority voters in 2017 matched their 2016 electorate share—for the first time ever there was no drop-off from the presidential to the gubernatorial election. The Democrats also expanded their margin of victory in Virginia from five percentage points in the 2016 presidential race to nine points in 2017's gubernatorial contest.

Majorities of voters of all races and ethnicities rejected anti-immigrant stereotypes as ugly and wrong. According to an election eve survey of voters by Latino Decisions, Latino voters said that Gillespie's MS-13 ads made them less enthusiastic about him by a 45-point margin. But it wasn't just Latino voters. By a 23-point margin (52 percent to 29 percent), whites in

Virginia also said the MS-13 ads turned them away from Gillespie, as did African-American and Asian-American voters by larger margins.[3]

Our data analysis of survey data paints a clear picture. Exposure to Gillespie's MS-13 ads actually helped drive white college-educated voters away from the Republicans. When we analyzed findings for white Independents and Republicans, voters who were aware of the MS-13 ads were significantly more likely to vote for Gillespie's Democratic opponent. What should be alarming for Republicans is that this effect wasn't limited to the governor's race. The Gillespie campaign had coattail effects, but of the wrong stripe. Across all racial groups, those who were aware of Gillespie's MS-13 ads were significantly more likely to vote for Democratic candidates for Virginia's House of Delegates.

Pro-immigration issue positions are not merely consistent with Democratic ideology, rather, they are also a strategically sound position for winning votes. Simultaneously, it sends a clear, welcoming message to Latino, African-American, and Asian-American voters, while also winning over enough of the white voters who also oppose immigrant bashing.

HOW MIGRATION STRUCTURED THE LEAD-UP TO THE 2018 MIDTERMS

There is no question the role played by immigration in the GOP rhetorical strategy in 2018. President Trump made attacking immigrants the main thrust of his midterm message. At campaign rallies, he unleashed on immigrants, tweeting that "we cannot allow all of these people to invade our Country."[4] In Nevada, he told a crowd that "illegal immigrants want to take over the control" of a California town.[5] In their closing arguments, many Republican candidates echoed Trump's xenophobia and nativism.[6]

Latino Decisions' pre-election polling suggested, earlier in the cycle, that this strategy would not work that well in 2018. Immigration rhetoric was overtaken by several visible developments, including especially anti-asylum and child separations policies, leaving over 1,000 (and now, we understand, many more) children as young as 12 months old parentless and alone in a government detention cell.

In July, we ran a 2018 midterm survey of more than 2,000 registered voters in the 60 most competitive congressional districts.[7] A majority of respondents opposed both the rhetoric and the policies. The administration's policy of separating children from their parents has defined this presidency on immigration. Among all registered voter respondents to our poll, 73 percent of voters said that the child separation policy made them angry. By a rate of 69 percent to 31 percent, white voters in swing districts also said that the policy made them angry. Not surprisingly, anger levels were higher still among minority communities, with 86 percent of Latino voters, 83 percent of black voters, and 79 percent of Asian-American voters saying that the child separations had made them angry.[8]

On balance, voters supported fixing our immigration system, not mass deportations. Seventy-seven percent of battleground districts voters supported the Dream Act, and by a two-to-one ratio these same voters reject spending billions on the border wall. Overall, 61 percent of whites in battleground congressional districts support a welcoming approach to immigration, with the highest marks coming from white college-educated women, a key group into which Democrats hoped to make inroads. Among this segment, there is overwhelming support for the idea that immigrants are just trying to provide a better life for their families.[9]

EFFECTS OF LATINOS IN THE 2018 MIDTERMS

Vote: Latinos were overwhelmingly supportive of Democratic candidates nationwide, and especially in competitive districts and states with Senate elections, and the net effects were substantial. Figure 11.1 illustrates Latino vote by location and overall. Nearly three-quarters of Latinos voting in the

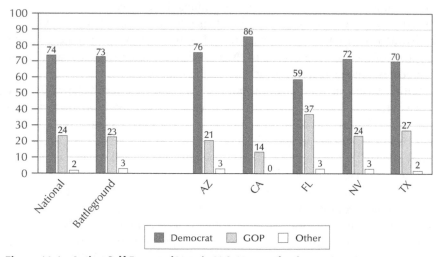

Figure 11.1   Latino Self-Reported Vote in U.S. House Elections, 2018. Source: American Decisions 2018 Election Eve Poll.

2018 election reported voting Democratic in their House race, against 24 percent reporting voting GOP. Numbers in just the most competitive battleground districts were similar.

In high-concentration states with important contests, California tops the list with an 86 percent to 14 percent Democratic preference, a two-party result that likely had historic effects across the California ballot. Democrats emerged in California with 46 of 53 House seats, both Senate seats, enlarged super-majorities in both chambers of the state legislature, and control of every statewide office. At the other end, Florida stands out as it often does, given the historic association of Cuban Americans with the GOP. Nevertheless, Democratic underperformance in Florida may have had significant effects on both the gubernatorial and Senate races there, which we will examine more closely.

Results in competitive statewide contests are reported in Figure 11.2.[10] Latino voters strongly preferred Democratic nominees in competitive gubernatorial and Senate elections. In California, Democratic Lieutenant Governor Gavin Newsom topped the performance of all statewide candidates with 77 percent of the Latino vote against Republican John Cox. Successful Democratic Senate candidates Jacky Rosen of Nevada and Kyrsten Sinema of Arizona, both members of Congress, won 71 percent and 75 percent, respectively. Rosen's partner on the Nevada ballot, Democratic Clark County Commission Chairman Steve Sisolak, was elected governor with 69 percent of the Latino vote.

Despite strong Latino voter support, some candidates were not successful. This included Texas where, with 74 percent of the vote among Latinos, Representative Beto O'Rourke fell short in his bid for a Texas Senate seat. Similarly, Democrat David Garcia's strong Latino showing in the Arizona gubernatorial race was not sufficient to offset his relatively poorer performance among other constituencies as he fell short in his challenge to incumbent Republican Governor Doug Ducey.

Turnout: Had this two-party preference been reflected among a customary midterm electorate, the net effects would not have been as great. Specifically, this Democratic performance is consistent with Latino vote shares for Democrats in recent years, since the political environment has become so poisonous for Latinos and the issue of immigration. But these vote shares have greater impact because of the growth of the electorate. In short, in most important locations and nationally, the evidence suggests a substantial increase in Latino turnout when compared with past midterm elections.

A careful post-election analysis of precinct-level vote data make two things abundantly clear. First, Latino total turnout was up, substantially. Second, and more importantly, in an election in which political interest and turnout

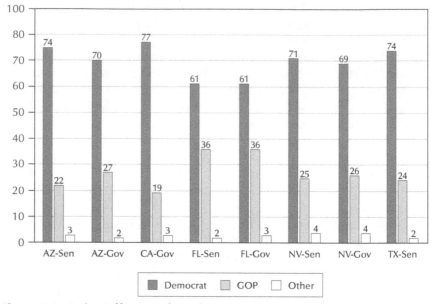

Figure 11.2   Latino Self-Reported Vote in Competitive Statewide Elections, 2018.
Source: American Decisions 2018 Election Eve Poll.

was up in all portions of the electorate, Latino vote increase was substantially greater than among non-Hispanic whites. Had all groups increased proportionately, there would have been no Latino-specific effect. But the substantially greater increase among Latinos meant that Latino voters were a larger share of the electorate, amplifying the impact of their two-party tilt to the Democrats.

Figure 11.3 illustrates the turnout differential for each individual precinct from 2014 to 2018. The y-axis is the percent increase in total votes cast between 2014 and 2018, and the hashed line indicates a zero percent change—that is, total votes cast in the precinct was unchanged between the two midterms. For each panel, the x-axis represents the share of the precinct's voters who are Latino. For the more than 20,000 precincts in these states, each dot represents a single precinct.

Two things are immediately clear. The first is that turnout was up for everyone. But more importantly, the turnout increase was uniformly greater in precincts with more Latinos. For each state, the line is a simple regression fit of y on x, the slope indicating the strength of the effect. The most pronounced effect was in Nevada, the least in Florida (where both Democratic statewide candidates ultimately failed in their bids), though even there, the slope is positive.

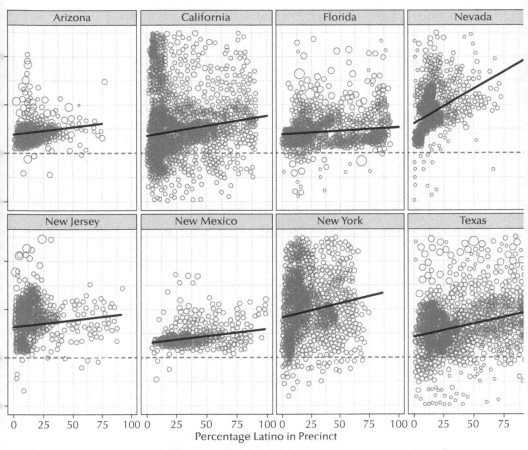

Figure 11.3   Precinct-Level Change in Turnout, 2014–2018. Source: UCLA Latino Policy and Politics Institute Post-Election Study.

Of course, percentage increase does not tell us whether the effect in raw votes was meaningful. For example, a precinct with 50 voters in 2014 would score a 100 percent increase if they had 100 voters in 2018, while a precinct with 400 voters in 2014 would score only a 25 percent increase if they had 500 voters in 2018, though the net effect is the same. We need to look at raw votes cast, and there the results again reveal substantial increases in Latino total votes cast.

Table 11.1 reports the average net increase in raw votes by Latino density in the more than 20,000 precincts reported in Figure 11.3. The results do not suggest that Latino precincts' increase was a result of a smaller increase in total votes case over a smaller 2014 base. In fact, the reverse appears to be the case. More heavily Latino precincts saw a greater increase in total raw

Table 11.1   Change in Total Ballots Cast 2014–2018 by Latino Density

% Latino in Precinct	2014	Avg. Votes Cast in 2018	Raw Vote Growth	Growth Rate	Precinct (n)
0–10%	422	636	214	51%	6209
10–20%	486	754	268	55%	4676
20–30%	431	683	252	58%	2541
30–40%	395	625	230	58%	1883
40–50%	355	574	219	62%	1497
50–60%	331	541	210	63%	1127
60–70%	360	578	218	61%	778
70–80%	386	630	244	63%	701
80–90%	443	746	303	68%	691
90–100%	294	550	256	87%	418

Source: UCLA LPPI analysis of precinct data in AZ, CA, FL, NJ, NM, NV, NY, and TX.

votes cast than in precincts more heavily non-Hispanic. While turnout appeared to spike across all segments of the electorate in 2018, there is little question that Latino increases—in total vote and as a percentage—were larger and that the Latino share of the electorate increased vis-à-vis 2014.

WHY THE GROWTH?

On average Latinos have historically reported lower levels of outreach by presidential campaigns, with that number tending to decrease during midterm elections. In week one of the NALEO Weekly Tracking Poll taken the first week of September 2018, we began asking whether Latino voters had been asked to vote, or if they had been encouraged to register to vote. At the time, only 40 percent of voters reported being contacted by a campaign of either party. By Election Day, and as noted in Figure 11.4, that number had increased to more than 50 percent. Note that minorities expressed a higher level of engagement than that of whites, which was a sign that party commit-tees were making good on their promise to engage minorities early and often.

Much of this can be attributed to robust efforts of the party committees, coupled with strong candidates who made Latino engagement a priority. The Democratic Congressional Campaign Committee (DCCC), for example, engaged with Latino Decisions well over a year in advance of the midterm election.

One other notable data point that caught our attention was the self-mobilization number in Figure 11.5. In our Election Eve poll, Latinos who

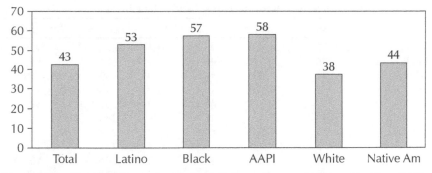

Figure 11.4 Reported Campaign Contact, By Race. *Source*: American Decisions 2018 Election Eve Poll.

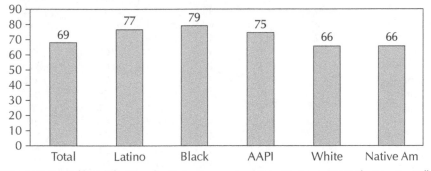

Figure 11.5 Self-Mobilization, by Race. *Source*: American Decisions 2018 Election Eve Poll.

reported encouraging their friends or family to register to vote or vote in the 2018 election was unusually high and at near parity with African-American voters. At 77 percent, that number was well above the average and over 10 points higher than that of white voters. In short, the stakes seemed higher for minorities.

Impact: What, if any, effect did this tilt in Latino vote and significant growth in Latino votes cast have on Democratic success in 2018? It is possible, for example, that the growth of Latino turnout was not sufficient to carry the day, as O'Rourke discovered in Texas. Nevertheless, taken as a whole, the data suggest that Latino turnout was pivotal in a substantial number of races, which we report in Table 11.2.

Table 11.2 lists the 43 House seats that shifted from Republican to Democratic in this last election, the composition of the electorate, and whether the margin of victory among Latinos exceeded the total margin in the race. In 29

Table 11.2   43 House Seats Democrats Flipped Red to Blue in 2018

State	District	Margin	R %	D %	Latino	Lat > margin
Florida	27	6.0	45.8	51.8	67%	YES
Florida	26	1.8	49.1	50.9	63%	YES
California	21	0.8	49.6	50.4	56%	YES
New Mexico	2	1.8	49.1	50.9	44%	YES
California	10	4.6	47.7	52.3	29%	YES
California	39	3.2	48.4	51.6	28%	YES
California	25	8.8	45.6	54.4	27%	YES
Arizona	2	9.4	45.3	54.7	21%	YES
Texas	7	5.0	47.5	52.5	20%	YES
California	49	12.8	43.6	56.4	17%	YES
New Jersey	11	14.7	42.1	56.8	16%	YES
California	45	4.2	47.9	52.1	15%	YES
California	48	7.2	46.4	53.6	15%	YES
Texas	32	6.3	45.9	52.2	14%	YES
New York	11	6.4	46.6	53.0	13%	YES
Colorado	6	11.2	42.9	54.1	12%	YES
New Jersey	2	7.7	45.2	52.9	10%	YES
Utah	4	0.2	49.9	50.1	10%	YES
New Jersey	7	5.0	46.7	51.7	8%	YES
Illinois	14	5.0	47.5	52.5	8%	YES
Virginia	10	12.4	43.8	56.2	7%	NO
Illinois	6	7.2	46.4	53.6	7%	NO
Oklahoma	5	1.4	49.3	50.7	6%	YES
Washington	8	4.8	47.6	52.4	6%	YES
Pennsylvania	17	12.6	43.7	56.3	6%	NO
Virginia	2	2.2	48.9	51.1	6%	YES
Kansas	3	9.7	43.9	53.6	5%	NO
New Jersey	3	1.3	48.7	50.0	5%	YES
Georgia	6	1.0	49.5	50.5	5%	YES
New York	19	5.2	46.2	51.4	5%	NO
Pennsylvania	6	17.8	41.1	58.9	4%	NO
Michigan	8	3.8	46.8	50.6	3%	NO
Iowa	3	2.1	47.2	49.3	3%	YES
South Carolina	1	1.4	49.3	50.7	3%	YES
Virginia	7	2.0	48.4	50.4	3%	YES
Minnesota	2	5.6	47.2	52.8	3%	NO
New York	22	1.8	49.1	50.9	3%	YES
Michigan	11	6.6	45.2	51.8	2%	NO
Pennsylvania	7	10.0	43.5	53.5	2%	NO
Minnesota	3	11.4	44.3	55.7	2%	NO
Iowa	1	5.1	45.9	51.0	2%	NO
Pennsylvania	5	30.4	34.8	65.2	1%	NO
Maine	2	1.0	49.5	50.5	1%	NO

of the House districts that shifted from Republican to Democrat, the Latino vote share was substantial enough to have made the difference.

Of course, we would not and cannot claim that Latinos are solely responsible for those outcomes, and this is particularly true in parts of the country with low Latino population shares. But in the districts reflected in the first 18 rows of Table 11.2, where Latinos are 10 percent or more of the electorate, their impact is critical. Latino surges were particularly important in California, where seven House seats flipped, some by extremely narrow margins.

NEVADA: JACKY ROSEN MAKES HER MARK

There were several candidates, including party committees, we credit with running effective Latino engagement efforts in 2018. However, there was one candidate that went above and beyond, complementing her efforts by utilizing every mode of communication afforded to her effectively. Not only did Democrat Jacky Rosen, who defeated incumbent Republican Dean Heller to flip a Senate seat in Nevada, employ unprecedented use of Spanish media, but she made it a centerpiece of her campaign, ceding no ground to Heller. Not surprisingly, her campaign was successful with healthy margins on Election Night and by effect, she positioned herself in a way that could make her a household name through continued outreach efforts in the Latino community.

Rosen engaged Latinos early in her campaign and started out with very low name ID in our first poll. Recognizing the urgency of increasing that number, her campaign immediately sprang into action and started running biography ads in Spanish around June 2018. The task of defeating an entrenched Republican with strong bona fides in the Latino community was not going to be an easy one. Heller was known for having a constant presence in the Latino community and, prior to Trump's election, for being pragmatic. Rosen's ability to define him early within the Latino community proved to be a lethal blow.

In the end, constant campaigning in Latino neighborhoods, in addition to over $2.5 million in Spanish advertising, proved enough to defeat Heller.

FLORIDA'S MISSED OPPORTUNITIES FOR DEMOCRATS

Any case study on Florida detailing how Democratic Senator Bill Nelson fell short on Election Day must begin with his campaign's reluctance to invest in

Spanish-language television. Then-Governor Rick Scott, Nelson's Republican opponent, spent nearly $5 million on Spanish television beginning in April 2018. This figure does not include third-party spending by groups like LIBRE, the Koch brothers–funded initiative aimed at attracting Latino support for conservative causes. During the World Cup alone, we were able to track spending north of $1 million on Scott's behalf during the one-month stretch. In contrast, Nelson surrendered the ground and would not go up on Spanish television until late August. This was a strategic mistake that proved lethal given that the race was decided by only about a tenth of a percentage point.

Spending on Spanish television alone was not the only factor propelling Scott to victory. In fairness, he made countless trips to hurricane-damaged Puerto Rico, making appearances alongside Governor Ricardo Rosselló at every opportunity. Ron DeSantis's decision to pick a Latina as his gubernatorial running mate also may have contributed to gains among Latinos.

In 2016, Hillary Clinton won 67 percent of the Latino vote in Florida, but in 2018 only 59 percent of Florida Latinos voted Democratic for Congress. That eight-point decline likely cost both Nelson and Democratic gubernatorial nominee Andrew Gillum in their very narrow statewide losses.

LATINOS ARE A BILINGUAL ELECTORATE

We just devoted a section to two Senate campaigns that maximized their reach into the Latino community by investing adequate resources into Spanish television advertising: Rosen, a Democrat, in Nevada and Scott, a Republican, in Florida. While we have precinct-level data as evidence of increased turnout where candidates invest in Spanish media, perhaps the strongest indication that investing in this medium pays dividends lies in the headlines. Earlier this year, NBC Telemundo reported a 300 percent increase in political campaign ad revenue from their 2016 presidential cycle.

According to Google, the top trending Election Day search was "where to go vote" in Spanish. According to our research, a majority of Latino voters rely on Spanish-language TV for news and information about politics. In fact, we've seen this in our qualitative research. In at least one focus group, when the question of who their most trusted media source is, participants overwhelmingly cited Spanish television networks and NPR.

SOME CONCLUDING THOUGHTS

In the 2018 midterm elections, Trump and the Republican Party charted out a campaign strategy that focused heavily on stoking fears about immigrants.

Their closing argument couldn't have been clearer. Republicans were blaring racist statements and ominous images of immigrants, calling them murderers, rapists, and invaders. They hoped these ads, run by Republican candidates up and down the ticket, would resonate with white Americans who would save their House majority.

But it didn't work. Enough whites did not feel motivated by Trump's immigrant bashing to vote for Republicans. On the other hand, millions of Latinos, African Americans, and Asian Americans were motivated by it to vote for Democrats.

This was the second major defeat during the Trump presidency for a campaign strategy centered on racism and attacking immigrants, even after it helped propel Trump to victory in 2016. In the 2017 election for governor of Virginia, the Republican candidate, Ed Gillespie, tried this same playbook, and it resulted in backlash from Latino and black voters, and no net gain in turnout or Republican votes from whites.

According to the 2018 American Election Eve poll of voters in the 70 most competitive House districts, which our firm, Latino Decisions, helped conduct, this is precisely what happened in the midterms too.[11] The Republican Party's anti-immigrant campaign failed to produce a white boost for its candidates.

Most political science research, including our own, concludes that in 2016, Trump did mobilize white voters who felt left behind and angry at immigrants, blacks, and Muslims. But in 2018, voters had had enough: In the Election Eve poll, 57 percent of white voters in swing districts said Trump's words and deeds made them angry. The net gain that Republicans thought they could count on from whites disappeared, with 50 percent now agreeing that Trump and the Republicans were using toxic rhetoric to divide Americans.

Likewise, no real evidence emerged in 2018 of a white base mobilized by attacks on immigrants. This is not to say that millions of white voters do not enthusiastically support Trump's anti-immigrant agenda; they do (49 percent said immigrants were a threat to America). But after two years of Trump's anti-immigrant policies, their numbers are getting smaller. Nationally, there was no evidence of a surge in white Republican votes for anti-immigrant candidates.

As Trump continues his anti-immigrant agenda in his fight with Democratic House Speaker Nancy Pelosi, it is important not to lose sight of just how thorough the defeat of anti-immigrant candidates was in the midterms. Sure, some anti-immigrant candidates won, but those were mainly in very heavily Republican districts, and even some supposedly safe Republicans lost. Prominent Republicans who championed Trump's immigrant bashing lost their election bids, from Kris Kobach in Kansas to Lou Barletta in Pennsylvania, and from Corey Stewart in Virginia to Dana Rohrabacher in California.

In Arizona, Republicans had high hopes for Martha McSally to hold Jeff Flake's Senate seat, but she ended up supporting Trump's full immigration agenda, and she lost, in part, because of Trump's anti-immigrant message. Although Ron DeSantis, an anti-immigrant Republican, won the governor's race in Florida, he was one of the few successes among a string of defeats. In Nevada, the incumbent Republican, Dean Heller, invited the president to stump for him. Trump railed against immigrant gang members. Heller lost to a proponent of immigration reform, Jacky Rosen.

So, did Republican attacks on immigrants mobilize any voters in 2018? Yes, but it came in the form of Latino voters who reversed their record-low midterm turnout in 2014 with record-high turnout in 2018. In the Election Eve poll, 73 percent of Latinos said Trump made them angry, while 72 percent said that they felt disrespected.

In 2001, the political scientists Adrian Pantoja, Ricardo Ramirez, and Gary Segura established that perceived immigrant attacks have a strong mobilizing effect among Latino voters. In 2018, Latino voters once again proved that thesis correct.[12]

In California, Latino voters increased their turnout enough to defeat six Republican incumbents and help Democrats pick up all of the seats in historically Republican Orange County. In Texas, Democrats won two House seats where Latino turnout was up. In New Jersey, Democrats gained four seats. Next door in New York, Democrats picked up three seats. There were two more Democratic pickups in Latino-majority districts in Florida, and one each in New Mexico and Arizona, while Democrats held on to two hotly contested seats in Nevada.

A recent analysis by the Latino Policy and Politics Initiative, a research center at UCLA Gary Segura and Matt Barreto helped found, revealed that across eight states with sizable Latino communities, the Latino vote grew by 96 percent from 2014 to 2018, compared with a more modest 37 percent in growth in the votes cast by non-Latinos.[13] In a postelection analysis, Latino Victory Project and the Democratic Congressional Campaign Committee noted that early voting among Latinos increased by 174 percent. The UCLA study also concluded that higher Latino turnout was influential in flipping 20 of the 43 of the Republican-held House seats Democrats gained.

As we noted earlier, when asked how they were engaged by the 2018 election, 77 percent of Latino voters in the 70 swing districts identified by the Cook Political Report said that they actively encouraged their friends and family to vote. But it was not just self-mobilization; campaign outreach mobilized Latinos. In these 70 competitive districts, 53 percent of Latinos said someone contacted them and asked them to register or vote, thanks in part to efforts by the DCCC, which invested $30 million in targeting minority voters in battleground districts. (Our firm, Latino Decisions, worked with the DCCC, although we did not work on any direct campaign efforts for individual candidates.)

So what does this mean for 2020? First, it's going to be much harder for Trump and Republicans to persuade Americans that immigrants are ruining our country. Before Trump took office, Republicans were more trusted than Democrats on immigration, but now it's Democrats who are more trusted.[14]

Nonetheless, Trump will continue attacking immigrants in 2019 and 2020. Indeed, he vowed to shut down the federal government to get his border wall. But as states like Texas begin to show signs of electoral shifts, Republicans will have to reassess their strategy. If their political dam in the Lone Star State ever gives, their path to 270 electoral votes is all but impossible.

NOTES

1. Otto Santa Anna, *Brown Tide Rising: Metaphors of Latinos in Contemporary American Public Discourse* (Austin, TX: University of Texas Press, 2002).

2. Matt A. Barreto, "Democrats Can Win on Immigration," *New York Times*, February 11, 2018, https://www.nytimes.com/2018/02/11/opinion/democrats-win-immigration.html.

3. "Virginia Election Eve Poll Results," Latino Decisions, November 8, 2017, https://www.latinodecisions.com/blog/2017/11/08/virginia-election-eve-poll-results/.

4. Brent D. Griffiths, "Trump: 'We Cannot Allow All of These People to Invade Our Country,'" *Politico*, June 24, 2018, https://www.politico.com/story/2018/06/24/trump-invade-country-immigrants-667191.

5. Tweet from Daniel Dale, @ddale8, Twitter, October 20, 2018, https://twitter.com/ddale8/status/1053721289779802113.

6. Manuela Tobias, "Senate Leadership Fund Distorts Heidi Heitkamp's Record on Immigration," PolitiFact, October 19, 2018, https://www.politifact.com/truth-o-meter/statements/2018/oct/19/senate-leadership-fund/heidi-heitkamps-record-immigration-sanctuary-citie/.

7. "Battleground Districts July 2018 Midterm Survey—Immigration Policy Attitudes," Latino Decisions, July 5, 2018, http://www.latinodecisions.com/files/7715/3245/4538/Topline_Immigration_Poll_July_2018.pdf.

8. An October 2018 *Washington Post*–ABC News poll found that the issue on which Democrats had the largest advantage over Republicans nationwide was immigration. This Democratic advantage has grown by 15 points since Trump began his presidential campaign in the summer of 2015. See: "*Washington Post*–ABC News poll October 8–11," *Washington Post*, October, 14, 2018, https://www.washingtonpost.com/politics/polling/

washington-postabc-news-poll-october-811/2018/10/14/48ad9e68-ce40-11e8-ad0a
-0e01efba3cc1_page.html.

9. A September poll by NBC News and the *Wall Street Journal* found that only 28 percent of registered voters thought immigration hurt our country. See: Mark Murray, "NBC News/WSJ Poll: Democrats Hold the Advantage in November's Elections," NBC News, September 23, 2018, https://www.nbcnews.com/politics/first-read/nbc-news-wsj -poll-democrats-hold-advantage-november-s-elections-n912046.

10. California's Senate race was excluded as the last remaining two candidates were of the same party. Texas's gubernatorial race was not viewed as competitive at any point in the cycle, in part because of funding differentials.

11. "American Election Eve Polling and Toplines," Latino Decisions, November 8, 2018, https://americasvoice.org/blog/latino-decisions-polling-2018/.

12. Adrian D. Pantoja, Ricardo Ramirez, and Gary M. Segura, "Citizens by Choice, Voters by Necessity: Patterns in Political Mobilization by Naturalized Latinos," *Political Research Quarterly* 54, no. 4 (December 2001), 729–50.

13. Matt Barreto, Sonja Diaz, Angie Gutierrez, Bryan Wilcox-Archuleta, and Ana Oaxaca, "Assessing Latino Vote Growth 2014–2018," UCLA Latino Policy and Politics Initiative, December 10, 2018, https://latino.ucla.edu/wp-content/uploads/2018/12/ LPPI_2018_vote2.pdf.

14. "*Washington Post*–ABC News poll October 8–11," *Washington Post*, October, 14, 2018, https://www.washingtonpost.com/politics/polling/washington-postabc-news-poll -october-811/2018/10/14/48ad9e68-ce40-11e8-ad0a-0e01efba3cc1_page.html.

12

Presidential Media and the Midterm Elections

Diana Owen

Much about the media's role in the 2018 elections defied established norms for midterm contests. The public was more interested in the midterms than usual, especially in the final weeks, and voters paid heightened attention to campaign news. Media coverage of election stories was notably more extensive than in the recent past. Cable news networks offered blanket coverage of the midterms, as the bulk of their political reporting was tied to the elections. Social media activity by candidates, political parties, commentators, journalists, and the public surged. Campaign advertising saturated television airwaves and digital networks to an unprecedented degree, as expenditures soared and tens of thousands of—mostly negative—spots were aired.

Still, the defining feature of the midterm media campaign was the prominence of Donald Trump. Off-year election campaigns traditionally are report cards on the chief executive's performance, and as such presidents tend to proceed with caution when entering the midterm media arena. Trump inserted himself into the midterms with abandon. He tweeted incessantly and stepped up his media appearances, especially on friendly sources like Fox News. He held rallies ostensibly for Republican candidates while trumpeting his own accomplishments and denigrating his rivals. His reelection campaign took the extraordinary step of running midterm campaign ads encouraging people to "Vote Republican" that focused on Trump's core issues of immigration and the economy. All the while, Trump dominated the national news agenda, as cable news treated his attention-getting antics as if they were must-see TV.[1] In red states, especially, media coverage of congressional and gubernatorial candidates was eclipsed by Trump's large shadow.[2]

Other factors were important to the 2018 midterm media story, especially those related to social media's rising significance. Misinformation and hoaxes, most often homegrown, were abundant and circulated widely on social media platforms. Serious attempts were made at suppressing voter turnout through adverse messaging.

NEWS COVERAGE

Midterm contests typically are characterized by low voter interest and involvement. As a result, mainstream media normally devote substantially less coverage to off-year elections than to presidential contests.[3] However, Americans became more attuned to political news than usual following the 2016 presidential election and the tumultuous times that followed. News organizations correctly anticipated that the hotly contested midterms would generate atypically high levels of voter attention, and thus devoted increased resources to coverage. Media outlets treated the midterms much like they would a presidential contest—a reasonable strategy given the looming presence of Donald Trump in the campaign.

Midterm coverage dominated cable news outlets and the nightly network news programs. Cable channels expanded their midterm coverage to include the entirety of primetime (8 to 11 p.m. ET) as opposed to the single hour (10 to 11 p.m. ET) that they dedicated to coverage of the 2014 midterms. Much of this additional time was filled with charged, often repetitious, debates among cable hosts, commenters, and political operatives. An inflammatory Trump remark or tweet could drive the cable conversation for hours, if not days. According to Nielsen, all cable and network news channels experienced a significant increase in their midterm election viewership, although the number of viewers was still roughly half of what it had been for the 2016 presidential contest.[4] Fox News had the largest audience for a midterm election in the history of cable news, while CNN and MSNBC attracted a record number of viewers to their midterm coverage.[5] Traffic to the websites of major news organizations, such as the *New York Times*, *Washington Post*, and CNN also escalated. National news sites overall experienced a 311 percent increase in traffic on Election Day over what they received on an average day in the month of October.[6]

MIDTERM MEDIA SPECTACLES

Unanticipated events created media frenzies with serious implications for the election that helped to fill the expanded cable news hole. In September, the

New York Times reported that deputy attorney general Rod Rosenstein had proposed secretly recording President Trump to document chaos in the White House and had recruited cabinet members to invoke the 25th Amendment to remove Trump from office for being unfit.[7] The news cycle was dominated by speculation that Trump would fire Rosenstein and endanger special counsel Robert Mueller's investigation into Russian interference in the 2016 election, a move that even his most ardent supporters on Fox News cautioned would be viewed negatively by the electorate. Conservative columnist Mark Steyn warned of a conspiracy during an appearance on Tucker Carlson's program on Fox: "This was deliberately leaked by an anti-Trump person to provoke Trump into firing Rod Rosenstein in order to assist the Democrats in the midterm elections."[8] Trump ultimately refrained from firing Rosenstein.

Another non-stop media spectacle was prompted by the Senate Judiciary Committee's confirmation hearings of Supreme Court nominee Brett Kavanaugh and the testimony of Christine Blasey Ford, who had accused him of sexually assaulting her when they were in high school. The highly contentious hearings made for explosive political theater that dominated the public's attention and sidetracked other campaign issues for three weeks.[9] Republican Senators Mitch McConnell of Kentucky and Lindsey Graham of South Carolina credited the "Kavanaugh effect" with galvanizing Republicans to vote against incumbent Democrats, including Democratic Senators Heidi Heitkamp of North Dakota and Joe Donnelly of Indiana, who had voted against Kavanaugh and ended up losing bids for second terms. Graham touted "Kavanaugh's Revenge" and commented on social media that "Liberal Democratic Senators and activists [sic] efforts to destroy Brett Kavanaugh ended up destroying Red State Democrats."[10] Aside from anecdotal evidence, however, it is unclear if a "Kavanaugh effect" was at work in the campaign as Heitkamp and Donnelly were facing difficult challenges from the outset.

VOTER NEWS PREFERENCES

Voters have become "news grazers" who get their campaign information from multiple sources.[11] People increasingly have been accessing election content from digital sources, including news websites and social media, as their preferences have trended away somewhat from print newspapers and television. These developments were apparent during the midterm elections. Television remained the main source of midterm election information. In fact, Trump supporters who decried the "fake news media" still tuned in to cable sources that were not limited to Trump-friendly Fox News.[12] Still, the percentage of people frequently consulting television news declined notably from 57 percent in 2016 to 49 percent in 2018. The percentage of the public listening regularly to radio news remained stable at around 25 percent.[13] At the same time, the number of people who get news often from news websites climbed from 28 percent to 33 percent as print newspaper use declined from 20 percent to 16 percent. Those relying often on social media for news grew from 18 percent to 20 percent between the two election cycles. Fully two-thirds of Americans used social media as a news source at least sometimes during the midterm campaigns, with almost half of the public getting news from Facebook.[14]

THE TRUMP FACTOR

Political scientist Gary Jacobson observed that "a sitting president has never been as central an issue in a midterm election as Trump is in 2018."[15] At the start of rallies in support of Republican midterm candidates, Donald Trump would proclaim, "Pretend I'm on the ballot!"[16] As far as the media were concerned, there was no need to pretend. Trump's behavior in the White House was an extension of his presidential campaign strategy. He featured prominently in midterm coverage, often stealing attention from candidates who were running. He overtly made the midterms a referendum on his presidency and would routinely tell his supporters, "A vote for [candidate] is a vote for me, and for our agenda to make America great again!"[17] He used the midterms as an occasion to promote his personal agenda and attempt to shore up support for his 2020 presidential reelection campaign. He drew inordinate amounts of press attention as he engaged extensively in the midterms through Twitter, made outspoken comments from the Oval Office, and hit the campaign trail. Trump bragged that he was using the midterms to get the word out to his supporters about his accomplishments. "One of the assets I have is I'm able to speak to people in tremendous numbers. I'm able to speak to them and often times it's on live television, you understand. So I'm able to get my word out."[18]

PRESIDENTIAL CAMPAIGNING
IN MIDTERM ELECTIONS

Conventional wisdom dictates that sitting presidents should distance themselves from midterm campaigns to avoid nationalizing elections that often are influenced by their performance in office. A president's popularity usually has dropped off since the beginning of his term, which was the case with Trump. The party in power generally loses congressional seats in off-year contests, and presidents prefer to situate the blame away from the White House. As a result, presidents tend to step gingerly into the primary arena.[19] An alternative perspective asserts that as the presidency increasingly has become a popular office that is associated more with personalities than parties, presidents have engaged strategically in midterm elections. They use midterms as an opportunity to shift the composition of Congress to serve their needs, to reshape and improve their own image, and to align their party with their personal ideological preferences.[20] In addition, presidents such as Bill Clinton have used the midterms to raise funds for candidates and their party. However, the president's contribution to fundraising has been limited somewhat in the era of Citizens United as there are no restrictions on independent campaign expenditures by corporations, labor unions, and other associations.[21]

Donald Trump's foray into the 2018 midterms was indicative of the revisionist perspective; however, his engagement in the elections took presidential involvement in state-level campaigns to a whole new level. Trump became immersed in the midterms beginning with the primaries. Presidents typically are more reluctant to participate actively in primaries than the general election to avoid fracturing party unity. Instead, Trump jumped into highly contested Republican campaigns. He targeted on Twitter sitting Republican members of Congress who spoke out against him. He weighed in at the last minute in Senate races where he felt he could rally his base to support a candidate that he viewed favorably. He also supported candidates who faced little opposition so that he could claim credit for their victories.[22] Sidney Milkis of the University of Virginia's Miller Center for Public Affairs observed that "Trump's involvement in the primaries was the most dramatic since the 1938 purge campaign"[23] At that time, Franklin Roosevelt attempted to punish fellow Democrats who did not support his New Deal policies by campaigning against them in the primaries. FDR's "purge campaign" was the first midterm contest that was nationalized by a president, and his efforts were unsuccessful.[24]

Trump stepped up his campaign efforts during the general election, especially in the final days. His unconventional level of midterm engagement, while welcomed by some in deep red states, sparked concern among Republican leaders who feared that the extensive media attention to Trump would derail their midterm strategy in tough races.[25] The "Trump Effect" on the midterms became a regular hook for news reports. Trump's presence on the campaign trail followed the formula that he had honed in the presidential race. His tweets and speeches at rallies were littered with attacks on political foes, including potential opponents in the 2020 presidential elections, such as "sleepy" Joe Biden and "Pocahontas" Elizabeth Warren. He aggressively leveled attacks on the "fake news media," even as the press covered his every move. Trump's message was amplified by his supporters who retweeted his posts, which spread widely through their networks. Fear appeals that Trump peddled during the 2016 presidential contest were reinvigorated for the midterm contest. He galvanized his supporters with exaggerated statements about a caravan of migrants who were making their way to the southern border. Without evidence, he characterized the asylum-seekers as an "invasion" of "stone cold criminals," "smugglers," and "trespassers," sparking chants of "build the wall!" at campaign rallies.[26]

In the final days of the campaign, Trump hosted many rallies in contested states, including events for prior political foes. The press spent significant time covering Trump's support for Ted Cruz, who faced a strong opponent in Democrat Beto O'Rourke for a Texas Senate seat. The Texas race became a national media event, as the upstart O'Rourke gave the high-profile incumbent Cruz a run for his money. The media discussed at length how Cruz had gone from "Lyin' Ted" in the 2016 presidential primaries to "Beautiful Ted" in Trump's assessment. At a rally with Trump, Cruz looked ahead to the presidential election, stating: "I am honored that President Trump is here endorsing and supporting my campaign and I look forward to campaigning alongside him in 2020."[27] The rallies for state-level candidates received considerable national coverage, although Trump lamented that even Fox News had backed off from hours-long live broadcasts on cable television.

Historically, when presidents have campaigned actively, the impact on electing candidates from their party has been either minimal or negative. Democratic president Andrew Johnson, who was at odds with the Republican-controlled Congress, embarked on an unprecedented speaking tour in the 1866 midterm elections. As one of the first candidates to engage in an off-year election, his campaign strategy backfired. More Republicans were elected to Congress, which enabled his impeachment in the House of Representatives.[28] Even Ronald Reagan, whose popularity was relatively high, was not able to sway midterm voters in 1986. Only five of the 18 Republican senatorial candidates for whom he campaigned won.[29] Donald Trump endorsed 75 congressional candidates mostly in Republican-leaning states either by tweet or personal appearances at rallies. Forty-two candidates—or 55 percent of his endorsements—were successful. Of the 36 candidates for whom he personally stumped, 23 won. As Brookings scholar Elaine Kamarck observed, "Consistent with his behavior since being elected, Trump made no effort to convert voters in this election, mostly playing to his base."[30]

ALL TRUMP, ALL THE TIME

During the 2016 presidential race, Donald Trump benefitted from far more press coverage than any other candidate. Trump received 63 percent of all primary campaign coverage and garnered 15 percent more coverage than Hillary Clinton during the general election.[31] A substantial portion of Trump's reportage was due to the media amplifying his social media postings—a trend that continued in 2018. Democrats sought to keep pace with Trump in the midterms and stepped up their social media game. A study conducted by the *New York Times* found that Democratic congressional candidates posted more messages and generated substantially more interactions (comments on posts and shares) on social media than Republicans. Over a 30-day period, Democratic Senate candidates prompted 10 million interactions on Facebook compared to 2.2 million for their Republican counterparts. Democratic House candidates bested Republican candidates with 3.5 million versus 1.5 million interactions.[32]

The number of social media posts and interactions is an imperfect gauge of candidate popularity or electoral success, but it is hardly inconsequential. Social media's function in political campaigns has broadened in reach, consequence, and complexity with each passing electoral contest. These platforms, especially Twitter, Facebook, Instagram, and YouTube, have become steady sources of election content for news outlets, especially cable channels with large audiences. This development has greatly benefitted Donald Trump. Even outlets that viewed Trump negatively give him countless hours of free publicity by showcasing his Twitter wars. The texts of his social media rants have become standard fare in the crawl on cable news screens. Despite the Democrats' advantage in the number of posts in the 2018 midterms, Trump's tweets received more media attention and generated more stories, especially on cable news.[33]

The tone and focus of news media coverage in the 2018 midterms bucked established trends. Generally speaking, media coverage tends to follow voter preferences as the winning party receives more favorable news coverage than the losing party. However, a study by Stuart Soroka of articles about the 2018 election in major newspapers found that the advantage in coverage went to the Republicans over the Democrats despite the outcome signaling a "blue wave." Soroka argues that the media's fixation on covering Trump is responsible for this anomaly. "One result of repeating the President's attacks against the Democrats is that the tone of coverage moves decidedly away from the Democrats—the balance of coverage no longer reflects the balance of public support for each party."[34]

SOCIAL MEDIA IN THE MIDTERMS

Donald Trump came to the 2018 midterms with a large social media follow-ing from his days on *The Apprentice* and his presidential bid that he used to his advantage. Trump supporters in 2016 were more inclined to follow news, engage in online discussions, and participate in campaign activities, such as recruiting volunteers, via social media than Clinton voters.[35] Trump loyalists remained receptive to his social media messages during the midterm campaigns, tuning in to his tweets with even greater frequency over time. His tweets were a primary source of election information especially for his followers living in "news deserts" where trusted local news sources have disappeared.[36]

CELEBRITIES ON SOCIAL MEDIA

Celebrities other than the reality television president were active on social media during the 2018 campaign, taking political stands and urging their fans to vote. The ability of social media influencers with large followings to have an effect on elections is up for debate. However, anecdotal evidence suggests that they can act as opinion leaders, especially for young voters, although their influence is more apparent for voter registration and turnout than vote choice.

Pop star Taylor Swift, who had 112 million followers on Instagram and 85 million on Twitter in 2018, posted a social media message encouraging people to register to vote. Four days later, 413,000 new voters had signed up, more than half of whom were ages 18–29, which far exceeded the 190,000 who registered in the entire month of October.[37] Swift, who had previously refrained from posting about politics, also urged supporters to vote for two Democratic candidates in her home state of Tennessee—Representative Jim Cooper (who was reelected) and Phil Bredesen for Senate (who was defeated). Swift's Instagram post attacked Bredesen's Republican opponent, Representative Marsha Blackburn, for her voting record in Congress, which Swift alleged failed to protect human rights. Donald Trump responded to Swift, tweeting, "I'm sure Taylor Swift doesn't know anything about her. Let's say that I like Taylor's music about 25 percent less now, okay?"[38] Swift's social media foray into politics, and Trump retort, sparked extensive, heated debate on social media and grabbed headlines on cable television and print media.

MIDTERM MISINFORMATION

As social media have become increasingly central to the electoral process, these sources have become more susceptible to spreading misinformation either intentionally or accidentally. Dissemination of misinformation through social media surged during the 2016 presidential election and continued to diffuse in its aftermath. Contributing to this trend has been the distribution of false content by automated accounts or "bots." Researchers at the Oxford Internet Institute found that "junk news," defined as "various forms of propaganda and ideologically extreme, hyper-partisan, or conspiratorial political news and information" that is verifiably false and presented as factual, grew as a problem during the midterm elections. More junk news was propagated during the 2018 midterms than in 2016. Users often did not distinguish between junk news and factual information, and they shared more junk than facts in their networks. People from a wider swath of the conservative political spectrum shared misinformation that previously was contained in the networks of Donald Trump's base and the alt-right. Less than 5 percent of the information sources referenced on social media in the midterms were from public agencies, experts, or the candidates themselves.[39]

The rise in misinformation, and the consequent implication of their role in the problem, prompted efforts by large social media companies to curtail the circulation of false content during the midterms. Facebook and Twitter instituted fact-checking initiatives and digital literacy programs. They developed algorithms to downrank false news.[40] Facebook established a "War Room" coordinating a team of 300 workers to stop the distribution of misleading content, conspiracy theories, and divisive propaganda, and to curb coordinated influence campaigns.[41] The company worked to mitigate "fake news" websites that were designed to look like legitimate news sources. It appears that these efforts curtailed the influence of foreign operations, especially Russian bots, from playing much of a role in the campaign. Thirty Facebook and 85 Instagram accounts were suspended due to their connections to Russian agencies.[42] However, the influence of these initiatives on social media users' experience was more mixed. User interactions with false stories on Facebook declined significantly between the end of July 2016 and July 2018. Sharing false stories on Twitter—Donald Trump's preferred social medium—rose considerably.[43]

Misinformation was abundant even on platforms designed to provide voters with accurate information. Twitter launched "The latest on the US midterm elections" page where users were invited to "Explore the latest news and top commentary, or join conversations about the issues, debates and candidates happening right now in each state." The page was designed to promote "conversational health" among voters, but it still contained tweets that pushed false information, conspiracy theories, and material circulated by bots. On its first day, interspersed amid legitimate information, the page included a tweet alleging that Democrats had paid for the caravan moving toward the Mexican border in order to "create another 'separating families' crisis" before the election. Erroneous claims were posted about illegal voting and candidates who were still in the running dropping out of the race. Trump-style personal attacks against candidates on both sides emanating from false accounts were attributed to politicians and celebrities.[44]

VOTER SUPPRESSION

Voter suppression through social media—attempts to depress turnout by disseminating misinformation—has become more prevalent in the digital age. In the 2016 presidential election, voter suppression messages, many of which originated in Russia, were posted across a range of social media platforms. They sought to divide Americans by targeting racial, religious, and ideological groups with messages meant to keep them from the polls. African Americans received posts in their social media feeds that said, "I WON'T VOTE, WILL YOU?" and "Everybody SUCKS. We're Screwed 2016." A study by the University of Oxford and Graphika found that the messaging clearly benefitted Donald Trump and the Republican Party and damaged Hillary Clinton's presidential bid. Voter suppression efforts had the effect of confusing and angering voters. They had the potential to influence tight races and undermine faith in the electoral process.[45]

There were legitimate concerns that social media were again being used as voter suppression tools in the midterms, especially from domestic sources.[46] False information about where to vote and how to file absentee ballots was circulated. Rumors were tweeted that federal immigration agents would be stationed at polling stations to check voters' citizenship status. Hashtags targeting particular groups appeared on Twitter, such as "#NoMenMidterms" and "#LetWomenDecide," which urged liberal men to stay home so that women could have more influence in the election. Doctored photos of long lines at the polls were posted to discourage turnout. Facebook and Twitter took some steps to deal with misinformation about voting when contacted by state election leaders and voting rights organizations. However, distinguishing coordinated voter suppression efforts from citizens exercising their free speech rights can be difficult.[47]

ADVERTISING

Advertising in the 2018 midterm elections reached new heights in terms of volume and negativity. According to the Wesleyan Media Project (http://mediaproject.wesleyan.edu), over 3.6 million congressional and gubernatorial ads were aired on television, marking a 109 percent increase in House ads and a 66 percent increase in ads for governor over the 2014 midterms. Further, there was a 61 percent growth in negative TV ads.[48] While television ads account for more than half of the $8.9 billion spent on advertising in 2018, digital ads proliferated. Over $1.8 billion was spend on digital ads in 2018 compared to $271 million in 2014.[49] Digital ads, especially, were used to increase turnout by targeting voting blocs. The independent group Next-Gen America backed by billionaire Tom Steyer, for example, spent over $4 million on anti-Republican ads in battleground states aimed at getting young voters to turn out.[50]

Negative ads long have been a staple of American election campaigns. However, the caustic tone of ads in the 2018 midterms exceeded the norm. The large number of competitive races, especially in the House, accounts for the increase in the amount and the more negative tone of spots. Ads in competitive campaigns focused on polarizing issues of immigration, health care, and identity politics.

Trump was featured in 22 percent of all midterm election ads for Republican candidates. His role in election spots differed markedly by the partisan composition of a state. Republicans running in states where Trump remained popular were most likely to feature him in their ads. Spots composed of clips of Trump making supportive statements during rallies, such as "Josh is a star" about Missouri Senate candidate Josh Hawley, were highly effective in mobilizing supporters in solid red states. According to Kantar Media, Trump appeared in over 11,000 television ads supporting Republican Senate candidates in the red state of Tennessee during the month of October. At the same time, Trump was mentioned in only three of the 13,000 Senate ads Republicans ran in the purple states of Wisconsin, Michigan, and Nevada.[51] Trump was mentioned in only 6 percent of Democratic candidate spots. Democrats most often chose to ignore Trump as opposed to even addressing him negatively.[52]

TRUMP CAMPAIGN ADS

Trump's presidential 2020 presidential reelection campaign took the unprecedented step of airing ads urging citizens to "Vote Republican" in the midterm contests. The first spot targeted college-educated, white women with whom Trump was especially unpopular. The ad had an uncharacteristically subdued tone that contrasted sharply with Trump's acerbic rhetoric at campaign rallies and avoided his stock divisive issue of immigration and crime. His campaign organization spent $6 million—$3.5 million on national television and $2.5 million online—to air the spot in the week before the election.[53] Trump himself did not appear in the 60-second ad, which is narrated by a white, suburban professional woman who credits Republicans with lowering unemployment and improving the economy. The ad used images designed to appeal to middle-class families, such as owning a home in a nice neighborhood and investing in their children's future. The narrator was seen marking a paper ballot for a generic female Republican candidate, "Tamara Tucker," who was running against the fictitious Democrat "William Cody," clearly an effort to show the Republican Party supports women. The tag line of the ad implored voters: "This could all go away if we don't remember what we came from."[54]

Five days before the election, however, the Trump campaign's final advertising push was an inflammatory, and largely misleading, anti-immigration web video. Trump himself tweeted the 53-second video that featured Luis Bracamontes, a Mexican immigrant who was in the United States illegally when he killed two law enforcement officials in California in 2014, making expletive-laced comments during his murder trial. Clips of Bracamontes smirking and bragging about the killings are interspersed with footage of a caravan of migrants walking toward the Mexican border. The video highlights a clash allegedly between the migrants and Mexican border authorities, although the caravan was many miles from the border at the time. The ad's unabashed message was that undocumented immigrants were criminals who posed a dangerous threat to the country. The ad claimed that "Democrats let him into our country; Democrats let him stay." However, Bracamontes had been deported on numerous occasions under both Democratic and Republican presidents, and last had entered the country illegally during Republican George W. Bush's presidency. He also had been arrested on drug charges in Phoenix and released by the office of then-Maricopa County Sheriff Joe Arpaio, a vocal supporter of candidate Trump who had been pardoned by President Trump after his conviction for violating a judge's order to stop racial profiling.[55]

CNN called the video, "the most racially charged national political ad in 30 years," and refused to post it.[56] The ad was subsequently pulled by Fox News, Fox Business News, NBC broadcast news, and MSNBC after it had aired. Facebook eventually blocked the ad from paid distribution, but otherwise allowed it to be posted.[57] The video/ad was reminiscent of the Willie

Horton attack ad which was aired in the1988 presidential election by an independent group supporting Republican George H. W. Bush. The spot depicted an African-American man convicted of murder who raped a white woman and stabbed her partner while furloughed from prison under a plan Bush's opponent, Democrat Michael Dukakis, had put in place when he was governor of Massachusetts. The Willie Horton ad, and a subsequent spot that showed convicts walking in and out of prison through a "revolving door" exploited racial stereotypes and fears and helped to label Dukakis as soft on crime.[58]

CONCLUSION

Campaign media in the 2018 midterm elections were anomalous in the extent to which presidential communication dominated. An usually energized midterm electorate, a highly polarized political climate, and especially a presidential personality that sought the media spotlight drove intensive press coverage. In many ways, election coverage reflected the chaos of the Trump presidency. An off-the-rails White House visit and endorsement from rapper Kanye West and the unexpected sexual assault controversy surrounding Supreme Court nominee Brett Kavanaugh were just a sample of the high-profile made-for-media events that spilled over to the electoral context. Donald Trump's unconventional use of social media to promote himself and upbraid his enemies continued unabated during the campaign. Candidates accelerated their Twitter use during the midterms, especially as Democrats sought to inundate the platform with posts. Despite their best efforts, they were unable to translate their tweets into press coverage to match that garnered by Trump. But in the end, the quantity of Trump's media coverage did not subvert the "blue wave" of Democrats that reclaimed the House of Representatives.

The trends witnessed in the 2018 midterms may represent the norm for the period of Trumpian politics. In many ways, they appear to be a product of a particular personality who honed his craft in the world of reality television. Whether they will persist beyond the Trump presidency is yet to be determined.

NOTES

1. Tessa Berenson, "President Trump's Midterm Strategy: Dominate the News," *Time*, October 11, 2018, http://time.com/5421823/donald-trump-midterm-elections-controversy/.

2. Ross Ramsey, "Analysis: The Most Important 2018 Candidate Isn't on the Ballot," *Texas Tribune*, August 8, 2018, https://www.houstonpublicmedia.org/articles/news/2018/08/08/299200/analysis-the-most-important-2018-candidate-isnt-on-the-ballot/.

3. Dan Schill and John Allen Hendricks, "Media, Message, and Mobilization: Political Communication in the 2014 Election Campaigns," in John Allen Hendricks and Dan Schill, *Communication and Midterm Elections: Media, Message, and Mobilization* (New York: Palgrave Macmillan, 2016), 3–23.

4. John Koblin, "Midterm Elections Deliver a Ratings Surge, with Fox News in the Lead," *New York Times*, November 7, 2018, https://www.nytimes.com/2018/11/07/business/media/midterm-election-tv-ratings.html.

5. A. J. Katz, "Fox News, CNN Split the 2018 Midterm Election Ratings Battle," *Adweek*, November 7, 2018, https://www.adweek.com/tvnewser/fox-news-cnn-split-2018-midterm-election-night-ratings-battle/383740.

6. Marisa Fernandez, "Traffic to News Sites Quadrupled on Election Day," *Axios*, November 16, 2018, https://www.axios.com/election-day-traffic-news-outlet-coverage-66d83267-bffd-4176-a206-045344ba6e36.html.

7. Adam Goldman and Michael S. Schmidt, "Rod Rosenstein Suggested Secretly Recording Trump and Discussed 25th Amendment," *New York Times*, September 21, 2018, https://www.nytimes.com/2018/09/21/us/politics/rod-rosenstein-wear-wire-25th-amendment.html.

8. John Cassidy, "Why Hasn't Donald Trump Fired Rod Rosenstein Yet?" *New Yorker*, September 25, 2018, https://www.newyorker.com/news/our-columnists/why-hasnt-donald-trump-fired-rod-rosenstein-yet.

9. Jeremy Gelman and Steven Wilson, "Will Kavanaugh's Confirmation Affect the Midterms? Here's What Showed Up on Social Media," *Washington Post*, November 5, 2018, https://www.washingtonpost.com/news/monkey-cage/wp/2018/11/05/will-kavanaughs-confirmation-affect-the-midterms-heres-what-showed-up-in-social-media/?utm_term=.880b43cf1074.

10. Kevin Breuninger, "Republicans Credit the 'Kavanaugh Effect" for Senate Wins against Red-State Democrats," CNBC, November 7, 2018, https://www.cnbc.com/2018/11/07/gop-credits-kavanaugh-effect-for-senate-wins-against-red-state-democrats.html.

11. Richard Forgette, *News Grazers* (Los Angeles: CQ Press, 2019).

12. Diana Owen, "Trump Supporters' Use of Social Media and Political Engagement," paper prepared for presentation at the Annual Meeting of the American Political Science Association, August 30–September 2, 2018.

13. Elisa Shearer, "Social Media Outpaces Print Newspapers in the U.S. as a News Source," Pew Research Center, December 10, 2018, http://www.pewresearch.org/fact-tank/2018/12/10/social-media-outpaces-print-newspapers-in-the-u-s-as-a-news-source/.

14. "Social Media Fact Sheet: Social Media Use over Time," Pew Research Center, February 5, 2018, http://www.pewinternet.org/fact-sheet/social-media/.

15. Elaine Kamarck, "Trump Endorsed 75 Candidates in the Midterms. How Did They Fare on Election Day?" Brookings, updated November 7, 2018, https://www.brookings.edu/blog/fixgov/2018/11/07/trump-endorsed-75-candidates-in-the-midterms-how-did-they-fare-on-election-day/.

16. Jeff Zeleny, "The 2018 Trump Factor: It's All about Him," CNN, October 22, 2018, https://www.cnn.com/2018/10/22/politics/trump-factor-all-about-him/index.html.

17. Anu Narayanswamy, Michelle Ye Hee Lee, Shelly Tan, Amber Phillips, and Lauren Tierney, "'A Vote for ——— Is a Vote for Me': Trump Has Endorsed These 2018 Candidates So Far," *Washington Post*, October 8, 2018, https://www.washingtonpost.com/graphics/2018/politics/trump-endorsements-rallies/?utm_term = .0dbf4eb3a4ff.

18. Berenson, "President Trump's Midterm Strategy: Dominate the News."

19. Brendan J. Doherty, *The Rise of the President's Permanent Campaign* (Lawrence, KS: University of Kansas Press, 2012).

20. Michael A. Julius, *Midterm Campaigning and the Modern Presidency* (Santa Barbara, CA: Praeger, 2018).

21. Olivia B. Waxman, "Trump Is Hitting the Midterm Campaign Trail Hard. History Shows That Doesn't Always Make a Difference," October 22, 2018, http://time.com/5419926/president-midterm-campaign/.

22. Narayanswamy et al., "'A Vote for ——— Is a Vote for Me': Trump Has Endorsed These 2018 Candidates So Far."

23. Waxman, "Trump Is Hitting the Midterm Campaign Trail Hard. History Shows That Doesn't Always Make a Difference."

24. Doherty, *The Rise of the President's Permanent Campaign.*

25. Jonathan Martin, Alexander Burns, and Maggie Haberman, "Trump's Role in Midterm Elections Roils Republicans," *New York Times*, April 28, 2018, https://www.nytimes.com/2018/04/28/us/politics/trump-midterm-elections.html.

26. Eugene Scott, "Before the Midterms, Trump Harped on the Migrant Caravan. Since Then, He Hasn't Brought It Up," *Washington Post*, November 8, 2018, https://www.washingtonpost.com/politics/2018/11/08/before-midterms-trump-harped-migrant-caravan-since-then-he-has-barely-mentioned-it/?utm_term = .b7904ccfaa98.

27. Patrick Svitek and Emma Platoff, "At Houston Re-Election Rally, Donald Trump Mocks Beto O'Rourke and Praises Ted Cruz as a Key Ally," *Texas Tribune*, October 22, 2018, https://www.texastribune.org/2018/10/22/Donald-trump-rally-ted-cruz-houston-eleciton-2018/.

28. Doherty, *The Rise of the President's Permanent Campaign.*

29. Jeffrey E. Cohen, Michael A. Krassa, and John A. Hamman, "The Impact of Presidential Campaigning on Midterm U.S. Senate Elections," *American Political Science Review* 85, no. 1 (March 1991), 165–78.

30. Kamarck, "Trump Endorsed 75 Candidates in the Midterms. How Did They Fare on Election Day?"

31. Thomas E. Patterson, "News Coverage of the 2016 General Election: How the Press Failed the Voters," Research Report, December 7, 2016, Cambridge, MA: Shorenstein Center on Media, Politics and Public Policy, Harvard Kennedy School, https://shorensteincenter.org/news-coverage-2016-general-election/.

32. Kevin Roose and Keith Collins, "Who's Winning the Social Media Midterms?" *New York Times*, October 18, 2018, https://www.nytimes.com/interactive/2018/10/18/us/politics/social-election.html.

33. Ibid.

34. Stuart Soroka, "How President Trump Helped the Media Lose the 2018 Midterm Elections," LSE US Center Daily Blog, November 30, 2018, http://blogs.lse.ac.uk/usappblog/2018/11/30/how-president-trump-helped-the-media-lose-the-2018-midterm-elections/.

35. Diana Owen, "The Digital Revolution and American Politics in the Trump Era," paper prepared for presentation at the 17th Annual Parliamentary Transatlantic Forum, NATO Parliamentary Assembly, National Defense University, Fort McNair, Washington, D.C., December 11–13, 2017; Diana Owen, "Trump Supporters' Use of Social Media and Political Engagement," paper prepared for presentation at the Annual Meeting of the American Political Science Association, August 30–September 2, 2018.

36. Ibid.

37. Hunter Schwarz, "How Taylor Swift Turned Her Instagram Into a Get-Out-the-Vote Fan Page," CNN, November 6, 2018, https://www.cnn.com/2018/11/06/politics/taylor -swift-instagram-gotv/index.html.

38. Amy B Wang, "Taylor Swift's Endorsement of Democrats Is Followed by a Spike in Voter Registrations," *Washington Post*, October 9, 2018, https://www.washingtonpost .com/arts-entertainment/2018/10/09/taylor-swifts-endorsement-democrats-causes-spike -voter-registrations/?utm_term = .5aed2eae8cad.

39. Nahema Marchal, Lisa-Maria Neudert, Bence Kollanyi, and Philip N. Howard, "Polarization, Partisanship and Junk News Consumption on Social Media during the 2018 US Midterm Elections," Data Memo, 2018, Oxford, UK: Computational Propaganda Research Project, University of Oxford, http://blogs.oii.ox.ac.uk/comprop/wp-content/ uploads/sites/93/2018/11/marchal_et_al.pdf.

40. Ibid.

41. Sheera Frenkel and Mike Isaac, "Inside Facebook's Election 'War Room,'" *New York Times*, September 19, 2018, https://www.nytimes.com/2018/09/19/technology/face book-election-war-room.html.

42. Max Read, "Facebook Stopped Russia. Is That Enough?" *New York Magazine*, November 8, 2018, http://nymag.com/intelligencer/2018/11/fake-news-on-facebook-in -the-2018-midterms.html.

43. Hunt Allcott, Matthew Gentzkow, and Chuan Yu, "Trends in the Diffusion of Misinformation on Social Media," Research Report, September 2018, Stanford, CA: Stanford University, Institute for Economic Policy Research, https://siepr.stanford.edu/system/files/ publications/18–029.pdf.

44. Ali Breland, "Twitter's New Midterm Election Page Highlights Hoaxes and False Information," *The Hill*, November 30, 2018, https://thehill.com/policy/technology/ 413905-twitters-new-midterm-election-page-highlights-hoaxes-and-false-information. Mallory Locklear, "Twitter's New Midterm Election Page Already Includes Fake News," *Engadget*, October 30, 2018, https://www.engadget.com/2018/10/30/twitter-midterm -election-page-includes-fake-news/.

45. Philip N. Howard, Bharath Ganesh, and Dimitra Liotsiou. "The IRA, Social Media and Political Polarization in the United States, 2012–2018," 2018, Research Report, Oxford, UK: University of Oxford, Computational Propaganda Research Project, https:// comprop.oii.ox.ac.uk/wp-content/uploads/sites/93/2018/12/IRA-Report-2018.pdf.

46. Nancy Scola, "Experts Warn the Social Media Threat This Election Is Home-grown," *Politico*, November 5, 2018, https://www.politico.com/story/2018/11/05/elec tions-social-media-american-trolls-959382.

47. Tony Romm, "How Facebook and Twitter Are Rushing to Stop Voter Suppression Online for the Midterm Elections," *Washington Post*, October 28, 2018, https://www.wash ingtonpost.com/technology/2018/11/02/how-facebook-twitter-are-rushing-stop-voter -suppression-online-midterm-election/?utm_term = .ff564f88 3665.

48. "61% Increase in Volume of Negative Ads," Wesleyan Media Project, October 30, 2018, http://mediaproject.wesleyan.edu/releases/103018/.

49. Frederika Schouten, "Politicians, Groups Turn to Digital Advertising in Race to Turn Out Voters for Midterms," CNN, October 15, 2018, https://www.cnn.com/2018/10/15/politics/digital-advertising-midterm-elections/index.html.

50. Sydney Ember, "Young Voters Could Make a Difference. Will They?" *New York Times*, November 2, 2018, https://www.nytimes.com/2018/11/02/us/politics/young-voters-midterms.html.

51. Craig Gilbert and Maureen Groppe, "The Election May Be about President Donald Trump, but Most of the Final Ads Aren't," *USA Today*, November 5, 2018, https://www.usatoday.com/story/news/politics/elections/2018/11/05/midterm-elections-president-trump-not-mentioned-most-ads/1885125002/.

52. Zeleny, "The 2018 Trump Factor: It's All about Him."

53. Caitlin Huey-Burns, "Trump Campaign Launches $6 Million Ad Buy for Midterms," CBS News, October 29, 2018, https://www.cbsnews.com/news/trump-campaign-launches-6-million-ad-for-midterms/.

54. Julie Hirschfeld Davis, "Why Trump Is Absent from His Own TV Ad," *New York Times*, October 29, 2018, https://www.nytimes.com/2018/10/29/us/politics/trump-ads-republicans-midterms.html.

55. Eli Rosenberg, "Trump's New Immigration Ad Was Panned as Racist. Turns Out It Was Also Based on a Falsehood," *Washington Post*, November 2, 2018, https://www.washingtonpost.com/politics/2018/11/02/trumps-new-immigration-ad-was-panned-racist-turns-out-it-was-also-based-falsehood/?utm_term = .20318be286c9.

56. Stephen Collinson, "Trump Shocks with Racist New Ad Days before Midterms," CNN, November 1, 2018, https://www.cnn.com/2018/10/31/politics/donald-trump-immigration-paul-ryan-midterms/index.html.

57. Adam Gabbatt, "Fox News, NBC and Facebook Pull Trump Ad Widely Condemned as Racist," *The Guardian*, November 5, 2018, https://www.theguardian.com/us-news/2018/nov/05/trump-anti-immigration-ad-pulled-fox-news-nbc-facebook.

58. John Hurwitz and Mark Peffley, "Playing the Race Card in the Post-Willie Horton Era," *Public Opinion Quarterly* 69, no. 1 (Spring 2005), 99–112.

13

Foresight in 2020

New Features of the Democratic Delegate Selection Rules

Joshua T. Putnam

The spotlight shone on the Democratic presidential nomination process during the 2016 cycle. Unlike the party's last competitive presidential nomination in 2008, however, a Democrat did not end up in the White House. Instead, the broader Democratic Party found itself locked out of the levers of power not only in Washington but in state governments across wide swaths of the country. Left wandering the wilderness, Democrats sought to pick up the pieces and begin their journey back to power.

As decision makers in losing parties are often motivated to do, their quest for the answers that would help begin reversing the party's fortunes took them down a path of reflection, reexamining the process that got Democrats, at least in part and at the presidential level, to the nadir of power following the 2016 elections. The scrutiny was widespread, but one spotlight in particular was again fixed on process. Presidential general election campaigns are built on foundations constructed during nomination battles, and the battle for the 2016 Democratic presidential nomination was waged against a backdrop of grievances about the rules. It reached a fevered enough pitch that the legitimacy of the process was called into question, and that, in turn, fractured the party to a degree that lingered into and out of the Democratic National Convention, affecting the party's ability to fully coalesce around its nominee.

None of this is unique to the Democratic Party before, during, or after 2016. Again, parties that find themselves out of power often look to fix the problems of the past in order to better shape the future. But that backward gaze may find remedies for bygone problems that are not often repeated under different conditions ahead. Like other parties before it, the Democratic Party of the 2010s found itself fighting the last battle and laying the groundwork through its nomination rules for future unintended consequences.

THE 2016 DEMOCRATIC RULES

If losing parties seek to fix the problems of the past in order to get back on top, parties that find themselves in power are motivated to maintain the status quo. Winning, after all, means that at least something was working. Coming off a 2012 election in which the party retained the White House and clung to a narrow majority in the U.S. Senate, the Democratic National Committee was content to stick with what helped it reap those spoils. The nomination rules that were crafted in 2009–2010 for the 2012 cycle achieved their goal: They not only successfully renominated Barack Obama, but he also was ultimately reelected in November.

No, President Obama did not face any serious challenge in the 2012 primaries and caucuses, and as a result, the nomination rules (and the changes instituted for that cycle in particular) were not stress tested in any significant way. That meant that at the 2012 Democratic National Convention in Charlotte there were the beginnings of only minor tinkering around the edges on the nomination rules for 2016. Importantly, the Convention Rules and Bylaws Committee did not charter a commission to examine how the nomination rules operated in 2012, as had been the party's custom for much of the post-reform era. Instead, the standing DNC Rules and Bylaws Committee handled the rules-making process for 2016 in-house. And by the summer of 2014, that yielded very little in the way of demonstrable change.

The biggest of the changes from 2012 to 2016 was a reduction in the number of base delegates to the national convention from which pledged delegates are apportioned to states. Throughout the post-reform era—from 1972 onward—the number of base delegates was set at 3,000. For 2012, however, that number was raised to 3,700. That increase had a couple of noteworthy impacts.

First, the base number of pledged delegates does not include superdelegates, the DNC members and elected officials who serve as unpledged delegates. They are free to align themselves with any candidate of their choosing at any time from before or during primary season and up to the convention itself. But raising the number of base delegates by roughly the same amount as the total number of superdelegates had the impact of diluting the voice and power of the superdelegates in the 2012 process, albeit during an uncontested cycle.

Moreover, it additionally had the effect of rewarding 700 more Democratic activists with trips to the national convention. And that reward is not without value to the national party. Those additional activists-turned-delegates often end up providing an integral foundation to the grassroots efforts of presidential general election campaigns. Yet, the addition also created a logistical nightmare for the DNC in planning, accommodating, and conducting a national convention. The problem was acute enough that the party sought to dial back the number of base delegates moving forward to the 2016 cycle. And that had the effect of recalibrating the balance between pledged delegates and superdelegates toward the latter.

Other than some minor technical changes to the rules, the decrease of base delegates from 3,700 in 2012 to 3,200 for 2016 stood as the biggest alteration in the delegate selection rules ahead of the 2016 cycle. But that change, finalized in the summer of 2014, was borne not of any calculation about how the 2016 process might progress, but of the practicalities of successfully managing a national convention at the end of that process. That change aside, however, the delegate selection rules for 2016 were basically the same as the rules that renominated President Obama in 2012; rules that were adopted in the summer of 2010.

THE 2016 DEMOCRATIC NOMINATION RACE AS A BASELINE FOR 2020 CHANGES

As the invisible primary period of the 2016 cycle heated up in 2015, those rules adopted in the late summer of 2014—much of which was, again, carried over from the 2012 rules finalized in 2010—became the source of some controversy in the race to determine the 2016 Democratic presidential nominee.

Superdelegates

There were three main flashpoints over which the 2016 campaigns clashed. The first began to reveal itself in the fall of 2015. An Associated Press survey[1] of the 712 unpledged superdelegates showed that Hillary Clinton had secured commitments from over half (359) and had a 45:1 advantage over her nearest rival, Independent Senator Bernie Sanders of Vermont, in the unofficial tally with fewer than one-third still unpledged. While that provided other candidates—Sanders and Maryland Governor Martin O'Malley—some room for growth, the advantage sent an early signal about where many in the establishment of the Democratic Party were with respect to who the 2016 nominee should be. Presidential candidates often make attempts at sending such signals via endorsements, fundraising, hiring, polling, and media attention as a means of warding off competition, but few have been as successful in those efforts from outside the White House as Clinton was during the invisible primary period of the 2016 cycle. And the sorts of endorsements that Clinton had racked up by that stage of the race have proven the best predictor of primary success in the post-reform era.[2]

As successful as the Clinton campaign was on that front, that success did not paper over the fact that the Democratic Party had not had an active nomination race in eight years and that there was demand for if not an alternative to the former secretary of state, then at least a race in general. This was evidenced by the shrinking polling advantage Clinton held nationally as the invisible primary progressed and primary season approached.

But that was the crux of the superdelegate problem in the 2016 Democratic process. The Clinton lead there was enough to keep Vice President Joe Biden out of the race. Although Biden considered a bid during the latter half of 2015, he and advisers around him judged that Clinton's advantages were too steep to overcome. Effective though that type of warding-off strategy is on establishment figures, it is hypothetically less meaningful to a disruptive candidate, and one who was picking up polling support throughout 2015, like Sanders. In large part, that was why Sanders and his supporters continually dipped into the well of discontent over the influence of early superdelegate support. More than half of those unpledged delegates were able to publicly weigh in on the nomination before any votes were cast starting in February 2016.

In many ways, the persistent Sanders question about the role of superdelegates in the Democratic process reopened old wounds revolving around similar themes that were raised during the more competitive 2008 nomination cycle. In addition to the pre-primary role, superdelegates could have an outsized influence later in the sequence as well. If the pledged delegate count was close enough—within a range of the total number of superdelegates or some fraction of them (see Figure 13.1)—those unpledged superdelegates, who are not bound by the results of primaries and caucuses across the country, could put a candidate with fewer pledged delegates or popular votes over the top. That issue dogged the 2008 process, with Clinton on the outside looking in.

The script was flipped for the former secretary of state in 2016, yet the superdelegate question remained, festering from the early endorsements and all the way to, through, and beyond the completion of primary season.

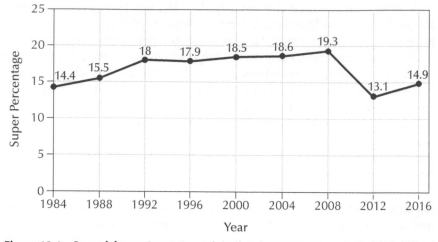

Figure 13.1   Superdelegate Percentage of Total Delegates to Democratic National Convention, 1984–2016.

Caucuses

But that was only one area within the structural setup of the Democratic nomination system that received scrutiny and drove inter-campaign division as the 2016 invisible primary transitioned into the more active primary season. And like the superdelegates question, there were echoes of 2008 in other areas of dispute. Unlike the superdelegates question, where Clinton went from 2008 disadvantage to 2016 upper hand, her campaign continued to struggle in caucus states beyond the earliest two. In Iowa and Nevada, two states where Clinton edged out Sanders, her campaign was able to organize well in advance. Elsewhere, however, Clinton fell short in the 2016 caucuses just as her campaign failed in 2008, out-organized in that format by the Obama campaign (see Figure 13.2 and Sanders' strong performance in the caucus column). Sanders, like Obama before him, excelled in caucuses, winning every caucus state after February 2016.[3] It was not that Clinton did not have support, but rather than Sanders had an intensity of support that translated better—just as Obama's support had—in those caucus states where the Clinton campaign was less organized than in the two carve-out state caucuses. The caucus process is more demanding of participants than primaries, requiring a more active role over a period of time that typically lasts longer than the lines and ballots at primary polling stations.

Underlying the Clinton caucus shortcomings in both 2008 and 2016 is an argument about the discrepancies in access between caucuses and primaries.

The demands are greater in the former and that, in turn, has some impact on the rate of turnout across modes of delegate selection. Just as in 2008, there were a couple of 2016 test cases of the theory that difference in contest type might impact the outcome of a state's delegate selection event. Both Nebraska and Washington State held caucuses *and* primaries. In both instances, the state Democratic parties opted to conduct their respective delegate selection processes through a caucus/convention system rather than through the state-funded primary. And in each case the primary was a beauty contest where the Democratic presidential candidates appeared on the ballot but the results had no impact on who the delegates from the two states were pledged to heading to the national convention. Obama in 2008 won caucuses in both Nebraska and Washington. In later, non-binding primaries with much broader participation that same year, Clinton won. History repeated itself in 2016 with Sanders coming out victorious in the earlier caucuses in Nebraska and Washington, but with Clinton winning the meaningless (albeit higher turnout) primaries in each state.

Contest Participation: Open versus Closed

While the caucus question was one that served again during the 2016 primary season as a drag on the Clinton campaign, it was not the only area broadly under the banner of access that received some level of scrutiny. However, issues with access (or lack thereof) was not something that was a consistent theme in one campaign or the other. From the perspective of the Clinton campaign, the limited access to caucus/convention systems was viewed as problematic, but it did not emphasize access more broadly than that. And while Sanders found success in caucus states, that did not keep his campaign from focusing on access in *primaries*. Sanders and his campaign made the argument that his candidacy was inviting a new and younger cohort of voter into the Democratic presidential nomination process; a group less likely to be directly affiliated with either major party, and thus, more likely to be shut out of the process in states that both have partisan registration and constrain participation to registered partisans only.

Moreover and to the Sanders campaign's point, Clinton did perform well in closed primary states, winning 12 of the 13 primaries in which only registered Democrats could participate (again, see Figure 13.2). Sanders was only making up for that closed primary deficit in a select group of more open states, those that only opened the door to unaffiliated voters participating. In true open primary states—those mostly southern states with no partisan registration and where crossover voting is possible—Clinton repeatedly bested Sanders. But that did not mute Sanders' point about broader structural

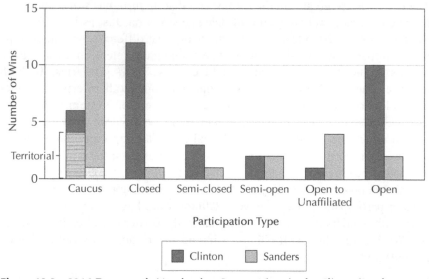

Figure 13.2   2016 Democratic Nomination Contest Victories by Clinton/Sanders Based on Contest Type.

impediments to participation like the New York requirement to change affili-ation six months in advance of the April 2016 presidential primary in the Empire State.

It is less clear that a change to a restriction like that in New York electoral law would have changed the outcome of the primary there, flipping the pri-mary and resulting delegate majority from Clinton to Sanders. As opposed to the example of states with both caucuses and primaries, there is no parallel contest conducted with alternate participation rules to even partially test that hypothesis. But the idea of that impediment to participation lingered, fitting neatly into the broader narrative that the DNC process was tilted toward Clinton. The primaries access issue alongside the superdelegates questions fueled the Sanders-led complaints about the process all the way to the national convention, raising questions about if, how, and in what ways the national party would respond for future cycles.

THE 2016 DEMOCRATIC NATIONAL CONVENTION CHARTERS THE UNITY REFORM COMMISSION

As primary season came to a close after Democratic voters in the District of Columbia were the last to weigh in on the nomination in mid-June, process questions remained. And they persisted into the convention the following month in Philadelphia. At least part of the motivation for Sanders to stay in the race once he had technically been mathematically eliminated in the pledged delegate count was to continue winning delegates to the convention. That presence would not be able to change the outcome of the nomination, but it could impact the procedural maneuvering at the convention, including the initial push for nomination rules changes for the 2020 cycle.

The divisions that developed and evolved during primary season carried over to the convention. During the weekend prior to the convention gaveling in, the Convention Rules and Bylaws Committee (RBC) considered the rules package it would send to the convention floor for a vote. Typically contained in that package are the rules for how the convention is to proceed and guidance for what if any rules changes should be considered moving forward. Quickly, the process of considering changes in the Convention RBC meeting devolved and began to exhibit the same battle lines as were highlighted in the preceding months of primaries and caucuses. Amendments were raised to eliminate superdelegates altogether, for instance, and then to attempt to reduce their role in the presidential nomination process. Both failed.

As that continued, a rough pattern emerged: For every two Sanders-aligned delegates on the Convention RBC voting for the amendments, there were three Clinton-aligned delegates voting against them. But rather than play hardball in rules vote after rules vote and risk the full convention devolving into divided camps when any resulting rules package would later come up for a vote, a number of RBC members on both sides of the Clinton-Sanders divide huddled and produced a compromise: a unity amendment that would charter the Unity Reform Commission to reexamine the rules of the DNC and the nomination process for the 2020 presidential election cycle.

Built around the three main structural flashpoints that developed between Clinton and Sanders during primary season, the unity amendment provided compromised guidance for how the resulting Unity Reform Commission would consider possible 2020 rules changes. The amendment was adopted by the Convention RBC and later the convention and laid the following groundwork:

1. No more than 60 days after the election of the next chair of the Democratic National Committee in early 2017, the chair will establish the Unity Reform Commission (URC).
2. Its membership will include Clinton surrogate, Jennifer O'Malley Dillon, as commission chairwoman and Sanders proxy, Larry Cohen, as vice chair. Clinton will fill nine additional slots and Sanders, seven. The newly elected DNC chair will select three additional members.

3. Consistent with the timeline of the Democratic Change Commission (the post-2008 rules body), the 21-member Unity Reform Commission will meet during 2017 with the goal of producing a set of rules recommendations to the Democratic Rules and Bylaws Committee by January 1, 2018.

4. The normal procedure is for the Rules and Bylaws Committee to consider those commission recommendations before sending them—potentially in an amended form—to the full Democratic National Committee for a final vote. That procedure remains intact. However, the URC retains the ability to place their recommendations directly before the full DNC if the Rules and Bylaws Committee "fails to substantially adopt" any of them.

5. Substantively, the unity amendment calls for another reconsideration of the caucus process. This was a Clinton campaign complaint after 2008 and is again in 2016. The question confronting the URC will be whether they come to a different conclusion than the Democratic Change Commission. The 2009 commission called for the development of a set of "best practices" for caucuses, but it ultimately left the primary versus caucus matter up to the states (in order to best tailor a process at the state level).

6. The amendment is less forceful on the parameters of discussion on participation in the nomination process. The commission's charter only calls for the development of recommendations that "encourage" increased involvement in the process. In the end, the directive on what essentially boils down to an open versus closed primary discussion is more passive. The Sanders proxies on the commission will likely push for something promoting more open primaries, but historically the DNC (and the RNC for that matter) have remained mostly hands-off on this matter, deferring to the states.

7. While the open primaries mandate was passive, the part of the amendment devoted to superdelegates had more teeth to it. In any event, there was more clarity as to the specifics of the superdelegates mandate of the commission. While the group will broadly consider the superdelegates' role in the process, it will specifically recommend that elected officials—Democratic members of Congress, governors, and distinguished party leaders (presidents, vice presidents, etc.)—remain as unpledged delegates. However, the second part of the recommendation shifts the remaining superdelegates (approximately two-thirds of them) out of the unpledged category and into a pledged group (to be proportionally pledged/bound based on the results of primaries and caucuses).

Structurally, the Unity Reform Commission (URC) was narrowly weighted toward Clinton and her surrogates to roughly reflect the balance of power among delegates at the national convention. But the true balance of the group would hinge on the three additional members the new DNC chair would install on the panel. A Sanders-aligned chair could tip the balance in Sanders' direction and thus be able to more aggressively push for changes. Former Obama administration Secretary of Labor Tom Perez's election as DNC chair over the Representative Keith Ellison of Minnesota, who had been one of the few superdelegate endorsements for Sanders in 2016, had the effect of locking in a slight Clinton advantage on the URC.

Moreover, another structural element designed to gain Sanders' delegates' approval at the convention was to empower the URC to circumvent the standing Rules and Bylaws Committee if the latter failed to adopt any part of the commission's recommendations. While the URC was granted that ability, it was not given any mechanism to force the full DNC to adopt any of its recommended changes. However, if the commission ended up near unanimous in its recommendations, that would potentially place some pressure on the RBC and/or the DNC and make any inaction by either more difficult.

Substantively, the unity amendment sought to address the three problem areas left over from the 2016 cycle but limited the URC's latitude on the superdelegate matter. The provisions on how to proceed on caucuses and on participation more broadly lacked the same level of specificity and thus provided the URC with a more elastic mandate in those areas. But ultimately, the provisions of the unity amendment colored how the URC would and could approach recommendations for 2020 rules changes.

THE 2017 UNITY REFORM COMMISSION
MEETINGS AND RECOMMENDATIONS

The First Four Meetings

After the DNC announced the members of the group in April, the first of five Unity Reform Commission meetings kicked off in May 2017 in Washington, D.C. While it proved to be more an introductory meeting than a work session, subsequent meetings in San Antonio, Chicago, and Las Vegas centered on the various "buckets," the four areas in which the URC was tasked with examining: caucuses, primary access, unpledged delegates, and party reform. Work was done, and subgroups were formed for each of the areas, but often the sessions were more instructional in nature. Each often served as an exploration of the limits of what a national party can mandate given the overlapping turf the DNC shares with the Republican National Committee, the state governments, and state parties in determining the patchwork of rules that constitute the presidential nomination process.

Although the question did not come up in any meaningful or actionable way during the Unity Reform Commission proceedings, the often thorny issue of Iowa and New Hampshire perpetually being at the front of the primary calendar queue is a noteworthy example of the national parties' jurisdictional sharing. State parties in the Hawkeye and Granite states on both sides of the aisle have a vested interest in maintaining the status quo. And the national parties know more of what they have in those two states after years of results or at least know better than they would if the states at the front of the line changed every cycle. Partly due to that and also partially because of the fact that there is not clear agreement across national parties as to which states would fill the void if neither Iowa nor New Hampshire were first, those states maintain a stranglehold on those coveted first two slots. But this serves as a guide not only to the trade-offs that the national parties have to consider, but the shared decision-making space in which they operate in finalizing the rules of the presidential nomination.

As the meetings continued through the summer of 2017 and into the fall, it was those types of procedural questions with which the URC dealt. But they continued to tackle issues left lingering from the 2016 race at the intersection of jurisdictions. At the October URC meeting that was held in conjunction with the fall DNC meeting in Las Vegas, the group heard testimony from Robert A. Brehm, the co-director of the New York State Board of Elections. In particular, some members of the URC were interested in what could be done about the very early deadline for changing partisan voter registration ahead of a primary election. Unlike the situation where a New York state party has some discretion over which voters (based on partisan registration) can participate in a Democratic primary, with respect to the rules and, in particular, the deadlines for registration, both the state and national parties are at the mercy of the state government. And the contours of that relationship between decision makers received a quiet nod in the unity amendment that chartered the Unity Reform Commission. There the emphasis was on the DNC *encouraging* changes to registration deadlines or trading out a caucus/convention system in favor of a state-funded primary rather than the DNC attempting to directly regulate the sorts of issues outside of party control.

The Final Meeting and URC Recommendations

If the early meetings had been more fact-finding in nature, the final Unity Reform Commission meeting in Washington, D.C., in December 2017 was a true working session. Based on its charter, the group was to have produced its recommendations for rules changes to the DNC Rules and Bylaws Committee by January 1, 2018. Over the course of the two-day meeting, the URC, despite is naturally fractious membership, came to consensus on most of what it would recommend to the Rules and Bylaws Committee. Yet, both the urgency of completing its task on time and the Clinton-Sanders divisions on the committee rose to the fore in varying ways in each of the three flashpoint areas that would potentially influence the 2020 presidential nomination rules.

With respect to the primaries discussion, the committee was in agreement that it would go on record as *encouraging* the wider use of primaries over caucuses (where actionable given state government partisan control). Still, the participation question from 2016 remained. Sanders surrogate and former campaign manager, Jeff Weaver, proposed an amendment that would *require* states to allow unaffiliated voters access to the Democratic Party process.[4] There was similar consensus in this area. Instead, the URC split along Clinton-Sanders lines in voting down the amendment 11–6 with the three DNC chair-selected members siding with the Clinton faction. And while the URC was divided in predictable ways, ultimately the participation question was met with a default obstacle: The DNC, or any national party for that matter, is limited in what it can require of states or state parties. Requiring a state party to take provable steps (such as having an affiliated member in a state legislature introduce legislation) toward changing state law is one thing. But requiring state parties to pursue expensive litigation against state governments is another matter altogether. This is especially true for typically cash-strapped state Democratic parties in states where the Republican Party is dominant in state government.

Consensus was reached in the area of caucuses as well. Most of the new encouragements for an assortment of actions, such as providing for an absentee voting option, received a green light from the group without dissent. The one exception came in how the commission wanted to recommend rules changes for states that have held caucuses despite the presence of a state-funded primary option. The initial draft recommendations from which the URC was working during its December meeting contained a plank that would *presume* state parties in bigger states—those with five or more congressional districts—would use a primary election, if available, as the means of allocating delegates to the national convention. This was a very narrowly targeted recommendation in its initial form. In its crosshairs, it had Idaho, Nebraska, and Washington, states that opted for caucuses in 2016 instead of the state-funded primaries. But even then, the original draft recommendation would have exempted both Idaho and Nebraska, both with fewer than five congressional districts.

However, Clinton proxy and former Clinton campaign delegate and ballot access director, David Huynh, offered an amendment to widen the scope of the recommendation to include *all* states with state-funded primaries at the state party's disposal. That amendment opened up an impassioned defense of caucuses from two Sanders-affiliated URC members, Larry Cohen (URC vice chair) and Nebraska Democratic Party Chair Jane Kleeb. Cohen, in particular, spoke of the need for state parties in heavily Republican states like Idaho and Nebraska to utilize the caucuses for party-building at the grassroots level. The organizational goals of the state party by his argument would be better served by caucuses than through the less engaging primary process.[5] In the end, a motion to table the amendment was made and deadlocked in a 9–9 tie. The chair and vice chair voted together to break the tie and table the amendment. The issue was never brought back before the group and thus the original recommendation aimed at states with five or more congressional districts was not ultimately included in the final URC recommendations to the DNC Rules and Bylaws Committee.

Finally, the group clashed over the superdelegates question. But where the URC struggled here was less about the extent to which the role of unpledged delegates would be curbed and instead centered on how the group would accomplish the goal handed to them in the convention unity amendment. Unlike the primaries and caucuses directives from the convention, the unpledged delegates mandate was explicitly laid out. The URC was charged with reducing the number of superdelegates by roughly two-thirds by shifting DNC members into a new pledged/bound category.

Two competing plans to accomplish that end were proposed and debated during the final December URC meeting. However, to set up the two plans, the URC first had to create new categories of delegates in order to implement the plans to treat them differently than a singular class of automatic unpledged delegates. The chartering document of the URC tied the hands of its membership, handing the group an end goal, but tasking it with the responsibility of determining how the newly pledged/bound delegates would be allocated. The resulting category one delegates—those elected officials, former presidents, and former DNC and congressional leadership—would be the remaining and reduced group of unpledged automatic delegates. In other words, this group, formerly one-third of the total number of 2016 superdelegates, would continue to be superdelegates in the conventional sense. But to create a new class of automatic but pledged delegates from the remaining former superdelegates—DNC members—the URC was forced to create two different categories based on how those DNC members are selected/elected. There is a difference between state-elected party members—state party chairs and national committeemen and committeewomen—and those at-large DNC members who typically end up as part of *state* delegations at the national convention but are selected by the DNC chair.

It was at this initial stage of consideration of the final recommendations where there was some dissension on the URC. Of all the draft recommendations, this one—the one creating different classes of automatic delegates—was where members from the Sanders contingent on the URC could voice their displeasure with the superdelegates system. Ultimately, there were two votes against adopting this recommendation. Nomiki Konst and Nina Turner, both Sanders-aligned URC members, voted no in the recommendation as a symbolic gesture against keeping *any* unpledged delegates in the recommendations (much less the ultimate 2020 delegate selection rules).

Other than that blip, there was unanimity within the group on the remaining recommendations in the superdelegates section of the draft Unity Reform Commission report. That included the two plans for allocating and binding the new classes of automatic delegates that the commission proposed sending to the RBC for its consideration. The first option laid out by the URC for binding, the Pooled Vote Option, borrows a concept employed by the RNC for the first time during the 2016 cycle. Essentially, the pooled vote option would do two things: 1) pool all of the category two and three delegates and 2) automatically have the secretary of the convention count their votes. This is akin to the binding mechanism the RNC instituted for the 2016 convention. And the intent in this case as in the RNC one is the same: to keep bound but conflicted delegates in line. Imagine a number of Sanders-bound but Clinton-sympathetic delegates at the Philadelphia convention, for instance, if this provision had been in place during the 2016 cycle. Those delegates would not be unlike the Donald Trump-bound, but Ted Cruz/John Kasich/Marco Rubio-sympathetic delegates who were locked into Trump votes by the convention secretary during the roll call vote at the Cleveland convention.

That was the simpler of the two options. Alternatively, a party/convention could employ a replacement strategy. This is what the DNC rules provide for in the case of all other pledged delegates. If, for example, a Sanders-allocated slot is filled with a delegate candidate who is not loyal to—or willing to vote for—Sanders at the convention, then the Sanders team would have the ability to replace that delegate candidate with one who would at least be more likely to support that outcome. It would be a different proposition altogether to replace elected DNC members than it would be to fill allocated pledged delegate slots with loyalists as has been the case for pledged delegates in the Democratic system.

And while the URC did not provide a full replacement option for the RBC to consider in lieu of the pooled vote option, it did attempt to thread the needle on a more complex alternative. The Alternate Vote Option would allow DNC member delegates to retain their actual voting privileges (rather than have the convention secretary automatically tabulate their votes) on the first ballot nomination vote while attempting to mitigate some of the conscience and replacement issues in ways that the pooled vote option would not. The end goal was to allow conflicted but bound delegates a way out and for candidates to have something closer to loyalists as bound automatic delegates.

In the end the adopted Unity Reform Commission report placed emphasis on increasing participation through structural alleviation. That came in the form of recommendations to provide, for instance, an absentee voting option in caucus states and encourage the easing of registration restrictions via same-day registration and party affiliation changes in primary states. But the report also proposed recommended changes for rebalancing the role and influence of superdelegates in the Democratic presidential nomination process.

THE 2018 RULES AND BYLAWS COMMITTEE MEETINGS AND RECOMMENDATIONS

As the baton was passed from the Unity Reform Commission to the DNC Rules and Bylaws Committee in January 2018, the priority of the rules-making task morphed from how best to change the rules of the 2020 process to a consideration of whether implementation of those changes was feasible or advisable. It was not that the URC had not reflected on implementation, but rather, that the group was differently configured and pressured—along Clinton-Sanders lines—than the RBC. As opposed to the URC, the RBC had to balance not only the Clinton-Sanders divide in the broader party coalition in weighing changes to the rules for 2020, but also the potential perception problem of maintaining the status quo, particularly on superdelegates, and finally in just how complex the rules fulfilling the recommendations would be.

Moreover, an additional pressure placed on the RBC was that the URC was nearly unanimous across the board in its recommendations. That signal would have been different had the report been the product of a divided group with the Clinton contingent on the panel limiting the scope of the recommendations, for example. And the RBC essentially acknowledged that it had received that message. In its interim report to the full DNC at the party's March 2018 meeting, the RBC noted that there was a perception problem surrounding the continued presence of superdelegates in the Democratic nomination system; that the role of that group of unpledged delegates should be revised and its perceived influence reduced. The RBC also stood in principle with the URC with respect to broadening participation and reducing restrictions to it in both primaries and caucuses.

But standing in principle with the URC does not transform recommendations into rules. And the RBC stage of the rules-making process, especially in cycles in which the DNC has impaneled a commission, is typically where the rubber meets the road; where tough decisions have to made about how to layer changes into a set of existing rules. As the RBC met over the intervening months after the March 2018 DNC meeting, it became clearer how the committee would tackle many of the issues raised in the URC report.

In the broad area of access to both caucuses and primaries, Frank Leone, DNC and RBC member from Virginia, proposed an amendment that would add many of the encouragements and other directives from the URC into Rule 2 of the DNC delegate selection rules. That maneuver codified those new encouragements and requirements recommended by the URC into the rule regarding RBC guidance to state parties in assembling their delegate-selection plans. And that would additionally set up a sequence whereby state parties would be required to show steps taken to address those issues like implementing absentee voting in caucus states to the RBC *before* the panel would approve the state delegate-selection plan. Should a state party be unable to demonstrate those actions taken toward the encouragements and requirements layered into Rule 2, then the plan would be questioned if not rejected by the RBC. That is a novel way of dealing with the URC recommendations without also adding penalties to the mix. Instead of a "do this or face delegate penalties" direction, it became "take these steps (where feasible) or not have a plan approved." The only drawback to that overall push by the RBC was that, if adopted by the DNC, it would mean an increase in the approval workload of the RBC during the May and June period in the year before the presidential election year when the RBC is considering state party-submitted delegate-selection plans.

Outside of that action, the RBC continued to wrestle with the superdelegates question as it met over the spring months of 2018. While there was agreement on the committee that the role of superdelegates should be revised and their perceived role reduced, the main roadblock to action on that front was the complexity of the rules that would bring about those changes. The two options recommended by the URC—the pooled vote option and the alternative vote option—were viewed by the RBC as problematic.

First, there was resistance to both plans among particular factions in the DNC. State party chairs on the RBC raised the administrative costs of the alternative vote plan, complaining that the process of replacement would be overly burdensome at a time when state parties are finalizing the delegate-selection process and transitioning preparations and delegations for the national convention. And RBC members also raised the fact that the Congressional Black Caucus opposed the pooled vote option because the provision instructing the secretary of the national convention to automatically tabulate the votes of automatic delegates disenfranchised not only black voices in the process but elected officials as well. For that reason, they favored the alternative-vote option.

Second, both options from the URC were full of complexities. RBC member and former DNC chair Don Fowler of South Carolina captured that sentiment by pointedly saying in the group's June meeting, "Try explaining either of these [two plans] in a bar or union hall."

Finally, there were also questions on the RBC about whether the two plans would require a charter change. That was meaningful to the RBC because it would shift the bar for passage at the DNC level up from a simple majority to a two-thirds supermajority if a charter change was required.

It was that combination of factors that gave the RBC impetus to explore options other than the two recommended by the URC. The new plan that gained steam was what came to be known at the third way plus as the third main option on the RBC's plate. Greatly streamlining the treatment of superdelegates relative to the other plans, the third way plus plan would keep the number of unpledged delegates the same but would bar superdelegates from the first ballot presidential nomination vote at the national convention in the event that either one candidate had a majority of pledged delegates or that no candidate received a majority of pledged or all (including superdelegates) delegates. Under the plan, superdelegates would only be permitted to participate on the first ballot vote if one candidate's margin of pledged delegates exceeded the total number of superdelegates, a scenario in which superdelegates if voting as a bloc could not overturn the decision from among pledged delegates alone.

Since it reduced a variety of complications that had become apparent in the URC options, the third way plus became the preferred option on the RBC. It was adopted in June 2018 in a near-unanimous vote with 27 votes in favor, one vote against, and one abstention. And that vote, the last major hurdle for the RBC, cleared the way for the full package of RBC rules recommendations to go back before the URC for its judgment about whether the RBC recommendations "substantially adopted" a series of rules amendments in line with the URC report. In a July conference call ahead of the August DNC meeting, the URC gave the RBC package the thumbs up, avoiding a potential clash of plans before the DNC. But that also cleared the way for a raft of changes on access to primaries and caucuses as well as reducing the role of superdelegates to be considered for adoption by the full DNC.

DNC ADOPTION AND UNINTENDED
CONSEQUENCES FOR 2020?

All of those actions between primary season in 2016 through the Rules and Bylaws Committee adoption of a package of amendments to the rules for 2020 set the table for the DNC to put its stamp on things in late August 2018. But for some lingering doubts, the party entered the summer meeting looking to adopt the rules changes. The Congressional Black Caucus opposed the superdelegates plan and there was still some question about whether that change would require a charter change and thus a two-thirds supermajority to pass the plan (instead of a simple majority). To that latter conflict, the superdelegate change had already been assessed as not requiring a charter change by the DNC legal counsel in July, something that had been followed by a sense of the committee voice vote in the RBC.

Although there was some dissension at the DNC meeting against the superdelegates changes in particular, the committee adopted the package of changes from the RBC. And while that specific change was labeled "dramatic"[6] in the press, the result is more nuanced than that. No Democratic convention has gone past the first ballot on the presidential nomination vote in the post-reform era. And many actors involved in the proceedings voiced as much throughout the various stages of the rules-making process. Under that reasoning, if a presumptive nominee is clear by the time of the 2020 convention, then the superdelegates are likely to participate in the first vote as usual, representing no net change relative to 2016 and other prior cycles.

However, with a larger field of Democratic presidential candidates in 2020 and a more frontloaded calendar because of California leaping from June to March, the potential is there, especially if the field does not winnow enough fast enough, that the pledged delegate count will be split in ways that could keep the superdelegates out of the first vote at the convention. The rules changes instituted in response to 2016, then, do not necessarily fit with the conditions of 2020, raising the likelihood of unintended consequences. This has been the nature of delegate selection rule changes in the post-reform era.

Nevertheless, that only addresses the reduced part of the role superdelegates typically play. The part that was so controversial in 2016 to Sanders, his allies, and supporters was left untouched by the DNC during its quadrennial tinkering with the rules. While superdelegate voting privileges may have been curbed under certain conditions, their role earlier in the process remained intact. Just as superdelegates lined up behind Hillary Clinton in 2014–2015, they retained the ability to do just that in the 2020 cycle.

The question is, will they continue to exercise that role? If they do, in whole or in part, that traditionally plays some role in how and how quickly the field of candidates narrows over the invisible primary period. But if any elected officials feel any pressure to remain silent, frozen by memories of the 2016 division over the role of superdelegates, then that may hinder the winnowing process. That, in turn, would make the split pledged-delegate-count scenario more likely and keep superdelegates out of that first convention vote. Early indications in 2019 are mixed. Candidates are jumping in early, but the vast majority of the small number of endorsements from superdelegates so far have been for home-state candidates. There is time for that to change, but if it does not or happens only slowly, then that could impact the subsequent sequence of events from winnowing to how the delegate count progresses to whether superdelegates have voting rights on the first ballot at the convention.

Yes, that was the big ticket item in the rules changes adopted by the DNC in 2018, but it was not the only rules change of consequence. The progress of the new encouragements for caucus states may have played some small role in nudging some traditionally caucus states toward primaries. Seven states—Colorado, Idaho, Maine,[7] Minnesota, Nebraska, Utah, and Washington State—have all made moves in the direction of conducting primaries in 2020. Five of the seven will have primaries, and work continued in Maine and Washington early in 2019. Although that change is consistent with the DNC encouragement of using primaries where available, the push seems to have been more bottom up from the states than top down and based on the rules changes. Four of the seven states made changes in or before 2017 prior to when the URC report was issued. And another, Idaho, chose the primary option before the DNC adopted the final rules for 2020. In many cases, administrative issues with overrun 2016 caucuses pushed state parties toward primaries. That is no small change. Again, it is consistent with the DNC push to increase participation in the process, but it does come at the expense of Sanders or Sanders-like candidates who can harness the enthusiasm of participants in the higher demand, lower turnout format.

One additional change that was not made and codified through the Democratic rules process as it was on the Republican side for the 2016 cycle concerned primary debates. That matter was handled by the chair but outside of the rules-making process. The rules devised in that area, too, may have an impact on how the 2020 Democratic nomination race progresses. Rather than separating candidates into tiers—a top and a bottom—like the RNC did for 2016, the DNC will randomly separate the candidates into two groups of no more than 10 candidates each. Additionally the qualifications for the initial couple of rounds of debates will be twofold and set a low bar. Candidates can qualify by polling at 1 percent or higher in any of three polls approved by the party or by the breadth of a candidate's grassroots fundraising base. The latter is set at 65,000 donors across at least 20 states with no fewer than 200 donors per state. Those debates may also have an effect on the extent to which the field of Democratic candidates winnows and how quickly, and that is particularly true if the DNC imposes incremental increases in what it takes for candidates to qualify.

As 2019 continues and the invisible primary wears on, it is that question about winnowing that matters most for how the 2020 Democratic process under a new set of rules will fare. If the field winnows some in that period and that continues to pick up pace as votes begin to be cast in 2020, then the changes will likely have a minimal impact. However, if that process is slow and multiple candidates hang around deeper into primary season, then that could make the rules changes made with 2016 in mind ill-fitting for a 2020 race waged under far different conditions.

NOTES

1. Stephen Ohlemacher and Hope Yen, "AP Survey: Clinton Holds Commanding Lead in Delegates to Win Party's Nomination," Associated Press, November 13, 2015, https://www.necn.com/news/national-international/Democratic-Superdelegates-Back-Clinton-347726851.html.

2. Marty Cohen, David Karol, Hanes Noel, and John Zaller, *The Party Decides: Presidential Nominations Before and After Reform* (Chicago: University of Chicago Press, 2008).

3. The emphasis there is on states. Sanders did win the remaining caucus states after Nevada, but Clinton was able to manage a number of wins in territorial caucuses.

4. Weaver's amendment:

The DNC and the party at all levels shall use all means including encouraging legislation, changing party rules and undertaking litigation to **require** that states permit non-aligned voters, also known as independent or no party preference voters, to participate in the Democratic presidential nominating primary. With respect to any state that does not permit non-aligned voters to participate in its Democratic presidential nominating primary, the rules of the party shall be amended to impose an appropriate penalty which could include a reduction in the number of pledged delegates to the Democratic national convention to which the state would otherwise be entitled or potential adjustments to state party support. State parties that are able to demonstrate that all provable steps including litigation as determined by the Rules and Bylaws Committee have been undertaken to require the participation of non-aligned voters but were not successful in the efforts shall not be penalized.

5. Of course there are trade-offs there. While caucuses may be good at actively cultivating partisans at the grassroots level, it comes at the cost of broader electoral participation in primaries, a goal also under the URC mandate in the convention unity amendment.

6. Brandon Carter and Don Gonyea, "DNC Votes to Largely Strip 'Superdelegates' of Presidential Nominating Power," NPR, August 25, 2018, https://www.npr.org/2018/08/25/641725402/dnc-set-to-reduce-role-of-superdelegates-in-presidential-nominating-process.

7. The 2016 adoption of a primary in Maine expired toward the end of 2018.

14

Was 2018 a Wave Election?

Sean Trende

In a particularly creative piece published shortly before the 2018 midterm elections, analyst Nate Silver walked his readers through two visions of the future.

The first future he described involved a rather disappointing night for Democrats. In the House, Democrats picked up only 16 of the 23 seats they needed to gain control of the chamber. Democrats won the House popular vote by six percentage points.[1]

In the Senate, Democrats lost seats in North Dakota, Missouri, and Indiana but held on in Florida. Republican Senator Dean Heller won in Nevada, and Democratic Senate candidate Kyrsten Sinema had an outside chance of winning the Arizona Senate seat in a recount; she trailed by 0.3 percent of a vote as of Election Night. Democratic Senator Jon Tester won by a large margin in Montana. Democrats still won the governorship of Florida, while Republican Governor Scott Walker of Wisconsin lost by two points. Republicans held on to the Ohio governor's mansion.

Silver also sketched out a contrary situation where Democrats had "a really, really good night." In this universe, Democrats picked up more than 50 seats in the House, winning the national popular vote by 12 points. Democrats held on to all of their competitive seats, including two open seats they were defending in Minnesota.

Beto O'Rourke became the first Democrat to win statewide office in Texas since 1994, defeating Ted Cruz in that Senate race. Democrats held their remaining seats; Democrat Jacky Rosen beat Heller by five points in Nevada, while Sinema won by seven in Arizona. Stacey Abrams won the governorship of Georgia for Democrats; in fact, Democrats won every competitive governorship except for Kansas and Alaska in this vision of the future for Democrats. Republican Governor Doug Ducey held on in Arizona, but it is close.

Obviously these were "on the fly" projections, but they nevertheless serve as useful markers for what expectations about the election were before people began the process of rationalizing the outcomes to serve their desires. The reality is complicated.

On the one hand, the House race results look a lot like a mild version of Silver's worst-case scenario. Democrats won the popular vote for the House by about 8.5 points, although that number is probably inflated a point or so by districts where Democrats ran unopposed, or where two Democrats were running in the November elections (this occurred in a number of races held under California's election system, where the top two vote getters in the primary election advance to the general election regardless of party).

Democrats didn't win 50 seats in the House, but they exceeded the expectations of many, and were much closer to 50 than the 16 seats he suggested in his "disappointing year" scenario. Many of the surprise upsets Silver describes didn't come to pass, but the elections were nevertheless close: Representative Duncan Hunter, running under the cloud of indictment, only won in his heavily Republican San Diego district by 3.5 points, while Chris Collins of New York, also running under indictment, won by less than a point. In the House, at least, this was a very bad year for Republicans.

Everything else, however, is a different story. A reasonable case can be made here that Democrats fell short even of Silver's "disappointing night for Democrats" scenario. Republicans not only won the Senate races in North Dakota, Texas, Indiana, and Missouri, but also in Florida. This marked the first time that the president's party had knocked off four incumbent senators from the other party in a midterm election since 1970, and the first time it had done so without defeating appointed senators since 1934. Democrats knocked off Dean Heller, but Kyrsten Sinema actually did trail narrowly on Election Night before winning her race. Jon Tester won, but by four points rather than nine.

Likewise, governor's races tracked Silver's "disappointing night" scenario. Losing gubernatorial races in Ohio, Oklahoma, and particularly Florida (which Democrats won in the "disappointing night" scenario) was not where the party expected to be.

This leads to the fundamental paradox of the 2018 elections. In the House, the results resembled, if not quite a wave election, then something very closely approximating one. Everywhere else, however, the results were substantially muted. While Republicans certainly could have had better nights in the Senate—a marginally more popular President Trump probably could have flipped seats in West Virginia and Montana and held Arizona—it still had to be regarded as a successful venture.

So was 2018 a wave election? This chapter seeks to explore that question. It begins by looking at previous elections that have been defined as wave elections qualitatively to get a sense of what we are trying to measure. It then explores a metric for district partisanship, and uses this metric to determine that 2018 probably ought not count as a wave election. It finishes by offering concluding thoughts.

A BRIEF HISTORY OF WAVE ELECTIONS

On the day after the 2018 elections, CNN political analyst Harry Enten intoned "[t]o butcher a quote from Newt Gingrich after 1994, if this isn't a wave, I'd like to know what a wave is. This is the biggest net gain for the Dems in the House since Watergate."[2] Maybe so. But before we set off to add a quantitative element to our definition of a wave, it is worth exploring things that have generally been considered waves in the past. The reason is simple; if a method we adopt were to return, say, 1990 as a wave election, we probably ought not adopt that metric. It might describe something interesting, but it isn't describing waves.

Even this is tricky, because it does seem to beg the question then of what definition people have used. For example, Stu Rothenberg prefers a holistic approach to defining a wave, but he has suggested that a wave is roughly a gain of more than 20 seats in the House by a party.[3] Using this definition, and beginning after the 1936 elections, we would see midterm waves in 1942, 1946, 1950, 1958, 1966, 1974, 1982, 1994, 2006, 2010, and 2018.

This seems as though it cannot be correct; a majority of the most recent elections would qualify as wave elections under this definition. If wave elections are supposed to be something unusual or quirky, then something that includes roughly every other midterm as a wave election seems like a poor classifier.

Nevertheless, if you spend enough time analyzing elections, you come across certain "canonical" wave elections. These are briefly described in what follows:

1938: After Franklin Delano Roosevelt's landslide victories in 1932 and 1936, as well as the Democrats' big midterm gains in the 1934 elections, Republicans were in actual danger of going extinct. There were almost as many Democratic senators (76) as there were Republican members of the House of Representatives (89). Ogden Mills, a Republican businessman, wrote to his friend Herbert Hoover in the wake of the 1936 elections that "[h]ow to revitalize the Republican party under such conditions looks almost impossible."[4]

Republicans were not, however, on the brink of extinction. Democrats overplayed their hands in the opening years of Roosevelt's second term, while bad monetary and fiscal choices led to a contraction in the money supply, and a nasty recession in the beginning of 1937. FDR embarked upon an ill-fated purge of Southern Democrats. It showed up in the results: Republicans gained 82 House seats, seven Senate seats, 11 governorships, and around 750 state legislative seats. This effectively put an end to the New Deal, since Republicans could form an alliance with Southern Democrats to control what moved on and off of the House floor.

1946: Over the next several cycles, Republicans did an impressive job of clawing their way back into legislative relevance. In 1942, they even won the popular vote for the House by three points, although they failed to gain control of the chamber. The GOP went from 16 senators in 1936 to 28 by 1940, to 37 after the 1942 elections (there were only 96 senators at the time).

FDR died early in 1945 and after an early period of success, his successor, Harry Truman, saw his popularity recede into the 30 percent range. On Election Day 1946, Democrats were soundly defeated, losing 55 House seats, 13 Senate seats, two governorships, and 440 state legislative seats. This period of Republican success was transitory, as the GOP lost control of the House and Senate in the subsequent election. But they proved that Mills' admonition was off base, and that Republicans had, in fact, been revitalized.

1958: The Eisenhower years are remembered as a period of normalcy, and the elections generally were consistent with this. Ike won his elections handily in 1952 and 1956, but, Ike's conservatism aside, the president acted as a fairly moderate Republican. His party lost control of the House and Senate in 1954, but the House and Senate seemed pretty stable.

Then came 1958. In the midst of a sharp recession, presidential scandals, and a series of ill-considered GOP right-to-work proposals, Republicans lost 48 House seats, 13 Senate seats, four governorships, and around 700 state legislative seats. This election had significant consequences, as it ushered in a number of liberal northern Democrats (Edmund Muskie, Philip Hart, Eugene McCarthy, and Clair Engle all hailed from this class) and gave Northern Democrats the numbers they needed to usher in the Civil Rights Act of 1964 and the Great Society.

1966: The Great Society ushered in a major transformation of American society, and the relationship between citizens and the government. Not all people were pleased with this, and the growing tension regarding the Vietnam War took a toll on President Johnson's approval rating. Notwithstanding the booming economy, Republicans gained 46 House seats, four Senate seats, eight governorships, and 548 state legislative seats.

1974: The Republican Party in the early 1970s looked to be ascendant. Richard Nixon won a landslide victory, losing only the District of Columbia and Massachusetts, and the South looked as though it was finally ready to flip to the GOP. Indeed, a number of Democratic state legislators in Virginia were planning to switch parties after 1972, which would have given Republicans control of that chamber for the first time since Reconstruction.

Then Watergate occurred. What began as a botched break-in of Democratic headquarters in the summer of 1972 spiraled into a major scandal that seemed poised to take down a presidency. Nixon's resignation in the summer of 1974 (after a series of Republican losses in special elections) combined with a growing recession and public antipathy toward President Ford's pardon of his disgraced predecessor led to a Republican wipeout in the fall. Republicans lost 48 House seats, four Senate seats, six governorships, and 700 state legislative seats.

1982: Republicans bounced back, as parties are wont to do, winning the presidency, Senate, and de facto control of the House in 1980. But a recession in 1981 hurt Republican President Ronald Reagan, and his party lost 26 House seats, seven governorships, and 214 state legislative seats. This is probably the weakest of the wave elections in the sample: Republicans gained a Senate seat, and many of the House seats lost were due to redistricting.[5]

1994: For 40 years, Republicans had been shut out of control of the House of Representatives. That streak came to an abrupt end in 1994, when Republicans wrested control of both chambers from the Democrats. The outcome was surprising, given that the mid-1990s were a time of relative peace and prosperity.

The aggressive liberal populism of the early Clinton years, combined with long-simmering discontent among conservative Southern Democrats, led to Republican gains of 54 House seats, nine Senate seats, 12 governorships, and 500 state legislative seats.

2006: Republicans had good elections in 2000, 2002, and 2004. Many Democrats were frustrated after the latter loss, concerned that their ability to win nationally had evaporated under the force of President Bush's personality and the genius of his aide, Karl Rove. Those concerns receded after the 2006 midterms.

Another win for the out-party in a time of economic growth, the 2006 elections represented a backlash to perceived corruption in the Republican Party, perceived incompetence on the part of the White House in response to Hurricane Katrina, and widespread discontent over the direction of the Iraq War. Republicans lost 30 House seats and six Senate seats, along with control of both chambers. Democrats enjoyed pickups of six gubernatorial seats, as well as 300 state legislative seats. As with 1958, the real impact of this election was felt in conjunction with a subsequent election—2008, in this case—which enabled real policy victories for liberals in the early years of the Obama administration.

2010: The legislative victories of the Obama administration were real, but they came with a price. While the economy struggled to recover its footing in the wake of the market crash of late 2008, the Obama administration's pursuit of unpopular policies, especially the overhaul of the health insurance markets that came to be known as "Obamacare," energized the Republican base while Democrats grew listless. Republicans gained 63 House seats—the most for a party in a midterm election since the 1938 elections—six Senate seats, seven governorships, and an astounding 712 state legislative seats, also the most for any party in a midterm since 1938.

There are other potential wave elections we could include. 2014, for example, "felt" like a wave election in many respects, because Republicans picked up nine Senate seats and a number of governorships in states where we would not expect them to win (Maryland, Illinois, and Massachusetts). The 1942 elections could also theoretically be added to the list. But in terms of "canonical" midterm wave elections, this list is comprehensive.

DEFINING A WAVE ELECTION

As noted above, the 2014 elections were unusual in that Republicans scored major victories in the Senate and governorships yet saw relatively muted gains in the House and state legislatures. Those small gains, however, were due to the fact that Republicans were already in a fairly strong position, as a result of the 2010 midterm wave. This led to a fairly vigorous debate over whether it should be treated as a wave election.

In the course of this, political scientist Matthew Green collected various definitions of wave elections.[6] He included the following proposed definitions of a wave election:

- A party gains 20 seats in the House;
- A party gains 40 seats in the House;
- A party makes "across the board" gains;
- A party makes "sizable" gains, combined with unexpected victories from weak candidates;
- The competitive seats all swing one way or the other;
- The election is nationalized, so that a single issue dominates;

- Above-average partisan swing;
- The swing in seats is large enough to influence the political status quo;
- A party wins control of a chamber, including in a state won by the president of the other party in the last election.

As you can see, there has not been much effort to formalize the definition of a wave. Outside of the cutoffs of 40 or 20 seats in the House, most of these proposed definitions are subjective, or even arbitrary. For example, having all of the competitive races break in one direction seems like a useful definition. It only works, however, if the races were properly categorized beforehand.

Likewise, the idea a wave election occurs if the swing in seats is large enough to influence the political status quo is only useful in a *Rick and Morty* episode, where we would be able to see counterfactuals where a party wins fewer seats. One of the most consequential election results was the decision of 509 residents of New Hampshire to vote for Maggie Hassan rather than Kelly Ayotte in 2016. Had Ayotte won, a number of narrow GOP defeats, including the end of the GOP attempt to repeal Obamacare and Jeff Flake's successful blockade of GOP judicial nominees in the lame-duck session of the Senate in 2018, might well have been avoided. The swing of this single Senate seat therefore had substantial ramifications for policy, and yet no one thinks of 2016 as a wave.

In an attempt to add some structure to our definition and interpretation of a wave election, I turn to a metric that I designed with one of the other authors in this volume, David Byler. As I've noted above, midterm election results can be broken down into four basic components: House, Senate, governorships, and state legislatures. For non-midterm years, we can add presidential results. Fortunately, most governorships are up in non-presidential election years, so we get a similar number of elections in on- and off-year elections.[7]

The idea is to measure the overall partisan strength of a party before and after elections. To measure this, our metric looks at all five segments of elections, excluding third parties. For the presidency, the metric includes an average of the popular vote share and Electoral College share. For the House of Representatives, we measure the share of seats in the House and average it with the party's share of the two-party vote. For the Senate, the metric takes the Republican share of seats in the Senate. For governorships, the metric takes the Republican share of governorships. Because third parties are excluded, if someone wanted to look at Democratic shares, they could just subtract the Republican share from one.

State legislatures present a more difficult task. A party can pick up a large number of seats, but if it doesn't translate to control of a legislative body, it does not matter much. Similarly, a party can gain control of a large number of legislative bodies while making minimal gains in seats. So, the metric averages the share of state Houses controlled, share of state Senates controlled, share of House *seats* controlled, and state Senate seats controlled.

Because each of the five measurements is expressed as a percentage with a theoretical maximum of 100 and a minimum of zero, we can easily add them together to create an overall index that runs on a scale of zero to 500. To ease interpretability, 250 is subtracted from the score, which means that a government that was perfectly divided between the parties would have a score of zero. A positive score favors Republicans, while a negative score favors Democrats. With that in mind, let's examine some different potential applications.

A case can be made that we should have weighted governorships by population. After all, winning the governorship in California is not the same as winning the governorship in Wyoming. But this ignores the reality of our federal system. For better or for worse, the small-state bias is a part of our system of government. Winning a Senate seat in California is theoretically a bigger deal than winning one in Wyoming, and yet we would not weight the California Senate seat any differently. This is a metric of political *power*, not of political popularity. As a final note, imagine that Republicans lose the California governorship, but win in Alaska, Arkansas, Delaware, Hawaii, Idaho, Iowa, Kansas, Maine, Mississippi, Montana, Nebraska, Nevada, New Hampshire, New Mexico, North Dakota, Rhode Island, South Dakota, Utah, Vermont, West Virginia, and Wyoming. Weighting by population would suggest no net change in party strength in governorships, but this does not seem correct. Perhaps most importantly, weighting by population really does not make that significant of a difference in outcomes; there are a few elections where things change by a reasonably large margin, but not many.[8]

So what does this have to do with wave elections? It makes sense if viewed in light of the discussion of previous wave elections. What we are really getting at with our definition of wave elections is that they involve a "sharp, unusually large shift in the national balance of power, across multiple levels of government."[9] If this sounds a lot like the definition of critical elections from realignment theory, it should. Indeed, wave elections are sort of built into the definition of a critical election, along with a requirement that the wave election have durable effects, and, in some tellings, occur roughly every 30 years.[10] This metric was initially conceived of as an attempt to give some structure to the "sharp change" prong of the realignment definition, although it obviously has other applications.

To measure the presence of wave elections, we can look at the shift in the index described above from election to election, for all elections going back to the founding of the Republican Party in 1856. Overall, the average shift in the index is 0.44, with 67 percent of the observations within one standard deviation of the mean and 5 percent within two standard deviations. In other words, the data are roughly Gaussian (or normally distributed). It also suggests that pro-Republican shifts in the metric over time are almost completely offset by pro-Democratic shifts in the metric.

This also sets us up for the ultimate question: How do we decide whether a shift counts as a "large" shift? Given the nice Gaussian distribution of our data, we can answer this with a tool typically used to analyze such distributions. Consider: The average American male is about 70 inches tall (5 feet 10 inches). This helps us know where the center of the height distribution is but doesn't really help us understand what would represent an unusually tall or unusually short American male.

For that, we would look at the standard deviation, which basically is a measure of how far observations in the dataset are from the mean. If the observations are clustered tightly around 70 inches, we would have very small standard errors. If we have lots of observations far away from that average, we will have larger standard deviations. With data that are Gaussian, one standard deviation from the average can be thought of as unusually tall, and two standard deviations from the average can be thought of as very unusually tall.

As it turns out, the standard deviation for American male height is three inches. So, using our rule of thumb for standard deviations, we might say: A man who is 6′1″ is tall, and a man who is 6′4″ is unusually tall, while a man who is 6′7″ is extremely tall. On the other side, 5′7″ is short, 5′4″ is very short, and 5′1″ is extremely short. Obviously we can have our differences about exactly where the cutoff should lie, but I think this basically lines up with how most individuals think about height.

So the idea would be this: Use the standard deviation of our election data to determine what constitutes an unusually large shift. Hopefully, some cutoff near our standard deviations will emerge.

WAS 2018 A WAVE ELECTION? PROBABLY NOT

Applying that rule of thumb to our data, there is only one election that is three standard deviations out from the average: 1932. Very few would disagree that FDR's first election constituted a massive wave. But only having one election fall under our definition of "wave" seems far too restrictive.

So let us look at elections that are two standard deviations from the mean.

We add three elections to our "bucket": 1860, 1894, and 1874. These represent two canonical realigning elections, plus one that probably should be in that bucket (1874).[11] Two standard deviations out would roughly reflect a 95 precent confidence interval, such as you see in public opinion polling. It is tempting to stop here, and say that a wave is an equivalent of a 6'4" male. The problem is, we are trying to figure out what people really mean when they talk about wave elections. This definition excludes all wave elections since 1932, which seems like a dissatisfying place to draw the line.

What about 1.5 standard deviations: calling a very tall man about 6'2½"? Most of what is added falls cleanly in our definition of a wave: We add 1920, 1938, 1994, 1922, 1912, and 2010. We've added only elections that people talk about as waves, without adding anything that isn't a wave.

Going one step further, to one standard deviation, includes a lot of elections. The first couple in the sequence pretty clearly should qualify as wave elections, but we also add a lot of elections that ought not be considered wave elections: 1958, 1948, 1966, 1974, 1930, 1870, 1890, 1910, 1980, 1856, 1968, 1942, 1882, 1964, 1862, 1954, and 1946. My instinct is to expand our definition of a wave election just beyond 1.5 standard deviations, to include 1958, 1948, 1966, 1974, and 1930. But reasonable minds can differ here. Regardless, that cutoff does include the bulk of the wave elections that we have discussed.

We do note that two elections that are widely considered wave elections—2006 and 1982—do not fall within our definition. Nor does 2014. And here we come to the virtue of our classification strategy: In any event, note that two widely discussed wave elections, 2006 and 1982, do not fall within our definition, nor does an arguable wave election, 2014. In fact, all three just miss a one standard deviation cutoff. In this case, we might just say that the commentariat got it wrong (especially 1982, where half of Republicans' losses can be chalked up to redistricting), unless people are also willing to accept 1942 (arguable) and 1954 (much less arguable) as wave elections.

So what about 2018? I think the answer is that, while it was surely a bad Republican year overall, it doesn't rise to the level of a "wave" election.

To reach the cutoff I set above, the index would have to shift roughly 40 points toward Democrats. The index, however, only shifts a little more than half of that. This places 2018 in between two years that we would consider "good years" for the presidential out-party overall, 1978 and 1970, and is in the ballpark of other "good years" such as 2014, 1950, and 2006, although it still falls short.

Democrats did quite well in the House; if you take their playing field into account, their win was probably as impressive as the Republican victory in

1994. But as described above, Democratic gains elsewhere were less impressive. In the House, the Democratic claim to a wave is absolutely the strongest. The Democrats' pickup of 40 seats marks one of the larger pickups in the postwar years, as does their win in the popular vote of around 8.5 points. Democratic gains here are on the higher end of "very good year," or on the lower end of "wave," depending on how you count. This is made all the more impressive by the fact that Democrats had to overcome some tough maps.

Democrats also had a good night in governorships, although the ground that Republicans lost largely came in seats that they held only as a result of the wave election of 2010 and the good GOP year of 2014: Maine, Illinois, New Mexico, and to a lesser extent, Michigan and Wisconsin. The only real surprise came in Kansas, where Kris Kobach—a problematic candidate in his own right—lost by an unexpectedly large margin. This represents a good night for Democrats, but it isn't the type of outcome we typically see in wave elections.

The Senate, however, was disappointing for Democrats. As noted above, this is the first time the president's party has knocked off four true incumbents in a midterm election since 1934. Democrats also either underperformed or ran roughly even with their 2012 showings in West Virginia, Montana, Michigan, and Ohio, despite facing lower-quality challengers in the latter three races.

We can chalk this up to the unfavorable map, but we should recall that Democrats won all of these seats in 2012 and many of them in 2006. Republicans had an unfavorable map in 2010, and many thought they would lose seats early on, yet they managed to make up for it by winning in places like Illinois and Wisconsin.

Finally, state legislative elections were not a great outcome either. Democrats picked up about 300 state legislative seats, which is actually a below-average performance in a midterm election.[12] One can try to chalk this up to unfavorable maps in state legislatures, but then one has to explain away Democrats's strong performance in House of Representatives elections while facing similarly unfavorable maps. Overall, this was most like non-wave years such as 1962 and 1950. It wasn't anything like we describe above, in years 1974, 2010, 1966, and 1958, where the president's party lost over 500 seats.

DOES IT MATTER?

The 2018 elections were unpleasant elections for Republicans, but they probably do not fit the bill as a wave election. We should end by asking ourselves:

Does it matter? The answer here is "probably not." Even though 1954 does not qualify as a wave election, it was still consequential, as it robbed Eisenhower of his Republican majorities. If 2006 was not a wave election, it still ended the domestic agenda of George W. Bush and set the stage for the large Democratic majorities of the 111th Congress. Regardless of how we describe 1982, it had the same effect on Ronald Reagan's presidency.

What this debate is really about is bragging rights. Parties want to be able to lay claim to a "wave" of popular affirmation, because it enables them to be able to cloak themselves in the mantle of the ever-elusive "mandate." But to the extent mandates exist—I am skeptical—they exist regardless of whether we label it a wave.

Regardless, for the wave moniker to mean something, it should represent an occurrence that is fairly rare, not something that happens every second or third election. Hopefully this chapter represents a small step toward a better understanding of this elusive phenomenon.

NOTES

1. "We're Back from the Future. Which of These Wildly Different Midterm Outcomes Would You Believe?" FiveThirtyEight, October 24, 2018, https://fivethirtyeight.com/features/were-back-from-the-future-which-of-these-wildly-different-midterm-outcomes-would-you-believe/.

2. Tweet from Harry Enten, @ForecasterEnten, November 7, 2018, https://twitter.com/forecasterenten/status/1060360046155087872?lang = en.

3. Stuart Rothenberg, "What Counts as a GOP Wave in 2014?" *Inside Elections*, October 28, 2014, http://insideelections.com/news/article/what-counts-as-a-gop-wave-in-2014.

4. Quoted in Clyde P. Weed, *The Nemesis of Reform: The Republican Party During the New Deal* (New York: Columbia University Press, 1994), 115.

5. Alan I. Abramowitz, "Partisan Redistricting and the 1982 Congressional Elections," *The Journal of Politics* 45, no. 3 (August 1983).

6. Matthew Green, "Some Observations on the Election of Donald Trump," November 11, 2016, https://sites.google.com/a/cua.edu/matthew-n-green/writings/legacy-blogs #WaveElection.

7. Sean Trende and David Byler, "Measuring the Strength of the Two Parties," RealClearPolitics, September 18, 2014, https://www.realclearpolitics.com/articles/2014/09/18/measuring_the_strength_of_the_two_parties.html.

8. Sean Trende and David Byler, "The GOP Is the Strongest It's Been in Decades," RealClearPolitics, May 19, 2015, https://www.realclearpolitics.com/articles/2015/05/19/the_gop_is_the_strongest_its_been_in_decades_126633.html.

9. Sean Trende, "What Is a Wave Election, Anyway?" RealClearPolitics, November 5, 2018, https://www.realclearpolitics.com/articles/2018/11/05/what_is_a_wave_election_anyway_138555.html.

10. Sean Trende, *The Lost Majority: Why the Future of Government Is Up for Grabs, and Who Will Take It* (New York: St. Martin's Press, 2012).

11. David Mayhew, *Electoral Realignments: A Critique of an American Genre* (New Haven: Yale University Press, 2004).

12. "State Legislative Elections, 2018," Ballotpedia, https://ballotpedia.org/State_legislative_elections,_2018.

Index

VEP (voting eligible population), 16, *25*
veterans, in 2018 midterm elections, *34*
voter engagement: of African Americans,
    199; in Democrat primary elections,
    2018, 61; of Latino voters, 214–15,
    215, 220–21; of Latino voters, by
    Nelson, 217–18; of Latino voters, by
    Rosen, 217; party polarization and, 55;
    in Republican primary elections, 2018,
    61; Trump's impact on, 2018, 47–48,
    55
voter suppression, social media and, 232
voter turnout: of African Americans, 2012
    compared to 2016, 189–90; of African
    Americans in Democrat victories,
    198–99; in Democrat primary elections,
    2018, 61, 76, *77–78*; early voting and,
    172–73; of Latino voters, 2018, 206,
    211–14, *212–14*; of Latino voters,
    precinct-level change from 2014–2018,
    212–13, *213*; midterm election factors
    of, 4–5; in midterm elections, 1962–
    2018, *25, 26*; in midterm elections,
    2018, 16, 27, 44; in Missouri Senate
    elections, 2018, 120; presidential elec-
    tions and, 55; in primary elections, 76;
    in Republican primary elections, 2018,
    61, 76, *77–78*; Trump's impact on,
    2018, 47–48
voting eligible population (VEP), 16, *25*
Vukmir, Leah, *20*

Wagner, Robert, 68
Wagner, Scott, *23*
Walker, Bill, 140, 147
Walker, Scott, *23*, 90, 146–47, 261
Walters, Mimi, 184
Walz, Tim, *22*, 148
Ward, Kelli, 126
Warner, Mark, 15
Warren, Elizabeth, *19*, 162, 173, 187
Warren, John, *71*
Washington Post, 224
Wasserman, David, 61
Watergate scandal, 265
wave elections: bragging rights of, 272;
    consequences of, 271–72; defining,

266–69; history of, 263–66; midterm
    elections as, 2018, 269–71
Weaver, Jeff, 251, 259n4
websites, as news source, 225–26
Weinstein, Harvey, 121, 180
West, Kanye, 235
West midterm results, Trumpian alignment
    compared to 2018, 92–95, *93, 94*
West Virginia Senate elections, 2018,
    127–28
Wexton, Jennifer, *110*, 184
Whitehouse, Sheldon, *20*
white voters: advertising targeting, 234;
    immigration policy and, 208–9, 219; in
    midterm elections, 2018, 81–82;
    Republicans courting, 192. *See also*
    race
Whitmer, Gretchen, *22*, 150
Wicker, Roger, *19, 67*
Wild, Susan, *110*
Wiles, Susie, 143
Williams, Pat, 153
Williams, Whitney, 153
Wilson, Jenny, *20*
Wisconsin gubernatorial elections, 2018,
    146–47
Wolf, Tom, *23*, 85, 151
women candidates: Democrat compared to
    Republican results of, 2018, 184–87; in
    Democrat primary elections, 2018, 70,
    181–83; diversity of, 2018, 183; in
    House and Senate elections, 2018,
    180–81; #MeToo movement and, 180;
    in 1992 compared to 2018, 178–80,
    179; in Republican primary elections,
    2018, 181–82; sexual harassment issues
    motivating, 179–80; Super PACs
    supporting, 181–82, 186; Trump's
    election motivating, 180; 2020 outlook
    for, 187. *See also* gender
Women Vote!, 181
women voters, advertising targeting, 234
Woods, William, 152

Zinke, Ryan, 101, 124
Zupan, Lawrence, *20*

About the Contributors

Alan I. Abramowitz is the Alben W. Barkley Professor of Political Science at Emory University and a senior columnist for *Sabato's Crystal Ball*. His most recent book is *The Great Alignment: Race, Party Transformation, and the Rise of Donald Trump*.

Matt A. Barreto is co-founder and managing partner of the polling and research firm Latino Decisions. He is a Professor of Political Science and Chicana/o Studies at UCLA.

David Byler is a data analyst and political columnist for the *Washington Post* Opinions Section. He was previously the Chief Elections Analyst at the *Weekly Standard* and an elections analyst at RealClearPolitics.

Rhodes Cook was a political reporter for *Congressional Quarterly* for more than two decades and is a senior columnist at *Sabato's Crystal Ball*.

James Hohmann is a national political correspondent for the *Washington Post*. He is the author of *The Daily 202*, the *Post*'s flagship political newsletter.

Theodore R. Johnson is a senior fellow at the Brennan Center for Justice and adjunct professor at Georgetown University's McCourt School of Public Policy. He's written on black political behavior for the *Atlantic*, *Washington Post*, *Politico*, and *National Review*, among other national publications. Previously, he was a fellow at New America and a naval officer.

Kyle Kondik is managing editor of *Sabato's Crystal Ball*, the University of Virginia Center for Politics' nonpartisan newsletter on American campaigns and elections. He is the author of *The Bellwether: Why Ohio Picks the President* (2016).

Albert Morales is a former official with the Democratic National Committee who has served under three DNC Chairmen over the last two decades and serves as senior political director for Latino Decisions.

Diana Owen is Associate Professor of Political Science at Georgetown University and teaches in the Communication, Culture, and Technology graduate program, and he has served as director of the American Studies Program. She is the author of *Media Messages in American Presidential Elections; New Media and American Politics* (with Richard Davis); and *American Government and Politics in the Information Age* (with David Paletz and Timothy Cook).

Madelaine Pisani is the gubernatorial reporter for *National Journal*'s Hotline.

Joshua T. Putnam is author of Frontloading HQ (http://frontloading.blog spot.com/), a widely-cited website that tracks both party's presidential nomination rules. He has taught political science at a number of North Carolina universities and colleges since receiving his PhD from the University of Georgia.

Larry J. Sabato is the Robert Kent Gooch Professor of Politics at the University of Virginia and director of its Center for Politics. He is the author or editor of more than twenty books on American politics and elections.

Gary M. Segura is co-founder and senior partner of Latino Decisions and is dean of the Luskin School of Public Affairs at UCLA.

Emily C. Singer is a senior political reporter for Shareblue. She has been covering campaigns and elections since 2012 at other outlets, including *Roll Call*, *Mashable*, and *Mic*.

Michael E. Toner is former chairman of the Federal Election Commission (FEC) and is chair of the Election Law and Government Ethics Practice Group at Wiley Rein LLP in Washington, D.C.

Karen E. Trainer is a senior reporting specialist at Wiley Rein LLP.

Sean Trende is the senior elections analyst for RealClearPolitics. He is the author of *The Lost Majority: Why the Future of Government Is Up for Grabs and Who Will Take It*, and he co-authored the *Almanac of American Politics 2014*.

CPSIA information can be obtained
at www.ICGtesting.com
Printed in the USA
LVHW082347141219
640544LV00037B/1508/P

9 781538 125274